THE GENESIS EFFECT

PERSONAL AND ORGANIZATIONAL

TRANSFORMATIONS

BRIAN P. HALL

Resource *Publications*

An imprint of *Wipf and Stock Publishers*
199 West 8th Avenue • Eugene OR 97401

Resource Publications
A division of Wipf and Stock Publishers
199 W 8th Ave, Suite 3
Eugene, OR 97401

The Genesis Effect
Personal and Organizational Transformations
By Hall, Brian P.
Copyright©2000 by Hall, Brian P.
ISBN: 1-59752-702-5
Publication date 5/19/2006
Previously published by Don Bosco Press, 2000

CONTENTS

FOREWORD

(New Edition 2000)

Since the first edition of this book, The Genesis Effect was published in 1987, a whole technology of how to measure the 125 values has been developed and validated. Since 1989, over 5000 executives have been coached using the new format. Additionally it is currently used in most European languages. Within a year, it will be translated into Japanese, South Korean and Chinese. Naturally this new reality has taught us a lot, yet for all of that the Genesis Effect is still valid with its ideas and concepts. In fact it has original material that only has not been superseded but also is current and useful to the new emerging measurement technology.

The basis of the values platform is now what is called the Cultural Assessment Database (CADB). What this means is that each employee of an organization completes a questionnaire on the internet, and a data base is created, that is confidential to the organization. All the information is confidential in that only an individual can download his/her own information. Nonprofit organizations have their own databases so that individuals can get personal profiles through their own church or adult education program. The measurement aspect of the values program was initiated at the University of Santa Clara since 1980, and was 90% complete by the time this book was written. This book is therefore a backdrop of invaluable information for the new technology.

In 1986 when the text was actually written the idea of Descriptors or the core of 50 values was new. We now refer to these clusters as Beliefs reserving the name of values to the 125. In the 90s a measurement technology based only on the 125 values was developed. It was felt that the new capacity of the computer allowed us to create a more complex measurement system. At the same time Benjamin Tonna in Malta continued to develop a methodology for measuring the values on an annual basis for the Republic of Malta, using a variation of the descriptor (belief) system.

INTRODUCTION

Now we are in the year 2000 and have worked with global companies such as Alcoa, Siemens and Wallenius-Wilhelmsen Lines. The values have been introduced through the CADB mentioned above, and have been used in executive coaching, team building, succession planning and merger and acquisition due diligence. The new methods require that the technology be delivered on line and be as simple in its outputs as possible – the consequence is a return to the *beliefs descriptor system* originally described in the Genesis Effect. The Genesis Effect is the only extensive explanation of that system – making it as valuable in 2000 as it was in 1987.

The explanation of the cycles of development was first addressed in this book and became a critical part of the measurement system. This book more than other books I have written integrated the psychological and psycho-analytical disciplines with that of religion and philosophy which are so critical to the face validity of the theory. As such the work is foundational and set apart from the later works such as Values Shift.

WHY VALUES AWARENESS IS SO IMPORTANT IN THE NEW MILLENNIUM

A key gift that the twentieth century gave us is that *knowledge is the key driver of economic growth for the foreseeable future.* Now we are told that power is in knowledge. We might say that for the economically developed countries the knowledge sector is taking on a far greater part of our lives than ever before. Certainly a key factor is that information and intellectual capital are the key resources in the new wealth creation. But knowledge has always been important – why is it different now, and what do we mean by knowledge in the modern context?

Knowledge creates knowledge when it is shared. Therefore, underpinning the new emphasis on knowledge is relationships. But it is also relationships between people who feel empowered in a manner that has not been evident in human history before.

The glue that holds any relationship together is the value priorities that we have. Ironically it is our values differences that stimulate creativity and insight. However if we do not have minimal values priorities in common the relationship will not be sustainable. What is required, then is to keep these two dimensions in constant tension. The Genesis Effect was written with this tension in mind. The ability to measure values is therefore a fundamental step in learning to manage knowledge. Being successful in life and business means having special knowledge . *Knowledge is always contextual and flows from a set of relationships that are underpinned, by minimal common value priorities.*

Ikujiro Nonaka and Hirotaka Takeuchi have pointed out there is Tacit and Explicit Knowledge. Tacit knowledge is subjective and known to the individual – it may even be partially unconscious as in the case of habits and skills. Explicit knowledge is coded and objective knowledge often written down. It is shareable and always flows from human relationships. Now given that our relationships are underpinned by values, values awareness leverages a whole new dimension to knowing and learning. Values awareness leverages our learning by:

1. Making our personal values priorities known, in a manner that they can be shared with others.

2. By sharing the values with others, a spouse, a team member or a fellow student, makes what was tacit explicit. Making it possible to see how we are different, so that the relationships can be better understood.

3. This process allows a couple, or teams to set their values priorities in common so as to leverage knowledge creation, or sharing.

Since 1990 not only has the technology developed and was made **THIS PUBLICATION** accessible via the internet but values as an essential aspect of organizational life is also much better understood. The critical relationship between the inner dimension of the human psyche and the external of culture although very much a mystery is more obvious as an important question for any executive to be aware of. The concept of leadership empowerment is better understood as a systems issue having to do with personal knowledge at the human level and the capacity to understand and align culture at a global and systemic level.

At a very practical level the growing community of values practitioners has now moved to an expanded knowledge of how values affect organizational culture. What has made the difference is the measurement of values and it's application in organizational development practice. What is interesting and humbling to me is the initial work I conducted with Fr. Benjamin Tonna with a number of global religious congregations such as the Franciscans, the Oblates of Mary Immaculate, the Sisters of Charity and over a hundred other groups.

Such was the groundbreaking work that led to this book, and created the platform for work now being carried out in global corporate entities like the Siemens and the Clarica Corporation in Toronto. The work reported in this book on the analysis of the Constitutions and the vows of religious congregations became, as an example, the foundation of our recent work on the formation of principles upon which the modern organizations functions. What I am suggesting is that relative to values studies this book is from the authors view point the most foundational of all my writing.

Over the years there were many points of despair. However what made it all possible was the community of practice. I could mention hundreds of people including all those mentioned in the original preface. However, special mention is given to those who have been so supportive in the last five years.

First of all my friend Benjamin Tonna and his relentless pursuit of the truth through his annual studies of the country of Malta have been a blessing. The work of Aurelio Villa Sanchez, Itziar, Elexpuro, Miguel Ayerbe and Roberto Pacheco at the University of Deusto in Bilbao, Spain, have been an inspiration to me. The quality of research that has come from Spain on entrepreneurial leadership and drug addiction based on this work is very impressive. In Germany special thanks goes to Elizabeth and Charles Savage for their pioneering work with Siemens . In the UK, I thank Mike Turner at Threshold for his work in executive coaching. To my son, Martin, who completed his doctoral work which included a massive validity study on the values work and the Universities of Hull and Lincoln in the U.K. My wife Elva deserves special mention for work done in the arena of executive coaching. She has made the The Genesis Effect the backbone of her work connecting to the Myers Briggs Indicator.

But what made this new edition possible is Ma. Bella Dumas and the International Values Institute in Manila, Philippines. Bella's tireless work over the last 12 years in the Asian region – in government, industry, education and the church – has done much to continue the interest of the professional community in the values work and the pursuit of excellence in human and institutional development.

The re-publishing of this book would not have also been possible without the help of the Salesian Fathers in Manila, Philippines particularly the dedication of Fr. Lazaro Revilla, SDB. As a values practitioner, he is relentless in his learning and positioning of the values work in his work as an educator and council member of his congregation. Gratitude is also extended to Fr. Manuel Guazon for facilitating the initial dissemination of the values technology when he was President of the Southeast Asia Interdisciplinary Development Institute, Antipolo, Rizal. Finally, thanks to Fr. Benjamin Mamawal, SVD for his continued interest in and support for the values work for over 15 years.

Brian P. Hall
May 2000

Notes

Notes

Notes

Notes

Notes

Notes

Notes

Notes

Notes

This book is the result of twenty years of research into the relationship of values to human and organizational development. The work began in 1965 with my first overseas assignment in Central America, with the Anglican Church of Canada. It was there that I met and was influenced by Paulo Freire, Ivan Illich and Erich Fromm.[1] Their main impact was to conscientize me to the dynamic relationship among languages, cultural, societal and institutional development. I suppose, more than anything, they forced me to rethink all my presuppositions about the nature of human development, which until that time had been predominantly psychoanalytical in nature.

My experience in Central America not only forced me to rethink my view of the world, but it also posed dynamic questions about the nature of human values. Are they really self-chosen, as I had always assumed, or are they imposed upon us by the institutions we live in and through?

I struggled with trying to discover a viable definition of values that could be pinpointed in human behavior. Naturally I was influenced by the Values Clarification movement, so popular in the 1960's. This resulted in three books titled *Value Clarification as Learning Process*, published by Paulist Press in 1973. The purpose of the books was to illustrate in a practical way the relationship between human development and values, particularly from an existential point of view.

THE EARLY STRUGGLE

The existential psychologists stress the immediacy and contingency of life, ignoring for the most part the developmental theories of human development. For them life is chosen and shaped by present choices and acts. Within this context values are the priorities we live by, reflected in our behavior, as we confront anxiety and choose life in the "now." From this point of view, Time, past, present and future, is an aspect of the present moment.

see Group Dynamics, chapter 8

After finishing my doctoral studies in 1969, the historical and developmental aspect of reality became my preoccupation. Growing up in Saint Albans, England, surrounded by the ruins of ancient Roman occupations and medieval cathedrals, left me with memories and a consciouness of history that could not be ignored. New questions arose. Am I simply the product of a developmental history—the shadow of past generations, bound by the influence of culture and family ties?

Additionally, during this period I engaged in serious personal psychoanalysis, half of which was done in Spanish with a wonderful psychiatrist by the name of Alfredo Sotela. This did two things. First, it helped my awareness of languages, and the fact that language is the repository of key words that I now call values. Further I became aware that value words such as Self-Esteem and Freedom transcend language, and occur in every person's meaning system, no matter in what culture he or she may reside.

Second, it heightened my awareness of my own developmental history: the influence of my parents, my culture and my religious formation. It taught me the importance of linear, or historical time. I became conscious of the fact that all I had learned had taken time, and further that to unlearn certain things would take time also. I discovered that the skills I had were learned in sequence. That is to say, I learned that "Rome was not built in a day." It takes time to grow up, no matter what the consequences or the final results.

A THEORY OF VALUES

In 1976 I published another book with Paulist Press called *The Development of Consciousness: A Confluent Theory of Values*. It reflected on a number of theories of human development, showing how the works of Maslow, Kohlberg, Erikson and others coincided with the development of values and consciousness in the human being. As far as I am aware this was the first time someone had tried to pattern out a schema, no matter how inadequate, of how values can be more specifically identified and related to stages of maturity in the person.

As I reflect back on this period, I realize that it broke open a whole new perspective on what values really were. I was working with a cross-disciplinary team. I was an Episcopal priest with all my religious and psychoanalytical heritage. With me were Eileen Cantin, a philosopher, Michael Kenney and Richard Kunkel, educators, Anthony D'Souza, S.J., from business science, and Benjamin Tonna, a sociologist. Bill Zierdt worked in leadership development and research with the United States Army, and Ewing Miller was the president of a local architectural firm. Additionally D'Souza and Tonna were very aware of the issues from political science and the cross-cultural perspective. It was at this time, also, that we began to do work in India and Europe.

We soon noticed that not only did certain values become priorities at different stages of maturity, but they also reflected various stages of faith development. This has now been well stated by James Fowler in a book titled *Stages of Faith*, published by Harper and Row.[2] Further, we realized that the values pointed to stages of leadership development in executives, and were reflected in the management design of different administrative frameworks.

With the help of Helen Thompson, Anthony D'Souza and Benjamin Tonna a series of publications resulted. *Developing Leadership by Stages* was published by Manohar in India in 1979. *God's Plans for Us* and *Leadership Through Values* were published by Paulist Press in 1980. *Shepherds and Lovers* was also published by Paulist Press in 1982.[3]

At this juncture in the journey we had a lot of information and an interesting perspective on values and human development. It was primarily an educational tool that gave persons a fresh perspective, and often led to problem solving, in counseling, in small administrative settings, and in educational curriculum design. It also linked counseling and spiritual direction.[4]

The problem was that we had gathered a great deal of information, but did not know how to make it practical. In 1979 I moved to Santa Clara University as a professor in the Graduate Division of Counseling Psychology and Education. I was also appointed the Director of Graduate Programs in Pastoral Counseling. Two major experiences occurred for me: an increase in cross-disciplinary interaction, and the introduction to computer technology. Suddenly, the last fifteen years of work took on an entirely new perspective.

GETTING
PRACTICAL

My friend and research associate Benjamin Tonna was the critical link. Benjamin is a sociologist and priest who lives and works in Malta and Rome. As Director of SEDOS, an international Documentation Center in Rome for seven years, Benjamin had written a book called *Gospel for the Cities*, published by Orbis.[5] He had carefully gathered comparative information on first and third world cities for some twenty years.

Together we had discovered approximately 125 value words in the written word that were borne out in several languages. (See Appendix.) Out of his own background in documentation we were able to put these words into a shorter list of 50 Value Descriptors. A Descriptor is simply the technical name, in this case, for a cluster of values. (See Appendix.) He was then able to analyze the data he had collected through this value screen, and immediately discerned patterns of growth and conflict at a global level. In religious language Benjamin called the values "signs." The value patterns, then, were signs of God's action in the world. In traditional spirituality this is called Discernment of Spirits.[6]

see Definitions as Descriptors and Values, Appendix

Although we felt that we were making some important discoveries and headway, the problem remained as to how to communicate what we had in a practical manner. This was particularly true when we were talking to persons who were suspicious of anything that looked religious. This is often exaggerated in a university setting where the disciplines are expected to be separate. It was clear to us that psychology, religion, business and technology are a part of a single whole. But to be able to communicate value related information across these disciplines is another question. This is particularly difficult in a competitive society.

In 1979 we began to consider the possibility of using video tapes to facilitate communication. With a grant from the Educational Division of the National Office of the Episcopal Church, and the support of Bishop Elliott Sorge, six tapes titled *The Leadership by Discernment Program* were released by Paulist Press in 1984.

A TECHNOLOGY
CONNECTION

At the same time we began to investigate the possibility of designing and writing a computer program that would translate all the complexity of an individual's values into a profile that would give practical and concrete feedback. With the aid of Bishop Sorge, Benjamin Tonna, and Dr. Irving Yabroff, a computer engineer and programmer, we set about the task. After four years of research, and considerable trial and error, we managed to develop an instrument named the Hall-Tonna Inventory.

The instrument is not a psychological test to measure what the values are of a given individual, but a documentation system based on 385 questions. Each question relates to a different value, so that an individual unfamiliar with the values is, in fact, documenting what his or her values are, and in what priority they are ordered.

Further, instead of designing a profile that gave the client direct information about himself or herself, such as one receives in a psychological profile, we produced a profile that gave partial information. This methodology was based on the science of documentation and traditional spirituality and it completely guards the confidentiality of the profile. The profile will state the person's values, his or her cycle of *see Discernment Questions,* maturity and his or her priorities, but then, instead of a given state-*chapter 4* ment about what this means, a series of direct questions are raised for every value that occurs. In this way the final meaning of the instrument only becomes clear as the client answers the questions. In the religious traditions this is called Spiritual Discernment. Its overall effect was to create an instrument that is helpful, confidential and non-threatening.

Reliability and validity studies have been carried out to standardize *see articles in Appendix by* the list of values, and to standardize their minimal common meaning. *Jeanine Kelsey, Barbara* Once the values of an individual were documented, we were then able *Ledig, Oren Harari* to write a program that placed them in cycles of maturity, that spelled out for the client what his or her particular value patterns indicated in terms of the information we had gathered over the years. In this way we were able to make very complex information understandable and practical for the individual without that individual having to understand all the theory and research that stood behind the values.[7]

see Retrieve, chapter 10 We administered about 1,500 of these instruments to persons in several different cultures, from different class structures, professions and disciplines. As we did this some interesting things occurred. We found first of all that what we had was a method for examining the reality of human development that was, in turn, giving us new and often contradictory information. The instrument began to inform us of our own theoretical mistakes about our own assumptions about the human condition. In other words we had discovered a method that was enabling us to investigate new insights about human and organizational development.

see Group Analysis, The interest in organizational development came about when we *chapter 8* wrote a program that took several individual profiles from a group of persons and wrote a composite profile. What was amazing was that the group profile, termed HT-Group, gave us new information not available on the individual instrument.

see Document Analysis, Additionally, a major Roman Catholic religious community invited *chapter 9* us to attempt to do a similar analysis, not of individuals or a group, but of their central management documents. When we did this we again found ourselves confronted with new and unexpected information and insights.

In the final analysis we discovered that after twenty years of re-

4

search into values, we were not dealing with value theory at all, but a far greater mystery—we called it the *Genesis Effect*. What the Genesis Effect is, and what insights it gave us about human, spiritual and organizational development, is what I want to share with you—the reader—for it is the subject of this book. I would like to express my gratitude to Kevin Lynch, CSP, president of Paulist Press, for his twenty years of support for our work, as well as to my editor, Robert Hamma. I also want to acknowledge the diligent work done by my associates Mary Lou Harrison and Barbara Ledig, and by my daughter Christy Hall, in the preparation of this book.

Introduction:

NOTES

1. Freire has had wide impact in developing countries where his pedagogical methodology is applied in programs with the economically deprived and illiterate. See the Bibliography for book references for authors Freire, Illich and Fromm.

2. Fowler (1981).

3. The present work brings together many of the concepts already expressed in these earlier ones.

4. For further understanding of the links between counseling and the art of spiritual direction see Leech (1977), Chapter 3.

5. See Tonna (1982) for a detailed analysis of urban life and the church's mission to the cities.

6. Richards (1970) in a translation from the French gives an historical summary of the practice of Discernment of Spirits and its present role.

7. See Hall (1982) for further discussion on the history and theory of values and their relationship to awareness and moral development.

THE GENESIS EFFECT:
Enabling Human, Spiritual and Organizational Transformation

In the beginning God created the heavens and the earth.
God created man in the image of himself,
in the image of God he created him,
male and female he created them.
Genesis 1:1 and 27. Jerusalem Bible

"All men by nature desire to know." With these words, Aristotle began his Metaphysics. But what is knowledge? What do people have inside their heads when they know something? Is knowledge expressed in words? If so, how could one know things that are easier to do than to say, like tying a shoestring or hitting a baseball? If knowledge is not expressed in words, how can it be transmitted in language? How is knowledge related to the world? And what are the relationships between the external world, knowledge in the head, and the language used to express knowledge about the world?
J.F. Sowa.[1]

GENESIS:
VALUES AS MEDIATORS OF
HUMAN AND SPIRITUAL DEVELOPMENT

The World thus appears as a complicated tissue of events, in which connections of different kinds alternate or overlap or combine and thereby determine the texture of the whole.

W. Heisenberg[2]

My life is a story of the self-realization of the unconscious. Everything in the unconscious seeks outward manifestation, and the personality, too, desires to evolve out of its unconscious conditions and to experience itself as a whole.

Carl Jung[3]

To introduce the reader to the "Genesis Effect" as it is reflected in ancient literature and modern life, and to show how each person has an inner and outer life connected in each of us through the values we hold. **PURPOSE**

A discussion of the human person as having an inner life of dreams and images that affects the way we live and shapes the world we live in. Demonstration of how values are priorities located in everyday spoken language, and that these values when identified give us valuable information about our lives and the institutions that influence us. **CONTENT**

This introductory chapter will continue in chapter two by showing how the same values also point and give us valuable information about our inner life. **LINKAGE**

We are on the edge of a new age of discovery, an age of convergence between the inner world of the human mind and our understanding of the world of people and things. New understandings of the working of the human brain would suggest the possibility of three dimensional images occurring at an unconscious level that prefigure all that we do—a sort of inner architectural planning room. It is even possible that every person contains the memory of the whole human race down through the ages in one's genetic code.

Quantum Physics is pointing out that the deeper we plunge into the study of material reality the less objective and real it becomes.[4] At the most basic levels beyond atoms and molecules we come to ghostly pockets of energy and the fact that each part can be described only in its relationship to the whole. In other words, the deeper we probe into the inner reality of material things, the more we find ourselves in contact with the whole.

Jung, a psychologist who spent most of his life studying the inner life of persons through the study of dreams (see above quotation) concluded that much of a person's inner life is unconscious. He also concluded that this inner reality was a creative energy that continually tries, in each of our lives, to express itself through our behavior and the way we act in the world. In other words, the world we human beings have created, civilization itself, in all its forms, from cars to interior design and the very structures of society, are a manifestation of our inner dreams and images.[5]

The bottom line is that life is not a series of related parts, but an intricately interdependent whole.[6] Even the inner world of images and dreams is related to the outer world of people, lovers, ships and cars. This connectedness and its creative consequence I call the Genesis Effect.

The Genesis Effect is the way the human being recreates the world he or she lives in from his or her internal images. This statement assumes that each person lives with his or her feet in two universes at the same time: the so-called external world of societies, institutions, family and friends, and the internal world of fantasy, images and the unconscious.

Science and technology has had a lot to say about the external world, especially during the last 100 years. Often it has ignored and even denied the existence of this other reality. This denial is, however, a recent phenomenon, and was not present during the foundation period of the sciences. Not only this but recent discoveries in physics and the social sciences are beginning to take a new look at the other reality.[7]

Since the beginning of human history religion and art have viewed the inner reality of the human being as the seat of wisdom and moral and spiritual potential. They have often looked down upon the empirical sciences. This is a recent phenomenon, since much of modern science grew out of the western spiritual traditions. Now there is a growing recognition of the interdependence of art and technology, science and religion. But what is it that mediates this inner reality, and enables it to reformulate itself into the world each of us creates?

During the last twenty years I have spent most of my time studying values in human and spiritual development. I am now convinced that values are the mediators between the inner world of images and the external and observable world of everyday life. Our values stand between the two worlds, and are a way of understanding both our inner life and our external behavior. This chapter will, therefore, take a look at what we mean by values, and how these values describe day to day behavior and how they point to our inner thoughts and images.

Finally, the Genesis Effect is also a phenomenon that has been described in religious literature for centuries. This title is taken from the book of Genesis, written in a place and time that was the initiating point of western civilization. The idea, as such, is very old, but our understanding of it may still be but at a beginning stage. We shall now examine this idea in more depth.

The Genesis Effect is the process whereby our internal images act upon and transform the world we live in. Values are those priorities which we act on that mediate those images and transform them into our everyday behavior. To make this clear the following Diagram 1:1 will help us understand the concept:

THE GENESIS EFFECT

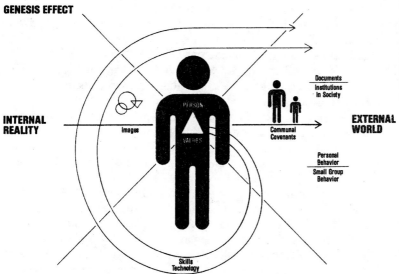

GENESIS EFFECT

INTERNAL REALITY

Images

PERSON

VALUES

Documents
Institutions
In Society

Communal
Covenants

Personal
Behavior

Small Group
Behavior

Skills
Technology

EXTERNAL WORLD

Diagram 1:1
THE GENESIS EFFECT
How our inner world of images and dreams becomes the external world of institutions and society.

In the diagram we see on the left side the Internal Reality. This would contain our unconscious inner world, and those elements of the unconscious that we become aware of through our dreams and intuitions. It is the world of internal images and hidden psychic forces. On the other side we see the external world. This would be my external behavior, my family and friends, my car, the company I work with, and everything outside of myself that is observed and recorded by my senses.

The diagram points out that the two are related in a circular fashion. For example let us consider a 24 year old woman graduating from college and beginning a new job. It is Sunday and she is to begin the job on Monday morning at nine o'clock. She quite naturally has some anticipatory emotions of fear and anxiety about the new job. We know that all feelings are accompanied by internal images, although they may remain unconscious.

Earlier that day she was asked by some friends why it was that she was so irritable and not talking very much. They asked the question: "What is the matter with you? Do you want to talk about it?" That night she has the same feelings, accompanied by a dream of being chased by a group of men in business suits.

The internal images of fear, in this case, become reflected in her external and observable behavior. We can also say that the original fear was initiated in the external world by the job that she had interviewed for and accepted. However, this is furthur complicated by the fact that her anxiety may also be due to her own expectations and internally generated fears, which may have little to do with the external reality.[8]

What comes first then, the chicken or the egg? Does the external world become internalized as images in the unconscious, or do the images shape our behavior and the interpersonal world we live in? The answer is surely both. One reinforces the other. Values then become the central criteria, to enable us to assess whether or not the images and the external reality are leading to a destructive or a creative life enhancing end.

see Skills, chapters 4 and 6 Skills are simply the flip side of values. When one looks closely at values, as we will later in the book, we find that one consequence is to discover a myriad of skills that lie behind them. Technology is the extension of skills into more complex and external forms.

The heart of the Genesis Effect is the way in which the values mediate the internal and external realities through the medium of language. This is what this chapter is about. The book of Genesis explains exactly what this phenomenon means. This is where we shall begin.

GENESIS: THE BOOK Genesis, which means beginning, is the first book of the Jewish and Christian sacred literature. It is also held in high esteem by all the Islamic writers and philosophers. Although it was probably written in the 6th century B.C., it is perhaps at least 3500 years old in origin.

The author of Genesis posits the idea that a personal consciousness, God, acted upon a formless void and brought order out of chaos. (See quotation at the beginning of this chapter.) The chapter continues with a series of sentences beginning with the phrase "God said" as follows:
"God said, 'Let there be light,' and there was light." (vs 3.)

"God said, 'Let the waters under heaven come together into a single mass, and let dry land appear.' '' (vs 9.)

"God said, 'Let the earth produce every kind of living creature: cattle, reptiles, and every kind of wild beast.' And so it was." (vs 24.)

"God said, 'Let us make man in our own image, in the likeness of ourselves, and let them be masters of the fish of the sea, the birds of heaven, the cattle, all the wild beasts and all the reptiles that crawl upon the earth.'

God created man in the image of himself,
in the image of God he created him,
male and female he created them." (*vs 26/27.*)

The author of these passages has in mind the notion that it is God's spoken word that is the instrument of the creation coming about. When God said, that is, when God spoke and named an entity, such as light or cattle and reptiles, so light, cattle and reptiles came to be. God's words or language, then, is the conveyer of the power that causes the world to be created.

The conclusions are striking, namely that language and consciousness are connected, and, further, that it is language that mediates the internal images into an external and recognizable form. In Genesis it is God's image of creation and humanity that is mediated through God's spoken word to become the created order. This reality described centuries ago is a latent gift that is given to each of us. It is this we call the Genesis Effect.

INNER IMAGES AND LANGUAGE

In their book *The Structure of Magic 1: A Book about Language and Therapy*, Richard Bandler and John Grinder note that each of us has an inner representational system, an image of what the world is really all about, that has been logically assembled by the mind as it tries to make sense out of all the data it receives through the five senses: "A number of people in the history of civilization have made this point—that there is an irreducible difference between the world and our experience of it. We as human beings do not operate directly on the world. Each of us creates a representational world in which we live—that is, we create a map or model which we use to generate our behavior. Our representation of the world determines to a large degree what our experience of the world will be, how we will perceive the world, what choices we will see available to us as we live in the world" (p. 7).

The concept is that each of us creates a practical map of the world based on our experiences. Each person's map then will be a little different, based on maturity and experience. Later they then go on to say: "All the accomplishments of the human race, both positive and negative, have involved the use of language. We as human beings use our language in two ways. We use it first of all to represent our experience—we call this activity reasoning, thinking, fantasying, rehearsing. When we are using language as a representational system, we are creating a model of our experience. This model of the world we create by our representational use of language is based upon our perceptions of the world. Our perceptions are also determined by our model or representation" (pp. 22–23).

What they are confirming is that there is a relationship between our inner world of images and representations, the so-called external reality, and the spoken language. Further we noted a little earlier that this would imply that language and consciousness are connected.

This relationship between the development of consciousness and language has important implications for each of us. Paulo Freire has written extensively of this connection in what he calls the *Pedagogy of the Oppressed.*[9] Julian Jaynes in his book *The Origin of Consciousness in the Breakdown of the Bi-Cameral Mind* has even suggested that consciousness of the world as the modern human being experiences it is as recent as written and recorded history.[10]

The concept of internal images prefiguring all of our external actions and reality is a little more challenging. Freire puts it this way, referring particularly to the economically oppressed:

"The oppressed, having internalized the image of the oppressor and adopted his guidelines, are fearful of freedom. Freedom would require them to reject this image and replace it with autonomy and responsibility. Freedom is acquired by conquest, not by gift. Freedom is not an ideal located outside of man; nor is it an idea which becomes myth. It is rather the indispensable condition for the quest for human completion."[11]

The concept of the oppressed here obviously has wider implications for all of us. Freire was particularly concerned with the illiterate. He discovered that in teaching illiterate persons to read and write, they came to a new awareness of their selfhood that enabled them to view their social situation from a new perspective, and do something about it.

The bottom line is that he discovered that language, particularly when it included literacy in the form of reading and writing, enabled persons to image the world differently. Language is then the mediator of inner images into the external world. But more than this, when persons are able to put their thoughts and ideas onto paper they see their reality differently. In his words they become Conscientized, or more self aware of their total reality.

What this implies is that there is something inherent within written and spoken languages that can alter a person's consciousness. This something is values. Let me illustrate this from a personal experience that I had in San Jose, Costa Rica, in 1968.

VALUES AND CONSCIOUSNESS

Early in my career I was sent by the Anglican Church to work in Costa Rica. I was assigned with my family to work in a small mission in Barrio Cuba, in San Jose. The barrio consisted of about 30,000 people. Most of them lived only on a few dollars a week. The cost of living at that time was about a third higher than in Canada or the United States. Naturally all the social problems that go along with poverty such as this were there.

14

I began working in the barrio with a value based model of community development, inspired by Freire. In his own work Freire had shown that if you use emotionally charged words unique to a language, and connected to a particular culture, to teach people to read and write, they learn very quickly. He took specific words and moved the letters around to make up new words that the learner would be taught to identify. Take for example the word "oppression." From this word we can make the words: pop, press, pin, sin and prison.

Freire discovered that by teaching people to read and write this way, they not only learned skills, but they also became aware of the deeper meaning of the word. In Freire's terms they became conscientized. What Freire was identifying was that certain words in the language are more central and powerful than others. These words we call Values.

Freire named the value behind this process "Word," because it was a life-giving experience that made the learners more conscious of their own oppression. In the Bible the word "logos" translated "Word" signifies the wisdom and creative power of God. For the Christian, Jesus was this Word of God incarnated, or made human.

This process gave people an awareness of their own power and potential, as well as their own oppression. In this sense, all human beings are oppressed until they become aware of their own creative potential. Freire's point was that every person, no matter how illiterate, has something to give and say to the world.

My original goal was simply to walk the barrio each day and talk to people, and try to discover what were the emotionally laden words in the language that they kept using. One such word did keep repeating itself: "problema," "the problem." In Spanish this means something like the dreadful most difficult problem. The identified problem was that children were being prostituted as early as nine years of age, in order to provide money for their family's survival. This meant that some families had up to twenty children, since more children meant more money. The result was rampant child abuse, abortion and malnutrition.

Over a period of several months I gathered the people together in the barrio into small groups to discuss the "problema." The group discussions in the barrio were based on the same idea of the motivating power of certain words in the language. These words we later identified and named "values." After several months of discussion the group decided that the "problema" was prostitution and too many pregnancies.

We decided to hold public meetings to discuss these issues. We even got media exposure and financial aid from a local United Nations agency. Many people came to the meetings, but there was something missing. I soon discovered people came to the meetings because the meetings were providing inexpensive entertainment. They were a welcome change to sitting in a one room dwelling, with ten other people, with no water or electricity!

At one meeting, after a long period of silence, during which time I had concluded that the venture was a failure, a woman stood up and said quietly: "At least when I am making love with a man, then at least I know that I am a woman." The group became silent for a few minutes.

Finally a middle-aged man very much respected by the group stood up and spoke: "The barrio is not home to us so much as it is a place where we have to live, and when I, too, touch a woman, then at least it is something to be a human being." We were able at that point to identify those two experiences with one word that had to do with being human: Self Worth.

The group came alive as a result of that experience. The meetings were now charged with energy. Now, whenever I think of the word Self Worth, I think not just of a word in the dictionary, but of a series of images and experiences I had with those people over the months we spent together. The group converged so much around that word and what it meant that in the following months they initiated a family orientation clinic that is still in operation there today.

In the 22 years since that experience a research team called Omega Associates researched and came up with a standardized list of 125 such values, which the reader will find in APPENDIX A. Number 125 was Self Worth. Each value came from a similar in-depth experience as the one explored above. The list is also in several languages including Spanish and English. What we found was that the values, since they come from common human experiences, actually transcend individual language differences.

In the development of computerized instrumentation, we found the list of 125 values cumbersome to work with, so we broke them down into clusters of common values (see Appendix A). The result was a short list of fifty values as follows:

SHORT VALUE LIST

1. SELF PRESERVATION.
2. WONDER/AWE.
3. SAFETY/SURVIVAL.
4. SECURITY.
5. SENSORY PLEASURE.
6. PROPERTY/ECONOMICS.
7. FAMILY/BELONGING.
8. SELF WORTH.
9. BELONGING (LIKED).
10. CARE/NURTURE.
11. CONTROL/DUTY.
12. TRADITION.
13. SOCIAL PRESTIGE.
14. WORK/CONFIDENCE.
15. WORSHIP.
16. PLAY.
17. ACHIEVEMENT/ SUCCESS.
18. ADMINISTRATION/ MANAGEMENT.
19. INSTITUTION.
20. PATRIOTISM/LOYALTY.
21. EDUCATION.
22. WORKMANSHIP/ TECHNOLOGY.
23. LAW/DUTY.
24. EQUALITY.
25. ACTUALIZATION/ WHOLENESS.
26. SERVICE.
27. AUTONOMY.
28. EMPATHY/GENEROSITY.
29. LAW/GUIDE.
30. PERSONAL AUTHORITY.
31. ADAPTABILITY.
32. HEALTH/WELL-BEING.
33. SEARCH.
34. NEW ORDER.
35. DIGNITY/JUSTICE.
36. ART/BEAUTY.
37. INSIGHT.
38. CONTEMPLATION.

16

39.	ACCOUNTABILITY.	46.	WORD/PROPHET.
40.	COMMUNITY/SUPPORT.	47.	COMMUNITY/
41.	DETACHMENT.		SIMPLICITY.
42.	CORPORATE MISSION.	48.	TRANSCENDENCE/
43.	RESEARCH/		ECORITY.
	KNOWLEDGE.	49.	CONVIVIAL
44.	INTIMACY.		TECHNOLOGY.
45.	WISDOM.	50.	RIGHTS/WORLD ORDER.

It is this shorter list that we will use to illustrate our findings in the rest of the book. If the reader wishes to review the longer list or the standardized definitions, you may do so by looking in Appendix A.

What we had discovered in this simple list of words was what occupied our research for the next twenty years. It was not just a simple list of words that, when used in the language, carry with them special meanings that conscientize people, but an enormous source of information about the nature of human beings and the institutions they create. The first discovery was that these values exist in our lives as priorities that reflect our behavior. Not only this, but they also exist in the institutions within which we live. This simple fact raises another question of whose values we live by: those we choose personally, or those given to us by others.

For persons who have grown up in western developed countries such as the United States or England reading popular psychology, the conclusion would no doubt be that mature persons choose their own values and their own path to salvation and happiness. On the other hand a cursory glance at history would suggest that our political and educational structures impose certain values on us. More cynical writers like Ivan Illich would suggest that the majority of values we hold are given to us through the institutions we live in.[12]

VALUES, PRIORITIES AND SELF IMAGE

In order to address this question we need to reflect a little more on the above experience. The result of the experience was that several persons, including myself, became affirmed and grew as a consequence. But in retrospect what I experienced was a little different than most of the others in the group.

I felt affirmed because the time and energy I had put into the experience was a success rather than a failure. The man and woman who stood up and spoke their piece were affirmed through the discovery that what they said was a common experience for everyone else. They experienced affirmation through solidarity and an increased sense of belonging. That is to say, over a period of time, they became aware that they were worth something as human beings. Was what we experienced really the same?

Self Worth is the experience of discovering that when others see me in depth, and see me as I really am, they will value me. It is a social value that occurs only when some in depth sharing occurs. Ideally this occurs early in our life in our family of origin. This of course only happens in a family that has time for quality sharing and mutual caring. Most of the families in Barrio Cuba only had time to think about day to day survival. As a consequence this was a new discovery for most of them that altered their consciousness of who they were and who they could become.

I, on the other hand, had a job and a profession, and only experienced this kind of human deprivation vicariously through the privilege of working with them. Self-worth was not a new revelation for me, but rather a confirmation of my value by being successful in the work that I was doing. The critical difference was not in the experience of the value of Self Worth, but where the value was as a priority in each of our lives. What we had discovered was that values mean very little in isolation. Values such as those listed above are descriptions of human images and behaviors that only make sense when you see them in relationship to other values as priorities. Let us illustrate the point.

I was initially worried that the experience was going to be a failure, and began to associate this with the possibility that I was not going to be successful in what I was doing. This is something common to most of us at one time or another. I was also afraid that my boss, the bishop, would feel I was wasting my time going to all those meetings that were leading noplace. Taking the above list I had three value priorities: ACHIEVEMENT/SUCCESS, SECURITY AND SELF WORTH. I experienced myself with two possibilities as follows:

Worry About Failure	Experience of Success
1. SECURITY	1. ACHIEVEMENT/SUCCESS
2. ACHIEVEMENT/SUCCESS	2. SELF WORTH
3. SELF WORTH	3. SECURITY

In the first experience I was feeling insecure because I was not succeeding, and hence felt of less worth. In the second experience my Achievement, or the success of the venture, made me feel worthwhile, and secure in my job. In the process my internal image of myself as a person changed, and as a consequence I was more confident in how I felt about my capacity to work with people in general.

The persons in the group, however, were dealing with a much more critical set of values. In addition to the discovery of Self Worth, which was not originally even in their consciousness, they were coping with the survival of their families in the barrio. Their values were minimally the following: FAMILY/BELONGING, SELF PRESERVATION, SAFETY/SURVIVAL, COMMUNITY/SUPPORT and SELF-WORTH. Before and after the experience we might imagine they were prioritized as follows:

Before the Experience	After the Experience
1. SELF PRESERVATION	1. SELF WORTH
2. SAFETY/SURVIVAL	2. COMMUNITY/SUPPORT
3. FAMILY/BELONGING	3. FAMILY/BELONGING
4. COMMUNITY/SUPPORT	4. SELF PRESERVATION
5. SELF WORTH	5. SAFETY/SURVIVAL

18

In my early experience of members of the group and the "problema," Self Preservation and Safety absorbed all the energy of most of the families. This was so extreme that the function of the Family was to provide what was necessary for survival, even if it meant bearing many children. In some extreme cases it led to prostituting the children. As such the values of Community and Self-Worth were, practically speaking, non-existent. The image that these people had of the world was that it was a very alien and hostile place. Their image of themselves was that "you look after number one first and last." Not only were people not to be trusted, but no one would ever love you for just being you.

In the second experience we see a major shift in the value priorities. A sense of the value of self is evident and is supported by the nurturing community. This in turn leads to a different image of what is understood by Family/Belonging, which now puts Self-Preservation and Safety in the second rather than the first place. This was underscored by the fact that this led the group to initiate, in the months to come, a family orientation clinic that provided family planning information, child development education and day care opportunities for families of mothers who wished to work.

For me Self Worth was an important but a secondary value. In the second experience it was Achievement/Success that was of primary importance to me. In the group's experience, Self-Worth was critically significant by its absence in the first experience, and powerfully significant by its presence as the first priority in the second experience.

What happened that caused so much creative energy? Minimally we can list the following:

1. There was the emergence and recognition of two new values: SELF WORTH and COMMUNITY/SUPPORT.

2. The people's value priorities changed.

3. The change in value priorities altered their internal perceptions and images of other people and of what was understood by FAMILY/BELONGING.

4. Their definition of their values of Family changed from something necessary for survival to something that nurtures and loves children and provides some belonging and comfort.

In other words when the priorities changed the quality of all their values changed. Putting it another way: their consciousness of themselves and the people around them changed. This in turn changed their behavior on a day to day basis radically. That is, they started using their time and energy in a different way.

This led me in earlier works (1973, 1976) to describe a value as "the priorities we choose and act on that creatively enhance our lives and the lives of those around us." I saw values at that time as being primarily a behavioral reaction to the environment.

Such a definition is supported by persons like Raths, Simon and Harmin (1966) who saw values as something we choose freely after considering the alternatives that we prize publicly, and that we act on immediately and repeatedly.

Both these definitions rightly point out the relationship between behavior, priorities and values. From this point of view values are priorities that are consciously evident in one's behavior. These definitions are also partly in reaction to educational and religious traditions that saw values as beliefs and aspirations, not always evident in a person's behavior. These definitions are helpful and do reflect much of the experience above. However there are other dimensions to the experience that are not covered in such a view. For example, these definitions do not address the transformational and institutional dimensions of the experience.

CONSCIOUSNESS AND COMMUNITY

The above definitions of a value stress the conscious nature of a value. A value is something that is conscious and consciously chosen. Reviewing the above experience as I have over a number of years, I realize that it is not to say that in the early experience of the group Self Worth was completely absent, and that in the later experience it suddenly appeared! Clearly, Self-Worth was a latent unconscious value that was brought to consciousness by the experience of the group.

Secondly, there is an institutional dimension that cannot be denied. It was not originally of a formal institution, although it developed into that later. Originally it was a small group that became a nurturing community of listeners with common concerns. But then is that not how all institutions in society begin?

In fact it can be argued that it was precisely the institutional dimension that permitted the group to transcend itself and grow productively. Clearly our values come from both places, each influencing the other. Living practically in today's world means learning to live and work in institutions. Family life is a form of institutional life. As such, it is the family that is the most basic unit of society, and it is in the family that we internalize our beginning values, as follows:

Diagram 1:2
Individual Values
The Person
Institutional Values

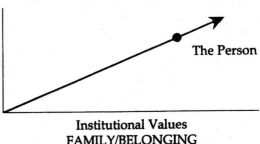

Individual
Values
SELF WORTH
SELF PRESERVATION
SAFETY/SURVIVAL

The Person

Institutional Values
FAMILY/BELONGING
COMMUNITY/SUPPORT

All of us as we grow have to negotiate the individual and institutional dimensions of our lives if we are to mature. Institutions can provide things that individuals cannot obtain on their own. This is another way of saying that we are interpersonal beings. In the early experience of the group this institutional dimension was present in the barrio, reinforcing the value of Self-Preservation. In the second or later experience it was also present but in a different way. Hence the communal institutional interaction was an ingredient of the conscientizing process.

What sense can we make of this? Perhaps we can point out that in the later experience of the group, the people became conscientized to new values that they were not formally aware of. All the group ever needed in this case was to become aware of some new values and re-prioritize their options. Ten years ago I would have probably argued that that was in fact the case. This in fact is only the case after the fact. In reality a major shift in consciousness occurred that is not explained by prioritizing the values alone. The prioritizing of the values occurred as a consequence of the shift in consciousness.

What then caused the shift in consciousness? I do not claim to be able to answer this to my or the reader's total satisfaction. But we have made some headway on the issue that may shed some more light. It was a significant shift in my own consciousness to discover the deeper reality—that values are but outward signs of an inner reality. They are but mediators that point to our behavior and the things we do, such as create institutions. They are the highway signs on the roadway, if you will, from the inner to the outer world.

In the last four years I have become aware that values form dialectical relationships. Dialectical simply means two entities talking to each other. I may give a point of view on what I feel family means. My wife may have another view, and together we may come up with a third and different understanding that satisfies both of us. This is the basis of dialectical discussion or reasoning. It seems that values do the same thing. Two values interact to form a third.

VALUES AND DIALECTICS

In other words not only are values the priorities that we live by, but they form dynamic clusters that can energize us, or perhaps destroy us! Consider our example above. The first experience gives us dialectic 1, from the the first three values, and the second experience gives us dialectic 2, as follows:

DIALECTIC 1
1. SELF PRESERVATION
> FAMILY/BELONGING
2. SAFETY/SURVIVAL

DIALECTIC 2
1. SELF WORTH
> 3. FAMILY/BELONGING
2. COMMUNITY/SUPPORT

In the first Dialectic Self Preservation interacts with Safety/Survival to form an image of Family, which in turn reinforces Self Preservation. That is to say, the Family becomes a tool or an arm of one's Self Preservation needs. Since that first experience I have seen such a dialectic operating in many families, and have seen its destructive effects as many times.

In the second dialectic, the person's sense of worth is enhanced by the community, which in turn gives a worthful or valuable view of the family. This reinforces the Self Worth and repeats the cycle, with the overall consequence of enabling the family to transcend itself in the community.

What is impressive here is the amount of energy that is produced in both cases. One, of course has destructive consequences, and the

21

other creative. Traditionally, it is a way of looking at the forces of good and evil.[13]

see Evil, chapter 10 We also notice in this example that not only are the values operating dialectically in pairs to produce a third, but there is an additional interaction between the personal and the institutional. It seems that it is this series of interactions that causes shifts in consciousness, either to the good and creative or to the evil and destructive side.

This then raises a lot of questions for which we do not always have answers. For example, if our values are not all self-chosen, but are more often the consequence of the interaction between what we choose and the values of those persons and institutions with whom we interact, then should we not be more aware of what they are?

What further might have occurred here? It would appear that since the values in the above dialectic are but mediators of a deeper reality, the real interaction is at this deeper level—namely, that behind each of the values lies a deeper inner reality, an image, often unconscious, of what that value represents. The value, whether in the written language or spoken word, is the tip of an iceberg. Self-Preservation and Self-Worth are prefigured, if you wish, in the unconscious as images of how our inner self views the world of people and things. Hence behind the dialectic there is an inner imaging and re-imaging process that is actually reorganizing the person's world view and all his or her consequent behavior. The values are simply external indicators of this process.

CONCLUSION: THE MEDIATION CONNECTION

What we are in the process of discovering is that values and the use of values is a way of retrieving information about the human condition. On the one hand, the values point to a deeper internal reality of the person and can give us information about human and spiritual growth. The values here point to the way in which each of us perceives the world.

On the other hand, values point to and underlie the way each of us behaves and acts in the world we live in. Values then are information technology mediating the inner world, and enabling it to express itself outwardly in our daily activity.

Also we noted that values are of little significance in isolation. They are priorities that are ordered in such a way as to enable us to cope with reality on a day to day basis. They also form dynamic clusters that can energize us or cause us to live our lives in creative or destructive ways.

Not only do our values reflect the various parts of ourselves, but they are also resident in those extensions of ourselves that influence our day to day living. That is, they are present in the very language we speak and write. They are also present in our institutions, and every expression of what we do, from building houses and the way we design them, to the very way we educate our children. We can now define a value more fully as follows:

"A value is a priority that is held by a person that reflects the internal images and world view of that person. Those values are also transported and contained in the products of human effort such as a work of art. In the human person the values are also chosen priorities that are acted upon daily in one's life that can recreate or detract from the development of that person and the community of persons with whom he or she lives and works. Values in isolation are always positive entities, but form dynamic clusters that can retard or enable growth. Values are units of information that mediate our inner reality into full expression in our everyday lives."

What the definition infers is that values can be specifically identified in language and people's behavior. Not only this, but we noted that when you know what the values are in a given situation, you have access to a lot of hidden information.

Since we do not simply choose our values in isolation but through interaction with other people and things, it is essential that we know as much about them as possible. How do we assess values in ourselves and those with whom we interact in order to produce productive outcomes?

More specifically we might ask: What value combination can insure a successful marriage, or a successful business? How is the management policy of my company or my school affecting my value system? Is there a way of setting up the value priorities of my institution so that creative energy will occur, rather than the opposite? What is the relationship between values, faith, and spiritual and human development? Exactly how can we assess what it is we are doing in this regard more clearly and accurately?

These questions and many others will be addressed in PART II of this book. But before we do that we need to review in more depth the exact nature of the Genesis Effect and its relationship to values as a technology for quality information retrieval. It is this that stands behind all the practical outcomes and insight we will share later. The Genesis Effect is the relationship of the inner to the outer world. The values are simply a tool to retrieve information and make this reality more accessible to us. The next chapter will review this phenomenon as it occurs in religion, science, the arts and technology.

Chapter 1:
Genesis: Values as Mediators of Human and Spiritual Development   NOTES

1. Sowa (1984), p. 1.
2. W. Heisenberg quoted in Capra (1982), p. 81.
3. Jung (1963), p. 3.
4. See Capra (1982), Chapter 3, "The New Physics," for a discussion of quantum physics.
5. Jung (1963).
6. See Capra (1982), Chapter 9, "The Systems View of Life."
7. For a brief historical essay by J. Theodore Klein see Hall (1982).
8. See Loye (1983), Chapter 13, for a discussion of the connection between our inner and outer worlds.

9. Freire (1972).
10. Jaynes (1976).
11. Freire (1972), p. 31.
12. Illich (1973 and 1978).
13. See Peck (1983) for an analysis of evil in the context of psychology.

THE GENESIS EFFECT AND INFORMATION RETRIEVAL

Down here in the depths of the unconscious are found the seeds or cores for the images that articulate and shape our lives. These image "seed-cores" were called archetypes by Jung.
David Loye[1]

Evolution suggests a pulsatory behavior that has devised a miniaturizing process for each step moving from matter to mind: miniaturization from unending and sparce cosmic existence to geological matter, miniaturization from geological matter to organic stuff, miniaturization from organic to organism, miniaturization from organism to animality, miniaturization from animality to reflectivity (man).
Paolo Soleri[2]

Discussion of the concept of Quality Information Retrieval and its relationship to the development of society on the one hand, and the development of a person's inner spiritual reality on the other hand. **PURPOSE**

The concept of Quality Information Retrieval as integral to the development of historical society, the scientific world view and modern life. The chapter further illustrates that each of us has a unique inner life, that is reflected in the ancient spiritual traditions, that is congruent with the recent findings of science and psychology, and that is integral to the spiritual development of each of us. **CONTENT**

The last chapter showed that the connecting point between the external world of history and society and the inner world of images is language and values in the language. This chapter expands that theme to show how values are also an important component of information retrieval which point to an initiating point within each of us—a unique inner reality full of potential wisdom and creativity. This chapter also forms a link with Part II of the book "Personal Genesis" which will explore the development of the individual in detail. **LINKAGE**

Critical to understanding the Information Age is to understand it as a meeting point of inner and outer knowledge systems. It is also the discovery of quality information, rather than quantity data collection. During the last thirty years we have seen the development of satellite television and personal computers that make unlimited information instantly available from any source.

The issue is not information collection and accumulation, but meaningful retrieval. John Naisbit has noted that "we are drowning in information but starved for knowledge." He goes on to note: "If users— through information utilities—can locate the information they need, they will pay for it. The emphasis of the whole information society shifts, then, from supply to selection."[3]

So now we have two processes that are an intricate part of modern society: information exchange and information retrieval. Both processes are changing our perception of the world, both are changing our internal images of how we see reality and how we act in the world as a consequence. The connecting mechanism is HighTec/High Touch. Put simply it is "the way modern society balances the wonders of technology with the spiritual demands of our human nature."[4] (*Megatrends*)

PRIVATE SECTOR INITIATIVE In 1976 I was invited to consult with a group that called themselves "Private Sector Initiative." It was a city-wide project of a large western city. The city's economy was dependent upon employment by the aero industry, which in turn was dependent upon large federal contracts. Overnight contracts were cancelled or reduced and massive unemployment ensued, threatening the life of the city. The purpose of "Private Sector Initiative" was, over a period of five years, to move major employment opportunities in the city away from the public to the private sector.

A committee was formed of representatives from unions, banks, universities, the churches, social agencies, politicians and local industry. Private Sector Initiative was then incorporated into its own agency to accomplish the task. It had a board of approximately 25 persons of influence. Within a very short time, they had their goals broken down into specific agendas and tasks—to be precise they had 300 such agendas and no way to prioritize them! Each group had its own agendas and priorities, making the task of the agency Executive Director impossible.

My job was to sort this information out, and so enable the group to decide on one or two priority goals and to initiate the projects. The task was accomplished in two days: a Friday evening, all day Saturday, and Sunday morning. First of all the group of 25 persons agreed to go away to an island retreat and think of nothing but the task at hand.

They were asked to reflect on what were the basic qualities and outcomes they would like to see as a consequence of the new agency. They were asked to do this by citing experiences, specific in time, from their own business interactions. Similar experiences were then clustered into common sets.

They were then asked to review a simple list of 125 values (see Appendix A), and, forgetting their own agendas, to describe the values behind the various experiences. Each person was then asked to review the values and answer the question: "Given Private Initiative was a success, what five values would you want the public to identify with that you would personally be proud of?"

Within an afternoon not only had each person identified five values, but the group came up with a consensus of eight values in a priority order. They included Work/Labor (more jobs), Collaboration, Human Dignity, Service, Productivity, Unity/Diversity, Security and Education/Certification. They were finally defined and became the working philosophy of the organization. Not only this, but as soon as the priorities were clear, the two or three priority projects to be initiated became self evident, without any political hassle.

The greatest lesson I learned from this experience was that in this day and age it is relatively easy to collect and accumulate data and information, but it is quite another thing to retrieve it in ways that are helpful. The fact is that all the data that the group had was impotent until it was placed through a value grid and retrieved in a non-partisan way. Another striking impression was that this was a city-wide pro- *see Corporate culture,* ject, and as such was affecting the history of that city. Individual val- *chapter 10* ues became group values or group mind, and as such became a part of what we shall refer to later as Corporate Culture.

INFORMATION RETRIEVAL

A friend recently bought a house in the mountains 50 miles south of San Francisco. He wanted the quiet and solitude of mountain life, but at the same time he wanted to stay connected with the world around him. For him that world is a global village. He bought a satellite dish, and had immediately available television programming and news networking from anywhere in the world. Without the dish he could not have retrieved any of the information.

Five years ago when I wanted a reference check done on "values and organizational development," I hired a team of research assistants to search library files for me. The search took a week to do. Now by connecting my computer with Dialog or several other resource systems, I can run a check on almost any subject matter from all the major library systems of the world without leaving my office. In this case, the retrieval was made possible by a combination of me and my computer.

We have just noted in the example that it is not information alone that is important, but our ability to read or retrieve it. Science, for example, is nothing other than the study of how to retrieve information from the natural world.

We noted in chapter I that the recent explosion of global information *see Book of Genesis,* networking was anticipated from the beginning of human conscious- *chapter 1* ness. In the book of Genesis it is God's spoken word that is the occasion for the created order to come about, and it was the development of language that created civilization. The sciences have aided us greatly in the last 100 years to gather more and more information. The issue for our time is the retrieval of quality information that will enable us to make creative decisions rather than destructive ones. This always involves the mediation of values.

We saw in the first chapter how values and language are connected. Consequently, it should not surprise us to see values reflected through the development of history. We shall begin by exploring this connection. The second thing we shall explore is Miniaturization and the connection between internal images and the external structures of historical society. Third and finally, we shall explore what religion has to say about the inner/outer connection through Detachment and Discernment.

QUALITY INFORMATION, VALUES AND HISTORY

Each historical period has its own code for understanding and processing information, and its own dominant values. These values reflect the image of reality, or the predominant world view of that period. Let us consider the last 200 years: the passing of the Industrial Age, and the coming of the present Information Age. Each has its own image of reality and its own unique values.

The Industrial period is something that is still very much with us. In fact, the idea that it is past and we are moving into a new age is a revolutionary thought to many. For this reason it will be helpful to see where the industrial period came from and what its dominant images and values are, especially as we experience them in the West. First it grew out of the development of a new world view discovered in the sixteenth century—empirical science.

THE SCIENTIFIC WORLD VIEW

Most of what a person experiences as science and technology today sprang from the emergence of the empirical sciences in the sixteenth and seventeenth centuries. Great thinkers like Galileo, Descartes, Bacon and Newton made an enormous discovery. It was a discovery that shook the predominant world view of their day.

They discovered that the external reality of the material world could be measured, and that its behavior could be predicted. What made this possible was Newton's basic discovery and premise: that "Time" was a constant.[5] That is to say, the duration of time from three o'clock to four o'clock will be the same every day from now to eternity. Put another way, they posited the idea that our reality is governed by a God-given set of prescribed laws. The concept that such laws are not God-given was a separation that only occurred later or within the last 100 years. It was an emphasis away from the internal religious to the external and measurable.

This may seem obvious to us now, but it was a revelation that was astounding at the time. Galileo, for example, observed that the sun did not go around the earth, but that rather the earth revolved around the sun. Church authorities placed him under house arrest for challenging the commonly understood view that placed the earth and mankind at the center of the universe.

28

This new scientific revolution also caused a psychological one that contributed to the French and American Revolution. At the heart of these revolutions was a new concept of human freedom that valued creativity, invention, and independence. These were all backed by the discovery that revealed knowledge, through scripture and church tradition, was only a part of the picture. As the medieval world view, dominated by the church, lost its power through the Reformation, a new source of measurable revelation was made accessible through the new science. Major values now appearing were: Independence, Equality/Liberation and Knowledge/Discovery/Insight.

THE INDUSTRIAL AGE

The English Revolution, also known as the Industrial Revolution, made the new insights practical and available to the masses through the development of technology. But behind technology stood a scientific image of reality that in the long run placed more value on the external world as the seat of reality, rather than on the world of revealed truth through scripture and church tradition.

An English school teacher by the name of Dalton in the early eighteen hundreds about 150 years after Newton, suggested that every whole can be predicted by the behavior of its parts. He asserted that all material matter is made up of invisible particles called atoms, which are the building blocks that aid us in understanding all matter. That is, it was suggested that any observable object can be understood if you can discover what the nature of its atomic parts are. One understands the whole by going to its smallest part. From these premises arose the technology of the industrial era that we are still living with.

Standardization and Specialization became the norm of the new industrial era. By breaking a machine such as a rifle or a car into hundreds of component parts, and standardizing the form of each part, so thousands of such products could be made and replaced when they broke down. Additionally each part took a specialized set of tasks with a whole range of special skills. As a consequence work and and labor increased, making a large amount of products available at less and less cost to more and more people. It was the backbone of the Industrial Revolution and of Capitalism, the critical values of which became: Productivity, Economics/Success, Education, Work/Labor and Technology.

Specialization meant dealing with parts, making the whole less and less evident. Consequently Sychronization and Centralization became essential additives to the new world view. The additional need for products by the general population as living standards increased meant the need for increased levels of productivity and efficiency. People, products, and energy resources had to be better synchronized, and centralization was one way of accomplishing it. As this view of the world grew, so did the values of Efficiency, Competition, and Administration/Management grow and become more important.

Many of the values from the past still continued to exist. One of these was that women were the weaker sex, particularly in the physical and emotional areas. As Anne Douglas, in an enlightening work called *The Femininization of American Culture* points out, the lack of

see Body Politic, Male Female chapter 3, Kelsey, Appendix

power by women and the loss of power by the clergy in the early eighteen hundreds led to an unconscious liaison between the two groups.[6] This later led to the Women's Rights Movement of the early twentieth century. These were, of course, linking with the general values of Independence and Equality/Liberation that were running through world society at that time.

But additionally Industrial society had a brutal side to it, from the enslavement of children and black Africans to colonial expansion with unfair trade practices, and the confusion of missionary work with cultural importation. God was for the most part unchanging and culturally bound to a particular denominational emphasis. He was also a God that ruled over a world of unlimited resources.

The women of this period may turn out to be the real heroes of the time, since it was they that instituted most of the educational, social and medical institutions of our day. Persons such as the Brontes, Beecher, Nightingale and Elizabeth Seton had untold influence on the humane and quality dimension of life in this period. The values they brought were Justice/Social Order, Empathy and Human Dignity.

Growth and development in every sector was seen as God's gift to the world. Industry and the church flourished, spreading its missions to all parts of the globe, vanquishing forever, so they thought, all poverty and ignorance.

One has to admit that much of what was envisioned did in fact take place. However, it also brought its failures and tragedies, such as the increased efficiency of war, deprivation of the environment, and a population explosion that has increased the overall number of hungry in the world.

Although it is true that this world view still exists for many, its failure is now overwhelmingly evident, due mainly to its success and a critical new discovery. Industrial success has confronted us with the fact that world resources are in fact limited and that as a consequence values of competition and unlimited productivity are counterproductive to the survival of the human race.

The critical discovery is that Newton's concept of the absolute nature of time was wrong! Time is not a constant, it actually contracts and expands. This brings us face to face with a new age, the one we are learning to live in: The Information Age. But like the Industrial Age it also began with a major paradigm shift in the way the average person viewed the world.

THE RELATIVITY OF TIME

New discoveries in Quantum Physics are now facing us with another revolution in human thinking as dramatic as the one that Galileo and Newton posed three hundred years ago, which is converging with new knowledge in the social sciences and religion.

It began in 1921, when Einstein published his theory of relativity.

see chapters 6 and 7 Most people think of Einstein as a brilliant mathematician, as he certainly was. But in fact, his mathematical theory was the language he used to convey a simple idea, an idea that challenged the total scientific world view of that time.

What was his thought or idea? Simply put, it was: "What would the world look like if I rode a beam of light?" Let me explain. If I were looking at a large clock on a church tower and it read nine o'clock, what I would be reading would be conveyed by a beam of light. Suppose now I rode that beam of light at the speed of light to a distant planet, and arrived on the planet ten minutes later. The clock would still read nine since its time is conveyed by the light. But for me it is surely ten past nine!

Einstein showed that time is flexible and actually expands and contracts, whereas it is only the speed of light that is a constant. What is seen and perceived by the observer is therefore relative, and not as objective and certain as had been presupposed. That simple initiating discovery has altered the whole world view of what constitutes reality. It has, in fact, brought us face to face with a new view of reality and a new Age that we are learning to live in: the Information Age.[7]

THE INFORMATION AGE

John Naisbitt notes: "Ten major transformations are taking place right now in our society. None is more subtle, yet more explosive, I think, than the first, the megashift from an industrial to an information age" (*Megatrends*).[8]

The spiritual traditions have understood for centuries that time and consciousness are intimately related. The potential of the industrial period was limited by its view of time, which was based on Newton's laws of motion. Time was linear and constant. Einstein exploded that view of time, and as a consequence altered our understanding of consciousness.

CONSCIOUSNESS, TIME AND INFORMATION

By consciousness we mean not only awareness, but awareness of awareness. It is the process of thinking about thinking, and has been a part of traditional philosophy for centuries. In the empirical view thoughts as images could not be proven to exist since they cannot be located in time and space.

Yet, we know they exist, since most people dream dreams. The concept of an unconscious as posited by Freud and Jung, therefore, seemed particularly heretical to many psychologists, since these were ghostly fantasies that had no empirical base. Yet, on the other hand, we know that these images and stories that appear in dreams are very energizing at times, and affect the external behaviors of the dreamer. We also know that a dream that feels like an hour in duration may have occurred in a split second. In other words time is experienced differently in the internal world of dreams than with our day to day conscious reality.

What is fascinating is that all this paradoxical information about the world of internal images is not a stranger to the world of Quantum Physics. In fact it parallels many discoveries that have occurred since the 1920's. The first and most obvious is the relativity of time itself.

Einstein, we noted earlier, pointed out that time was elastic and changed depending on the motion of the observer. The closer to the speed of light a person moves, the quicker one moves through time. In recent years that has been validated in a number of ways. It has been demonstrated, for example, that a moving clock runs slower than a stationary one. It has also been shown that gravitational pull also has an effect on and alters the experience of time.

Itzhak Bentov reports of an experiment with time in the use of bio-feedback during meditation states.[9] He noted that when a person produces Theta waves, which is a deep meditative state, and keeps his or her eyes open and on a clock with a second hand, the second hand slows to a point of almost stopping.

see Harari, Appendix Not only does this information raise questions about our traditional view of time, but it is the same view of time we experience in the world of images and dreams. What is also fascinating is that the left and right side of the brain function on different views of time. The left side orders the world in a linear and manageable way. Its view of time is the way in which we normally view it, namely that time is a constant on which we rely for our day to day business.

On the other hand, the right side of the brain does not think in space-time continuums. Often the subject and the object occur together as one observes oneself in a dream. The experience of time is summed up in a moment. Consequently what appears to be a long dream may have occurred in a split second.

Interestingly enough this parallel has occurred in theories of human development, such as with the developmentalists and the Existential-*see Part II* ists. Developmental theories of human personality posit the idea that human growth is related to the completion of certain tasks at different stages of one's maturity. Such theories relate these tasks to the aging process. There is a lot of stress on understanding the psychology of the maturing process from childhood to middle age to retirement. Time, here, is linear and left brain orientated.

see Harrison and Prendergast, Appendix On the other hand the Existentialists view all time as being in the present moment. Counseling means dealing with the now. The past is present in memory, and the future is present as one imagines what it will be. This view is clearly right brain thinking, relative to our understanding of time.[10]

It is now clear that both views are right. The truth would appear to be a blend of both. But in the old empirical world view, truth tended to be one thing or the other. It had a lot of difficulty dealing with paradox. Quantum Physics is pointing out that we have to live with both most of the time. In other words time is both linear and non-linear at the same time. To think this way is new to us. The critical link is information retrieval. When one thinks developmentally, one retrieves one set of information; when one thinks existentially, one gets another set of information. Both are a part of one whole.

This became particularly evident when physicists tried to study the nature of atoms. The concept until recently was that atoms were tiny particles that were composited in different ways to give us everything from sulphur to steel. But closer examination showed that the atoms consisted of more and more sub-atomic parts that looked less and less like the objective material reality expected.

What was odd was that these sub-atomic entities behaved as particles when the observer was looking for particles, and behaved as waves when the observer was looking for waves. The same phenom-

32

ena occurred for light. Sometimes it behaved as if it were made up of particles called photons, and at other times it behaved like waves which are spread out over a large area. Nils Bohr suggested that both realities were true at the same time. He called it his theory of complementarity.[10a]

Not only can we have differing expressions of reality, which seem to our finite minds to be opposites, but it also seems that the observer's attitude can actually alter the reality that he or she will see. The more these sub-atomic particles were studied, the more it became apparent that the concept of individual and isolated particles made no sense. Bohr finally concluded that isolated particles are but abstractions. The reality, he said, was that their properties could only be defined as they interact with other systems.

This led another scientist like Gregory Bateson to suggest that nothing we know can be defined or understood, except in how it relates to other things.[11] In other words, the more we move to the inner nature of things whether it be sub-atomic particles, or dreams, we end finding ourselves connected to the whole. Life, if you wish, is one undivided whole.

Unfortunately, we live in a world where people often feel that only one way is right, and cannot conceive of a world view that lives with paradox as the norm. The world is full of people who live by the rules of narrow ideologies, and who feel that they, and they only, have the truth. In the new world view they might all be true. In other words, INFORMATION IN THE INFORMATION AGE IS BY ITS VERY NATURE PARADOXICAL.[12]

Quantum physics has led to the inescapable conclusion that consciousness is the consequence of and an intentional part of the evolutionary process. The human being's inner world of dreams and images is an inescapable part of that reality. For this reason it should not surprise us that there are obvious parallels between the paradoxes of the inner life of myth and dream, and what is being discovered about the nature of reality through the new physics. This is causing a new revolution in information where the information is the consequence of an inner and outer process.

From 1900 on there was a slow but growing awareness through the behavioral sciences of a new in-depth understanding of the human being. Psychoanalysis, group dynamics, the sociology of marriage, and management science all contributed to a new perception of the human being. In the religious sphere a reaction to the mass institutionalism of religion stirred a new interest in meditation and the commonality of the eastern and western traditions.

Through the 1950's and into the sixties people's perception of what constitutes the quality of living had changed, and a whole new set of values began to emerge as the norm for many people such as intimacy, empathy, sharing/listening/trust, contemplation and play.

This period was also characterized by a reaction to the conformity of the passing industrial era, plus a major mistrust of large corporate entities. This was dramatically symbolized by the Second Vatican

THE INFORMATION AGE: THE OUTER CONNECTION

Council of the Roman Catholic Church in the mid nineteen sixties. One of its critical acts was to return to the legitimate historical practice of having the priest face the people during the Eucharist, rather than conduct the majority of the service with his back to the congregation. This theologically meant a shift from the priest in hierarchical authority standing between God and the people, and acting as representative on their behalf, to inviting the congregation to participate with him in a community of equals.

The consequence was not a few ritualistic changes, but a major value shift from a beauracratic system to a participative system of management. The immediate overall result was chaos, as hundreds of priests and sisters rebelled against dress code, teaching methods and basic management structure.

They, however, contravened a basic law of human systems: namely that individuals are able to change far more rapidly than it is possible for a system to change—especially one like the Roman Catholic Church which has 700 million members! The basic value shift was from institutionally dominated values such as Work, Service, Efficiency, Duty, Hierarchy and Law to a new emphasis on the interpersonal dimensions of quality Community, Intimacy, Accountablity, Justice and Human Dignity. I am not suggesting that these are mutually exclusive, but only that there was a major cultural priority shift.

Another major change occurred in 1945—the dropping of the atomic bomb on Hiroshima. In the medieval period wars were fought by paid mercenaries. War was also viewed as a short-lived phenomenon that occasionally broke up normal day to day life. In 1914, for the first time in history, ordinary lay people were conscripted into wars between nation states. Yet even as late as 1939 when Germany declared war against several European communities, England had several months to prepare. War was something that one took time to get ready for. This all ended at Hiroshima when a new and dreadful global entity was created: the security state and its economic symptom, the arms race.

Should war be declared by a major power, the threat would be instant and the build-up time would be zero. Hence, since 1945 we have spent more time and money on weapons of destruction annually than we did for the totality of World War II.

Therefore, in addition to the chaos of rapid change due to the new enlightenment values, we have an increase of the values of Self Preservation, Security and Safety/Survival that affects everyone on the planet earth.

What makes the Information Age particularly unique is the rapidity with which it is changing the world we live in. For the first time in history information is immediate and global in its source and impact. Images of persons and situations are everywhere available through satellite television. Computers are forming global networks that speak to each other instantly from Italy to Japan. What the information age might be then is a new breakthrough in consciousness. John Haught in referring to new discoveries in the field of molecular biology suggests:

"Throughout most of human history our universe has been viewed as a repository of meaning. It is not entirely out of the question that modern molecular biology is but one of many recent scientific developments that have made it possible for us to rehabilitate this intuition in a fresh way. The specific sequence of vibrations gives an electron its character or an atom its properties. The specific sequence of nucleotides determines the various kinds of life that appear in evolution. Perhaps our universe is closer to an embodiment of 'intelligence' than we have been accustomed to think."[13]

At the heart of the matter is the fact that information can be life-giving or destructive. How it is used is dependent upon how we view the world. It is here that we note that there has always been an inner connection. After all, no idea was ever formed except from within the recesses of the human mind. Bronowski has given an excellent historical portrayal of how the ascent of the human being has been a long process of one idea connecting to another, shaping the very world we live in.

"Man is a singular creature. He has a set of gifts which make him unique among the animals: so that, unlike them, he is not a figure in the landscape—he is a shaper of the landscape. In body and in mind he is the explorer of nature, the ubiquitous animal, who did not find but has made his home on every continent."[14]

GENESIS EFFECT: THE INFORMATION CONNECTION

The historical survey we have just completed confirms the idea that values are very much in our environment affecting history, shaping our institutions of learning and of war. In fact they affect and reflect all our external behavior. But this information is in fact made real by its connection with another entirely different set of data coming from within. Jung called this inner source the Psyche.

Let us return first to our original diagram to keep the overall perspective clear. In the Diagram the Internal Reality is basically what Jung and others have referred to as the unconscious. It has its own unique process and information. The external world contains all the information we gain from our senses. This includes the accumulative information of history that we reviewed above. (See next page.) Earlier we also noted that this picture is really a whole, and that the external and the internal are really related interdependently. They are not separate parts, but parts of a whole. But at face value they seem as though they are totally different realities: the external world of history and the internal world of the Psyche. What is this Psyche and what is the nature of the information that it carries? And what is the process by which it is decoded. The process called Miniaturization?

THE INNER CONNECTION: SOMETHING FROM JUNG

The psychoanalyst Carl Jung was born in 1875 and died in June 1961. His interest was in a study of the unconscious. Near the end of his life in a book called *Memories, Dreams, Reflections*, he wrote the following:

"My life is a story of the self-realization of the unconscious. Everything in the unconscious seeks outward manifestation, and the personality too desires to evolve out of its unconscious conditions and to experience itself as a whole."[15]

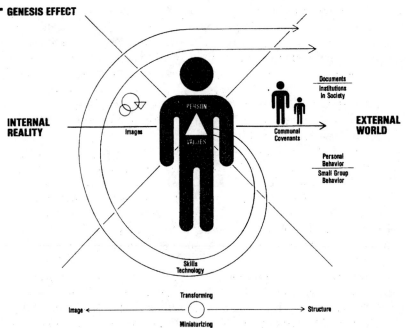

Diagram 2:1.
THE GENESIS EFFECT II
How complex information is processed internally by a human being and transformed by values, skills and technology into new external realities we call institutions and society.

see Ledig, Appendix

For Jung, the imagination is the innate ability of the brain to generate images, images that are largely unconscious, but that come to our consciousness in the form of dreams. These all constitute an inner part of our reality that is ninety percent unconscious, and actually has a life of its own. This entity is called the *Unconscious*. This is what Jung himself had to say:

"The rationally explicable unconscious, which consists of material that has been made unconscious artificially, as it were, is only a top layer, and that underneath is an absolute unconscious which has nothing to do with our personal experience. This absolute unconscious would then be a psychic activity which goes on independently of the conscious mind and is not dependent even on the upper layers of the unconscious, untouched—and perhaps untouchable—by personal experience. It would be a kind of supra-individual psychic activity, a *collective unconscious*, as I have called it, as distinct from a superficial, relative, or personal unconscious."[16]

He also noticed that in his own life journey, as well as in those of thousands of clients that he observed, the more integrated and mature a person became, the more these dreams and images became conscious. It was as if, in his words, the unconscious of a person was not only striving to be known by the conscious part of a person, but striving to be meaningfully focused. This is what a number of psychologists and theologians now refer to as the Self.[17]

36

David Loye, reflecting on image formation and recent discoveries about the brain, adds the following in reference to Jung:

ARCHETYPES AND TWO DREAMS

"Jung also contended that the images underlying our thoughts and behavior do not arise solely within the limits of our single skulls. The most powerful of these images, shaping the destinies of humans and of nations, arose from a 'collective unconscious' wherein we are, like swimmers holding hands in the sea, hooked into the unconscious of one another. To compound this heresy, he further contended that these large images, the 'archetypes,' are passed on generation after generation through genetic codes."[18]

This was illustrated to me recently over a two year period, with two dreams I had recorded. The first dream was written while I was on a three day holiday at a point when I was feeling a lot of stress in my life.

The dream occurred in 1982. In the dream I was observing myself in a lotus or meditation position wearing no clothes except for a pair of linen shorts. I was sitting in the middle of a white circle which was divided into five segments, each with writing on it. The first said: Your birth and the expectations of your school teachers and parents. The second said: Your teenage years and your expectation to conquer the world. The third said: Your marriage and your years of striving for success. The fourth said: Years of questions, stress and possible despair. The fifth and last segment read: Years of aging, detachment and possible rebirth. The last segment then pointed back to the first. I then looked up and said: "What can I do?" The answer came, "Seek the friendship of the Bear."

I wrote the dream down in my diary and for the most part forgot about it. Its obvious meaning for me at the time was that I was stressed because of my undue worry about success and what others expected of me, and that I had always had that tendency. The segment on detachment had specific meaning for me since meditation was an important factor in my life that I had neglected. Detachment is a method of meditation. The statement about the Bear meant nothing at the time.

Eighteen months later at a time when there was a considerable increase in opportunity for financial success in my life, I had this second dream.

THE SECOND DREAM

In the first scene I was standing on the side of a mountain, completely alone, among a sparsely scattered group of tall Canadian pines. Then there appeared, about one hundred yards away, a huge black stallion. It just stood there staring at me. I felt fearful, and fled to a cave lower down the mountain.

I now viewed myself sitting on the floor of a huge, well lit cave. In the center there was a circle of green short grass. I was sitting cross-legged in the circle, relaxed with my back erect, staring at the cave entrance. In front of me, on the edge of the circle, were several baby bears sitting upright. At the entrance to the cave was a very large brown bear guarding the entrance. A voice said: "Do not fear for you are a friend of the Bear."

Suddenly, outside the cave there was a roaring noise as the black stallion and a great herd of horses came down the mountain and ran in front of the cave. As I looked out through the entrance, in the dust I saw the history of humanity passing in front of me. On the horses there appeared knights and soldiers of many ancient wars, from ancient Rome to horse-drawn cannons of World War I. The large brown Bear simply stood there making sure that they passed by, and that we were protected. The voice repeated itself again: "Do not fear for you are a friend of the Bear."

The scene changed for a third time. I saw myself sitting in the same cross-legged position on a patch of grass on a ledge overlooking a pool of water which was being fed from a gentle waterfall, some twenty feet high. Sitting beside me, upright and staring at the waterfall, was the brown Bear. Once again the voice repeated: "Do not fear for you are a friend of the Bear."

I was greatly moved by the dream, but did not know why. In talking to a faculty member who specializes in dream analysis and imagery, some aspects of the dream became clearer. In Jung's terms it was a myth made up of many images, some of which were archetypal, like that of the Circle, the Bear and the Horse.

The Horse is a very ancient motif, and is familiar to us in the myth of the centaur—half man and half horse. It is probably connected to the fact that a major alteration in the development of civilization occurred at the point horses were tamed and used for transportation and means of power as instruments of war. Consequently, the horse is often felt as a symbol of masculine power. In riding the Horse, ancient civilizations were able to cross the globe as conquerors.

The Bear appears to be another archetype that is even more ancient. It is felt by some to symbolize the very "ground of caring being." It is the image of stable protection and care, such as a strong parent may give to his or her children.

The circle or mandala is the most common of all archetypes and represents the process of integration. Water is, of course, a common archetype of cleansing and purifying, as in the waters of baptism. We could go on and explore the dream, but that would distort our purpose. The two dreams simply illustrate how the psyche continues with a life of its own. The theme of the bear occurred in the second dream as a continuation of the first, even though it had no obvious meaning to me at the time.

But as I examined the dreams from a personal value perspective, much more came to light. Values such as Integration/Wholeness, Care/Nurture and Security were important to me. In fact the Bear represented very clearly the last two values for me. Integration/Wholeness was in both dreams as the circle. But more than anything, my friends were able to say that it was clear to them that when I took time to sit and be quiet, and reflect as the water scene indicated, my own creative life did in fact improve.

What we are dealing with is information that comes for each of us from two sources, an inner world of racial memories and mythical insights, and an outer world of sensory perception. For hundreds of years this connecting point has been the crux of the spiritual life, and the discipline of the ancient art of contemplation.

The assumption is that reality encompasses both an inner and an outer reality. Reality is not one or the other. What is required is that both realities be seen as a balanced whole which must be in harmony with each other. Something has to mediate the two realities. That something is called values. It is the values that we have that carry the life-giving energy of the inner world into the external world of family and society. But although it is true that the values mediate this process, something else also happens; it is called Miniaturization.

The par excellence examples of miniaturization comes from the arts. One of those great artists was Michelangelo, who in 1501 sculptured his famous statue of David. Kenneth Clark, in writing about Michelangelo's work, says the following:

MINIATURIZA-TION: CONSCIOUSNESS MADE MANAGEABLE

"Seen by itself the David's body might be some unusually taut and vivid work of antiquity; it is only when we come to the head that we are aware of a spiritual force that the ancient world never knew. I suppose that this quality, which I may call heroic, is not a part of most people's idea of civilization. It involves a contempt for convenience and a sacrifice of all those pleasures that contribute to what we call civilized life. It is the enemy of happiness. And yet we recognize that to despise material obstacles, and even defy the blind forces of fate, is man's supreme achievement; and since, in the end, civilization depends on man extending his powers of mind and spirit to the utmost, we must reckon the emergence of Michelangelo as one of the great events in the history of western man."[19]

What Michelangelo accomplished in this one work of art was to take all his internal images, ideas and reflective thinking about Greek and Roman antiquity, all his thought about the Old Testament and the person of David, and convert that through personal skill and the technology of the stone mason into one external representational form. The result was the statue: David.

Basically, miniaturization is the continual process from complexity to simplicity. It is taking complex data, like all of arithmetic and simple mathematical equations and accounting problems that would fill several text books, and shrinking all that data into one two by three inch hand-held calculator. The calculator is simple to use, and does not require so much knowledge to use it as the original mathematical principles did. Here we see that arithmetic has in fact been miniaturized.

But something else has happened in the process. All the mathematical symbols and processes that the calculator is able to potentially carry out appear in an external physical form as a the calculator. Obviously, there has been a translation process.

First of all the brain in all its complexity took not only all the mathematical data, but also all the technical data about calculators to formulate the final idea. We do not know how this occurs; we only know that an original act of creation does occur. Again, internal images become an extraordinary and totally different external structure that miniaturizes the task in a new way.

39

Another way to view this is that the brain processes thoughts, ideas and images that are really ways of collating external sensory data, and reorganizes such data with internal unconscious information into a new miniaturized form. But is this all we have? Surely Michelangelo's David is more than an information unit. First of all, art conveys not only information that is, in the everyday sense, practical, but feelings and spiritual messages that go beyond the normal limits of sensory perception. That is what makes art art. When this happens something else has occurred.

When I look at the statue of "David" or use my pocket calculator I have access to information that I did not have before. Also, I am able to do things and experience things that were not accessible to me before. As an owner of a small business who never learned sufficient accounting skills, I suddenly find I have information at my fingertips that enables me to be more successful and more confident in what I am doing.

The sensitive observer of Michelangelo's statue will view David and even the Psalms of David in a different light. In other words, miniaturization has the consequence of expanding human awareness. It develops consciousness. I call this process "Minessence." It is the process of simplifying complex data and translating it into new forms.

Minessence is the value that has as its goal the precise process of converting the internal world of ideas and images, as information, into unique external structures, such as calculators, houses and institutions. It has the consequence of developing human consciousness. It is an integral part of the life process that we have called the Genesis Effect.

But since it is the value priorities that we choose that enable us not only to retrieve information, but have some governance over our lives, how we make value choices becomes a central and critical issue. In the ancient traditions this was called discernment.

DISCERNMENT AND THE PROBLEM OF INFORMATION RETRIEVAL

Oddly enough since the dawn of history, information retrieval, or, more precisely, how to make the right decision given the information available, has been at the heart of religious tradition. It was termed "Discernment of Spirits."

It is here that we shall now turn for additional information as a way of concluding this chapter. Discernment of Spirits, unfortunately for many, conjures up images of rigid religious fundamentalism, based on narrow interpretation of the scriptures. Historically and traditionally this is not the case.[20]

see Grassi and Schmitt, Appendix

The origin of the term appears to come from a time in history when it was believed that any choice that a person made was informed or influenced by the spirits or gods. This is still true in some parts of the world today, where primitive cultures still exist. When a person made a choice that led to productive ends, the conclusion was that he or she must have been informed by the good spirits. If the choice happened to be a bad one, then the bad spirits must have been at work. Hence, the origin of the term "Discernment of Spirits."

Historically, leaders would seek out wise men or women to discern

40

the spirits for them before they made major decisions. One of the most famous was the Oracle at Delphi in Greece that was a great center for learning and discernment for centuries before the birth of Christ.

The concept of discernment is as we have noted very ancient. But additionally it has always been linked with wise leadership since the time of King Solomon which dates back to about 600 B.C. The following quotation from the first book of Kings speaks for itself in this regard:

"At Gibeon the Lord appeared in a dream to Solomon during the night. God said, 'Ask what you would like me to give you.' Solomon replied, 'You showed great kindness to your servant David, my father, when he lived his life before you in faithfulness and justice and integrity of heart; you have continued this great kindness to him by allowing a son to sit on his throne today. Now, Lord my God, you have made your servant king in succession to David my father. But I am a very young man, unskilled in leadership. Your servant finds himself in the midst of this people of yours that you have chosen, a people so many in its number that it cannot be counted or reckoned. Give your servant a heart to understand how to discern between good and evil, for who could govern this people of yours that is so great?' " (1 Kings 3:5–10).[21]

In the Hebrew tradition the question became how we can distinguish good prophets and kings from the false ones. This was at a time when there were many prophets—it was a way of making a living for many. A methodology was set up by which the prophet's value was measured behaviorally. A good prophet, for example, would follow the commandments, be a person of prayer, and even perhaps be able to heal people. In other words, discernment slowly became recognition of certain behaviors codified into rules, later described as the law.

The discerner or prophet was one who read the "signs." He or she read available information called "signs" and interpreted the outcome. A prophet such as Jeremiah in reading the signs or the behavior exemplified by the local king and his political allies was able to predict the fall of Jerusalem. From a purely secular point of view, he was insightfully reading the signs of the times. From the religious point of view, he was also doing that, but was additionally informed by the Spirit of God within.

In the Old Testament, but particularly in the New Testament era, God was present in many forms through dreams. One sees this with Joseph and the King of Egypt (Genesis 40) and with Daniel and King Nebuchadnezzar of Babylon (Daniel 2). In the New Testament the popular story of the Angel visiting Mary in the night to tell her of the birth of Jesus was in the author's term a manifestation that occurred in a dream (Luke 1:26ff). In Matthew Mary's husband decided to divorce her when he found out she was pregnant: "Joseph was an upright man unwilling to expose her to the law and decided to divorce her quietly. Such was his intention when suddenly the angel of the Lord appeared in a dream" (Matthew 2:19bff—NAB).

The only point I wish to make is that in the biblical world view dreams are the place where the spirit of God, as well as the spirit of evil, speaks and moves. This point has been very adequately researched in a volume titled *Dreams: The Dark Speech of the Spirit*, by Morton Kelsey.[22] He also documents that the same attitude persisted in traditional spirituality until quite recently—that is, the last one hundred years.

Not only this, but the eastern traditions had a similar orientation. Ancient Buddhist writings reflect the same discovery about the inner and external nature of things. The four truths of Buddha speak of the nature of suffering. The first truth is that all the world is suffering. The second truth deals with the cause of suffering which is attachment to inner desires. For example, if one is suffering anxiety due to the discovery of a terminal illness, its cause would be due, according to the Buddhist doctrine, to the expectation that I should live a long life.

The third truth deals with the cessation or removal of the suffering. By removing this inner need to expect that I should live a long life, I eliminate the suffering. The fourth truth describes the "Way," or the method by which persons detach themselves from those desires and needs that cause this erroneous view of reality in the first place.

CONTEMPLATION AND DISCERNMENT

see Simplicity and Spiritual Growth, chapter 6

In Western spirituality, especially as influenced by the Gospel of Saint John, the concept was that behavior and rules were indeed important, but that contemplation was equally important. That is to say, attention to the inner life, as in the Buddhist tradition, was of equal importance.

In the East the methodology was stressed. In the West the theology and exactly what you believed was of primary concern. However, the point was that the quality of one's inner life, through ascetical practice, must be of the highest order if true discernment was to be a possibility.

In the terms of Christian mysticism it is only as one experienced intimacy and union with God, or with the divine, that one would be able to see God's purpose for the created order clearly. In the eastern experience and methodology it is this experience that detaches one from all one's negative desires, whether they be sexual, anxiety related, depressive, the need for power, or whatever, and enables one to be at one with inner and infinite wisdom.

see Stages of Mystical Development, chapter 4

Either way, from the point of view of the mystic, the end result is the same: the right behavior, combined with contemplative practice, gives rise to the kind of wisdom that allows a person or community of persons to discern wisely about global affairs. An additional result is the right use of human resources relative to a just and environmentally harmonious world.

see Schmitt, Appendix

In the West, a high point in the practice of the discernment of spirits was Ignatius of Loyola, who constructed a brilliant training method that made extensive use of feelings and imagery.[23] This was in the 16th century and, as such, very advanced for the time. He developed a four week process that moved the young novice or trainee to a point of commitment to a life plan and direction. Sometimes, of course, such a plan was not possible. The point is that the discernment process assumed a formal set of minimal behaviors and a concrete commitment to a given value stance.

Finally a concrete difference between the Western Christian orientation and the East is the communal dimension. In the West especially from the writings of Paul there is the assumption that this overall discernment process is communal first and individual within that context. In other words there is a set of values that the group or the community is committed to as well as the individual.

There are some very obvious connections between discernment and human and organizational growth that we need to note. But before we do that I feel that we might need to set the record straight on some historical abuses that some readers may be aware of or have had to live with. *see Corporate Genesis, Part III*

For some, the term Discernment of Spirits held by certain religious personalities or groups conjures up legitimate fears of the rigid impositions of certain values and ideas. For some it conjures up the thoughts and ideas of control through values of special interest groups. These fears are totally valid, but they are not at all related to this work, or the interest of the author.

Discernment is being used specifically in the historical way in which I have explained it. Values, as was explained in the first chapter, are here understood as priorities that will better enable us to retrieve quality information. Having said all that, I want to make it clear that informed religion and science have a lot to learn from each other. With that out of the way let us proceed with some conclusions about this chapter.

It seems that we have now come round in a circle. In the first half of the chapter we looked at the macro effect of values as they affected historical society. We concluded by looking at Discernment of Spirits. At the societal level, we noted that we are drowning in information, giving rise to the problem of selection, or to retrieval of information. Similarly, we are drowning in values, also giving rise to the problem of selection, as knowing what are the right values we need to guide our decisions by.

CONCLUSIONS: THE IMPLICATIONS FOR PERSONAL AND CORPORATE GENESIS

Benjamin Tonna, a Maltese sociologist, was the director for some ten years or more of a documentation center in Rome, called SEDOS. His job was to collect and categorize global information to aid foreign missionary efforts. It was he who first pointed out to me that it was a relatively simple matter to collect data, but it was quite another thing to collect quality information that could be retrieved in helpful ways and that would enable persons to make sound discernment decisions. In making a study of the city at the global level, and particularly in the third world, he suggests that values are signs of God's intentions for our world. He writes as follows:

"What type of solution offered by the predominant values in the city is in alignment with the master plan of God? In what way? In what modalities? This brings us to a true and full reading of the city-sign as a point of entrance into God's plans for contemporary urbanization. We must again examine each of the major components (values) of contemporary urbanization, to see if it is coherent with what we already know about that plan of God."[24]

Tonna is simply returning back to our intitial theme of Genesis and

43

the Genesis Effect. After all, the central message of that book is that, no matter what one's religious disposition is, we have a responsibility for the earth and what we do with it.

In recent literature the macro dimension of values, as they relate not only to culture but also to the internal culture of an organization, has also become a central focus. This is something that we will be concentrating a great deal on in Part III of this book. William Ouchi has the following to say in this regard:

"Tradition and climate make up a company's culture. More than that, culture implies a company's values, such as aggressiveness, defensiveness, or nimbleness—values that set a pattern of activities, opinions, and actions. Managers instill that pattern in employees by their example and pass it down to succeeding generations of workers."[25]

We noted in the central section of the chapter the importance of internal sources of information from what Jung called the Psyche. We also noted that by analogy at least there are a lot of parallels between the new physics and the nature of the psyche particularly as we examine concepts of space and time.

Often this takes on the complicated and fascinating form of miniaturization which not only translates the internal reality into a new form, but conscientizes the person into new levels of awareness at the same time. We called this process "minessence."

What this implies is that each human being is continually experiencing data from two sources, simultaneously, from the Psyche and from the external world of sensory perception. Values stand in between as a brokerage unit assessing and enabling the brain to synthesize the information into the common everyday decision making processes.

Clearly, then, values are of central importance. But the problem is that we are bombarded by them every day of our life. What we have done through our research is develop a method of not only identifying what the values are, but, more importantly, learning to read what they mean when one is confronted with them.

It turns out that there are a limited number of significant values that affect our lives on a day to day basis, and they fall into predictable and readable patterns. In Benjamin Tonna's terms they really are signs, once one knows how to read the language. We will begin by moving to Part II of the book, "The Personal Genesis," which will examine how the value patterns affect human and spiritual development. Part III will move into the Organizational Dimension.

NOTES **Chapter 2:**
The Genesis Effect and Information Retrieval

1. Loye (1983), p. 127.
2. Soleri (1973), p. 5.
3. Naisbit (1982), p. 24.
4. Ibid., p. 4.

44

5. See Capra (1982), Chapter 2, for more information on the New-tonian world view.

6. Douglas (1977).

7. See Loye (1983), Chapters 4 and 5, for a fascinating discussion of time. In these chapters he treats of the different inner biological rhythms from which the mind selects its time referents, appropriate to the "time sense" demanded. Serial time, spatial time and "timeless time" are elucidated in a clear manner.

8. Naisbitt (1982), p. 11.

9. Bentov (1977).

10. See Yalom (1980), p. 346, for an application of the existentialist's "time emphasis" to the process of psychotherapy.

10a. See Capra (1982), pp. 79–80.

11. Bateson (1972).

12. See Schumacher (1977), Chapter 10, "Two Types of Problems," for an analysis of coping with paradox.

13. Haught (1984), p. 59.

14. Bronowski (1973), p. 19.

15. Jung (1963), p. 3.

16. Campbell (1971), p. 34.

17. See Bolen (1984) for an examination of archetypes in women, using myths of Greek goddesses in conjunction with the Jungian per-spective.

18. Loye (1983), p. 77.

19. Clark (1969), pp. 123–124.

20. See Richards (1970).

21. The Jerusalem Bible, 1 Kings 3:5–10.

22. Kelsey (1968).

23. See De Guibert (1964) for a full treatment of the method and un-derlying values of the training of his followers by Ignatius of Loyola, founder of the Society of Jesus.

24. Tonna (1982), p. 129.

25. Ouchi (1984), p. 195.

THE PERSONAL GENESIS

Change is but a mode of existence, which follows on another mode of existence of the same object; hence all that changes is permanent, and only the condition thereof changes.
Immanuel Kant.[1]

Man has lived in close contact with change since he first appeared on earth. During every one of the thirty-six million minutes of his life his own body alters imperceptibly as it moves from birth to maturity to death. Around him the physical world too is in constant change, as seasons pass: each day brings visible evidence of the annual cycle of growth, fertility and decay.
James Burke.[2]

Part II of this book, on personal genesis, is directed at the understanding of human and spiritual development, using value based methods and information retrieval methods. Reference in this section will be made to several other developmental theories. The value perspective is not offered as an alternative, but rather to illustrate that all such theories are naturally related. The primary purpose of this section is, however, to offer some of the insights that we have gained from the use of our own instrumentation in working with people on a personal and corporate level.

INTERIM
REFLECTIONS

Introduction

The next five chapters are called personal genesis because I am treating the material from the primary perspective of the person. In fact we are always related to the greater whole of the institutions that we work in, or to our family and friends with whom we live. Therefore this greater dimension is assumed and will be continually alluded to. In fact we will continually address the issue of leadership which has obvious institutional dimensions.

see Institutional Perspective,
Part III

Values, we have continually stressed, stand between the inner and outer dimension of a person's life.[3] As such they are an enormous source of information once the value patterns can be deciphered and discerned. What the next four chapters are about is precisely what these patterns are and how they can be utilized to give us valuable discernment information.

There are, however, some assumptions and themes that will run through these chapters which we will review at this point, in order to aid the reader's understanding of the text. The following assumptions grow out of the first two chapters, and the processing of hundreds of personal case interviews using specific value related instrumentation.

One of the elementary facts about being human is that we develop, and we develop intellectually, emotionally and spiritually by collecting and utilizing information. If one looks dispassionately at the human body, one cannot but notice that it is designed from head to foot most beautifully to propagate itself and survive in a biologically orientated world.

Assumptions

The five senses not only react to information by assessing sight and smell, but they also reach out and touch things with a sense of wonder and awe from the moment the small child is born into the world. It is as if, then, the body is a communicator, or an instrument of information retrieval. Sexuality is a significant aspect of this in that it is a way of not only communicating to another person, but actually disseminating oneself through him or her.

The Self

see The Inner Connection, chapter 2

What I am suggesting is that behind the body lies an entity that we earlier called the "Self." This Self is a dynamic center of the motivating energy and emerging consciousness of each person. Self is the highest point of human evolution. It is in a sense a self-perpetuating energy field that requires the physical body as we know it to be fully operational. That is to say, it exists only as the consequence of relationship. To put it another way, it is a unique whole that exists because of the peculiar relationship of the body to conscious and unconscious (internal) information.

This view of the Self posits a reality that can function outside the space time continuum, as in the experience of dreams, and that in essence may be neither male nor female. Whether or not it perpetuates its existence after the life of the body raises significant questions that have been the bases of theology and religion for centuries.

Male and Female Psychology

The suggestion that the Self is not male or female is based on the premise that this energy source, as we know it, becomes more conscious and focused as we develop through the stages of maturity that we encounter as we grow up. What I am suggesting is that it is the body that is primarily female or primarily male. This does of course make a difference!

see Kelsey, Appendix

The Self of the female person, then, develops differently than the Self of the male, but in the long run the fully developed human being must integrate both components into the Self. In this sense the body is a limiting factor whose own life cycle would appear to be essential to the spiritual growth process of human beings.

Life and Death Issues

Death, or the final breakdown of the human biological form, is a relatively new phenomenon within the total time span of life on earth. Simple one-celled life forms such as the amoeba do not die; they simply perpetuate themselves through continual cell division. Death, then, within the overall framework of biological life, must have occurred for a reason. Fritjof Capra puts it this way:

"Birth and death, therefore, now appear as a central aspect of self-organization, the very essence of life. Indeed, all living things around us renew all the time, and this also means that everything around us dies all the time. . . . But for every organism that dies another one is born. Death, then, is not the opposite of life, but an essential aspect of it."[4]

This is a scientific affirmation of the cycle of Birth, Death and Resurrection, which is not simply a life after death issue, but a description of the inherent nature of the created order.

At birth then, the largely unconscious self is molded and develops in reaction to the external environment. Any inner life is minimal at this stage. The first experience of this is going to be the child's own body—male or female. In ancient Greek, one of the earliest languages in the civilized world that is still extant, the female noun was identified by that which one enters into. House and woman would therefore be female. At the dawn of each person's life, as in the dawn of history, that same awareness exists, giving rise to two psychologies: a feminine and a masculine form.

The feminine by its very nature is going to have the beginning point of vulnerability—for she is entered into. In addition, as Carol Gilligan has pointed out, she is physically the same as the mother, whereas the boy is different, initiating a masculine psychology based on separation.[5] As we shall see in the following chapter the consequence is that different values are stressed by the feminine personality than by the masculine, at different stages in the life cycle.

Some of our basic assumptions are, then, that 1. Each person has a unique Self system that is developed and nurtured through life experiences. 2. That psychological development has a female and a male component, and that both have to be recognized and nurtured for a person of either sex to be fully integrated. 3. That death is a part of the life cycle, suggesting that the Self may be able to transcend time and sexuality.

Evelyn Underhill has noted that the two dimensions of the development of well integrated persons are the qualities of Being and the constant reality of Becoming.[6] In theories of human development it is the Existential position that emphasizes Being, and it will be presented in Chapter VII. The Becoming dimension is represented by the developmentalists, and this approach to human and spiritual development will be presented in Chapters IV and V. Behind the theme of Becoming and Being are hidden several other themes that will run through the next four chapters: Perspectives on Time, and Issues for Human and Spiritual Integration.

Themes: Being and Becoming

In the great spiritual traditions time was always at the center of human integration. Dom Gregory Dix in referring to the medieval worship called it the Sanctification of Time. And now Quantum Physics views time as the fourth dimension.

Perspectives on Time

Basically time can be viewed in two different ways: as a space time continuum or linear time (T1), and as something that is relative or a fourth dimension of what we normally consider to be space (T2).

see The Industrial Age, chapter 2

Chapters III through V will be based on the concept of linear time which assumes, with the left side of the brain, that all of life is a continuous sequence of events, one after the other from birth to death. Human and spiritual development is viewed as a maturing process related to the passages of time and the integration into one's life of certain skills and tasks. Unhealth is simply the consequence of blocks to this process or the inability of the individual to integrate into his or her life the necessary building blocks.

Chapter VII will view time through the eyes of the existentialists and mystics, as does the right side of the brain. Here, time is relative and is transcended as past and future become now. As such space and time become one, so that one travels a thousand miles in the blink of an eye. Human and spiritual development here is viewed as the capacity

see Harrison and Prendergast, Appendix

of the individual to face central life issues including birth and death, and choosing values that enable one to transcend the difficulties of everyday life.

The point is that both points of view are legitimate, reflecting two sides of one reality. As such, each orientation gives rise to a different set of information about ourselves and the world we live in. In reality we move backward and forward between both experiences of time. *see chapter 7* We call this phenomenon *The Oscillation Effect*. Although each perspective on time is given in separate chapters, the concept of time as including both will continue throughout the book.

Issues for Human and Spiritual Integration A question asked frequently is: what is it that we need to do to grow in a developmentally healthy way? The answer is that while we do not know all the factors, we know some of them, and knowing that can at least help us make fewer mistakes. The basic elements that have to do with our development are: positive reinforcement from the environment, skills and inner integration. These will be constantly mentioned throughout the next five chapters.

Positive reinforcement from the environment implies that growth involves support from the outside, from our parents, our peers, and particularly the institutions that make up the fabric of our society. Skills and inner integration relate to what Ken Wilber calls Manna and Taboo.[7]

see Manna and Taboo, chapter 4 and Integrated Development, chapter 7 Manna is food and we need it to grow. Manna is basic human sustenance such as food and shelter, but it is also basic skills for living, choosing and journeying that can enable each person to fulfill his or her maximum potential in a creative manner. Taboo reflects the necessity of each person to deal with his or her inner and sometimes darker side.

What we present is not the whole story but another addition to our understanding of the human condition. But the basic presupposition running through all these themes and assumptions is that each person is a whole reflected through the parts.

The reader should be aware that Chapters III, IV and V are fairly long and detailed, since they form the basic foundation for the rest of the book. Chapter III will share the information we have gained from our research about the perception of the Self and the concept of different World Views that we all hold at different stages of our lives.

Chapters IV and V extend this idea into an initial theory of human and spiritual development that underlies most current theories of human growth. This is the place where we begin to pay more attention to the question of values as a system of information retrieval. That chapter will reveal specific information about dialectics, leadership styles, skills and personality profiles.

Chapters VI and VII begin to deal more directly with overall insights that we have gained about human and spiritual integration through the varied examination of time and skills. We call those two chapters "Time Traveling." Let us now begin with Chapter III: "Discern: Looking Through a Mirror."

Part II:
The Personal Genesis

1. Immanuel Kant, "The Critique of Pure Reason." Hutchins (1952), p. 76.

2. Burke (1978), Introduction.

3. See Moustakis (1956), p. 7, where he points out: "When the individual is free to be himself his acts are always consistent with his values."

4. Capra (1982), p. 283.

5. Gilligan (1982).

6. Underhill (1955).

7. Wilber (1983). He describes good manna as integrative, healthy and binding. Taboo is separative and at its most fundamental it is death.

DISCERN:
LOOKING THROUGH A MIRROR

When I was a child I used to talk like a child, and think like a child, and argue like a child, but now I am a man; all childish things are put behind me. Now we are seeing a dim reflection in a mirror; but then we shall be seeing face to face. The knowledge that I have now is imperfect; but then I shall know as fully as I am known.

Paul's First Letter to the Corinthians: 13:11 and 12.

Conceptions of the human life cycle represent different attempts to order and make coherent the unfolding experiences and perceptions, the changing wishes and realities of everyday life. But the nature of such conceptions depends in part on the position of the observer. . . . When the observer is a woman, the perspective may be of a different sort. Different judgements of the images of a man . . . imply different ideas about human development, different ways of imagining the human condition, different notions of what is of value in life.

Carol Gilligan.[1]

PURPOSE To demonstrate how the human being and his or her unique "Self" has the potential to develop through Four Phases and eight Stages of development, transcending the most basic need to survive to the possible development of higher consciousness.

CONTENT The chapter relates how human beings grow through stages of development, all of which are undergirded by specific identifiable values. Although there are many theories of development, they are all aspects of one single developmental reality. The chapter notes that although we all have basic needs and growth requirements in common, there is a uniqueness in the way the female and male develop, each complementing the other.

LINKAGE This chapter links with Part I of the book that demonstrated how values are an invaluable source of information that connect the human being's inner life to his or her external reality. This chapter extends this concept to show that specific clusters of values reflect the world view and maturity of a person, giving us invaluable information about human and spiritual growth, male and female development. The next chapter will extend the information connection even further, showing how the values are also indicators of factors such as management and leadership style.

Basic to our understanding of the human person and his or her potential for destruction and creation is the fact that everything we have learned points to the human being as a medium of purposeful information retrieval. The purpose appears to be to recreate itself and the world in a life-giving way. When this being becomes stressed the creative side becomes an expression of preservation, which in turn subverts the creative into a destructive side.

Both the element of information retrieval and the positive and negative consequences of this will be a constant theme in this and the following chapters. The basic medium for information retrieval will be the values analysis that stands behind all that we are discussing. However the values are but a doorway into a deeper understanding of human and spiritual development.

DISCERN is the name we give to a personal value analysis. Using a computerized instrument called the Hall-Tonna Inventory we have processed over a thousand individual value analyses. The result was to confront myself and my fellow workers with a number of insights about human development that I am going to begin to share in this and the following three chapters.

PHASES OF DEVELOPMENT

The first insight was that our internal images of reality fall into four main categories of what we shall call World Views. Not only this but the World Views are developmental and are related through time to the aging process. Each World View also has a particular set of values associated with it which become a focal point for different stages in our life cycle.

We called the four world views and the values that lie behind them, Phases of Development. The Phases of Development and the values that lie behind them are the foundation stone of what became for us a growing awareness of the patterns of cyclical growth that lie at the heart of everyone's development. These will be reviewed in the first half of the chapter.

The Phases, so it turned out, were composed of two stages each: an A and a B stage. This eight stage sequence is illustrated in Diagram III.1 below. This became the foundation of all our later work.[2] As we worked with hundreds of individuals since that time a series of additional patterns emerged.

First we noticed that contrary to most of the developmental psychologists, there was not a natural movement from one Phase to the next. Rather, individuals remain in one Phase integrating the values of that stage of maturity. The concept precludes growth and development.

Let us begin then with the Phases of Development. Diagram III.1 gives us an overview of the Four Phases of Development. We will however spend much more time on Phase I since it is the main point of departure from which an understanding of the other Phases will flow. It, as we shall see, initiates a developmental pattern of interactions that continues through all the other Phases and Cycles.

The Four Phases of Development are the backbone of our understanding of the development of human and spiritual consciousness. Each Phase is going to be presented separately. How one moves from one Phase to another will be discussed later. Human beings construct a perception of their world in order to cope with the world they live in. This in turn begins to shape the individual's "Self" image. Therefore the content of this World View and our Image of the Self changes with each Phase.

The following description of each Phase will be an expansion of the following Diagram III.1. The description will begin by listing the values by Stage for that particular Phase of development. (A complete list of the values by Phase can be found in Appendix A.) This will be followed by a description of the individual's perception of the world, the image of the Self, and the felt human needs.

WORLD VIEW, VALUES AND DESCRIPTORS

Diagram 3:1
THE FOUR PHASES OF DEVELOPMENT
Concise description of a person's World View, Needs and example Values at each Phase.

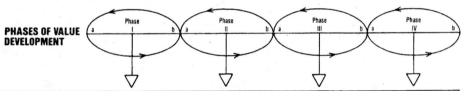

PHASES OF VALUE DEVELOPMENT	Phase I	Phase II	Phase III	Phase IV

ELEMENTS IN CONSCIOUSNESS	PHASE I	PHASE II	PHASE III	PHASE IV
How THE WORLD is perceived by the individual.	The world is a MYSTERY over which I have NO CONTROL.	The world is a PROBLEM with which I must COPE.	The world is a PROJECT in which I must PARTICIPATE.	The world is a MYSTERY for which WE must CARE.
How the individual perceives its SELF FUNCTION in the world.	The self EXISTS at the center of a HOSTILE WORLD. The self struggles to SURVIVE in an ALIEN, OPPRESSIVE, CAPRICIOUS ENVIRONMENT.	The self DOES things to succeed and to belong in a SOCIAL WORLD. The self seeks TO BELONG in a SIGNIFICANT HUMAN ENVIRONMENT and TO BE APPROVED by other SIGNIFICANT PERSONS.	The self ACTS on the CREATED WORLD with conscience and independence. The self strives to RE-SHAPE the NATURAL, SOCIAL, CULTURAL ENVIRONMENTS with CONSCIENCE and INDEPENDENCE.	Selves GIVE LIFE to the GLOBAL WORLD. Selves ENLIVEN the GLOBAL ENVIRONMENT through the UNION of INTIMACY and SOLITUDE within and the HARMONY of SYSTEMS without.
What HUMAN NEEDS the self seeks to satisfy.	The self seeks to satisfy the PHYSICAL NEED for FOOD, PLEASURE/SEX, WARMTH and SHELTER.	The self seeks to satisfy the SOCIAL NEED for ACCEPTANCE, AFFIRMATION, APPROVAL, ACHIEVEMENT.	The self seeks to satisfy the PERSONAL NEED to EXPRESS CREATIVE INSIGHTS, BE ONESELF, DIRECT ONE'S LIFE, and OWN ONE'S IDEAS/ENTERPRISES.	Selves seek to satisfy the COMMUNAL NEED for GLOBAL HARMONY by nurturing persons and communities from their phase of consciousness.

TYPES OF VALUES	STAGE I A	STAGE I B	STAGE II A	STAGE II B	STAGE III A	STAGE III B	STAGE IV A	STAGE IV B
Primary GOAL Values	Self-Preservation	Security	Family/Belonging Self-Worth	Self-Competence/ Confidence	Life/Self-Actualization Service/Vocation	Being Self Human Dignity	Intimacy/Solitude	Ecority/Beauty Transcendence
MEANS Values	Safety-Survival		Instrumentality	Education	Empathy Health Independence	Accountability/ Mutual Responsibility	Interdependence	Convivial Tools/ Intermediate technology

THE VALUES.

The Values that lie behind the first Phase are as follows:

PHASE I CONSCIOUSNESS
see Value Lists and Definitions, Appendix

Stage A Goals

1. SELF PRESERVATION
2. WONDER/AWE

Stage A Means

3. SAFETY/SURVIVAL

Stage B Goals

4. SECURITY

Stage B Means

5. SENSORY PLEASURE
6. PROPERTY/ECONOMICS

The person at the first Phase, as the diagram illustrates, grows by continually trying to integrate the values in the A and B Stages. We can best understand what the significance of these values is by looking at the World View that lies behind them.

THE
WORLD
VIEW
AND THE
FUNCTION
OF THE
SELF

The world in Phase I is perceived as a mystery over which the individual has no control. For the newly born child it is an awesome world of constant change and surprise, filled with giants on whom he or she is totally dependent. Since the child is dependent on his or her mother for all sustenance, and since the child is without skills in all regards, it is a world over which he or she has no control.

Stage A in each of the Phases relates to the personal dimension, that is to say, how the "Self" views its basic needs as it reacts to what it sees in the environment. As we can see from the values, it is double-edged with a sense of wonder and awe and a need to be safe and survive.

Stage B in each Phase is how the Self views its basic needs as it acts on the environment. This is an inner creative response to cope, mold and recreate the world we live in. Security and Property/Economics is the way historically and individually humankind has initiated control of its surroundings. The very basis of family life is to provide a secure environment in which to live and grow. This very often includes buying property and creating a physical home through personal economic resources. Sensory Pleasure includes the whole realm of sexuality and the literal will to create children.

Diagram III.2 illustrates this natural tension between the Stage A and B values of preservation and creation. On the one hand all persons have a natural inner creative drive to be their own self; on the other hand they have to preserve their Self from the possible negative effects of the external world of nature and society.

Diagram 3.2
**SELF
PRESERVATION
AND GROWTH**

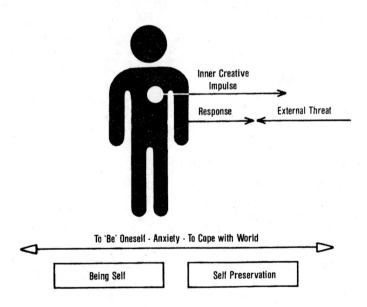

58

On the other hand there is in each of us an innate curiosity that goes right down to the DNA structure that pushes us from within to reach out and touch the world outside of ourselves. It is marvelous to watch a child of one or two weeks of age reach out and touch a colored object or feel a person's face or hair.

At the very heart of every person is the innate need to be oneself by relating to persons and things outside of ourselves. But this requires that we also preserve the self. Human development then is a constant tension between the will to relate creatively to the world and the need to preserve oneself.

What we are seeing then in the birth of an individual is the birth of a conscious dynamic pocket of energy within each of us called the "Self." It comes into being through a sensory system called the body and develops humanly and spiritually as it grows in relationship to itself (its body, male or female) and to its family and the wider world around it.

As Lawrence Kohlberg has pointed out, this Phase, which he calls *see Introduction, chapter 4* the Pre-Conventional Level of Development, is characterized by the person making choices out of a need for physical protection or satisfaction.[3] Hence, the values of Self Preservation, Security and Sensory Pleasure are present. Consequently, the person with these values is very self centered.

For the adult at this level the world is a hostile and alien place, or, as Diagram III.1 says, an alien, oppressive and capricious environment. This is well illustrated in a high percentage of movies that exploit this world view. The negative extreme is pornography that very often links a distorted view of sensory sexual pleasure with material needs and violence.

A series of movies like those of the James Bond 007 genre well illustrate how we are all captured by this Phase as adults. James Bond's whole life style is one of physical delight and physical survival for Queen and Country. He delights in the best food, brandy, clothes and cars, and he treats women as physical objects whose only purpose is to satisfy his sexual needs. At the same time he is a one man army against the forces of evil, with all the advances of technology at his finger tips.

EVOLVING DESIGN

The values in Phase I are not only divided in Stages A and B, but also in Goals and Means. What does this additional information signify? The values at the top of each column, in all the Stages, are long term Goals. This means that they are initiated at the point that they appear in the Phases and then continue on through a person's life. The Means values on the other hand are more limited: they are the means by which the Goals values become actualized at each stage of development.

For example, Self Preservation at Phase I, Stage A involves a sense of wonder and awe and requires safety and survival skills at a strictly physical level. But the feeling experience of Self Preservation continues all through one's life; the only thing that changes is our ability to

Diagram 3:3
THE VALUES IN THEIR PHASES OF DEVELOPMENT (THE CONSCIOUSNESS TRACK)

The diagram illustrates how the 50 values fall into specific Stages of maturity (Stage A and B) for each of the Four Phases.

PHASE I.

STAGE A GOALS	STAGE B GOALS
1. Self Preservation.	4. Security.
2. Wonder/Awe.	

STAGE A MEANS	STAGE B MEANS
3. Safety/Survival	5. Sensory Pleasure.
	6. Property/ Economics.

PHASE II.

STAGE A GOALS	STAGE B GOALS
7. Family/ Belonging.	14. Work/ Confidence.
8. Self Worth.	15. Worship.
	16. Play.

STAGE A MEANS	STAGE B MEANS
9. Belonging/ (Liked).	7. Achievement/ Success.
10. Care/Nurture.	8. Administration/ Management.
11. Control/Duty.	9. Institution.
12. Tradition.	20. Patriotism/ Loyalty.
13. Social Prestige.	21. Education.
	22. Workmanship/ Technology.
	23. Law/Duty.

PHASE IV.

STAGE B GOALS	STAGE A GOALS
48. Transcendence/ Ecority.	45. Wisdom.

STAGE B MEANS	STAGE B MEANS
49. Convivial Technology.	46. Word/Prophet.
50. Rights/Word Order.	47. Community/ Simplicity.

PHASE III.

STAGE B GOALS	STAGE A GOALS
34. New Order.	24. Equality.
35. Dignity/Justice.	25. Actualization/ Wholeness.
36. Art/Beauty.	26. Service.
37. Insight.	
38. Contemplation.	

STAGE B MEANS	STAGE A MEANS
39. Accountability.	27. Autonomy.
40. Community/ Support.	28. Empathy/ Generosity.
41. Detachment.	29. Law/Guide.
42. Corporate Mission.	30. Personal Authority.
43. Research/ Knowledge.	31. Adaptability.
44. Intimacy.	32. Health/Well-being.
	33. Search.

Copyright: Brian P. Hall, January 1984.

preserve the Self in more sophisticated ways. Diagram III.3 shows all the values by Phase to help you to see the overall pattern.

We note that the Diagram is not linear but in a square for easier reading. At Phase I Self Preservation is seen by the Self as being synonomous with physical survival. At Phase II it is survival of my Self as reflected through the eyes of an accepting family and peers. To lose my job at that Phase would put myself into a feeling state of Self Preservation. A threat to my creativity and independence would feel like

60

a threat to the survival of my Self in Phase III. At Phase IV Preservation of the Self would be co-extensive with the Preservation of the Selves of the human race.

Additionally, we noticed that the Goal Values form similar values at the different Stages, slowly extending and transcending the meaning of the original value as we grow and mature through time. For example, Self Preservation expands into Self Worth and Self Confidence in Phase II. In Phase III it expands into Self Actualization and Being Self. In Phase IV it becomes transcended to mean Self as Wisdom.

One way of looking at this phenomenon is to realize that all the values are inherent in us from birth. They are our potential futures, which will be worked out differently for each of us. Erik H. Erikson in looking *see Introduction, chapter 4* at human development through the eyes of psychoanalysis calls this the *epigenetic principle:*

"Whenever we try to understand growth it is well to remember the *epigenetic principle* which is derived from the growth of organisms *in utero.* Somewhat generalized, this principle states that anything that grows has a *ground plan,* and that out of this ground plan the *parts* arise, each having its *time* of special ascendancy, until all the parts have arisen to form a *functioning whole.* At birth the baby leaves the chemical exchange of the womb for the social exchange system of society, where his (her) gradually increasing capacities meet the opportunities and limitation of his (her) culture. How the maturing organism continues to unfold, not by developing new organs, but by prescribed sequence of locomotor, sensory, and social capacities, is described in child development literature. Psychoanalysis has given us an understanding of the more idiosyncratic experiences and especially the inner conflicts, which constitute the manner in which an individual becomes a distinct personality. But here, too, it is important to realize that in the sequence of his (her) most personal experiences the healthy child, given a reasonable amount of guidance, can be trusted to obey inner laws of development, laws which create a succession of potentialities for significant interaction with those who tend him."[4]

HEALTHY AND UNHEALTHY DEVELOPMENT

We noted earlier that Phase I is the beginning of mixed blessings. The Self emerges as a creative entity striving to be itself on the one hand, while striving to preserve itself on the other hand. If Self Preservation takes the upper hand, then a state of mistrust is developed, destroying a person's sense of well-being.

Erikson calls the first stage of human development the stage of *Basic Trust versus Mistrust.* This leads directly to a second stage called *Autonomy versus Shame and Doubt.* Both of these stand behind the first phase of development. The concept is simple, namely, that in order for the child to grow and develop into a healthy person, its early experiences of its mother in breast feeding and its parents in toilet training must be securing and loving. In this way, according to the psychoanalytical viewpoint, trust and a capacity for autonomy will be initiated. For Erikson, these become the foundation for all future growth relative to a person's creative interaction in the world.

On the other hand, if the early experiences are painful or frightening to a baby, then mistrust of the environment is built into its development. The consequence is that a lack of confidence develops that makes autonomy difficult, setting into motion feelings of doubt and consequent experiences of failure. This can then affect the rest of that person's life.

This approach, of course, sees development very much as a left brain phenomenon bound by the processes of linear time. Another limitation of this viewpoint is that it does not take into sufficient consideration that men and women develop a little differently. This is what stands behind, in part, the quotation from Carol Gilligan at the beginning of this chapter.

"Conceptions of the human life cycle represent different attempts to order and make coherent the unfolding experiences and perceptions, and the changing wishes and realities of everyday life. But the nature of such conceptions depends in part on the position of the observer. . . . When the observer is a woman, the perspective may be of a different sort. Different judgements of the images of a man . . . imply different ideas about human development, different ways of imagining the human condition, different notions of what is of value in life."[5]

PHASE ONE NEEDS: THE SELF, NARCISSISM AND GRACE

While it is true that Erikson's approach gives us invaluable information about this first Phase of development, to understand it fully, as the foundation of the other Phases, we must go back to what lies beneath this process. The beginning point is, as Carol Gilligan notes, the internal images of what reality is about. The developmental process is the consequence of how each person's Self responds to his or her experience of the world.

As we noted in the introduction to Part II the "Self" is neither male nor female. But human development is, since the first external environment the "Self" encounters is the body, and it, of course, is sexual in nature. But even before the experience of the body the "Self" experiences itself as the all-important center of the universe. Freud called the phenomenon narcissism, but theologians call it Grace!

We can suppose that the newly born infant is not aware of sexual differences, that it is a boy or a girl. But it is aware of its needs and acts as if the entire world was created for him or her. Indeed the very nature of the birth and nurturance process for a human, unlike most animals, requires the presence of the mother for at least a year if the child is to survive physically. Each child, then, is born with the knowledge that he or she is the center of the universe and as such is invaluable.

This has been well illustrated by the popular children's series by A.A. Milne, who in 1928 wrote *The House at Pooh Corner*. Milne wrote the story from the psychological perspective of the small child. Each character in the story, including Pooh Bear, is really a toy of the small boy named Christopher Robin. In the story *Tiggers Don't Climb Trees*, Roo a Kangaroo is talking to Tigger, who is a Tiger.

And as they went, Tigger told Roo (who wanted to know) all about the things that Tiggers do.

62

"Can they fly?" asked Roo.

"Yes," said Tigger, "they're very good flyers, Tiggers are. Stormy good flyers."

"Ooo!" said Roo. "Can they fly as well as Owl?"

"Yes," said Tigger. "Only they don't want to."

"Why don't they want to?"

"Well, they just don't like it, somehow." . . .

"I can swim," said Roo. "I fell into the river, and I swimmed. Can Tiggers swim?"

"Of course they can. Tiggers can do anything."

"Can they climb trees better than Pooh?" asked Roo stopping under the tallest Pine Tree, and looking up at it.

"Climbing trees is what they do best," said Tigger. "Much better than Poohs."

"Could they climb this one?"

"They're always climbing trees like that," said Tigger. "Up and down all Day."

"Oo, Tigger, are they really?"

"I'll show you," said Tigger bravely, "and you can sit on my back and watch me." For of all the things which he had said Tiggers could do, the only one he really felt certain about suddenly, was climbing trees.[6]

For the small child the world is there for them, not the other way around. What is right is what they choose to do that satisfies their physical needs and their perspective of wonder, curiosity and awe at the world around them. The small child through Tigger literally knows no boundaries, for imagination, fantasy and external reality are still undifferentiated. In the story poor Tigger climbs the tree, but finds that he can't get down and has to be rescued by his friends. For Milne this is the process of growing up from childlike narcissism to a recognition of our limitations.

In Christian theology this is the concept that each person is of infinite value. God became flesh in Jesus of Nazareth to prove this point. The problem is that if this awareness of one's worth is not transferred to others we become narcissistic and grandiose.[7] Maturation is the process of overcoming one's personal needs, recognizing that we are in fact of infinite worth, and moving on to recognizing that therefore all persons are of infinite worth also. This process will become clearer as we move through the other three Phases. If we do not grow out of this however, then the destructive side of development enters in.

EVIL AND THE DESTRUCTIVE SIDE OF NARCISSISM

Freud saw the experience of narcissism in adults as a condition of severe mental unhealth. Some modern psychologists and analysts such as Erich Fromm and Scott Peck[8] see this in the adult as an expression of evil.

The narcissism in its most demonic manifestation is a form of behavior whereby the individual, rather than integrating into himself or herself the demands of family, friends and society, forces or manipulates them into conforming to his or her view of reality. Many historic characters have fallen into this category as Erich Fromm points out:

see Framework for Discernment, chapter 10

63

"A particular instance of narcissism which lies on the borderline between sanity and insanity can be found in some men who have reached an extraordinary degree of power. The Egyptian Pharaohs, the Roman Caesars, the Borgias, Hitler, Stalin, Trujillo—they all show similar features.[9]

An example would be the Roman Emperor Nero, who played music to the burning of Rome. Nero set Rome on fire in order to put a new architectural plan into action, killing thousands in the process. The Emperor Caligula, also related to Nero, went to the extremes of sexual immorality and butchered his own pregnant sister. Both Emperors were convinced they were immortal and could do anything, as did Tigger (although with more moderation) in the quotation from A.A. Milne. Both died violently, Nero by suggested suicide and Caligula by assassination. Rampant narcissism, in the adult, is really a condition whereby the individual sees all the world as an extension of oneself.

At the heart of adult narcissism, as Alexander Lowen has pointed out, is denial of the self with an over-investment in one's image. It is characterized, more than anything else, by a denial of reality and an absence of feelings. What is frightening from a religious perspective is that as the self disappears from the psyche it can become possessed by a negative self, a force of such destructiveness that it has led even a psychologist like Erich Fromm, who claimed no belief in God, to call the phenomenon Evil.[10]

In an earlier work, *Shepherds and Lovers,* I noted that in my opinion the phenomenon of evil is a phenomenon that is related to the development of systems.[11] It reaches its extreme in the experience of possession. Dictators like Hitler and Nero for example did not live in isolation, they fed on others and were destructive of not just simply themselves but hundreds and thousands of other human beings. Hitler in perceiving himself as the savior of mankind, and a new Emperor God, was perfect, giving birth to a perfect Aryan race. Those who did not fit his perception of perfection, like all Jewish people, had to be exterminated.

The values, at this level, rather than causing growth, reinforce reflect a pathology that culminates in the destruction of the self, as follows:

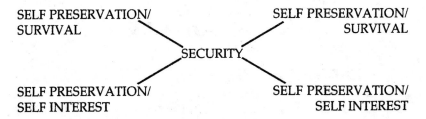

SELF PRESERVATION/
SURVIVAL

SELF PRESERVATION/
SURVIVAL

SECURITY

SELF PRESERVATION/
SELF INTEREST

SELF PRESERVATION/
SELF INTEREST

see List of 125 Values, Appendix Self Preservation as the experience of survival when combined with narcissism, which as a value is Self Interest/Control (see long list of values in APPENDIX A), causes an added need for Security, which then leads to a greater need for Self Preservation and Self Interest. In other words it perpetuates itself, so that the person sees himself or herself more and more as the center of the universe. The following example will explain this a little further.

Janet had been married twice, and recently married for the third time, and she was already (after six months) experiencing tension and conflict with her husband. In doing a value analysis with Janet I found that she placed the three values above as her first three priorities. Surprised, since I had not seen anything as stark as this before, I asked her to explain.

She told me she had been married twice before, and in her words explained the values as follows:

"I really got screwed over by my last husband in the divorce settlement—he took the money and the car, and I got some broken down furniture and the kids."

"What has this to do with the values?" I asked.

"Survival is the name of my game," she noted, "and looking after number one is how I view my new marriage." (Looking after number one is the value of Self Interest/Control.)

"But what do you and your husband get out of it?" I asked naively.

"Hell," she said, "he gets sex and food, and I get security, but I keep my tabs on him so he does not get out of line."

She denied that there could be any other way of doing things, even though I pointed out the potential emotional harm that would be caused to the children, let alone the marriage. Four years later I read in the newspaper that she had been killed by one of her children, who also severely injured her husband.

Denial, in effect, is the way in which this infinitely beautiful entity the "Self" will go to infinite ends to defend itself when its world view gets sufficiently distorted. When the experience is carried over to a significant group, then the phenomenon is even more terrifying.

Scott Peck, in a book called *People of the Lie*, traces the experience of Mylai.[12] Mylai occurred at the end of the Vietnam War on March 16, 1968. At that time Task Force Baker, Charlie Company was a part of that Task Force involving about 50 soldiers. Although no enemy were actually identified, villagers including women and children, were herded together and slaughtered with grenades, rifle and machine gun fire. Peck was one of three psychiatrists appointed to a committee to investigate the incident and make recommendations. He noted that one man Lieutenant William L. Calley was eventually found guilty some four years later for the incident.

Peck notes that minimally fifty persons were involved, there were numerous coverups, and with almost total denial by the army. Even the persons involved denied that anything wrong had occurred. Why? Dr. Peck makes the following observation:

"We were villains out of ignorance. Just as what went on at Mylai was covered up for a year primarily because the troops of Task Force Baker did not know they had done something radically wrong, so America waged the war because it did not know what it was doing was villainous."[13]

Peck identifies this with the condition of evil. Ignorance here was not that they did not actually recall the event, but that they denied that it had happened, and actually unconsciously displaced totally all compassion and moral sensitivity during the event—they had been possessed. Put another way the individual selves became displaced by a communal or archetypal image of reality which was savagely destructive.

BODY POLITICS

When the person grows in a healthy way, the values of Self Preservation and Security become the foundation of an individual's future potential. As the self emerges it first encounters its own body, through which it first develops its predominant masculine or feminine character.

As we noted earlier in the chapter feminine perceptions of the world develop differently than that of the male. The girl is like the mother, and is physically vulnerable. Her physical role is to receive and then to nurture within her body the new born creation.

see Kelsey, Appendix   The male, on the other hand, at an early age, recognizes that he is different than his mother, and grows up initiated by a psychology of separateness with the role of the one who penetrates or initiates.

In the last twenty years I have spent considerable time consulting to religious communities of celibate men and women celibate sisters. In comparing the two and in particular noting the values that tend to predominate at the first Phase of Development, I could not help but notice some distinct differences.

For the male the value of Self Preservation leads in later Phases to Achievement/Success, Work/Confidence, and New Order. Now this, of course, is with a particular population (see Diagram III.3 above). But this theme also relates historically to the male as the hunter and provider for the tribe, while the female nurtures and preserves the whole tribe through child bearing.

What was particularly interesting was that the majority of the female religious population, unlike the male population, had the value of Wonder/Awe in the first Phase. Many objected saying that this was too primitive a value for them. We have elsewhere defined that value as: overwhelming feelings of reverence, admiration and fear about the natural order. (See Appendix.)

see Kelsey, Appendix   In a survey of 905 men and women we found that the women placed Wonder/Awe as their first value with 844 responses, for Phase I values. Their second value was Security with 479 responses. The men interestingly enough had the same first two values, but the order was exactly reversed.

In fact the value is a Phase I Goal, meaning it is initiated at this point and continues on through the Phases depending on where a person's stage of development is. Further it is really the initiation of a religious feeling in the human being. It is that value that denotes the first religious act of recognition that an "Other" exists. It is a high point of vulnerability that leads to values such as Worship in Phase II, Intimacy and Contemplation in Phase III, and Wisdom in Phase IV (see DIAGRAM III.3. above).

Ironically, many of the early writers in psychology, such as Freud, saw women as weaker and morally inferior to men. Recent writers like Erikson and Kohlberg have consistently stressed a masculine bias.[14] With Erikson, for example, Intimacy is the first stage of adult development that normally occurs at the age of 21 years or older. I am sure that he would point out that it might take years to develop, and that its initiation would depend on the level of integration of the individual.[15]

However, the values would suggest that Wonder/Awe anticipates the skills of intimacy at a much younger age for women. It is also clear that weakness and vulnerability have been confused. In my own experience it is clear that women seem to have a much higher capacity for intimacy and the contemplative arts, leading them to an equal concern for Justice as men, but via a different route.

On the other hand, they are not so strong in the early Phases of maturity in such things as Achievement/Success. Since they operate more on an ethic of responsibility rather than separateness and competition, they often find it more difficult to confront others and assert themselves in an organizational setting than men.

One consequence of all of this information was to enable us to realize the need for the feminine component in spiritual development. It is really the need for a feminine spirituality—not a spirituality for women, but a spirituality for men and women that appreciates this component. The following DIAGRAM III.4 is taken from an earlier work of the author: *Shepherds and Lovers.*

The concept is as follows. The values on the left hand side of the diagram of Self Preservation, Security and Self Interest (listed as self as Center) represent the basic needs in our lives if we are to survive in this world.

Family, Work and the productive life are seen here as extensions of Preserving One's Self in this world. In the same way Security is extended into our reality through the experience of comfort, and our ability to control our lives personally and institutionally through sound management, which in turn contributes to how we see our Worth in the world. Self as Center is the same as Self Interest mentioned earlier and is extended into everyday life by the experience of hierarchy at the institutional level and the need for prestige on the personal level.

These elements are the basis for survival in society. But as we have noted earlier these very elements can conspire dialectically to cause destructive narcissism. In the diagram, if the experience of Self Preservation becomes increased due to difficulties in the work area, such as unemployment, so the family is affected, and the need for Security increases at the next level. The more insecure the person becomes, as for example when the unemployment continues, so the person becomes more and more controlling with less and less sense of his or her Worth.

When this happens the person moves down to the third level. This is where Self Interest and narcissism become predominant. The per-

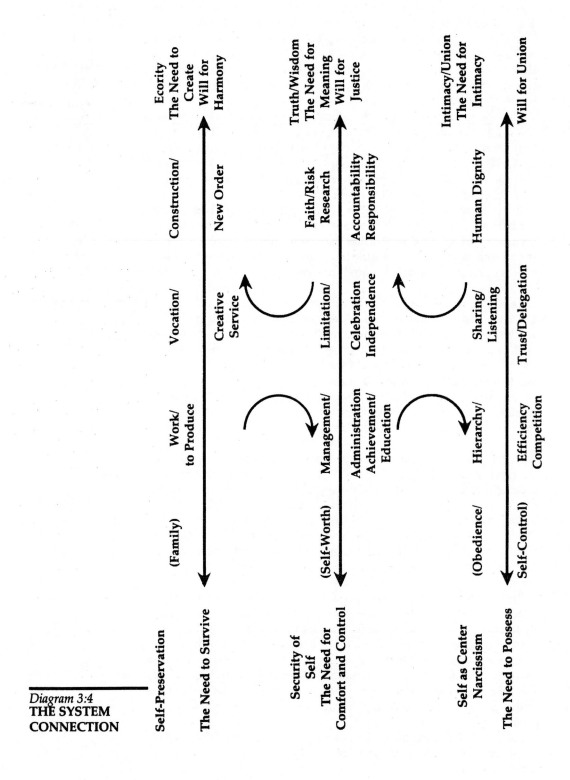

Diagram 3:4
**THE SYSTEM
CONNECTION**

68

son may withdraw or simply become more and more controlling—the purpose is the same—to make and control all the decisions. In an institutional setting this becomes unreasonable hierarchy.

The most common example of this in my own experience has been with executives under increasing stress, who feel that their basic reality is one of Self Preservation and Survival. Over a period of time they become more and more withdrawn and authoritarian, even though this is not their original style or value inclination. In its most extreme condition as with persons like Nero and Caligula, and many others I have personally experienced, the person concludes that the only decent decisions that can be made must be made by himself or herself. Such persons become so insulated that they will listen to no one who does not agree with them—the Bible calls this Possession.

What is interesting is that the initiating point is Self Preservation which is a basic need for everyone, but it is also a masculine value of acting on the world to Preserve Self and Family. To discover the feminine influence we must go to the right side of the diagram.

The idea is that each value on the left side is initiated in Phase I, and is on a continuum to Phase IV. Therefore, the values on the right hand side of Ecority, Truth and Intimacy all appear in the fourth Phase from the list of 125 values. *see List of 125 Values, Appendix*

As such Self Preservation becomes the preservation of the whole created order, which is the value of Ecority on the first continuum. Being personally creative, and creative through one's service to others and the natural order are therefore a component of this. In religious terms this is the experience of Hope.

The second continuum goes from Security to Truth and Wisdom. Security at its extreme is what Paul Tillich called a state of "Unfaith." As such it emphasizes control, comfort and stratification of the status quo. The opposite is therefore "Faith" which is the central character of this whole continuum. Faith implies personal risk, and therefore includes some independence. But ultimately the opposite of Security and its extension in Self Worth is to give worth to others through the exploration of Truth/Wisdom and their essential consequence: Justice.

The last continuum goes from Self as Center, or total Self Love to the unconditional love of others in Intimacy. This in the language of the mystics was also the ultimate possibility of being loved and in love with the Divine—experienced as Union with the Other.

What is interesting is that we have discovered that in the same way the values on the left hand side can coercively bring about a condition of evil termed possession. One would think by looking at the diagram that the solution would be at the opposite end of the continuum, namely that the solution to Self Preservation would be in creative alternatives on the Ecority side—but what this does in fact is increase the anxiety and the feelings of Self Preservation!

The first continuum is basically masculine in its initiating emphasis. The solution to the issues that arise out of Self Preservation interestingly enough begins on the opposite side in the opposite corner, which is basically feminine—namely with the value of Intimacy. This causes a creative coercive dialectic in the opposite direction as follows:

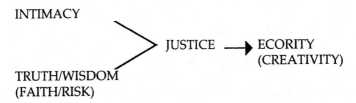

INTIMACY

JUSTICE ⟶ ECORITY
(CREATIVITY)

TRUTH/WISDOM
(FAITH/RISK)

Diagrammatically when the experience of Self Preservation and control through security is responded to with Intimacy as trust in the individual and delegation at the institutional level, this is experienced as putting Faith in others. This is trusting in the Wisdom of others, and of course takes the skills of the wise person to delegate and trust the appropriate persons in the first place.

The resulting experience is of persons feeling that life is meaningful and that they are being treated Justly. In fact the two critical experiences in anyone's meaning system is Intimacy and the ability to make creative choices in one's life. The result of this dialectic, then, is to enhance the creativity of the person. The extension of this at the higher levels of development is Ecority.

There is of course a significant difference between a person becoming creative because of this dialectic, and a person working to alter the creative balance of the planet as is expressed by the values of Ecority—this is a developmental issue that we shall begin to address as we look at the other Phases.

The main point I wish to make at this juncture is that the beginning point for creative development and spiritual growth in a stressful world is on the feminine side of the diagram (right side). In the continuum it is that line of development that begins with the values of Wonder/Awe, which are the precursors to Intimacy and Union. Religiously this is the continuum of vulnerability or love and Charity. Saint Paul said: "Faith, Hope and Charity, these three are essential to our spiritual growth, but the greatest of these is Charity." (1 Cor 13:13)

These integrations of modern psychology, values and spirituality are ultimately suggesting that spiritual and human development will only occur in healthy ways as men and women learn to integrate both *see Interim Reflections,* masculine and feminine values into their lives. This will become in- *Part II* creasingly evident as we move on to look at the other Phases.

PHASE ONE SYNOPSIS Phase I is the story of the emergence of the Self as it expresses itself in the world through the body. The world is viewed as a mystery over which we have no control. The lack of control of course is directly related to the immaturity of early growth and the lack of skills and awareness that an individual has at that stage.

At the same time the Phase I experience is equally possible at any age of one's life. It is not a description so much of what happens early on in our life, although that is a part of it, as it is a description of what a person's experience is with a particular set of values. If the environ-

70

ment is threatening enough as it was at Mylai, the person will start to react out of that world view and perspective, no matter how old he or she is.

We ultimately return to this Phase at some level of experience as we get older and begin to encounter the aging process. Diagram III.3 is drawn in a square with Phase I next to Phase IV for this reason.

This extensive treatment of Phase I was necessary because from it emerges all our life patterns. It is here that we run into a first time warp. On the one hand Phase II values and all the later Phases emerge from the first Phase experience in time, from childhood to old age. On the other hand all the values are present, in seed form from the beginning of our existence, so that as we grow the earlier values on the Consciousness Track (the name for the value patterns shown in Diagram III.3) affect and give form to the values we are presently living with.

see The Oscillation Effect, chapter 7

We are now going to review the World View, the function of the Self, and the Needs of the Self for the other three Phases. We will begin each Phase with a review of the values as a way of grounding the discussion. They are also a way to consistently retrieve information about the Phase and Stage that we are dealing with. Let us explore this more by starting with Phase II.

THE VALUES.
The Values that lie behind the second Phase are as follows:

PHASE II CONSCIOUSNESS
see Value Lists and Definitions, Appendix

Stage A Goals	Stage B Goals
7. FAMILY/BELONGING	14. WORK/CONFIDENCE
8. SELF WORTH	15. WORSHIP
	16. PLAY

Stage A Means	Stage B Means
9. BELONGING (LIKED)	17. ACHIEVEMENT/SUCCESS
10. CARE/NURTURE	18. ADMINISTRATION/ MANAGEMENT
11. CONTROL/DUTY	19. INSTITUTION
12. TRADITION	20. PATRIOTISM/LOYALTY
13. SOCIAL PRESTIGE	21. EDUCATION
22. WORKMANSHIP/ TECHNOLOGY	23. LAW/DUTY

As illustrated in Diagram III.1 the Stage A values are integrated with the Stage B values as the individual grows. Clearly at this Phase the primary concerns have moved beyond individual survival to social perspective taking. That is to say, the other's point of view is beginning to be considered. The critical values for understanding this are the Goal values; the Means are, in a sense, extra-dimensions of these values.

see Ledig, Phase II, Appendix

The general movement from the A to the B side can be viewed as a movement from a personal needs perspective to a more institutional perspective. Self Worth is a value that every person needs to grow in a healthy manner. Its actualization, however, comes about for persons through their family of origin, no matter what configuration that may take. Family might mean having a mother and father for the duration of one's childhood, or it may mean an orphanage. Nevertheless it is the device whereby each of us grows socially.

see Introduction, chapter 4 Self Worth is beyond Preservation and includes knowledge that I am loved and respected by those I know and respect the most. This is the condition for Erikson's concept of Basic Trust and Autonomy. The social environment of the family is, therefore, essential to this coming about. This value becomes well formed in the person precisely through the means values of Care/Nurture and Belonging. This means that the person is trained to be caring and nurturing, as well as receiving these for himself or herself.

For Erikson this then allows a person to take initiative and to begin to be industrious and productive at school and later at work. Control/Duty includes values such as dexterity and discipline and respect for others. These are basic values necessary for coping and surviving in society in order to learn what is necessary to survive on one's own.

Tradition, of course, is an essential part of one's Social Self. Social Prestige is the beginning of success and affirmation beyond one's family of origin as one moves into the world of work where one provides for one's own family in Phase IIB. Stage A represents those values that the Self needs to sustain itself as it reacts to the home environment, and the environment of friends and those it trusts.

Stage B is more representative of how the Self begins to act on the environment through Work, Education and Play. The environment here is civilized society which is made up of a network of Institutions. The social sphere has expanded clearly. Self, as being of value or worth, gives one an increased ability to give worth to others and even God in the value of Worship, which in its original derivation meant Worth-ship.

The experience of being a child in a family in Stage A moves to the experience of initiating one's own Family, to the experience of managing a job to provide for that family in Stage B, through such values as Workmanship/Technology and Achievement/Success. Family/Belonging and Tradition become Patriotism and Loyalty. As a parent I can become the governor of an Institution or an Administrator or Manager. To see these patterns with more clarity let's turn to the World View and the function of the Self at this Phase. (See APPENDIX for the definition of the values.)

THE WORLD VIEW AND THE FUNCTION OF THE SELF

The world view for the Phase II individual is that the World is a Problem with which I must cope. (See Diagram III.1.) As the values indicate, the world is primarily social in orientation. The function of the Self, then, is to learn how to Belong, in order to survive and succeed. The word survive here, however, is not physical survival as in Phase One so much as it is coping socially in a difficult world. Survival is coping adequately in society by having sufficient social and job related skills.

The individual joins with the world by winning approval of friends and family. As a small child he or she begins to venture out of the home, onto the block, and into the neighborhood and local school to learn the skills necessary to finally support himself or herself in society. This involves four basic processes: 1. Identifying with one's family and other significant groups, 2. Modifying one's behavior and learning to live by the rules of the family and groups in society with which one becomes acquainted, 3. Learning social and professional skills through one's family and school, and 4. Learning how to achieve and succeed in the community and society within which one has to live.

For Lawrence Kohlberg what is right and what is wrong at this Phase is based on living up to what others expect of me. This is a natural consequence of living in a world conditioned by the value of belonging. Being good is therefore important, as is sustaining relationships through loyalty and mutual respect.[16]

KOHLBERG

see Introduction, chapter 4

As the person develops into the B Stage so loyalty to individuals moves to the group level as respect for rules, duty and the common law. This is more sophisticated in that the person differentiates between what society demands from what is interpersonal and more subjective.

For Erikson this is where the person moves into the final stage before adulthood which he terms Identity. It really involves a minimal integration of the previous stages of Basic Trust, Autonomy, Initiative and Industry. To the extent that these have been taken care of, so will the young person successfully move into adulthood. However, as Erikson is quick to point out, it is more than that:

NEEDS AND ERIKSON

"The integration now taking place in the form of ego identity is more than the sum of childhood identifications. It is the inner capital that accrues from all those experiences of each successive stage, when meaningful identification led to a successful alignment of the individual *basic drives* with his *endowment* and his *opportunities*. . . . The sense of ego identity, then, is the accrued confidence that one's ability to maintain inner sameness and continuity (one's ego in the psychological sense) is matched by the sameness and continuity of one's meaning for others. Thus, self esteem, confirmed at the end of each major crisis, grows to be a conviction that one is learning effective steps toward a tangible future, that one is developing a defined personality within a social reality which one understands."[17]

From a value perspective this means that minimal internalization of the values at this phase, with minimal skills to actualize those same values with others, is necessary for healthy human integration. For example, Care/Nurture involves caring for others, and the capacity to accept care from others.

For Erikson when Identity does not occur due to a lack of integration at the earlier stages, Identity Diffusion occurs. At its worst it results in the negatives of all the previous stages, namely lack of trust, inability to make decisions and be self initiating, resulting in a lack of confi-

NARCISSISM AND VALUE IMBALANCE

dence and guilt. For Erikson, this leads to difficulties with adult relationships and the first stage of adulthood, which for him is Intimacy versus Self Absorption.[18]

see Phase One, Narcissism, chapter 3 Lack of identity integration leads to a denial of the Self as a person tries to discover other selves by attachment to external objects such as heroes in groups and even alcohol or drugs. Denial of self leads us back to the phenomenon of narcissism and the dominance of the value of Self Preservation. An interesting phenomenon is that in the same way that an overdose of Self Preservation in the first Phase leads to narcissism in the adult, so can it also be carried over into the second Phase.

Family can simply be a mechanism for survival as was illustrated in Chapter I and in the experience of the families in Costa Rica who were forced to prostitute their children. Historically, whole families from the ruling Caesars to the Mafia have become small isolated units of Self Preservation viewing the outside world as hostile and alien. We see the same sickness in racism in the United States and in its extreme in South Africa.

MALE AND FEMALE

Mythologically the archetype of the Great Mother has been with us since the dawn of history. This was in turn supported in the West through the attention Christians gave to the Virgin Mary as the sorrowful contemplative at the Son's side as he died on the cross. In the medieval period a lack of correct anatomical information led people to believe that impregnation came solely from the male. This meant that women were receptacles of male semen designed to care and nurture the male creation.

see Body Politics, chapter 3 The consequence was to see the vulnerability of women as an inherent weakness. They were important creatures who had to be protected, but who for the most part were seen as "the weaker sex" with—from Freud's point of view—inferior moral stamina.

Anita Spencer, in a very clear little book called *Mothers Are People Too*, documents in a very clear way how in the West this led to the Victorian ideal of the place and role of woman in society.[19] It is rooted in two concepts: Momism and the Cinderella Complex. Momism is the idea that the woman's total fulfillment should come through her children. The implication is that a second career would be destructive to family life, and in particular to the psychological development of the child. In its extreme it suggests that the woman whose life is not totally satisfied by her children is somehow inferior or even unstable.

The Cinderella Complex basically implies that real happiness and success is going to come from outside of one's self—by being rescued by a Prince Charming. This is a natural follow up to Momism. Since the Woman's role is primarily that of a Mother, it follows that she should not have a career, and should dedicate herself to her home and husband. She should anticipate all the needs of her husband and children, and deny herself.

What is fascinating about this, although it is very sad, is that this brings about the same process that is at the root of narcissism—denial of the Self. As Anita Spencer says, this causes the woman to become

74

a dependent child and "becoming more of a child and using tactics of a child in maintaining control over one's life is not conducive to emotional maturation."[20] In fact, she points out that the result is to retard her own development, which in the long run is helpful neither to her husband nor to her children.

The idealism of the Victorian view of women was a cultural and social distortion that was detrimental to the overall growth of women and men. What is important is that the second Phase of development tends to reinforce these problems due to the predominant world view that stresses surviving in the social sphere, by belonging and making a living.

The values in Stage A tend to reflect the current stereotype of the woman as a dutiful caretaker silently enduring her suffering for her family. The values in Stage B reflect the masculine stereotype of the successful achiever in society through work and loyalty to God and Country.

We did an analysis of 950 men and women and compared their values from this Phase of Development. They were all professional persons with graduate education and a career. Their values were in fact very similar with one or two exceptions. High in the women's priorities was the value of Endurance/Patience, which is defined as the capacity to bear difficult and painful experiences with calmness and stability. (See APPENDIX.) On the male side the same priority position was substituted by the value of Productivity, which is defined as achieving one's external goals and expectations. *see Kelsey and Harari, Appendix*

What our team of researchers concluded about this is what now seems obvious, namely that it is everyone's growth task to fully integrate all the values of the A and B stages at each Phase of Development, and that when such integration does not take place, personal and social aberrations occur such as racial and sexual discrimination.

We can also see from this discussion that the sexual issue of male and female perception is not simply an aspect of development, but central to our understanding of how the Self actualizes in the world.

THE VALUES

The Values that lie behind the third Phase are as follows:

PHASE III CONSCIOUSNESS
see Value Lists and Definitions, Appendix

Stage A Goals

24. EQUALITY
25. ACTUALIZATION/ WHOLENESS
26. SERVICE

Stage B Goals

34. NEW ORDER
35. DIGNITY/JUSTICE
36. ART/BEAUTY
37. INSIGHT
38. CONTEMPLATION

Stage A Means

27. AUTONOMY
28. EMPATHY/GENEROSITY
29. LAW/GUIDE
30. PERSONAL AUTHORITY

Stage B Means

39. ACCOUNTABILITY
40. COMMUNITY/SUPPORT
41. DETACHMENT
42. CORPORATE MISSION

Stage A Means	Stage B Means
31. ADAPTABILITY	43. RESEARCH/
32. HEALTH/WELL-BEING	KNOWLEDGE
33. SEARCH	44. INTIMACY

see Ledig, Phase III, Appendix The entrance of a person into the third Phase marks a great change in values orientation. We remember from Diagram III.1 that the A and B stages in each Phase are in the process of cyclical integration. The norm is not simply to move from one Phase to the next, but the tendency is to stay in one place. The actual cause of development will be discussed in the next chapter. At this point we do need to notice the strong patterns of emergence from the previous stages and the interconnections between the values in Phase IA, IIA and IIIA, and Phase IIB and IIIB. In order to do this I will refer to the value list above and make some references to the longer list of 125 values that can be found in the APPENDIX.

We have noted earlier that the A stages are an expression of how the Self sees itself as it reacts to the world around it. The beginning point is Self Preservation, which becomes Self Worth in the second Phase. This depicts the Self surviving in a social context, since, in fact, Self Worth is needed by everyone to grow up in a mentally healthy manner. Self Worth leads to the development of Self Actualization, a value that appears under Actualization/Wholeness in Phase IIIA above.

The values in the B stages are more representative of how the Self operates in an institutional world, and how the Self acts on, rather than reacts to, that world. Consequently Self Worth graduates into Self Confidence, a value under Work/Confidence in Phase IIB. Also Self Actualization graduates into a high point of Being Self, a value under Insight in Phase IIIB above. In order to understand this pattern, and understand why this occurs, we will need to proceed to look at the World View of Phase III first.

THE WORLD VIEW AND THE FUNCTION OF THE SELF

The world here is perceived by the Self as a project in which I must participate. (See Diagram III.1.) Rather than a world that is a "given," as in the first two Phases, Phase III consciousness perceives a world that is a "created" human project in which the Self must participate.

The individual in Stage A is motivated by a personal need to express feelings and creative insights, to be self initiating and directing. This is a revolution for Self perception, because for the first time one's authority comes from directly within, and not from the authority of others external to the Self.

Phase II is a movement from an individual's critical choices being determined by external personal authority, normally vested in one's parents, to ever widening systems of external authority such as one's teacher, boss, or bishop. The key alteration in Phase III is that the nexus of authority comes from within the person. The person is self initiating and assertive about his or her creative role in the world.

Self Actualization in IIIA is defined as the self initiating experience of fulfilling one's own potential, and seeing this as related to a process

76

of becoming emotionally and physically integrated and whole. Being Self in IIIB is an extension of the latter value by adding the objective awareness of one's strengths and limitations, plus the ability to act both independently and cooperatively within institutional settings. All the other values in these two stages are really expansions and extensions of these two values.

These values could only emerge out of an entirely new consciousness of the self around its self initiating role in the world. Stage A is really self initiating personal growth. Stage B is initiating change in the external world through personal creative projects, concern about Human Dignity and Justice, and taking authority for institutional and corporate development through such values as Corporate Mission and New Order.

The needs as expressed in Diagram III.1 are to satisfy personal self expression relative to self direction and personal ownership over ideas and one's creative enterprises. The two words that best express this are Independence and Integration.

NEEDS: INDEPENDENCE, INTEGRATION AND CONSCIENCE

Independence, which is also a value under Autonomy (see longer Value list in the APPENDIX), expresses both the positive and negative possibilities of this Phase. Independence is a very positive component of any experience of emancipation, either at the personal or societal level. The American Declaration of Independence is a strong positive example. It begins as follows:

"When in the course of human events, it is necessary for one people to dissolve the political bands which have connected them with another, and to assume, among the powers of the earth, the separate and equal station to which the laws of nature and nature's God entitle them, a decent respect for the opinions of mankind requires that they should declare the causes which impel them to the separation."

This same independence is recognizable in many political movements in our day relative to racial and sexual rights. Lawrence Kohlberg refers to this Phase as the Post-Conventional Stage of Moral Development.[21] It is characterized by the formation of conscience. That is to say this is the first time a person has had the consciousness and skills to make self intitiating decisions relative to what he/she thinks is right or wrong, without undue reliance on outside authority. The person for the first time clearly recognizes that there are different points of views on significant issues, and begins to move toward specific faith and value commitments. For Kohlberg, the emphasis is on a rational objective view of Truth and Justice that transcends the individual.

KOHLBERG
see Introduction, chapter 4

It is my experience that when a human being is not well integrated, independence as misplaced autonomy and power connects once again to the inherent narcissistic side of each of us. As the value of Self Preservation becomes exaggerated within a person, it manifests itself primarily through power and autonomy (Independence) in the third Phase. It can be expressed as the unwillingness to cooperate, or it can

INDEPENDENCE AND NARCISSISM
see Phase I, Narcissism, chapter 3

become the actual manipulative use of values. For example, a person can use Empathy and even appear generous, but really is acting out these values in order to accomplish some other end, such as selling a product.

Narcissism at this level, then, is misuse of power for personal gain. Excellent examples of this are found in advertising. Advertising will be expressed through values in order to sell the product. Sometimes they can be so manipulative that the product appears to be totally secondary. Most advertising is going to be directed at the earlier Phases of Development because that is where most of the population is. Let us look at a couple of examples.

A number of years ago a shampoo manufacturer wanted to create a larger market for its product by selling to a younger audience than its present audience of 18 years and older. In its advertising it showed two young girls of thirteen or fourteen years of age. One was smiling with a beautiful made up head of hair. The other one was sad and showed a very untidy straggly head of hair. Under the photograph was the name of the shampoo, with the caption: "Which of these two has been loved?"

The advertisement was playing very heavily on a young person's Phase I Self Preservation values, and Phase II values relating to the need to Belong and the need to competitively succeed, in order to survive. But the real object was to sell the product! This is of course blatant manipulation. Let us now take a look at a recent woman's perfume advertisement that appeals to all three Phases up to the value of Autonomy and Independence in Phase IIIA.

The advertisement begins with a beautifully made up woman sitting in a very expensive bright red, open topped sports car. The car looks like a Ferrari which would sell for a minimum of sixty thousand dollars. The door is open, and the camera moves through the door to focus on the gear shift and the woman's side, from her thigh to her knee. She pulls up her dress, and then raises her other leg, presently hidden from our view, so that we can see everything from her knee down to her thigh.

She then takes the perfume product that is being sold, and sprays it up and down slowly on the inside of her leg. Finally she slams her foot down on the clutch, turns the ignition key, puts the car in gear, and accelerates the car at a neck breaking speed. As she does this, exciting music accompanies a woman's voice, singing: "Independent Woman!"

The sexuality from her thighs to the gear shift is suggestively orchestrated and designed to seduce men. It is the Phase I dimension. A sixty thousand dollar car and the expensive perfume product are reflection of Phase II Image, Prestige, Success and Achievement. These all add up to a narcissistic symphony appealing to an exaggerated Independence and liberation in Phase III. In that it is designed for men using the woman model, it is a subtle continuation of the Cinderella Complex mentioned earlier. It demeans women, and distorts Phase Three values to sell the product.

The critical aspect that makes narcissism impossible and spiritual growth possible is the integration that can occur at this Phase. The best way to explain this is for me to repeat a quotation that I made in a previous work *Leadership through Values*, from Ira Progoff's book *The Symbolic and the Real*. In the quotation he is referencing the trial and death of Socrates.[22]

The trial and execution of Socrates took place in 399 B.C. at Athens by the conquering army from Sparta. Cicero said of Socrates that he was the first man to call philosophy down from heaven. He was a nobleman, a great warrior, but above all a great thinker. The motto "Know Thyself" often imputed to Saint Augustine was actually Socrates' motto that he got from the temple of the Oracle in Delphi. In his defense Socrates:

"described his intimate feeling of why it was important for him to live his life as he had been living it. It was not a question of intellectual philosophy, but of a calling that came to him from two sources, an outward source and an inward source, which Socrates understood as ultimately not separate at all from one another. The outward source of his calling was the Gods of the Greek Pantheon, and to this the Oracle at Delphi testified. The inward source of his calling was the oracle within himself. He describes this as the 'divine faculty of which the internal oracle is the source.' To Socrates the inward and the outward were two aspects of a single principle. It was in the light of this unity that he could state his belief 'that there were Gods in a sense higher than any of my accusers believe in them.' "

Phase III is that point in human development where the Self begins to recognize the presence of the inner world of the psyche, and integrate it with the external world of nature and society. For this reason it is the most critical point in human and spiritual development.

see Ledig, Values and Personality Integration, Appendix

This inner and outer integration becomes evident as we review the values. Those values that stress internal development are: Actualization/Wholeness, Autonomy, Empathy, Personal Authority, Expressiveness/Flexibility, Search, Insight, Contemplation, Detachment and Intimacy. On the other hand, the external piece is emphasized by: Equality, Service, Generosity, Law/Guide, Health, Dignity/Justice, Accountability, Art/Beauty, Community/Support, Corporate Mission and Research.

As we shall see in the next chapter, the consciousness of a person at this level is becoming more global in its orientation. Minimally a person thinks across culture, sex and race. The person is then able to understand the concept of systems better relative to institutions and Nations.

When we surveyed the value priorities for men and women at this Phase we also found more integration in that the differences were not so pronounced, but there were still some differences that were surprising to some of us. First of all, on the male side Intimacy was a higher value need than it was for women. On the feminine side there was much more attention paid to Justice related values than by the men. What would account for the difference?

see Introduction, chapter 4 Erikson states that the Stage of Intimacy is the first of the adult stages. But Erikson, like Freud, is coming out of a masculine bias, as is Kohlberg whose original research was all conducted on male subjects![23]

Kohlberg stresses the rational as the seat of moral decision making. The values stress a balance between reason and the interpersonal dimension. The rational emphasis is also a partial male bias. What is really needed is a minimal balance between the reasonable intellectual side of a person and the feeling interactional side.

Carol Gilligan in her incisive work: *In A Different Voice,* shows that Erikson is correct in saying that the passage of Identity from adolescence is critical for everyone, but it is different for both sexes. "These different perspectives are reflected in two different moral ideologies, since separation is justified by an ethic of rights while attachment is supported by an ethic of care."[24]

see Kelsey, Appendix The passage from Identity to Intimacy leads to an ethic of rights, and is primarily a male rite of passage. The female Self from the very beginning of development shared a form of intimacy with its mother. For this reason, the stage of intimacy and the value of intimacy are much more natural to the woman. Therefore, it makes sense that Intimacy was less of a priority at this Phase for women, since it has already been taken care of.

The higher emphasis on justice values such as Human Dignity and Justice/Social Order would appear to support the notion that the female perspective leads to an ethic of care, and would in this Phase at least appear to transcend the average male orientation. This of course is based on a limited survey of 950 professional men and women, but is interesting nevertheless. In Phase III at least the weaker sex would appear to be the stronger sex!

PHASE IV CONSCIOUSNESS

see Value Lists and Definitions, Appendix

THE VALUES
The Values that lie behind the fourth Phase are as follows:

Stage A Goals	Stage B Goals
45. WISDOM	48. TRANSCENDENCE/ ECORITY

Stage A Means	Stage B Means
46. WORD/PROPHET	49. CONVIVIAL TECHNOLOGY
47. COMMUNITY/ SIMPLICITY	50. RIGHTS/WORLD ORDER

The values at this Phase of Development are particularly difficult to understand because they are represented in a small population of persons. I have not experienced more than 20 persons operating at this level out of at least 4,000 interviews.

The A Stage is the perception of the Self as it experiences, not only the external environment, as in all the other Phases, but a new integration of the inner and outer world. It is in fact a mystical level of the experience of what we originally called the Genesis Effect. In order to explain these values we will need to look at what values appear in the Goal area from the list of 125 values in the APPENDIX, and to get more differentiation. They are as follows:

Stage A Goals	Stage B Goals
45. WISDOM	48. TRANSCENDENCE/ ECORITY
65. INTIMACY AND SOLITUDE AS UNITIVE	36. ECORITY/ AESTHETICS
16. TRUTH/WISDOM INTEGRATED INSIGHT	115. TRANSCENDENCE/ GLOBAL EQUALITY

The values with the capital letters are from the short value list, and the ones below are values in that category from the long list, serving to give more differentiation to what the value can mean. In our survey of 950 men and women these were prioritized according to sexes at this Phase. That is to say a statistical analysis was done of 950 HT-Inventories, and a mathematical priority was worked based on the frequency of choices of Phase IV values for the men, and for the women.

The first value was the same for both sexes: Intimacy and Solitude as Unitive. The value is at the heart of mystical experience and the life experience and practice that leads up to what many mystics speak of as an experience of union, intimate union, with the Divine.

Such persons speak continuously of the balance in their lives between solitude, understood as the daily ongoing practice of the ascetical contemplative arts, and the capacity for high degrees of human intimate interaction. Intimacy here is not understood genitally so much as it is as a reciprocal sharing of feelings and internal images, hopes, failures and ideals between two peers.

There are two behavioral norms that make such practice authentic. The first is that the experience is one where the individual feels a loss of meaning when the ascetical solitude and the intimacy are not in harmony. The second is that the experience leads to new insights and actions that are global in consequence.

Gandhi, for example, struggled all his life with Intimacy and Solitude as they are here described. One might argue that he never fully integrated the first. However, the point is that he had these sufficiently in harmony to alter the course of history. His ascetical practice led to the methodology of peaceful resistance that has been used by millions ever since.

It should be noted also that the eastern and western approaches to what causes the final outcome of mystical union differ greatly. The east stresses the way as a method or means by which the mystical state is arrived at. It stresses very much the various methods of ascetical contemplation. Western writers like Poulain stress that although such methods are necessary, the final outcome is from the other side. Poulain notes: "We apply the word mystic to those supernatural acts or states which our own industry is powerless to produce, even in a low degree, even momentarily."[25] Poulain called the method the Ascetic. The value is descriptive of both the method and the experiential consequence of the value of Intimacy and Solitude as Unitive.

TRUTH AND TRANSCENDENCE

The second and third priorities were reversed for men and women. The men had Truth/Wisdom/Integrated Insight as the second priority, and the women had Transcendence/Global Equality.

Truth/Wisdom/Integrated Insight is basically the pursuit of truth and understanding above all other activities. Transcendence is the ability to experience and comprehend the infinite at a minimally global level, and the finite at the minimal level of sensitive human interaction. What Transcendence/Global Equality means then is knowing and working on the problem of the relationship between human oppression, freedom and creative global development. It is taking authority for injustice in the world at a global level and trying to do something about it.

Now our statistics did not say that most of the women we surveyed were working at global justice, and that most of the men were radically pursuing Truth. What it said was that these two orientations were seeded in that population's mind as a possible future direction if they develop to those levels of spiritual maturity.

What is fascinating is that Carol Gilligan's observation seems to hold even at these high levels of integration, namely that males continue to be ethically drawn to an ethic of rights by probing for the Truth, while the feminine continue to be based on an ethic of care via social justice. It should also be noted that both values were held by men and women; it is simply that the order was different. The male prefers to enter into justice issues at his level through reasoned investigation, the female through caring acts followed by reasoned investigation.

The last value held by men and women in the Goal area was Ecority/Aesthetics. Ecority is the mandate to the human race in Genesis 1: "Take authority for the created order." This is in essence the heart of the Genesis Effect. The value is defined as: the capacity, skills and personal organizational or conceptual influence to enable persons to take authority for the created order of the world and to enhance its beauty and balance through creative technology in ways that have a worldwide influence.

The other values in the means area are an extension of these goals. We will refer to these in a little more detail as we review the World View and the function of the Self in Phase IV.

THE WORLD VIEW AND THE FUNCTION OF THE SELF

The World View is described as a Mystery for which "we" must care. Rather than the function of the Self we speak of the function of Selves that purposefully enliven the global environment. The key factor for this Phase is harmony—harmony of the Self through a balance of intimacy and solitude, and harmony in the total created order.

The concept of mystery at this Phase is related to the experience of mysticism as the experiencing of the Divine, from the religious per-

82

spective, and being in contact with the creative life forces that make ecological balance on the planet possible from a scientific point of view.

This Phase of Development is beyond Kohlberg's final stage of development which is characterized as a rational conscience orientation of an individual whereby a person chooses right and wrong based on internalized universal moral principles. This occurs in Phase III. Here, what is required is the additional consciousness of how global ecological systems interact and work. The level of development requires that choices always come from a "We" perspective. From a religious viewpoint, "We" includes an experience of divine energy.

KOHLBERG AND ERIKSON

see Introduction, chapter 4

This Phase also moves beyond Erikson, whose last two adult stages include Generativity versus Stagnation in one's middle years, and Integrity versus Despair as one copes with the end of one's life. Erikson intentionally related his schema to emotional growth as it relates to the normal life cycle. It was never his intention to explain all other issues that are related to ultimate human potential. However, what he says does help us better understand this Phase of Development.

Erikson's last two stages are a part of the third Phase. Generativity implies that as one grows up, and marries or decides to remain single, then one encounters the need to be meaningfully productive in one's life. When one succeeds emotionally and in one's work, so one's life becomes enriched, and one enriches and gives meaning to other people's lives.

Integrity is the coming to grips with the limitations of one's body and one's ability to accomplish something in a given life span. For some, this is a confrontation with what life's ultimate meaning is all about. For others, it is the disappointment of not accomplishing enough, not succeeding sufficiently in one's chosen career, or never being able to overcome personal tragedy such as the loss of a loved one. Integrity is the ability to confront and transcend the reality of limitation and be at home with who and what one is. The failure to do this is the experience, for Erikson, of despair and disgust.

Erikson also feels that the experience of integrity is based largely on the ability of the person to have integrated all the previous tasks at the various stages.[26] This all occurs in Phase III, but is relevant here as an explanation of the minimal conditions for Phase IV to occur which is the capacity on the part of the person to: 1. Recognize and be able to act on universal moral principles, 2. Have experienced generativity as an expression of personal creativity and productivity, and 3. Have recognized, confronted and come to grips with one's limitations as a way of developing one's gifts and potential.

Whereas Independence and Autonomy characterize Phase III thinking and perceiving, Interdependence (a value under Community/Simplicity) characterizes the fourth Phase. The individual Self is transcended as a person acts interdependently with other selves. In other words the "I" has become "We."

NEEDS AND GLOBAL HARMONY

see Ethics as a Global Issue, chapter 11

In much of the popular literature and story telling that one sees on television and the movies there is a stress on individual accomplishment. James Bond is a man against all odds. Popular American democracy often hearkens back to the days of the early settler forging his way across the wilderness, supported by a wife and children who make this possible, and carry on the tradition. Every American is then told that anyone who is a citizen can become president, or be an astronaut.

Phase IV perspective makes it clear that independence only goes so far—as far as one's back fence. That is to say it is a personal value that involves others only to a very limited extent. On the other hand, Interdependence implies a high degree of cooperation. It is this that makes space travel and responsible government happen. Not only this, but the emphasis on independence that stood behind the freedom movement in the industrial and American revolution is one of the causes in the western world of rapid depletion of global biological resources from trees to oil.

As in the last three Phases, Self Preservation and narcissism can raise its head here as elsewhere. In fact, at the later Phases the difficulty in integrating one's life in a harmonious way becomes more difficult and complex. Therefore the presence of Self Preservation comes closer. The idea is a familiar one: "absolute power corrupts absolutely!"

Hitler had a global perspective and influence. He appreciated the pursuit of Truth and talked about all the values in Phase IV, but they were all in the service of the Preservation of a unique super-race, which was an extension of himself. He tried to alter the whole world to conform to his view of it. He became a god, as did the Roman emperors, modeling himself after that image. The consequence was a form of narcissism that was more terrifying and destructive than anything before in history.

In other words the global environment is facing the human race with Phase IV values, which at the global level are needs. *To put it another way, what makes Phase IV unique is that it circles around and connects with Phase I,* as is illustrated in Diagram III.3. More details on this connection and a phenomenon that we call the "Onion Effect" will be the subject of the next chapter.

CONCLUSIONS AND INSIGHTS

I first wrote about the Phases of Development in 1976. Since that time the insights that we have gained have transformed all our former thoughts and ideas about values, and human and spiritual development. What we have reviewed in this chapter, however, still remains the foundation for most of what will follow.

When I first wrote about the Phases I thought I was writing about a theory of values. I have since discovered that this is not in fact the case. The values are simply the bridge between the two universes that we live in so aptly described by Socrates over 2200 years ago. He asked the same question that we persist in asking over and over again: What is the nature of reality? Is what we perceive, what the Self perceives, real?

What the Phase theory does is say yes, but it is changing as we change. That is to say, our view of the World changes as we change and develop. The values are important because they allow us to get a handle on this change process, and enable us to grasp a little bit of reality. We noted that the Phases represent four world views. Are there only four? one might ask. My response would be that there are as many world views as there are people to think about reality. The world views that we have presented are general categories of how people perceive the world at clear stages of development. Within these four schemes there are a myriad of individual forms. But the four Phases serve us well as a way of getting an overall perspective on reality.

Phase I is a world view in which the Self is struggling to survive, and has a limited view of anything beyond personal physical satisfaction and needs. Phase II is quite distinct in that the Self now realizes that survival requires social interaction, and requires that interest and attention be given to the perspective of others as we negotiate our place in society.

Phase III is revolutionary in that the Self now begins to act on the environment in creative ways, and not simply react to it. Phase III is a stage of essential integration as the Self feels conscience and recognizes that it exists not in reaction to the external only, but also to the internal world of psychic energy. As the person engages the Fourth Phase, so the world gets bigger both within and without. Without it becomes global and galactic, and within it becomes infinite.

Each Phase is distinct, and unique, but within its own framework is an infinite number of possibilities for everyone. As we move on to the following chapters we shall see that this is but a framework for dozens of emerging patterns of behavior. Some insights that we have gained from the Phases alone are as follows:

1. Each Phase can be described by a set of values represented by an A and a B Stage. The A stage is the way in which the Self reacts to the world, while the B stage is the way in which it acts on the world. The concept of development is not an orderly movement from A to B as many psychologies have suggested, but an increasing of the levels of integration in a cyclical manner of the A and B stages. As such, homeostasis is the norm at the personal and institutional level. Change is a natural ongoing process, but development in the integrated sense takes an act of the creative will, and is not natural. Human and spiritual growth requires additional dynamics other than the aging process alone.

2. Each Phase represents a different world view with a different concentration of values. Within each world view, and within its limits of expression and choice, there are individual human perspectives. One major difference in perspective is between the male and the female of the species, leading to different ethical orientations. The female tends to have an ethic of care, while the male is orientated more to an ethic of rights.

3. Since each Phase is different in the world view it follows, and it is our experience, that persons of differing world views can fail to communicate meaningfully if they are not aware of this basic difference. They will use the same words, but since the values carry different meanings, the meanings behind what they say are different. Examples of this will be stressed in later chapters.

One example is a person using the word "Work" in Phase III to convey the idea of personally meaningful and creative labor that is a part of one's life vocation. A Phase I person would use the word "Work" to mean doing anything to make enough money to survive. The two persons could speak to each other, use the same word, but have nothing in common, relative to their understanding of the word "Work."

Critical to understanding this is the idea that the Goal values are initiated at a particular Phase, but also continue on in a person's life no matter what Phase one is at. Interestingly enough, a Goal value can also go backward on the scale, becoming even less of what it was intended to be.

For example let us consider the value of Family. In Phase II Family is a value that implies parental consistency, to engender and develop belonging, self esteem and education in the children, in order that they might survive and make a positive contribution to society.

At Phase I the Family loses the loyalty aspect and becomes as it is in much of the world, a primitive group of persons feeding off one another for mutual physical survival. Wherever there is insufficient food to feed a population, this will inevitably be the case.

In the other direction, Family in Phase III becomes an expression of an intimate union between two or more people such that the maximum creative potential of all those involved can be enhanced.

4. An extension of this concept is the fact that all the values appear to be potentially implicit in a person from birth. As a consequence we notice that for any given Phase there is a pattern of development relative to particular value strains or tracks from all the previous Phases. Self Preservation, for example, appears in a new and developed form as Self Worth, Self Actualization and Being Self. Although these are all distinct values there is a clear pattern of emergence of these values from Phase to Phase. They are like offsprings of energy born from the original value.

5. We also notice that having values is not the same thing as being healthy or integrated. Certain value combinations will describe a destructive disposition, and others a healthy one. What it is that makes the difference will be described in the next four chapters. We did note that when the Phase I values such as Self Preservation become unbalanced it can cause an increasingly destructive form of narcissism at each Phase. Once it reaches the fourth Phase its power of destruction is global, and its name becomes "evil."

Now that we have explored the foundation we can move on to the main purpose of the book, which is to see how all this enables us to discover patterns of information about human, spiritual and organizational development. In the next chapter we are going to look at Cycles of human and spiritual development, discernment questions and the development of skills.

Chapter 3:
Discern: Looking Through a Mirror

1. Gilligan (1982), p. 5.
2. Hall (1976).
3. Kohlberg (1981).
4. Erikson (1980), pp. 53–54.
5. Gilligan (1982), p. 5.
6. Milne (1928), pp. 62–63.
7. See Lowen (1983) for a full discussion of the narcissistic individual.
8. Peck (1983) states the importance of "naming" or diagnosing evil as a condition in order to render it curable. Evil he claims is also a curable disease. It is caused by hereditary factors (parents' actions etc.) or it is chosen.
9. Fromm (1964), p. 76.
10. *Ibid*. and Lowen (1983).
11. Hall (1982).
12. Peck (1983), p. 214.
13. *Ibid.*, p. 249.
14. Gilligan (1982) pp. 6, 7, 11, 12, and 18 criticizes the male bias of Erikson (leaning on Freud) and Kohlberg in whose case she claims, ". . . in his research from which he derives his theory, females simply do not exist."
15. Erikson (1980), pp. 87–93.
16. Kohlberg (1981).
17. Erikson (1980) pp. 94–95.
18. *Ibid.*, pp. 94–104.
19. Spencer (1984).
20. *Ibid.*, p. 48.
21. Kohlberg (1981).
22. Progoff quoted in Hall and Thompson (1980), pp. 42–43.
23. See note 14 above.
24. Gilligan (1982), p. 164.
25. Poulain (1978), p. 1.
26. Erikson (1980).

THE CYCLES OF DEVELOPMENT I

Each life stage offers new growth resources and possibilities as well as new problems and losses. Wholeness is a lifelong journey of becoming. . . . The gift of growth is received when we choose to develop our options intentionally. The process of growth, although deeply fulfilling, often involves pain and struggle.

Howard Clinebell.[1]

As I looked at the living creatures, I saw wheels on the ground, one beside each of the four living creatures. The wheels had the sparkling appearance of chrysolite, and all four of them looked the same: they were constructed as though one wheel were within another. They could move in any of the four directions they faced, without veering as they moved. The four of them had rims and I saw that their rims were full of eyes all around. When the living creatures moved, the wheels moved with them: and when the living creatures were raised from the ground, the wheels also were raised.

Wherever the spirit wished to go, there the wheels went, and they were raised together with the living creatures: for the spirit of the living creatures was with the wheels.

NAB. Ezekiel 1:15–21. 600 B.C.

PURPOSE To examine human and spiritual development as a cyclical process of integration and transformation that is reflected through our values, our skills and the questions that we ask ourselves.

CONTENT The chapter begins with a look at human development through the eyes of Kohlberg, Erikson and the Mystics to raise the question: What is integrated development? The assumption by many theorists that we naturally ascend through a hierarchy of stages of development is challenged, as the concept of Cycles of Development is presented. The idea of Seven Cycles of Development is introduced through the first or Primal Cycle. The discussion illustrates how the Cycles give unique information about the nature of discernment, skills and leadership styles.

LINKAGE This chapter shows how the Phases of Value Development discussed in the last chapter are a foundation for understanding human and spiritual development as represented through Seven Cycles of Development. The Cycles are a process of integration and transformation, where the future is always a function of a transformation process that includes a continual return and reintegration of the past. This chapter introduces us to the first Cycle, and links us to Chapter V, that continues the journey by looking at the next six Cycles.

This chapter is about the Seven Cycles of human and spiritual development. The four Phases constitute the basis and foundation for human and spiritual development as it stands on the threshold between
the inner and outer world of each person's universe. We noted that
there were also eight stages of development: four Phases with an A
and B stage for each Phase. What is the connection between all these
pieces?

In our original research we studied over 40 theories of development
and tried to elicit the common themes and underlying values that related to the various stages that different theorists would propose.
Writers like Lawrence Kohlberg and Erik Erikson had their proposed
six and eight stages of development. They in turn had grown out of a
long history of thinkers before them, like Piaget, Dewey, Freud, Sullivan, Adler, Jung and others.

Each was studying the human being from a slightly different framework.[2] The Structural Developmentalists from which Kohlberg was
spawned were interested in child and adult education. They were interested in the concrete structures of how a person grows in knowing
and learning. Kohlberg basing his studies on the work of Dewey and
Piaget wanted to know how the human person rationally and cogni-
tively chooses and makes a judgment as to what is right and what is
wrong in a given situation. He concluded that moral choices alter according to the developmental level of the person, which was a radically different point of view from traditional moral philosophy. He
concluded there were six such stages of development.

Erikson on the other hand had come from a 100 year tradition of
psychoanalysis beginning with Freud and his associates like Jung and
Adler. This tradition studied the human being from the perspective
and presupposition that the human being is purposefully driven from
within, by partially unconscious forces. Further they saw development as psychosomatic. That is it was tied to the physical development of the body on the one hand and the emotional imaginal
dimension on the other hand. The growth process was seen as a series
of struggles and integrations between the inner psychic forces and the
external demands of the social world. Since a part of the framework
was that humans are goal and need directed, ill-health becomes an un-
natural blocked condition of their natural growth process.

Different thinkers picked up on different aspects of these new and
very radical ideas about the human condition. Jung studied the inner
psychic processes, Adler and Sullivan placed special emphasis on the
interpersonal dimension. Erikson integrated some of these and placed
his emphasis on identity and development. Erikson posited eight
stages of development for the human life cycle from birth to old age.
The following Table IV.1. will give us an overview of the stages of de-

velopment as represented by Erikson and Kohlberg as they were discussed in the last chapter.[3]

ERIKSON	KOHLBERG
LIFE CYCLE STAGES	STAGES OF MORAL DEVELOPMENT
	PRE-CONVENTIONAL LEVEL: Moral Value resides in external happenings.
1. TRUST VERSUS MISTRUST. Initial need for securing caring physical/emotive environment.	1. EGOCENTRIC VIEWPOINT. Right is what physically satisfies self.
2. AUTONOMY VERSUS SHAME AND DOUBT. Need for parental care and affirmation of will.	2. CONCRETE INDIVIDUALISTIC PERSPECTIVE. Right is to do what is in one's self interest.
	CONVENTIONAL LEVEL: Moral Value in performing right role and maintaining the expectation of others.
3. INITIATIVE VERSUS GUILT. Need for positive role models who affirm creative fantasy.	3. SOCIAL PERSPECTIVE TAKING. Right as living the Golden Rule—do unto others as you wish they would to you.
4. INDUSTRY VERSUS INFERIORITY. Need to experience success in tasks at school and work.	4. SOCIETAL PERSPECTIVE. Right is following the system's rules.
5. IDENTITY VERSUS IDENTITY DIFFUSION. Adolescent need to integrate past tasks in order direct one's life.	POST-CONVENTIONAL LEVEL. Moral resides in integration of self with a personal conscience.
6. INTIMACY VERSUS ISOLATION. Need of male to develop new level of Trust with equal.	5. RATIONAL RELATIVE PERSPECTIVE. Rights as value specific but relative to individual point of view.
7. GENERATIVITY VERSUS STAGNATION. Family development and career path completion.	
8. INTEGRITY VERSUS DESPAIR AND DISGUST. Final stage of meaningful life satisfaction.	6. CONSCIENCE PERSPECTIVE. Rights based on objective set of moral principles that are universal.

Historically the concept of development and change has been around since the beginning of civilization. Heraclitus stated nearly *see Introduction, chapter 8* 2500 years ago: "All is change." In the religious traditions of spiritual direction there have been models of development around in Eastern and Western Mysticism for centuries. They are all remarkably similar and show amazing convergence. The most ancient are from the Hindu and Buddhist traditions. Western mystical tradition grew more out of the Jewish, Christian and Islamic faiths from the second century on.

The Stages of Mystical Development, unlike the stages of development described by Kohlberg and Erikson, are not related to the aging process, but to experiences of higher consciousness. Historically five Stages[4] of Mystical experience are described by a range of Eastern and Western Mystics. The first Stage is the *Primal Stage* and the last is that of *Union*. The *Primal Stage* is simply initial human and psychological development. It would be equivalent to Erikson's and Kohlberg's first four stages. The second Stage is normally called *Conversion*, and relates to an individual's initial awareness of the transcendent dimension in life. It is followed by a commitment to a Faith center with a particular value focus. It is a coming to clarity around specific values that one must have to grow to unusual heights of spiritual development.

STAGES OF MYSTICAL DEVELOPMENT

The third Stage is *Purification*. It is following of "A Way of Life" initiated by the experience of Conversion, where the individual is involved in a discipline that enables the person to be conformed to the chosen value orientation. At the best this relates in part to the final two stages of Erikson and Kohlberg. The comparison is not direct however, since these are experiences that are really beyond what the psychologist intends to deal with. In the value framework this would be Phase III.

The Mystical Stage of *Illumination* relates to the values in Phase III. It is the description of an increased state of internal integration. It is an increased awareness of one's life being intimately related to a transcendent energy form—in Christian terms the Divinity of Christ. Other religions describe the same experience but call it by a different name. The consequence of the experience is illuminative insight about one's Self and the nature of reality.[5]

The Unitive Stage. The fifth and last stage is an experience of Union with this Divine energy. It is called by some the Unitive experience; others refer to it as the *Ultimate or Causal Stage*. It is often described as an overwhelming experience of love, an experience of intimacy and union with an-Other, to be at-one with the ground of all being. This experience is anticipated by the values in the fourth Phase of Development, but is by no means the same thing. After all such experiences transcend human description. However at the practical level the values of such integrated human beings have the consequence of global influence, and wise insights about the the world that have traditionally affected the human race.

91

The Phases of Development transcend the various developmental theories by suggesting that they are undergirded by a common set of values. In other words any stage of development, whether it be described
by Erikson or Kohlberg or the mystics, is in fact a stage in life that reflects a particular value framework or emphasis.

A natural assumption is that all the above theories of development,
whether Mystical or Psychological, are a part of one single wholistic
process. This, I have concluded, is partly true. Our Value orientation
does provide, hopefully, an overall picture. The former assumption
that I and others made that each of these theories runs on a parallel
track is questionable.

This would assume, for example, that Kohlberg's second stage
would always somehow reflect a similar early life stage for a given individual using Erikson's approach. After all since we live within a
common time framework, from birth to death, and are all physically
constituted in a similar manner, would we not expect this to be the
case? Over the last five years I have had research students doing comparative analyses of the biographies of famous people comparing values development, with the Faith development schema of Fowler,
Kohlberg's works and that of Erikson,[6] as well as one or two other theories. Our discovery was that our second assumption was false; the
frameworks did not compare in any orderly way!

In fact we found that it was in the discrepancies and differences between them that we had the most valuable information. It is true that
a healthy person needs to be morally and emotionally integrated as in
Kohlberg and Erikson, but it does not follow if you have one you will
have the other.

see Ledig, Appendix   This raised the question: What is integrated development? One conclusion is that all such theories of human development are but aspects
of a greater integrated whole. Therefore any particular theory is going
to have a particular value bias. This raises a major ethical issue, since
many of the authors of such theories especially as they are applied to
psychotherapy claim they are value free, which is of course nonsense!
In fact any theory by any author, including this one, is assuming a set
of values by which his or her theory is constructed.

In 1979 I published a book in India called *Developing Leadership by
Stages.* It came out of a practical study to try to determine how different
styles of executive leadership might be related to the eight stages of
values development. The assumption was that the eight stages probably correlated with Erikson and others and that logically there would
also be a similar experience in the examination of leadership styles.

Again my assumption was false! Taking common leadership styles
ranging from the more autocratic to the participative and collaborative
forms of management, and analyzing the values under various styles,
we found there were distinct styles that clearly lined up with the four
World Views at each Phase. But when we tried to line them up for each
value stage (eight altogether) we were unable to find any satisfactory
correlation. There seemed to be other possible stages that did not fit
the Phases but were in between them!

Further analysis revealed that the stages of leadership development see *Retrieve, chapter 10* became very clear when we paired the value stages. In other words the first leadership level was Phase IA and B. The second was between the first two Phases: Phase IB and IIA. The third became IIA and B, and so on, to give us a total of seven leadership levels.

After several years of working with this we found that we had actually put the cart before the horse! The seven leadership levels were really Seven Cycles of human and spiritual development, and the leadership stages were simply one aspect of what was a far greater whole.

In the next section of this chapter we are going to look at Seven Cycles of Human and Spiritual development, based on the four Phases described in the last chapter. The idea is not to just add another theory but to look at the underpinnings of all developmental frameworks, in order to begin to put them in an overall perspective. As such we shall also look at the relationship between psychological and spiritual development.

We shall look at the various factors that cause development, using in part the framework proposed by Ken Wilber in a book called *A Sociable God*. He uses the word "Translation" to mean that process that causes integration at a particular stage of development. The two main processes for this to occur are Manna and Taboo. Manna means food, and indicates the gifts and skills that cause health and integration at a particular stage. Taboo involves the negative factors that block development, including the skills that can result from the attempt of an individual to adapt and survive in an abusive environment at each stage.

Wilber uses the word *Transformation* to indicate those processes that enable a person to transcend a particular stage and move on to the next. We will indicate that there are a number of factors including a peculiar dialectical relationship between the values and the skills that help this occur.[7]

THE SEVEN CYCLES OF DEVELOPMENT

Viewing the values once again as a system of information retrieval we conclude that in order for a person to grow from one Phase to another he or she had to pass through Seven Cycles of development, as illustrated in Diagram IV.1 on next page.

In the top half of the diagram we see the four Phases each with a Stage A and a Stage B. The values in each Phase go through a cyclical process of integration as a person grows in that world view. In the second part of the diagram we see that between each Cycle is posited see *Diagram III.1* an in between Cycle giving rise to the Seven Cycles indicated.

Time as it is used with the Cycles is not related to the physical process of growing up, for the most part. It is regarded more as a continuous cycle of Human and Spiritual development potentially accessible to anyone, but chosen by very few past the fourth cycle.

The Seven Cycles will introduce us to an intricate network of values patterns. This, then, is the beginning of a more concentrated look at the retrieval of information through values as they reflect the Genesis Effect. Each of the Seven Cycles has its own Values, World View,

Diagram 4:1
CYCLES OF HUMAN AND OF SPIRITUAL DEVELOPMENT
The diagram shows how the Four Phases represent separate World Views, but that they are all connected by in-between cycles made up of the "b" and "a" stages of each Phase, giving rise to Seven distinct Cycles of Development.

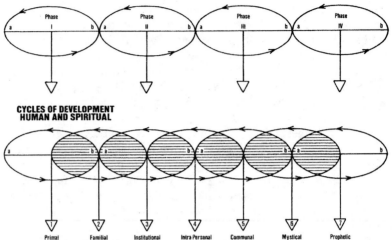

Leadership and Follower style and Skills. Additionally each set of information raises its own set of discernment questions.

The World Views and the values will be reviewed very briefly since they were covered for the most part in the last chapter. They are reviewed once again because the context, as we shall see, is different. Explanation of the other aspects will be covered in more detail in Cycle One as an introduction to the other Six Cycles.

CYCLE ONE: THE PRIMAL CYCLE
see Value Lists and Definitions, Appendix

THE VALUES: Stages 1A/1B as in Phase I.

Stage A Goals	Stage B Goals
1. SELF PRESERVATION	4. SECURITY
2. WONDER/AWE	

Stage A Means	Stage B Means
3. SAFETY/SURVIVAL	5. SENSORY PLEASURE
	6. PROPERTY/ECONOMICS

PROFILE OF THE PRIMAL CYCLE
see Phase I and Phase I Synopsis, chapter 3

This is the first cycle of growth. The person views the world as an alien and mysterious place ruled by distant authority. The adult is motivated by the need for Security and material ownership, and the struggle for physical survival. Ethical choices are based on Self Interest which is viewed as the most practical way for all to survive. It is important that at this stage a creative and positive imagination be developed for a healthy movement into future stages. Religiously God is Savior, who is viewed as awesome, present in nature and ruling this world from a distant place.

The profile, then, is the direct consequence of how a person will perceive the world and act toward it when he or she is living in an environment where the above values are the priorities. A detailed explanation of this Cycle was given as Phase I in the last chapter.

The purpose of the discernment questions is to elicit in a confidential manner more information about the values that a person may have. For example if persons place a lot of emphasis in their life on Security, but are not aware of it, they will exhibit a lot of insecurity in their behavior. If you as a spiritual guide or counselor, or even a friend, say to them "What is making you so insecure?" they are likely to become even more defensive. On the other hand they may be able to respond to a series of objective discernment questions about that value.

The discernment questions in this and the following chapter will appear on a separate page in each section. Look at the discernment questions related to the value of Security, as an example.

The concept of counseling an individual by discernment is one of the oldest methods of giving Spiritual Direction or Guidance. The concept is that ultimate wisdom is found from within. In religious terms it is a seeking out of the will of the spirit of God within.

see Grassi and Schmitt, Appendix

The difference between this and psychological counseling is that spiritual counsel is directed to enabling persons to fulfill their total potential, by discovering their unique gifts and deciding how to actualize those gifts in the service of others. This may include utilizing all the skills of psychological and career counseling. Generally speaking psychological counseling is more directed to removing barriers to individual or family growth and development. Spiritual counsel ultimately differs from this by adding the assumption that each person is called to fulfill his or her potential in a particular way as a child of God.

Discernment became more specifically a psychological art form with the work of Ignatius of Loyola the founder of the Jesuits in the late 16th century.[8] He designed a particular 30 day series of spiritual exercises that combined experiences of the active imagination, reflection on scripture and personal counsel, for the purpose of leading the trainee to new levels of value commitment. The commitment in this case was to service within the Society of Jesus.

The principles of discernment had three dimensions which are applicable to anyone today as they were then: Congruence, Confirmation and Convergence.

VALUE: SECURITY

Questions:
- Are ordered surroundings important to you?
- Is comfort and certainty important to you?
- Is a minimal amount of certainty and security important to you?
- Is the future uncertain to you?
- Does worry or anxiety take a lot of your energy at this time?
- Do you feel that you are more controlling than you need to be?

CONGRUENCE

Psychologically Congruence means that what I feel within, and what my external behavior indicates are the same to any outside observer. For example if Security is a value I should be able to identify those times recently when I felt insecure or anxious. In fact the more mentally unhealthy a person is the more these two become separated. For example a person will do small annoying things to someone, indicating an angry attitude, but deny any such feeling.

Ignatius would help an individual to examine his or her feelings, especially those of elation or consolation, and those he called "desolation" which would be closer to despair, depression or frustration. His methodology was to then enable the person to raise discernment questions about the meaning of this feeling.

A feeling of despair may be positive if a person's behavior warrants it. In the same way a feeling of consolation may be inappropriate if the person is mistaken about an idea or possibility for himself or herself. The values are simply a modern entrance into the same discernment framework, and as such an aid to a person to gain important information about himself or herself and his or her life direction.

CONFIRMATION
see chapter 2

Confirmation occurs as the questions that the values pose tend to repeat themselves. For example if you the reader would care to mark the questions that are the most important to you as you go through the Seven Cycles you will notice a repetition of similar ideas. This will help you in turn identify the values which are important to you, and specify the direction in which you can move to fulfill your potential. Be careful, however, only to mark the really important questions. In any set of questions in the next few pages pick no more than two priorities.

The experience of Confirmation is not only a question of the repetition of the questions but also a confirmation of your own experience. If the question asks if you are overcontrolling of others and a friend recently confronted you on the same issue, then you are experiencing a confirmation of the same inner question. It is simply a way of collecting important information about one's life in order to try to understand what it is you are being called to through the question.

CONVERGENCE

Convergence is the introduction of the idea that a repetition of confirmatory questions and experiences is pointing to patterns in your behavior, relative to what you are being called to from within. Again this convergence is not simply with the questions but with all the other things you know about yourself.

For example a person might experience a common pattern of questions about personal anger on the one hand, and lack or recreation and play on the other hand. These two are probably related, in that they are both symptoms of stress. Additionally they may also be internal symptoms of a call to change one's life style, or even one's life direction. That is to say when one has sufficient play and relaxation one is less likely to be stressed and frustrated.

If you answer several of the questions in the next section, put them all together on a separate sheet of paper and see if you can discern the underlying patterns—and discover some convergence. Let us now look at some of the discernment questions related to the values in Cycle One.

Each Cycle of Development not only gives rise to an individual way of operating in the world, as evidenced above, but it also gives rise to the style of leadership a person will have.

Leadership is used here to signify the way in which the person influences others. Due to the survival nature of the values at the Primal Cycle the leadership style is going to be necessarily *AUTOCRATIC*. The person feels that all major decisions have to be made by himself or herself. Leadership and Management feels that they need to keep control in order to function properly.

Survival on a day to day basis, and control of property, profit margin and financial flow, are of utmost importance. Loyalty to the organization through its leadership whether it be a church, a corporation or a family is seen as a number one priority and the overriding criterion for ethical choices.

Robert Townsend, with tongue in cheek, put it this way: "The best two guarantees that the chief executive will work full time are hunger and fear. He has to hunger for the company to succeed; and he has to have so much of his own money and ego tied up in the company that fear of failure is constantly with him."[9]

This level and experience of leadership is absolutely essential when the environment is alien. In other words when the values of survival and self preservation are objectively occurring then a dictatorial leadership style is probably the only thing that will work. If one is in charge of a jungle search team in war time Vietnam the leadership had better be autocratic. If one's house is burning and the children are trapped, someone has to be dictatorial to avoid disaster!

SELF PRESERVATION:

Questions:
- Is life a daily physical struggle for you?
- Do you have sufficient control over your life?
- Is looking after your own welfare taking a lot of energy at this time?

WONDER/AWE:

Questions:
- Do you see life as mysterious and awesome much of the time?
- Do you feel that fate rules your life?

SAFETY/SURVIVAL:

Questions:
- Do you feel that outside forces are threatening your survival?
- Do you feel unsafe at times?

SECURITY:

Questions:
- Are ordered surroundings important to you?
- Is a minimal amount of certainty and security important to you?
- Is the future uncertain to you?

SENSORY PLEASURE:

Questions:
- Is being touched and held important to you?
- Is physical appreciation of nature important for you, and is this part of your life satisfactory?

PROPERTY/ECONOMICS:

- Is property ownership important to you?
- Do you have sufficient skills in money management?
- Is your financial future a problem at this time?

THE FOLLOWER. Whenever a particular leadership style is operative there is always a consequence for those who are working for the designated leader. At the Autocratic level leadership is hardly ever elected; it is usually appointed out of survival necessity.

Churchill was asked to be Prime Minister at the beginning of World War II, but as soon as the War was over he was voted out of office. Why? Dictatorial leadership was needed in the War years. However, the consequence for the follower at this level is always the same: the experience of oppression. Therefore when the environmental threat is removed the people if they have a choice will change the leadership—as they did with Churchill.

I remember being on an overseas assignment in Central America for a Canadian Company twenty years ago. I was with my wife and a small child. All our baggage had been lost for six weeks, and we had heard nothing from our superiors in Toronto for two months. It was in August and they were on holiday! Relative to the work that I was doing there were a lot of serious questions from local people in Costa Rica about what we were doing there in the first place. I put my concerns in a letter to my boss asking for an urgent reply.

A short letter came back three months later which said: "Hall, please remember, we are all members of a Soccer team, and you are one of the linebackers. Team members do not ask questions, they wait for orders. Hope all is going well. Yours sincerely. . . . " Followship at this level is primarily an experience of distance from the leadership with a lack of interpersonal sensitivity.

The point of the story is not only the feeling of oppression and of being ignored that a person experiences under Dictatorial leadership but the fact that it is particularly disturbing when the environment is not in fact oppressive!

In Phase I, world view survival and self preservation are expressions of physical threat. Hence when the leadership operates Autocratically in a physically non-threatening environment it becomes Dictatorial and destructive.[10] Persons with Phase I values and Autocratic leadership styles need to be certain that their circumstance really demands that such a style is essential. When this is not the case, then the situation is mentally unhealthy for the followers and the leadership.

The tendency at this leadership level is for the leader to be overcontrolling of employees and possibly of his or her family and friends. Primary loyalty of the leader is going to be to one's self and closest confidants. There will also be a tendency to confuse business and personal relationships, and place unrealistic expectations on others. What is called for at this Cycle is attention to stress reduction and physical health, and a need to develop a positive imagination relative to future responsibility.

Failure to do this will disenable a person to see the realities and pressures one has to deal with in a sufficiently comprehensive manner. Several leadership discernment questions are raised for this level.

THE SKILLS

The ability to function at a given level and the ability to develop to another level are dependent very much on the skills that an individual has. By skills is understood something akin to what Aristotle understood by virtues. That is the power (*virtus*) to act with ease and the ability to respond to and manage the environment—internal and external.

Skills are the other side of a value. That is to say any value can be described as an inventory of skills. For example Self Preservation is an important value for anybody who is going hiking and camping alone in the mountains of northeastern California in the winter. At the same time that value could be defined as a long set of Instrumental or professional skills directly related to that value.

These skills would include knowing how to use a compass, knowing what light weight protective clothing one needs, knowing how to negotiate steep areas and what kind of terrain to avoid, knowing how to read a map of the area, knowing what food to take, and how to prepare it, knowing how to avoid bears at night and prevent them from stealing all your food. In this setting all these skills and others constitute one aspect of Self Preservation.

We need to be careful to point out that although a value consists of a series of virtues or skills, the composite of them does not necessarily insure the formation of the value. For the value of Self Preservation to occur you would need the skills and the will and motivation. On the other hand the value cannot come to fruition without the skills.

In categorizing the list of 125 values into skill areas we found that they broke down into four main categories, all represented in a rudimentary form in the first Cycle. They are called: Instrumental, Interpersonal, Imaginal and System Skills. Let us review them briefly for this Cycle and as a preparation to understanding the next six Cycles. *see chapter 6* They are defined as follows:

a. **Instrumental Skills.** These are the skills of the mind and the hands—of cognition, craftmanship and my profession. They are developed in my early years and through formal education. The origin of instrumental skills relates to the historical development of tools, and the personal physical dexterity to use them. The Primal Cycle is basically characterized by these skills as represented in the values: Self Preservation, Safety/Survival and Property/Economics.

LEADERSHIP DISCERNMENT QUESTIONS CYCLE ONE

- Are you finding that it is impossible to delegate work?
- Do you feel that you cannot trust people at this time?
- Do you have difficulty sleeping? Do you have high blood pressure?
- Do you have any recreation or play time?
- Do others tell you that at times you do not value others' opinions sufficiently?

b. Interpersonal Skills. These are skills with the emotions that bring about human cooperation rather than isolation. They enable us to objectify and identify feelings so as to enhance social interaction. We learn them through our family of origin and through other forms of social conditioning and training.

These are underdeveloped in this Cycle but their rudimentary beginnings are anticipated in the values of Security and Sensory Pleasure. Although these values are interpersonal, at this level they are primarily experienced as physical rather than emotional.

c. Imaginal Skills. These are the skills of generating new ideas and images through the creative evaluation of disparate data. It is that skill whose primary job it is to integrate internal fantasy and information with external information gathered by the five senses.

d. System Skills. System skills involve the ability to see and understand how all the parts of any complex organization of data or of an institution relate to the functioning of the whole.

These skills also include being able to make decisions based on a knowledge of the whole organization rather than on its parts. This value is only experienced at this level as a partial aspect of Property/Economics. It is for the most part a skill that will develop in later Cycles.

MANNA AND TABOO

see Issues for Human and Spiritual Integration, chapter 3; and Integrated Development, chapter 7

Manna is the positive skills that persons need at a given Cycle.[11] In the Primal Cycle the basic skills are Instrumental skills around preservation and the securing of the system in order that one might survive. Developmentally this means learning the basic skills for physical functioning. It also means learning the rudimentary skills of survival education in society such as reading and language, writing and arithmetic. Above all this cycle requires the learning of minimal skills in pain tolerance.

These skills are the basic foundation of what competence a person will have later. Without minimal positive tolerance of pain, Erikson's level of Trust is never transcended. Autonomy becomes a virtual impossibility. Negative skills can also be formed at this Cycle reinforcing the experience of Taboo. Taboo is basically an avoidance and denial of one's inner feelings, images and life. Naturally it is most likely to appear in its most negative form in this first Cycle. This is the problem of Narcissism discussed at length in the last chapter.

At the skill level Taboo in the Primary Cycle can cause an aberrative *see Narcissism, chapter 3* form of behavior which is traditionally classified as mental illness. One form of this is narcissism as previously discussed, which results in a demagogic form of leadership that would be an extreme form of dictatorship. Basically we are talking about a negative skill formation that would involve the denial of self for the purpose of perceived survival, at a time when the environment was in fact secure.

The denial might take other forms also relative to chemical dependence such as alcohol. At a more moderate level the negative behavior takes on the form of manipulating others into doing what one wants without directly asking for it. This as Hellmuth Kaiser points out takes the form of "Domination" or "Dependence."[11a]

Domination is a form of manipulation where the individual bullies or threatens persons into doing what he or she wants. In leadership this has been historically very common in persons such as Hitler and Napoleon.[12] The opposite form less common in leadership is the dependent personality that uses guilt and personal martyrdom to persuade others to care and feel sorry for him or her.

As Diagram IV.1. above indicates, Cycle 2 consists of the B stage values in Phase I, and the A stage in Phase II. It is this connecting point that begins to aid the development from one Phase and World View to the next.

Let us examine this more closely by moving to the other six Cycles, beginning with Cycle Two, in the next chapter: The Cycles of Development II.

Chapter 4:
The Cycles of Development I

1. Clinebell (1981), pp. 16–17.

2. See Ryckman (1978) for a series of essays on the different theories of personality and its development.

3. Erikson (1980) and Kohlberg (1981).

4. Underhill (1955).

5. Johnston (1974) discusses similar stages in the "journey of a soul." A more scholarly work is that of Poulain (1978).

6. Fowler (1981), Kohlberg (1981), Erikson (1980).

7. Wilber (1983).

8. de Guibert (1954).

9. Townsend quoted in Hall & Thompson (1980), p. 56.

10. See Bullock (1971) for a revealing examination of the destructive quality of Adolf Hitler's language and thought. Even in defeat ". . . .

we should drag half the world with us." We see here the inherent nihilism of the autocrat.

11. See Wilber (1983).

11a. Kaiser, (1965).

12. Bullock (1971).

THE CYCLES OF DEVELOPMENT II

The testimony of the mystics, however, and of all persons possessing an "instinct for the Absolute," points to the existence of a further faculty—indeed a deeper self—in man; a self which the circumstances of diurnal life usually keep "below the threshold" of his consciousness, and which thus becomes one of the factors of his "subliminal life." The hidden self is the primary agent of mysticism, and lives a "substantial" life in touch with the real or transcendental world.

Evelyn Underhill.[1]

Personality can be said to develop according to steps predetermined in the human organism's readiness to be driven toward, to be aware of, and to interact with, a widening social radius, beginning with the dim image of a mother and ending with mankind, or at any rate that segment of mankind which "counts" in the particular individual's life.

Erik H. Erikson.[2]

PURPOSE To discuss the last six Cycles of Development, beginning with the Familial Cycle, and how they can furnish us with unique information about the positive and negative sides of human and spiritual transformation.

CONTENT The chapter looks at each of the Cycles of Development beginning with the values and the peculiar dialectical relationships that they form that can enable or disenable growth at this point in an individual's life. The relationship of value related discernment questions to leadership styles and skills at each of the Cycles is also examined.

LINKAGE The nature of the Cycles of Development and a review of the first Cycle was the subject matter of the last chapter. This chapter continues this journey by looking in detail at the other six Cycles—from the Familial to the Prophetic. In Chapter VII we will go a step further and try to determine what factors cause healthy or integrated growth and development as phenomena we call the "Onion Effect."

The last chapter discussed the relationship of the four Phases of Development, their values and World View, and their relationship to the Seven Cycles of Human and Spiritual development. Since we are exploring a developmental view of the person, it was necessary that we give quality attention to the first Cycle. This chapter is going to look in detail at the other six Cycles, their values and discernment questions, their leadership and skill requirements, and their special relationship to the development of the self.

CYCLE TWO: THE FAMILIAL CYCLE

THE VALUES: Stages 1B Phase I/IA Phase II.

Stage B Goals (*Phase I*)	Stage A Goals (*Phase II*)
4. SECURITY	7. FAMILY/BELONGING
	8. SELF WORTH

see Value Lists and Definitions, Appendix

Stage B Means (*Phase I*)	Stage A Goals (*Phase II*)
5. SENSORY PLEASURE	9. BELONGING (LIKED)
6. PROPERTY/ECONOMICS	10. CARE/NURTURE
	11. CONTROL/DUTY
	12. TRADITION
	13. SOCIAL PRESTIGE

see Diagram I/III II.1 and V.1   This is a Cycle that is in between the Phases moving from a physical orientation to the world to a more social orientation, stressing Family and security. The question that is addressed here and that will be continually addressed in the following chapters is what causes development to occur.

Clearly it is a combination of many factors. But a central underlying factor in our experience of hundreds of individual profiles examinations is the dialectical connection between stages, particularly as they cross the Phases, as is the case in this Cycle.

Let me illustrate with a common example. As the values in the first Cycle become integrated, the individual, whether a child confronted by the family environment, or a businessman confronted with the demands of the marketplace, is brought face to face with the values reflected in the next stage.

The child discovers frankly that he or she will not survive if minimal courtesy and affirmation is not accorded to his or her parents, and not simply the other way around. The business man or woman finds that survival must include others, and must include the valuing of others if he or she is to gain their cooperation. Two dialectics will illustrate the point:

104

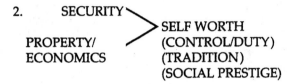

1. SECURITY

    SENSORY PLEASURE
    FAMILY/BELONGING
    (BELONGING [LIKED])
    (CARE/NURTURE)

For the new member of a family, which could be a child, or equally a newly married couple, security and the sense of pleasure and comfort one gets from being touched, hugged and held is one of the things that make life worth living. But unless it moves into the social reciprocal stage (stage B) the person soon discovers that pleasure and security are not forthcoming. Family/Belonging implies that one belongs, is cared for and nurtured, as one cares and nurtures others, and makes them feel they belong. We note that the Means values are dimensions of the Goals.

2. SECURITY

    PROPERTY/
    ECONOMICS
    SELF WORTH
    (CONTROL/DUTY)
    (TRADITION)
    (SOCIAL PRESTIGE)

In this dialectic a business manager, for example, in order to be secure in his or her job, by keeping the office running well and making a profit (Property/Economics), would not survive without crossing Phases into the A stage of this Cycle. The reason is that the successful manager is going to need to affirm the value (Self Worth) of those he or she needs to cooperate with in order for them to do the same. This in turn means using traditional management skills (aspects of Tradition and Control/Duty) and be confirmed by his or her peers that he or she is doing a good job (Social Prestige).

A positive experience of these values as the dialectic moves across the Phase is one of the descriptions of how development occurs. What is fascinating is that that once an individual is able to see the dialectic, as in the latter examples, they are very often able to convert these into images, usually as a description of a personal aspiration or hope for the future.

For example in the first dialectic above a young couple who were in premarital counseling were able to talk about their dream, using the first dialectic, but occasionally substituting Property/Economic as follows.

    SECURITY

    SENSORY PLEASURE
    PROPERTY/
    ECONOMICS
    FAMILY/BELONGING

Janice spoke from the dialectic and simply said the following: "It captures my hopes for Joe and me. We have both had a difficult upbringing. My father died when I was seven years old, and Joe's mother was divorced and remarried twice before he was fifteen. So we are hoping to buy some property in the country and build our own house slowly, by buying more materials each month from the money we make in our business. (They owned a small fish shop.)

"We get a lot of pleasure just being with each other and cuddling up in front of the fire or the television at night. Anyway we want to have several children and build a family for all of us, so that they can have what we could not have—a place where we belonged and felt secure."

Obviously the values are being defined by Janice as she speaks. Also the values here are a mere reflection of the depths of feelings that she had about the internal images she expressed. The dialectic then is a shadow of an internal reality, that is, in turn, a plan for future behaviors. It is the loop from internal to external that we call the Genesis Effect.

This attachment to a dialectic or cluster of values that enpowers the person to grow is what James Fowler calls a Faith Center.[3] This Faith Center is also developmental and will be dealt with in depth in a later chapter. At this point let us continue and briefly describe the rest of Cycle 2.

PROFILE OF THE FAMILIAL CYCLE

see Phase I and II, chapter 3

The World View of this cycle is a blend of Phase I and II, where one's living situation, my home and my friends shelter me from an unfriendly or uncaring society. The predominant task is to integrate personal security needs with those of family and friends. Respect for legitimate authority is important.

Ethical choices are based on fairness and mutual respect. We are "good" when we follow the rules that fair authority has laid down. In this cycle, education, and the avoidance of perfectionism through objective study, and hospitality are essential for spiritual growth. This Cycle is moving in the direction of personal and familial integration. Religiously God is my Master and Teacher known to me through stories and tradition.

DISCERNMENT QUESTIONS

The discernment questions for the Phase IB area have already been addressed as a part of Cycle One. Additional example questions relative to the other values from Phase IIA for consideration are listed herein.

CYCLE TWO DISCERNMENT QUESTIONS

FAMILY/BELONGING

Questions:
- Is your family a priority concern for you?
- Do you have sufficient skills in family management?
- Is your home living arrangement satisfactory?

SELF WORTH.

Questions:
- Do you feel sufficiently respected by those who know you?
- Are there aspects of yourself you do not feel good about?
- Are you embarrassed to share yourself with others?

BELONGING (LIKED).

Questions:
- Is being liked by others an important issue for you?
- Do you have good friends you see regularly?
- Do you have enough emotional support from others?

CARE/NURTURE.

Questions:
- Do you feel cared for?
- Is caring for others a major issue for you?
- Is courtesy and hospitality important to you?

CONTROL/DUTY.

Questions:
- Do you have a strong sense of duty?
- Do you have sufficient skills in orderly discipline relative to your health and spiritual life?

TRADITION.

Questions:
- Are family traditions and annual festivals important to you?
- Do you enjoy historical reading, drama and film?

SOCIAL PRESTIGE.

Questions:
- When you make a decision do you wonder what others will think?
- Is how you dress and look to others important to you?

At this cycle Leadership style is one of CARING AUTHORITY, or BENEVOLENT MATERNALISM AND PATERNALISM, where the tendency is to be maternal or paternal. The style is Autocratic, as in the first Cycle, with an emphasis on careful listening.

LEADERSHIP
see Leadership Level, chapter 4

The leader is very much aware that she or he is ultimately responsible for decisions. Consequently loyalty to designated superiors and following the rules they set down is important. Credibility, resistance to change and perfectionisistic behavior often mark the leader's style.

The primary orientation of the leader is to be authoritarian and parental. He or she is caring of the employee but would never consider what the follower or employee has to say to be of any significance as far as decision making is concerned. Therefore the leadership style here is always hierarchical.

The FOLLOWER still feels oppressed relative to expression of ideas or personal authority, but feels cared for much like a child to a parent. This is a very common style in many administrative settings, and was the normal style of operating for most religious executives up until the late 1960's.

This style of leadership is most appropriate in an environment where the founder or executive of the organization is highly skilled, and the support persons are not. In this setting the leader very often has to take a parental or teacher role in order for the system to survive. However this role format would be a disaster with competent peers.

SKILLS
see Chapter 6 The positive Manna skills for this Cycle are all the skills that are required relative to rote learning. As in Cycle One, Instrumental skills are the highest priority, from mathematics and language to the particular skills one needs as a basis to do one's professional work. For example growth in this Cycle requires that the person have competence in basic administrative skills. Anything that a secretary could do a person in a leadership role should be able to do.

see Manna and Taboo, chapter 4 and Contingency chapter 7 Skills in rote learning are an ongoing necessity for survival at all the following Cycles, as pain tolerance is in the first Cycle. The reason is that once formal education has ended it is the ability to keep learning on one's own that is essential.

For example in today's world where so much of what is done is out of an international framework, it is necessary for a person to be able to rote learn, if necessary, a new language or new information about a culture or a foreign made product.

LEADERSHIP DISCERNMENT QUESTIONS CYCLE TWO

Questions:
- Do others feel you listen well to them?
- Do you delegate sufficiently without checking up on others?
- Do you have sufficient administration skills, or skills of completion?
- Do you have sufficient play/work balance, and are you at home enough as far as your home base is concerned?
- Are you respected by persons in authority, or those you respect?
- How important is it to you that others are loyal and respectful?
- How important is learning about new things for you at this time?
- What is your attitude toward rules and law?

In spiritual development this is the point where a person needs to gain the basic information about his or her religion and minimal skills in the ascetical life, theology and daily discipline. These are the basic skills that become the foundation of later levels of personal integration.

Interpersonal Skills and a positive imagination need to be nurtured at this level in a person. Depth sharing of feelings is not a part of this Cycle, but the necessity of being courteous and well mannered are important.

Care needs to be taken that a person does not become overly per-
fectionistic or rigid in adherence to the rules. The issue is not conformity but the nurturing of an integration of the interpersonal values of
Self worth, Belonging, and Care and nurture at this Cycle. Knowing
how to affirm and value persons is important. Care should be taken
not to compromise one's values, or to make decisions based on belonging or personal preference, rather than what fairness and the situation demands.

The negative Taboo skills at this level involve what has classically
been termed neurosis, which is developed to defend the Self against
external threat. It involves a mistrustful attitude to the world with an
over attention to perfectionism and a fear of failure. Its most direct
negative consequence is an overt resistance to change and learning
anything new.

It is a state of high anxiety coupled with circular feelings of guilt,
anger and depression. The dynamics will be dealt with in more detail
in chapter seven. The consequence at this point is to block growth by
a tendency on the part of the individual to be cliquish and isolated
from a wider range of persons.

Commonly it can also be experienced as arrogance and discrimination against other persons. At this cycle it very often takes on the form
of sexual and racial discrimination. Let us complete this Cycle by reviewing the discernment questions directed at Cycle Two leadership.

THE VALUES: Phase II A and B.

**CYCLE THREE:
THE
INSTITUTIONAL
CYCLE**
*see Value Lists and
Definitions, Appendix*

Stage A Goals

7. FAMILY/BELONGING
8. SELF WORTH

Stage B Goals

14. WORK/CONFIDENCE
15. WORSHIP
16. PLAY

Stage A Means

9. BELONGING (LIKED)
10. CARE/NURTURE
11. CONTROL/DUTY
12. TRADITION
13. SOCIAL PRESTIGE

Stage B Means

17. ACHIEVEMENT/SUCCESS
18. ADMINISTRATION/
    MANAGEMENT
19. INSTITUTION
20. PATRIOTISM/LOYALTY
21. EDUCATION
22. WORKMANSHIP/
    TECHNOLOGY
23. LAW/DUTY

The values and world view of Cycle Three are the same as that of *see Diagrams III.1 and IV.1*
Phase II covered in the last chapter. An additional piece of information
comes to light at this cycle relative to the dialectics and their relationship to development. There are hundreds of possible combinations
that reflect the development across the Phases. We will illustrate the
point with one example.

Consider the following dialectic which is not uncommon with many people as they grow and develop:

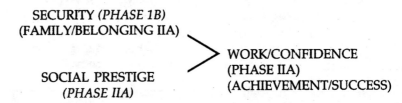

SECURITY *(PHASE 1B)*
(FAMILY/BELONGING IIA)

SOCIAL PRESTIGE
(PHASE IIA)

WORK/CONFIDENCE
(PHASE IIA)
(ACHIEVEMENT/SUCCESS)

This scenario is a continuation of Janice and Joe, the couple with the small fish restaurant in the example above. The only difference is that they have now been married for two years.

Joe is working on Security by doing well in his business. He spends a lot of time in the community making himself known (Social Prestige) and as a consequence feels he is achieving and succeeding through his work. The result is that he feels more confident. What was originally an experience of insecurity about his work is becoming an experience of security through the family. This in turn altered his image of himself, and how he perceived the future.

Looking at this closer along with dozens of other individual cases several insights about human and spiritual development came to light. The traditional understanding of development assumes that we grow in relationship to our emotional and physical maturing processes, by completing different task at different stages.

This is really a hierarchy of tasks where integrated development comes about as these tasks are completed, at each stage of maturity. Circling back to earlier tasks is constantly alluded to by Erikson, Fowler and others. But basically it is a redressing of past incompletions. We are suggesting something more than this as DIAGRAM V.1 will illustrate (see next page).

In the diagram the first ball I1 represents the first half of our dialectic above. It is the integration of the Phase IB and IIA values. In our example it would be the circling around and integrating of Security in IB, and Social Prestige IIA. This in turn leads dialectically to the Phase IIB value of Work/Confidence, designated by the shaded ball I2.

This is also a shift in consciousness from a Phase IB stage to a IIB stage. This new Consciousness is designated by C1. In other words the first integration of two values across the Phases alters the consciousness of a person to see the future and its possibilities differently. But let us continue with the analysis.

The second larger circle from the second ball indicating Achievement/Success in IIB now returns (in the diagram) back to IB past the arrow pointing to C2, to its new position C3. What does all this mean? What I am trying to illustrate is that at the point Joe began to understand and experience Achievement and Success his past as presently perceived and experienced in his imagination was altered. He had a new consciousness of all that had been before, which we call C2.

As we shall see in chapter seven mystical consciousness and existentialism view all time as present. In this way the past concept of Se-

DEVELOPMENT a/b/a

I₁ Integration of Two Stage
I₂ Integration of Next Stage
C₁ Consciousness of New Skill Requirements
C₂ Consciousness of Present Skills (Past)
C₃ Consequence of New Integration I₂

Note I₂ now repeats I₁ at New Level.

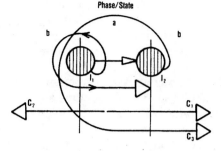

Phase/State

Diagram V:1
DEVELOPMENT a/b/a
I₁ Integration of Two Stage
I₂ Integration of Next Stage
C₁ Consciousness of New Skill Requirements
C₂ Consciousness of Present Skills (Past)
C₃ Consequence of New Integration I₂

Note I₂ now repeats I₁ at New Level.

curity alters as it becomes upgraded and connected with Family for Joe and Janice in a new way. Finally this new internal re-imaging of reality moves into the future as C3, giving Joe a whole new confidence about his work and himself.

In other words the dialectical process is not only a bridge to the internal images we have of reality, and how we express them behaviorally, but it is also a part of the dynamics of the development of consciousness. Not only this but it would appear to be an energy form that at times transcends the space/time continuum, rewriting the past and the future for a person.

see Harrison and Prendergast, Appendix

The world is viewed as a problem, but one with which I am able to cope by becoming educated and by making an adequate living. My chief struggle is to be successful and to please those who control my future and at the same time to be able to take enough time to be with my family.

My ethical choices are based on what the law and respected institutions of government and authority say is right. In this Cycle growth in interpersonal skills, skills of administrative effectiveness and the ability to look critically at the values of my family and the policies of respected institutions are important.

The direction of this cycle is from the personal to the integration of institutional demands in the market place. For the religious person God is my Law-giver and my Master who leads me through my needs to belong to the Church where I depend upon the help of Her Ministers, to a sound and secure faith community to guide me in my journey.

PROFILE OF THE INSTITUTIONAL CYCLE

The discernment questions that are raised here are those from the IIA values covered in Cycle 2, and those from Stage IIB.

DISCERNMENT QUESTIONS

For a person in a leadership position the style at this Cycle is related to the Organizational Person, and is called EFFICIENT MANAGEMENT. Business is seen as ordered, efficient, and productive. It is therefore managed bureaucratically through the principles of scientific management. Management by objectives would be an appreciated style and methodology. As such, respect for superiors and the rules and policy of the organization are viewed as being of paramount importance.

In Cycle Three institutional authority has replaced parental author-

LEADERSHIP
see also Leadership Level, chapter 4

ity. Good experiences of institutional leadership are necessary for a person to develop into the later and more complex leadership styles. This is the last of the autocratic styles and as such is characterized by set hierarchical structures that view the system as being made up of leaders and FOLLOWERS.

The FOLLOWER experiences the leadership as considerably less distant than in Cycles One and Two. The leader at this level is at his or her best a sensitive listener who takes into consideration everything that the follower says, as long as what is said reflects loyalty to the institution and is helpful in making the system more effective relative to its given tasks and goals.

In the same way that the Primal Cycle is to the Self Preservation of the individual, so this Cycle is the perpetuation and survival of the institution. In other words a form of institutional narcissism can occur where the system begins to protect itself against any kind of change. This is the negative aspect of institutional development.

During the medieval period for example the Western Christian Church often saw itself, through the eyes of many of the Bishops, as the Kingdom of God on earth. The Roman Empire before that saw the City of Rome as eternal and often saw the Emperors as Divine. When in the late 1960's many priests and sisters began to leave the Roman Catholic Church following Vatican II, the reaction of many of the leaders at that time was to see those who left as traitors turning their back on God.

CYCLE THREE DISCERNMENT QUESTIONS

WORK/CONFIDENCE

Questions:
- Do you feel competent in the work you do?
- Have you done well in supporting your family, or do you feel you could have done better?

WORSHIP

Questions:
- Do you attend a church or synagogue regularly?
- Does Sunday or weekly worship give you a sense of meaning and stability to your life?
- Are your church's beliefs very important to you?

PLAY

Questions:
- Do you feel the need for recreation?
- Do you feel guilty about enjoying yourself, and doing nothing for a day or so?

ACHIEVEMENT/SUCCESS

Questions:
- Do enjoy competitive sports? Is winning important to you?
- Does your competitiveness ever get in the way of other priorities in your life?
- How important is succeeding to you?

ADMINISTRATION/MANAGEMENT

Questions:
- Are you comfortable in a management role, or do you lack some administrative skills?

INSTITUTION

Questions:
- Is loyalty to the institution a high priority for you?
- Can you function well in a bureaucratic setting?
- Are ordered levels of management important to you?

PATRIOTISM

Questions:
- Is loyalty a high priority for you?
- Is pride in your country a high priority for you?

EDUCATION

Questions:
- Is continual learning important to you? What are you doing to see that this occurs?

WORKMANSHIP/TECHNOLOGY

Questions:
- Do you have sufficient skills with your hands, around car and house repairs, sewing and cooking?
- Is technology a mystery to you, or do you have all the skills and knowledge you need in this area?

LAW/DUTY

Questions:
- Do you think of yourself as "living within the rules"?
- Do you have difficulty with persons who refuse to be accountable to the rules?

see Cycle Two Discernment Questions, chapter 5

Interestingly enough, when I was younger and refused a particular mission assignment by the Anglican Church, in the early sixties, I was accused of the same thing. I have counseled a number of persons who have had exactly the same experience within different fundamentalist denominations in the last several years.

In the last chapter we discussed the Mylai incident in Vietnam and the coverup by the government and the military. If you live in Russia or any of the communist bloc countries today and you want to succeed in life you must join the "Party." Those who do not belong are often suspect, and are seen as a threat to national security.

see Evil and The Destructive Side of Narcissism, chapter 3

What am I saying? Well I am not saying that the churches are suspect, or that all military leaders are in a continual state of coverup, or that government is bad. I am simply saying that a negative aspect of this Cycle is the possibility of institutional narcissism, no matter what institution you are talking about. It is present when the system begins to deny that change is occurring, and when its leaders begin to consider that the system is more important than the sum of its members. It is no more evident than when the very life of an institution is being threatened.

Witness the denial of any fault whatsoever by both partners equally during the tragedy of family divorce proceedings. Witness parents up in arms at the closing of a local school that should have been closed ten years ago. It is as if the system is human and is struggling to survive by denying its own death. A partial reason why this occurs comes to light when we look at the skills of this Cycle.

SKILLS

see Manna and Taboo, chapter 4, and Contingency, chapter 7

The positive Manna skills involve organizational survival, with skills of administrative completion and interpersonal management, that stress efficiency in the work environment. The leader is learning new interpersonal skills, but at this cycle this is primarily the ability to negotiate cooperation between persons in order to further the efficient functioning of the institution.

There is a tendency to be over competitive and alienating of persons who are not loyal to the system. Management skills are related to a bureaucratic and hierarchical view of systems. It is important to realize that a positive experience of an efficient institution is necessary to gain these skills.

see Skills in Chapters 4 and 6

The Instrumental skills associated with this Cycle of Leadership are highly developed. Success in corporate management depends on proficiency in such technical skills as communications, data processing, bookkeeping and all the aspects of sales and marketing. But at this level all these skills are within the setting of human interaction.

The consequence of this stage is to push the manager or executive hard in the development of Interpersonal skills. These include improved listening and clarifying skills, and keeping calm during times of conflict. At this Cycle peer support is important, with an emphasis on pleasing others, being friendly and outgoing. It is not, however, until the next Cycle that in depth interpersonal skills begin to develop.

The area of Taboo relates to problems of institutional narcissism explored above. In terms of skills two things can happen. The first is a poor experience of an institution, the second is excessive dependence on institutional life with minimal skill development.

Some institutions like the Church, the military and sometimes the government, are totally inclusive relative to a person's life. This is very common in some of the major Japanese industrial Corporations. By inclusive is understood that all one's education, medical bills and life needs from family security and recreation to death are taken care of.

In industry it is not unusual for some companies to expect the same loyalty from an executive as a religious community expects from one of its superiors. In such a situation a very negative experience of leadership becomes life threatening and even damaging to the person's meaning system if that person is not well developed emotionally. Such an experience can lead to passive aggressive behavior that manifests itself negatively in later experiences of leadership by the individual.

The second circumstance of Taboo at this Cycle is where a person is excessively dependent on the institution and at the same time has

114

gained all his or her skills from that setting, but in a narrow spectrum of accomplishment.

I have known several persons who did well in the electronic field, and were making so much money that they did not finish their education. The skills they learned were so esoteric and specialized, that when the company collapsed they were unable to get another job. What is even more critical, and what will be discussed in depth in the next chapter, is that when a full range of skills is not developed in the Instrumental, Interpersonal, Imaginal and System skills areas, the personal spiritual growth of the individual is retarded.

Finally let us review this leadership area by looking at some discernment questions that are relevant to the Efficient MANAGER.

Questions

- What is your physical health and work/play balance like?
- How well do you understand management structures?
- What are your administrative skills like in the areas of computer, finance, writing, typing and filing?
- Are you able to take a project to paper completion in a professional manner?
- How do you handle anger and failure?
- Is achievement important to you?
- Does your competitive spirit get in the way of your achieving all you want to at times?
- Is the time management of work and home life harmonious enough for you?
- Do you have sufficient education and skills to do what you want to do?
- How do you feel about disloyalty to the organization?

LEADERSHIP DISCERNMENT QUESTIONS CYCLE THREE

In some discussions of organizational and personal leadership styles it is fashionable to divide them into two camps: the Autocratic Authoritarian and the Participative Collaborative Style.

This language has been particularly popular in the organizational development of religious institutions. For example in the literature of the Center of Planned Change[3a] in the mid 1970's leadership persons were described as Authoritarian, Therapeutic and Collaborative. This was related to the idea of the Pre-Vatican II Church, which was primarly Autocratic in Style, and the new Post-Vatican II Church described as Participative and Collaborative in its philosophy.

The same kind of distinction has been made in other management literature. McGregor talked about *Theories X and Y*, in the late 1950's in a book called *The Human Side of Enterprise*.[4] Theory X is the primitive concept of the human being that would be expressed through an exaggerated Autocratic mindset. In this view management is responsible for organizing all the functions of the productive enterprise, including

AUTOCRATIC AND PARTICIPATIVE LIFE STYLES

115

the people involved. In this view people as workers are seen as being basically indolent and lazy only working when they are compelled to do so. They are viewed as dependent and preferring to be led. Finally they are seen as less intelligent than the leadership and resistant to change. Management's job is to assume that they are naturally resistant to the organization's needs, and to control their work though punishment and reward systems that will get the job done.

On the other hand Theory Y views people positively. The worker is not by nature passive and dependent, but is this way in reaction to his or her experience of the Theory X Institution. In this view the goal of management is to organize the conditions of the Institution such that an individual's motivation and natural capacities and potential skills can be manifest. The idea is that when these conditions are present the worker will naturally want to aid and assist in the development of the organization.

Basically what is being recognized in these discussions is that each leadership style has its own consequence on the follower's experience. And that this is due primarily to the fact that a particular leadership style based as it is on particular values, has a world view that leads it to view the worker or its membership in a particular way.

In our schema the first three Cycles are in these terms various forms of Autocratic Leadership, and are all characterized by a leader-follower format, in which management governs normally through carefully designed hierarchical structures for the consequence of efficient institutional functioning.

Cycles Five, Six and Seven on the other hand would be considered as participative or collaborative styles. Cycle Four is an in between Cycle that is therapeutic in nature, in some of its aspects.

The point that needs to be made is that it is important not to so oversimplify our understanding of leadership that we ignore its essential developmental nature. The first thing to note is that the Autocratic and Participative modes are general descriptions of several styles of leadership. It is not just a matter of one or the other.

Secondly it is very important to note that the reason that some organizations are run Autocratically and some Collaboratively is because the environment and the situation demand it, not because someone just decides to do things that way.

Each style of leadership suits a particular set of circumstances which make that style the necessary style for that given set of circumstances. The difference in the philosophy of authority and management that arose from Vatican II did not do so in a vacuum.

Pre-Vatican II Autocratic management was not isolated to the Roman Catholic Church; it was the form of leadership in all institutions, and reflected the values embedded in a rapidly changing western society. The Participative mode of Vatican II simply reflected a massive change in the values of western post-World War II society. In other words the management philosophy grew out of a new perception of the world brought about by a change in societal values.

Our final point is that *any style of leadership is the symtematic consequence of the values of the individual leader in relationship to the corporate*

116

setting, and its membership, as reflected by a particular Cycle of Human and Spiritual development. It is not the other way around. Therefore if an organization wants to be participative in style it must have leaders with a given value orientation for it to occur. It is not just a matter of designing a different management style.

It is critical to understand that the concept of "follower" is itself a *see Retrieve: Explanation and Development, chapter 10* judgment that only occurs in the first three Cycles. It is a perception by functional leadership of the membership of an institution, and a view of leadership and management by the membership. It is a description of how each perceives and behaves toward the other by virtue of their understanding of reality—their world view. That is to say the leadership and membership are bound together symbiotically as a whole; they are in fact dependent on each other, not separate, as the world view of these Cycles would lead us to believe. In fact, as we shall see later in the book, leadership as a group and the membership as a group can transcend their Cycle of development by the way they act and cooperate together. As an example: the whole trade union movement is surely based on this premise!

We will now review Cycles Four, Five, Six and Seven. Each of these Cycles involves higher levels of integration of the skills, and consciousness of the human, spiritual and organizational dimension of day to day living. These special Integrative dimensions will be dealt with in the next chapter titled: Time Travel: Simplicity and the Onion Effect. Therefore we will at this point only briefly cover these four Cycles, revisiting them in more depth in the next chapter. With these points in mind let us review Cycle Four: The Intrapersonal Cycle.

THE VALUES: Phase II B and III A.

CYCLE FOUR: THE INTRAPERSONAL CYCLE
see Value Lists and Definitions, Appendix

Stage B Goals *(Phase II)*

14. WORK/CONFIDENCE
15. WORSHIP

16. PLAY

Stage A Goals *(Phase III)*

24. EQUALITY
25. ACTUALIZATION/ WHOLENESS
26. SERVICE

Stage B Means

17. ACHIEVEMENT/SUCCESS
18. ADMINISTRATION/MAN- AGEMENT
19. INSTITUTION
20. PATRIOTISM/LOYALTY
21. EDUCATION
22. WORKMANSHIP/TECH- NOLOGY
23. LAW/DUTY

Stage B Means

27. AUTONOMY
28. EMPATHY/GENEROSITY
29. LAW/GUIDE
30. PERSONAL AUTHORITY
31. ADAPTABILITY
32. HEALTH/WELL-BEING
33. SEARCH

There are many dialectics as before that enable the developmental *see Diagrams III.1 and IV.1* process to proceed. Two common examples from recent consultations are as follows. A 26 year old woman executive who loved her Work as an Administrator found that increased sensitivity in Empathy through some counselor education at the University led her see her work as Service. This in fact altered the way she worked with people on the job. Her dialectic would be represented as follows:

WORK/CONFIDENCE
(ADMINISTRATION/MANAGEMENT)
> SERVICE
EMPATHY/GENEROSITY

Pat a housewife started to study philosophy and spirituality as a way of developing her play dimension by going to a local Junior College in the evenings. Her purpose was to search out new meaning for herself. It not only gave her a whole new lease on life but it altered her image of herself and her ability to express her inner self in a new way. Her dialectic was as follows:

PLAY
> ACTUALIZATION/WHOLENESS
SEARCH

CYCLE FOUR DISCERNMENT QUESTIONS
see also Cycle Three Discernment Questions, chapter 5

EQUALITY.

Questions:
- Is the question of personal equality important to you and do you have sufficient assertiveness?

ACTUALIZATION/WHOLENESS.

Questions:
- Are you working on personal integration, through health and emotional development?
- What are you doing to develop yourself in the areas of reading, meditation and relaxation?

SERVICE.

Questions:
- Is your job satisfactory as a life vocation?
- Is your work meaningful and energizing to you?

AUTONOMY.

Questions:
- Are you sufficiently your own person, or are there some decisions you need to make?
- Is being assertive or initiating your own course of action difficult for you?

EMPATHY/GENEROSITY.

Questions:
- Do others experience you as saying what you feel, or are your feelings held back at times?
- Do others experience you as being able to imagine their circumstance in helpful ways?

LAW/GUIDE.

Questions:
- Do you feel the law or rules are a necessary beginning point, or are you too dependent on the rules?

PERSONAL AUTHORITY.

Questions:
- Do others see you as a person who defends your own rights? Can you do this without upsetting others?
- Do you feel you have a sufficient sense of your own authority?

ADAPTABILITY.

Questions:
- Do you have all the skills you need for coping with constant change?
- Is creative expression a high priority for you?
- Are you able to express your anger creatively?

HEALTH/WELL BEING.

Questions:
- Do you relax when necessary, or is this difficult?
- Do you pay sufficient attention to overall physical health—diet, exercise and minimal leisure?

SEARCH.

Question
- Do you have a set of principles that you live by, and that make life an adventure for you, or do you have pressing unanswered questions?

PROFILE OF THE INTRAPERSONAL CYCLE

see Phase Three, chapter 3

The world view is one where the person stands between the strong institutional values of Phase IIB and the strong personal values of Phase IIIA causing feeling of uncertainty in the area of decision making. Values appear relative so that I have to search to find my own place and meaning in the scheme of things. In whatever institutional framework I find myself my task is to try to assess my successes in relationship to the new revelations and doubts I am having about myself, my gifts and my vocation.

Ethical issues no longer seem black and white and I try to reason my way to appropriate decisions. It is often not easy for me to make commitments without any reservations. Growth in this stage is dependent upon learning to establish a balance between a need for independence and a predilection for reasoning on the one hand and giving appropriate expression to interpersonal, emotional and intuitive needs, on the other hand.

Attention and commitment to a particular life sustaining value system is growing in importance, such as the study of justice issues. This Cycle is moving in the direction of significant personal growth, which must at the same time integrate the institutional demands one is faced with.

The religious person is beginning to discover that God is Friend and that he or she needs to re-evaluate many elements in his or her past faith stances. Such persons need to find a center for their faith by which they can really live and be sustained in all circumstances. The discernment questions that the third Cycle presents are from the values of Phase IIB and IIIA. The questions from IIb were presented earlier. The remaining questions from Phase IIIA will be presented subsequently.

LEADERSHIP The leadership style is one of ENABLER and should be regarded as an interim style, due to its conflictual nature. The leader is caught between adherence to what the institution demands, and a new view of human dignity and sense of self. The leader/follower distinction is not clear for this person.

SKILLS For the person who wishes to exercise a leadership role, or grow stronger in this area, integration of the skills in IIB management, with the personal dimension of IIIa, resulting in a more dignified view of community and institutions, is necessary. Note that it is not a question of IIIA being higher than IIB; it is a question of cycles of development that result in more integrated levels of Human and Spiritual development.

LEADERSHIP DISCERNMENT QUESTIONS CYCLE FOUR

Questions:
- Is what you want to do contrary to what others whom you work with need?
- Do you have an intimacy support system—someone who is an equal you can share at any level with, as a peer, on a regular basis?
- Do you have a work support team to whom you can delegate anything you do in times of stress?
- Do you have a peer professional group or person you can talk to on a regular basis?
- Do you have sufficient group dynamic skills?
- What do you do with your anger? Or do you ever get angry?
- How are you at sharing and objectifying feelings?
- What do others report to you about your ability in this area?

At the personal level of search and personal development, a new awareness of persons, but insufficient SYSTEMS skills and awareness can cause stress. Emotional support systems are essential to insure growth. Interpersonal and imaginal skills development is critical.

At the leadership level this becomes translated into Group Dynamic and Human Relations Training skills. The particular need is in small group facilitation and the processing of feelings as well as cognitive information. Skills in clarification, brainstorming and project planning and management are required.

In the Taboo area persons have difficulty in this cycle with accountability, confusing equality of person (dignity) with equality of skills. As such the leader is a good community builder but may have difficulty in delegating responsibility.

For persons in human relations work and counseling this can become a natural style of leadership, and as such it should be monitored to insure that it does not prevent further spiritual growth. To avoid stress and distortion the person in this Cycle needs strong support systems. The negative consequences of this Cycle are over stress, withdrawal and possible regression down through the Cycles. The issue of support at this level is covered in the next chapter. Let us get a little more clarity by reviewing the discernment questions for this leadership level.

THE VALUES: Phase III A/B.

CYCLE FIVE:
THE COMMUNAL
COLLABORATIVE
CYCLE
see Value Lists and Definitions, Appendix

Stage A Goals

24. EQUALITY
25. ACTUALIZATION/
    WHOLENESS
26. SERVICE

Stage B Goals

34. NEW ORDER
35. DIGNITY/JUSTICE
36. ART/BEAUTY
37. INSIGHT
38. CONTEMPLATION

Stage A Means

27. AUTONOMY
28. EMPATHY/GENEROS-
    ITY
29. LAW/GUIDE
30. PERSONAL AUTHORITY
31. ADAPTABILITY
32. HEALTH/WELL-BEING
33. SEARCH

Stage B Means

39. ACCOUNTABILITY
40. COMMUNITY/SUPPORT
41. DETACHMENT
42. CORPORATE MISSION
43. RESEARCH/KNOWLEDGE
44. INTIMACY

The dialectics that enable development at each Cycle are multiple in possibilities and increase as the Cycle gets higher, since the number *see Diagrams III.1 and IV.1* of values increases. A couple of examples from the values in this Cycle will illustrate the personal development of this Cycle.

At each Cycle the first Stage in the Cycle determines the nature of the Cycle. For example Cycle Four was dominated more by the institutional reality as a person began to consider the more personal human dimension. This Cycle is primarily personal as the individual begins to look at institutions a little differently.

For example, Georgina was a 30 year old divorcee who was going to Law school. She was very concerned and angry about women's rights and her own sense of EQUALITY. Through her studies she began to mature beyond her anger and became concerned about all people's rights. She joined a law agency that provided free legal advice on JUSTICE and civil rights to persons who felt that their rights were being violated, but who could not afford legal advice. She now saw LAW as a guide. She drew her dialectic as follows.

At the same time she began to look after her HEALTH, lost about 30 lbs and felt some real changes in her own personal spiritual development (ACTUALIZATION) as she gained a number of INSIGHTS about herself. She explained her second dialectic as follows.

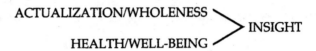

PROFILE OF THE COMMUNAL COLLABORATIVE CYCLE

At this Cycle the world is viewed as a project in which the person needs to participate and to which he or she has something unique to offer. Such persons find that they have suddenly become acutely aware of their gifts and of ways in which they may be used productively.

These persons see that they must discover new ways to integrate their gifts with the demands of society. They have also become intensely aware of the importance of making institutions more human. Ethical choices are based on a personally meaningful center of values to which the person is clearly committed and which he or she can articulate. Actions, as a consequence, are guided by a personal conscience. Rules and lawful guidelines are important, but the person modifies them if necessary based on personal conscience.

Spiritual growth at this stage is strongly dependent upon establishing a right balance between time devoted to work and to leisure. The person needs to get personal affirmation from peer groups which helps to counterbalance the ever present possibilities of disillusionment, as one's choices and vision of reality grow. See the discernment questions for the B Stage of this Cycle.

CYCLE FIVE DISCERNMENT QUESTIONS
see Cycle Four Discernment Questions, chapter 5

NEW ORDER.

Question:
■ Are you sufficiently aware of the consequences of the development of your institution on society?

DIGNITY/JUSTICE.

Questions:
- Do you place high priority in your work on the dignity of others, and is this balanced with a personal sense of dignity, relative to time management and time with intimates and friends?
- Are global and national injustices a concern to you?

ART/BEAUTY.

Question:
- How actively appreciative of art and beauty are you?

INSIGHT.

Questions:
- Do you have the skills to be yourself in front of others such that they become themselves also?
- Is your growth connected to insights from study?

CONTEMPLATION.

Question:
- Are the disciplines of contemplative or meditative prayer important to you—do you allow sufficient quality time, and do you keep your physical and emotional life in balance to make this possible?

ACCOUNTABILITY.

Question:
- Is mutual accountability important to you among your employees and peers?

COMMUNITY/SUPPORT.

Questions:
- Do you have a supportive community at work?
- Do you have a community of peers who are supportive?

DETACHMENT.

Questions:
- Do you have the skills to separate yourself from your emotions, ideas and physical limitations such that your best self consistently emerges? Do you put the time aside for this process?
- Are you discovering that a simpler life style is necessary for life to be meaningful at this time?

CORPORATE MISSION.

Questions:
- Are you able to fully delegate anything you do at this time?
- Is interdependence of skills and peer authority more important than competition for you at this time? Are you acting on this structurally in the organization?

RESEARCH/KNOWLEDGE.

Questions:
- Is original research and investigation important to you, and do you have the support you need?
- Are you viewed by others as an innovator and pioneer in your field? Do you have the human support systems you need?

INTIMACY.

Questions:
- Are you able to smile at your own limitations and admit them to others?
- Do you have all the skills of interpersonal intimacy that you need, or is this a difficult area for you?

The direction of this cycle is to move beyond personal issues to integrating a human systems perspective. The religious person sees and feels God as a Friend with whom he or she must spend more time and to whom he or she has a vocational responsibility.

LEADERSHIP
see Leadership Level, chapter 4, and Leadership Discernment Questions, chapter 5

The leadership style for one in this Cycle is CHARISMATIC LEADERSHIP, which sees itself as democratic but is often overtly independent. It is at a point in life when the person's value focus is clearer and Imaginal and Systems skills are releasing new energy. A person at this Cycle often has difficulties with time management, resulting in the possibility of stress. Critical growth factors are:
1. Time Management.
2. Support Groups at Work and Leisure.
3. Clarity about value focus—present and future.

see Leadership, chapter 5

This leadership style to function well must be built on internalized skills from Cycle Three: the EFFICIENT MANAGEMENT style of leadership.

SKILLS
see Manna and Taboo, chapter 4 and Contingency, chapter 7

The positive Manna skills at this level are ones of moving from a more interpersonal approach to problem solving and group interaction, to a full system orientation and appreciation that sees the whole first and the parts second. The person sees the parts in perspective as they relate to the whole. This system orientation is necessary for a non-stressful existence at this Cycle. The skills are therefore at two levels:

1. New skills in system management and small group facilitation, goal and climate setting.
2. Skills in stress management.

see also chapters 4 and 6

The Taboo side of development at this stage is the corrupting influence of power, particularly as manifest in the person's inability to accept personal limitations. The consequence is crippling problems of time management, stress and over commitment and extension.

124

The basic protection against this is delegation and involvement in personal support structures of persons who are not afraid to point out one another's limitations. The natural tendency of a person in this leadership style is to be overly independent, due to over commitment. The leadership discernment questions will help to clarify this further.

Questions:

- Do you have an intimacy support system—someone who shares regularly with you and is a peer?
- Do you have a work support team to which you can delegate anything you do in times of stress?
- Do you have a peer professional group or person you can talk to on a regular basis?
- Do you have sufficient group dynamic skills?
- Do your interpersonal skills need improvement:
    a. Skills in processing feelings in a group?
    b. Objectifying your feelings?
    c. Accurately identifying others' feelings?
    d. Making others accountable?
- Can you express your anger creatively, make others accountable and still remain relaxed?
- Do you have sufficient team building skills?
- Do you have skills in planning, goal setting and management design?
- Are you aware of methods of stress reduction?

THE VALUES: Phase IIIB and IVA.

Stage B Goals *(PHASE III)*

34. NEW ORDER
35. DIGNITY/JUSTICE
36. ART/BEAUTY
37. INSIGHT
38. CONTEMPLATION

Stage A Goals *(PHASE IV)*

45. WISDOM

Stage B Means

39. ACCOUNTABILITY
40. COMMUNITY/SUPPORT
41. DETACHMENT
42. CORPORATE MISSION
43. RESEARCH/KNOWLEDGE
44. INTIMACY

Stage A Means

46. WORD/PROPHET
47. COMMUNITY/SIMPLIC-ITY

see Diagrams III.1 and IV.1

Cycle Six is a level of development accessible only to a few exceptional individuals. At one time such persons were known only through history, such as a Gandhi or a Saint Francis. But now because of global communication and enormous advances in education there are many such individuals in the world.

see Phase III and Phase IV, chapter 3 A more detailed explanation of the values that lie behind Phase IVA were covered in chapter three. The dialectic in this Cycle are once again moving to the personal level. The person tends to be primarily institutional in orientation but moving in this Cycle to the highest point of Human and Spiritual development, when the person is an integrated individual. The opposite is also possible. A positive example of a dialectic is illustrated in the following example.

The person I have in mind that we shall call Ron was the Superior General (Chief Executive) of an international religious Order. His day to day work involved stressful administrative decisions relative to international conflicts that were entirely new to him. The overall consequence was a severe heart attack, during his first year in office, which he survived. He felt that the values were dialectically as follows prior to the heart attack.

Being in this new position, with the expectation that he would be a new and great leader (NEW ORDER) like many of the previous executives in his position, he would "by the Grace of God" without any training be able to manage well (ADMINISTRATION/MANAGEMENT). This however led him to feel stressed, even to the point of physical survival (SELF PRESERVATION), which finally led to his heart attack.

After some personal counsel I met him a year later. He was doing very well in the same job. He was still leading the international community and very enthusiastic about the work they were doing (NEW ORDER). The difference was that he had moved out of his old quarters, which were next to his office, and was living very happily with a community of friends (COMMUNITY/SUPPORT). He expressed his new dialectic as follows:

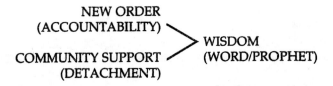

His spiritual discipline had improved which involved taking four days off a month for recreation, prayer and solitude away from everything (DETACHMENT). This not only led to new WISDOM about himself, but it resulted in his having increased intuitive insights about the international situation that he was in. He became in fact as the years went by a prophetic figure in his community.

126

Critical to this Cycle even more than before is the need to be able to Detatch one's self from the stress one encounters, through meditation, a sound work and leisure balance, and an appropriate away from work support group.

PROFILE OF THE MYSTICAL CYCLE

The person now sees all of humanity and the physical/material world as a sacred gift in which he or she must be responsibly involved. Of critical importance for life is the struggle to find a suitable balance between the time devoted to work and the occasions that are set aside for intimacy and ascetical solitude.

Ethical choices are now informed by awareness of the rights of all human beings. The person finds himself or herself compelled to be more actively critical of unjust organizations in society—especially the injustices found in those organizations in which he or she is personally participating. Growth at this stage requires careful attention balancing involvement in organizational development based on humane values, and time devoted to the kind of intimacy and solitude which are truly energizing.

Growth is also dependent upon having several different life projects which prevents over absorption in any one particular project and so facilitates the development of a global world view. The person finds that he or she has a new perspective on the created order. For the religious person God is seen as both Lord and Friend. It is as though she or he sees the world as God sees it. See the discernment questions for the A stage of this Cycle.

CYCLE SIX DISCERNMENT QUESTIONS
see Cycle Five Discernment Questions

WISDOM

Questions:
- Is life difficult for you when your meditative discipline and intimacy are out of balance?
- Are you gaining more insight through a balance of meditative solitude and pursuit of the truth?

WORD/PROPHET

Questions:
- Are you discovering that your discipline of meditative non-attachment enables you to gain better global perspective?
- Do others see you as prophetic and global in what you have to say? Do you have the human support systems you need? Do you have time for solitude and intimacy?

COMMUNITY/SIMPLICITY

Questions:
- Does your living situation enhance your creativity and sense of interdependence with the others in the group?
- Are you convinced that the wisdom of two minds can always yield more than is possible by one, and do you act sufficiently on this?

LEADERSHIP
*see Leadership Level,
chapter 4*

The leadership expression at this Cycle is called SERVANT LEADERSHIP. Primarily this Cycle involves interdependent governance by a peer team, which manages a system on the basis of pre-chosen value clusters. This Cycle relies on a minimal global perspective, and an ability to see how the parts of one's institution support and affirm through the values each individual person in the system or institution.

Servant leadership is different than all the earlier forms, in that it not only moves beyond any form of autocratic tendency, but it also transforms the value of independence into interdependence. It recognizes that peer professional interaction at high levels of trust and appropriate intimacy causes synergetic creativity in the group that cannot be obtained by any one individual alone. In other words leadership at and beyond this Cycle is always plural in its form.

In an earlier work I described this style of leadership as follows: "The servant-leader is distinguished by the kinds of questions he or she raises institutionally."[5] The Cycle Six executive uses the concept of limited design criteria in planning for the organization.

His or her role is to create a management design that maximizes the possible development of all individuals within the system, that guards the efficiency of the organization, and that tends to the good of society as a whole.

The servant-leader is interested not only in what is produced by the organization, but also in the quality of interaction within the organization and the impact of the organization on the quality of life in society. The Phase Four vision of the world underlies the activities of the servant leader as he or she seeks to give life to a global world.

SKILLS
*see Manna and Taboo,
chapter 4 and Contingency,
chapter 7*

The positive Manna expression of skills assumes a healthy work leisure balance already in operation, and peer support groups at the intimate, professional and work level. The stance of the leader is as Wise Enabler, who governs with a team on the basis of values related goals, objectives and norms. Skills in developing such norms at a total system level are therefore required, plus constant attention to both physical and emotional health. The discernment questions in the last Cycle give us a clearer explanation of the exact nature of these skills.

see also chapters 4 and 6

At the Taboo level, when one is living at this Cycle, with one foot in Phase Four, integration is not guaranteed. The demonic can as easily occur, as was well illustrated in the last chapter. That is to say, as the value of Self Preservation rears its narcissistic head great destruction can occur because of the high level of skills a person is likely to possess.

**LEADERSHIP
DISCERNMENT
QUESTIONS
CYCLE
SIX**

Questions:

- Do you have sufficient balance between ascetical solitude and intimacy with friends you can relax with?
- Do you have skills in value based planning, goal setting and management design?
- Is your professional life congruent with your values?

- How does the grass roots access your life?
- Are you sufficiently aware of, and do you have quality information on, different cultural groups you are dealing with?
- Do have the ability to risk when questions of Justice are at stake?
- Do you live and encourage system wide collaboration?

The most negative possibility at this Cycle, then, is misuse of power, and governance by values that are detrimental to the individuals working in the system and to society as a whole. Critical to this concept of leadership is clarity about one's values as they enable the leader to transcend at a personal level institutional pressures, placing them in a global and prophetic perspective. See the discernment questions that relate to this stage area.

THE VALUES: Phase IV A and B.

Stage A Goals	Stage B Goals
45. WISDOM	48. TRANSCENDENCE/ ECORITY

Stage A Means	Stage B Means
46. WORD/PROPHET	49. CONVIVIAL TOOLS
47. COMMUNITY SIMPLICITY	50. RIGHTS/WORLD ORDER

CYCLE SEVEN: THE PROPHETIC CYCLE
see Value Lists and Definitions, Appendix

This Cycle of Development strangely enough is often more evident *see Diagrams III.I and IV.I* than the one before it, except that the individuals are too often highly stressed. The reason is that the peculiar nature of this Cycle is that it cycles all the way around to the first Cycle.

At this point Phase Four connects with Phase One. Hence the person *see Phase One, chapter 3* who is integrated transcends this Cycle and reaches persons at all the other levels. On the other hand since this Cycle also engages Phase One the danger for the demonic and what we called possession in chapter three is also a high possibility. This is in present human and spiritual development the most difficult place to be in.

In order to illustrate the dialectic I will also use the list of 125 values in the APPENDIX to expand the options, since the Cycle like the first has a more limited selection of values. We will look at some examples to illustrate.

A very bright inventor that I know had researched a computer software program that interfaced with biochemistry in such a way as to greatly improve a range of tests needed before major surgery. He had the ideas in fact for years, but had not been able to set up either the technology or the management structure through an organization to enable the idea to be actualized. When he finally accomplished his dream it took the original WISDOM through his research and practical (CONVIVIAL) TECHNOLOGY to bring it about. But it also took the Interdependence of working with others in product development,

129

marketing and sales to really enable the idea to become a practical reality. INTERDEPENDENCE is a value under the Value Descriptor COMMUNITY/SIMPLICITY. The consequence was to effect that component of medicine globally (TRANSCENDENCE/ECORITY)—I am assuming in a positive way. The dialectic was presented as follows:

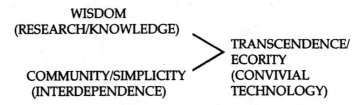

WISDOM
(RESEARCH/KNOWLEDGE)

TRANSCENDENCE/
ECORITY
COMMUNITY/SIMPLICITY
(INTERDEPENDENCE)
(CONVIVIAL
TECHNOLOGY)

Another simple example would be from the life of Gandhi. His own spiritual discipline and consequent WISDOM, lived out in a simple communal Ashram of supportive peers, including his wife, led to the emancipation of millions from British Rule. That dialectic would be as follows, using the longer 125 values list:

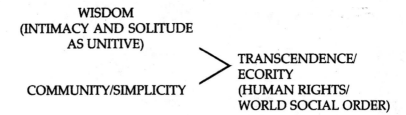

WISDOM
(INTIMACY AND SOLITUDE
AS UNITIVE)

TRANSCENDENCE/
ECORITY
COMMUNITY/SIMPLICITY
(HUMAN RIGHTS/
WORLD SOCIAL ORDER)

PROFILE OF THE PROPHETIC CYCLE

The person now views the world as a mystery for which "We" must care. I say "we" because such persons are acutely aware that their vocation is a global one requiring nothing less than the collaboration of all concerned institutions.

The person finds himself or herself continually challenged to match a prophetic vision with practical applications which comes out of a global vision that must be put into action at the local level. My ethical choices lead me to be involved in activities which are designed to effect an improved balance between the material and the human world. Global distribution of goods to meet human needs is essential.

Critical to spiritual growth in this Cycle is an awareness of the whole field of consciousness with peer representation at each active Cycle. The religious person appreciates God's Lordship over the whole creation and realizes that He is calling all people to co-operate with Him in establishing a more just and ecologically balanced order in the world. See the discernment questions for this final Cycle.

LEADERSHIP AND SKILL LEVEL
see Leadership Level, chapter 4

The leadership expression at this Cycle is called PROPHETIC LEADERSHIP. Primarily this Cycle involves interdependent governance by a peer team, who manage a system on the basis of pre-chosen value clusters. This Cycle relies on a global perspective, and an ability to see how one institution relates to other institutions in global society.

TRANSCENDENCE/ECORITY.

Questions:
- Do you spend much of your life working on ecological issues?
- Do you have sufficient knowledge of technology and its ethical and ecological consequences globally?

CYCLE SEVEN DISCERNMENT QUESTIONS
See Cycle Six Discernment Questions

CONVIVIAL TECHNOLOGY.

Questions:
- Is your work with global economics balanced with quality times in intimacy and solitude? Do you have first hand knowledge of the international consequences of your work? Are you aware of the ethical implications, and are you clear about your own position?
- Is the technology you are developing simple enough for the uneducated to be able to use in third world countries?
- Have you considered the long term moral and social impact of your work on other societies?

RIGHTS/WORLD ORDER.

Questions:
- Are you a part of an international peer group that enables you to address Justice issues with less stress?
- Have you found a way of relaxing when you are constantly traveling?
- Have you had sufficient experience of poverty and oppression to be able to appreciate that experience? Are you a careful listener at that level?

Examples of this style are illustrated above in the dialectics. The integrated leader at this level is also a spiritual leader no matter what the person's religious preference. It is primarily characterized by the ability to integrate Phase Four with Phase One and Two.

The whole person at this Cycle therefore integrates the values of survival, security and self preservation as they are experienced by others at a global level. The consequence is always therefore to be concerned about the *Genesis Effect* as global world order at the human and environmental level. Issues of world peace and poverty are going to be major action concerns.

At the Taboo level which is here more power than skill related the values of security and self preservation become personalized into the need for global control and domination. Examples range from Alexander the Great who killed his own brother when he questioned his opinion to Hitler who killed millions to prove himself right. Basically the person attempts to alter the world at a global level to look like himself or herself. At this Cycle the narcissistic leader seeks world domination.

SKILLS

see chapters 4 and 6
The skills assume a healthy work leisure balance already in operation, and peer support groups at an international and intimate, professional and work level. The stance of the healthy leader is as a wise and prophetic enabler, who governs with a team on the basis of value related goals, objectives and norms.

Skills in developing such norms at complex Corporate levels are required. The person at this Cycle works in and with several systems at a time, having a concern for the global issues. The ability to be clear about complex value systems and their ethical consequences to the planet and beyond are primary factors for this person. Ability therefore to be in touch with the right format and to be well educated in the religious and philosophical norms that stand behind global ethical issues is important. More than any other Cycle there is a need for clarity about one's own faith center, within the context of a support group that insists that the person's intimacy and solitude are in maximum creative balance.

The most negative possibility at this Cycle is misuse of power, and governance by values that are detrimental to the individual working internationally and in society as a whole. Critical to this concept of leadership is clarity about particular values as they are translated into institutional policy that can be amended and creatively criticized at every level in an institution to insure an integrated perspective. Some further discernment questions are listed herein.

LEADERSHIP
DISCERNMENT
QUESTIONS
CYCLE
SEVEN

Questions:

- Do you have skills in value based long term institutional and social planning at an international level?
- Is your professional life congruent with your values?
- How does the grass roots access your life?
- What is your attitude toward inter-institutional collaboration for global societal improvement?
- Have you integrated at a skill level experiences of survival that relate meaningfully to the populations you are dealing with?
- Are you able to convert ideas into practical outcomes at every level of economic development?
- Are you sufficiently aware of the philosophical and religious norms that impact the ethical concerns that are apparent to you relative to global concerns about such issues as: balance of power, global poverty and ecological balance?

CONCLUSIONS

Chapter four and five have basically been a review of the Seven Cycles of Development, exposing us to personal discernment questions and acquainting us with some of the conditions for integrated development and growth. This chapter with the last one gives us the majority of basic information that we need, in order to begin to explore in depth the connections between Human Growth and Spiritual and Organizational Development, which we shall now do, beginning in the next chapter.

The major question that now addresses us is what causes the integrated or healthy development of a person to occur. This question inevitably is going to bring us back to the problems of Time and Time travel. These questions and the insights that we have gained about them will be explored in the next chapter: Time Traveling: Simplicity and the Onion Effect.

Chapter 5:
The Cycles of Development II

1. Underhill (1955), p. 67.
2. Erikson (1980), p. 54.
3. Fowler (1981).
3a. The Center of Planned Change is now called Inter-Community Consultants, located at 1225 Maryhurst Drive, St. Louis, Missouri 63122.
4. McGregor (1960).
5. Hall and Thompson (1980), p. 80.

6

TIME TRAVELING:
SIMPLICITY AND THE ONION EFFECT

For many a year it was my impression that I had passed through several different states: All those going backward, or all those going forward, Show themselves equal in their astonishment.
Sharafuddin Maeri 1263–1381.[1]

After passing through all the phases of world-experience and self-experience, the individual reaches consciousness of his true meaning. He knows himself the beginning, middle, and end of self-development of the psyche, which manifests itself first as the ego and is then expressed by this ego as the self.
Erich Neumann.[2]

A cycle of learning is being completed. The time of withdrawal is moving into a time of return. The exploration of new ways of being is a movement that arises from the awakening of compassion—the dawning of realization that the fate of the individual is intimately connected with the fate of the whole.
Duane Elgin.[3]

PURPOSE To examine the concept of the development of Skills and their relationship to Simplicity as a critical juncture in the spiritual formation of the human being through what we shall term the "Onion Effect."

CONTENT The chapter examines the nature of integrated growth and development of the human being, by looking at the formation of Instrumental, Interpersonal, Imaginal and System Skills. The integrative nature of the imagination is explored in its relationship to the development of consciousness. Finally time is re-examined through the Cycles of development through the notion of the "Onion Effect" where a form of time travel becomes a real possibility.

LINKAGE In the last chapter we looked in detail at the Cycles of Development. In this chapter we will look at them more wholistically to see what overall truth they hold, relative to processes of integration and the limitations of time from a developmental perspective. In the next chapter "Being" rather than "Becoming" is examined, where time becomes a vehicle for exceptional growth, as we enter the faith dimension.

In the last two chapters we have reviewed a lot of information about the individual's World View and Cycles of Development. In this chapter we are going to look at the insights we have gained from working with this material. We are also going to review some of the practical implications of these insights for personal and spiritual growth.

In the last chapter we looked in detail at the Seven Cycles of Development. We looked at them through the eyes of what we might call psychological time. That is we assumed that there was a relationship between our individual aging process and the level of maturity that I might possibly be at. One point that does emerge is that persons can be healthy and spiritually integrated, or they can be narcissistic and destructive no matter what the Cycle of Development. That is, the battle between the good and the evil is present all the time at every value stage.

We also noted that as persons develop they not only become aware of their futures as they dream of success or family, or new creative projects, but they rewrite their past at the same time. As I grow and view the world differently so my whole past, contained in my internal images, is also rewritten.

These observations raise several practical questions that we are now going to address. The first is: What factors contribute to integrated rather than destructive growth? A beginning response to this has to do with the nature of skill development as it relates to our values. We will revisit the four skills: Instrumental, Imaginal, Interpersonal and Systems skills and how their interrelationship with other developmental factors can cause a rapid growth in consciousness. This growth is primarily characterized by a conversion of complexity and busyness in one's life to an experience of simplicity and harmony. This will be the subject of the first half of the chapter.

The second question is in regard to the idea of transformation, or development from one Cycle to the next. We shall pose the question as follows: Can time be transcended and development be speeded up? This will introduce us to what we call the "Onion Effect," which will differentiate between normal human and psychological growth, and exceptional or spiritual growth. This we will cover in the second half of the chapter.

One of the key factors in making any science practical, whether it be the study of chemistry or spiritual direction, is the ability to break down an entity into its smaller component parts. The chemist, by imagining matter as consisting of small parts called atoms and molecules, is able to develop a practical theory of chemical interaction that has permitted the development, for example, of new life saving drugs.

We stated earlier in the book that the Genesis Effect uses values to underlie and interconnect both the internal images and the external behavior that each of us has. What is equally important is that these values are only really transferable as they are in turn translated into sets of skills.

In a recent example of this I was counseling a young married couple. Julia loved her husband a lot, and even wrote love poems to him in several letters, that she never gave him, to express her feelings. She was also disappointed that they were unable to buy some furniture to replace some of the second hand tables and chairs they had.

Bryan had aspirations to be in management in the electronics industry, and wanted very much to buy his own house. He was not earning a high enough salary to accomplish what he wanted, and she after six months of marriage was complaining and communicating to him that she was sorry they ever got married. In short they were both doing the opposite of what they wanted.

They were both experiencing some insecurity and frustration. He had started a fairly good job without finishing High School. In fact he only had one class to finish. She on the other hand had completed two years of college and had given it up to get married, and was additionally frustrated at the job she had as a part-time secretary.

In order for Bryan to succeed into management training in his company, he was told he would need a high school certificate, and to be enrolled in a University or College with the intention of getting a degree in either science or business. The company was even willing to pay his way on a part-time basis. Bryan was willing to do this but was afraid to tell his wife because he felt that she had already given up college to marry him.

She on the other hand was actually angry at him because he was not trying to improve his education. She did not say anything, because she was also angry in her job, where it was difficult to get anywhere as a woman in a man's world, especially without a degree.

The difficulties in this particular instance were basically all skill related. Many of the values that they had were really Visionary. If I have certain values that I hope and long for, like being successful, but I lack the skills to actualize the values, then they are really what we call Vision values. Values that we have the skills to fully actualize are called Act values, because we are acting on them. The person who believes in honesty and is careful to be frank and honest in all he or she does would be modeling his or her Act Value. DIAGRAM VI.1 will assist us in understanding the problem.

The width of the circle from the Past to the Future indicates each individual's value and skill range. Values that we have not lived out yet but are important to us we call Vision Values. The values that were inspiring this young couple were in the vision area! The bottom line is they both wanted their own house, new furniture and successful self chosen jobs. It was a simple matter to identify values of Education, Self Confidence, Family, and Achievement/Success. But it was not until we began to convert the values into skills that we made any practical headway.

When we looked at the skills that they already had they were im-

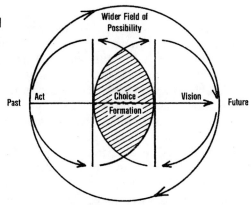

Diagram 6:1

Circle 1: Range of Present Skills.
Circle 2: Direction of Present Choices/Skills.

pressive. Julia had excellent skills with writing, typing, bookkeeping and some crafts such as finishing old furniture. Bryan was very good at mathematics and calculus, and mechanical things around the house. In the Act area they both had a lot of basic Instrumental skills ranging from crafts to basic educational skills.

The problem areas were in the emotional and imaginal sectors. Bryan had a problem historically with not completing things. He had a negative imagination that made him overly fearful that he would fail in anything to do with school work. She on the other hand was very rational and competent but did not share her feelings and concerns about him in a way in which he could hear her without being defensive and getting angry. In the diagram their difficulty lay in the Choice area, which is the one where what we want to do and accomplish (Vision) intersects with what we can do well (Act).

As we examine the skill connection a little later in the chapter we will see how all the skills tend to be interconnected. A development of a particular skill will often release many potential skills in a person, or in this case a couple. This is what happened in this particular instance. Bryan's negative imagination and Julia's lack of emotional sharing could be seen in traditional mental health terms as a possible indication of historically formed internal defenses. In this instance it was not a health issue but a growth issue.

What helped them was a simple training session for 30 minutes in brainstorming and planning. Without discussion between each other Julia and Bryan wrote down on a large sheet of paper what it was they wanted to accomplish. They did this with my support. Then we prioritized what was on the paper in order of importance and reflected on the values that lie behind what they had written down. Within an hour, with a few tears, Bryan was able to state his need for Achievement and Success required some schooling. Julia was able to say that she wanted to finish college but felt that Bryan should finish High School and do a couple of years of college first.

Next they brainstormed the same way on what they had to offer each other and what their limitations were. This was done again on a large sheet of paper with the care and support of myself. The difference this time was they reported on their experience of each other. Once everything was written down we looked at the skills that lay behind what they had written down. This was in a second session, and was a little more delicate than the first.

Finally they put the skills together with their goals from the first session and came up with a strategic plan. They did this at home. I saw them only once after that—we ran into each other several months later while shopping. They reported that Julia had assisted Bryan with a written English examination to complete his High School Certificate which he did in less than a month after the second session. Further he was enrolled in a local Junior College with an emphasis in science. Since the classes were free Julia was enrolled in one of the classes with him; this enabled him to be supported while she continued to work on her own education. Additionally they were planning on buying an inexpensive broken down house, and rebuilding the inside of it themselves.

What was interesting to me was the following remark from Julia: "You know we are still using that goal setting technique we used in the counseling session. It's funny but when we write things down and look at them we can laugh at each other easier. But what is really nice is the way in which Bryan thinks about himself now." "What do you mean?" I asked. "What she means," piped in Bryan, "is I don't have such a crummy attitude toward myself like I did before. You know I almost do as well in Math as she does, and I am getting better at it. We also talk more now—well not more exactly, but deeper maybe."

This is a pleasant example of how skills are important to growth. Naturally not all counseling and guidance sessions turn out this way. But it does illustrate that what is often felt and seen as a problem is very often a lack of skills. Sometimes the lack of skills is due to an inability or unwillingness to learn. This relates to the Taboo area that we will address in the next chapter. The skills in this example are those that were simply needed, but were absent because they were not learned due to a lack of awareness or resources.

In terms of our Diagram above, both Julia and Bryan had a strong residue of Instrumental Skills in the Act areas. They had internalized values and skills related to crafts, education and success in the past. They had a great deal that they brought to the relationship that was already in place. This is what we mean by the ACT area. Clearly the counseling revealed that their hopes and VISION were being frustrated. The Vision area is that area where we lack the skills to bring about the dreams, hopes and VISION that motivates and makes life worthwhile for us in the present.

What the Diagram also illustrates is that the ACT and VISION areas always intersect at a middle ground called the CHOICE area. The whole movement, then, is from past to future as I build on my present gifts, by Choosing to learn the skills now that will produce the future Vision that I hope for. This whole process is a process of Spiritual Formation. In this sense Time can be transcended or at least accelerated as I bring the future into the present more quickly. The critical skill that this couple had to learn was an Imaginal Skill. To see why this is we are going to revisit the four skills and their interrelationship in more detail.

The development of all skills is related to the development of the imagination, and as a consequence Imaginal Skills are critical to a person's growth. We know that memory is stored in images. We know that images prefigure language and therefore rational thinking and discourse. Many great thinkers like Einstein noted that they primarily thought in images first, and in logic and language second.

THE GENESIS OF SKILLS

see Diagram VI.2

Piaget a French pyschologist did considerable work to establish the stages by which a child gains knowledge rationally of the world around himself or herself.[4] He noted that the child's imagination or use of the imagination develops in stages from rudimentary fantasy, to the ability to differentiate between quantity and quality, to the ability through language to categorize and order data, and finally to think abstractly as in theology, mathematics and philosophy. The skill component here was for Piaget primarily skill of cognitive reasoning, a part of what we call Instrumental Skills. Clearly the imagination is what makes reasoning skills possible.

see Skills, chapter 4

James Fowler in his book *Stages of Faith* suggests that the imaginal capacity of a person can mean more than this: "Our use of the word *image* requires some explanation. I maintain that virtually all our knowing begins with images and most of what we know is stored in images. Several points must be developed here. First, evidence from a variety of sources suggests that our knowing registers the impact of our experiences in a far more comprehensive way than our own consciousness can monitor."[5]

IMAGINATION AND THE IMAGINAL SKILLS

This is close to what Jung refers to as the Intuitive side of the personality, which is more developed in some people than others. Basically it is an unconscious process of reading the external data that one has before oneself, and making insightful, intuitive (unconscious) conclusions about what the information means. For Jung the logical connections are actually made unconsciously by the Psyche.

Further for Jung the imagination has a transcendent dimension where it not only synthesizes information in new ways, but does it by adding additional archetypal information.[6] What we have done in our work is to make a composite of all these dimensions, and have additionally suggested that the imagination can and is enhanced through the developmental processes as a skill.

The Imaginal Skill is the ability to create images. It is a peculiar blend of internal fantasy and feeling that enables a person to externalize one's ideas and images in an effective manner. Basically it is the ability of the person to transform internal images into external structures that are workable in the world. In this sense it is the heart of the Genesis Effect in a person.

IMAGINAL SKILLS: A DEFINITION

Its direct practical consequence is that it enables a person to make sense out of increasingly complex data, and synthesize into new

139

wholes. It is particularly central to human and spiritual development in that it has the peculiar quality of synthesizing all the other skills. A specific example inventory of Imaginal skills is as follows:

- ability to sythesize new facts
- ability to initiate new and unthought of thoughts and ideas from seemingly unrelated data
- ability to perceive hidden meaning in disparate data
- ability to transform complex data into simple ideas
- ability to generate external practical structures from internal images and ideas.

Critical to understanding Imaginal Skills is to recognize that they develop with spiritual maturity. This process begins as the imagination and the skills related to its development blend, first, with Instrumental Skills and then with Interpersonal Skills. Not only this but the skills tend to be related to the Cycles of Development.

INSTRUMENTAL SKILLS

Instrumental Skills are basically skills with the hands and the head. They are a peculiar blend of intelligence and manual dexterity, that enables the person to survive at home, in school and finally in his or her chosen profession. It is basically the ability to manipulate that which appears objective and external such as ideas and physical tools, like pens, hammers and cars.

As was indicated above the imagination is an integral part of the formation of the Instrumental Skill. Intelligence is in fact a blend of imagination and sensory data in a loop effect, which is a movement from inner images to external data and back again—it is an information feedback loop.

Sensory data is received from the environment, such as a small child being taught how to hold a spoon. This combined with the conscious and unconscious activity of the psyche enables the child to learn and know. This is the development of thinking and intellect.

Once language develops the process is accelerated because the person can now transfer inner images into the external world in precise knowable ways, and can at the same time begin to actually experience the inner world of others through imitation and then later through conversation and dialogue.

Instrumental skills are always body and tool related. From the primitive history of the human person going back into pre-history the tool was an extension of the body, such as the flint rock swung by the arm as a hammer, or down across an animal skin as a cutting implement. Clearly the physical condition and the physical dexterity of the person with his or her own body as a tool was also important.

Slowly through history the tools became separate from the body, extending the body over greater distances. For example the aborigine's spear or boomerang extends his or her powers to touch and slay an animal at a great distance. These tools are examples of the extension of the arm and the body. What we are now aware of is that all tools we use are extensions of the body in some form. For example the Television is in fact an extension of someone's inner fantasies as we watch a comedy or a drama. Light bulbs when turned on are an extension of a part of our optical system.

Tools through time have also become very complex. The body's ability to adapt to temperature change was extended by animal furs, and eventually into modern clothing. A more complex version is the development of primitive shelters as an extension of group clothing, eventually leading to houses, and even the modern complex city. The modern hospital is a very complex combination of hundreds of tools which is an extension of the body's ability to heal itself.

Instrumental skills are then a combination of the tool with the intellect. Any profession takes a combination of these. For example persons who work in crafts such as rug making must have the imaginal and intellectual component in place in order to think of a design, and at the same time they have to have trained dexterity with their hands and fingers to do the job. A plumber must know about the design of houses and the sizes and material composition of piping, and he or she must have the physical skills to accomplish the given tasks.

Each of the skills is held together and integrated through the imagination, as we have just noted with the Instrumental Skills. This becomes even more evident when we look at the interpersonal area.

Whereas Instrumental Skills develop in the first three Cycles of Development, Interpersonal Skills begin to develop at the second Cycle but really become an important factor in one's life in the third and fourth Cycles.

INTERPERSONAL SKILLS

Interpersonal skills are the ability of a person to act with generosity and understanding toward others. The high point is empathy which is the ability to enter into another's imaginal world and to be with that world, so that the other person feels that depth of acceptance to the roots of his or her very being.

In the third Cycle of Development understanding is more a language issue. As persons move into Cycle Four they become skilled with, and gain the facility to mobilize, their feelings creatively. At first it is the ability to recognize and objectify one's own feelings—for example the ability to state feelings of anger in a controlled manner to another person within a short period of time, so as to enhance cooperation rather than isolation from that person.

Critical to the mature development of interpersonal skills is self awareness and knowledge of one's emotional and imaginal life, in the past and the present. Such an awareness plus the skills that come with it is not something that is learned intuitively; it has to be learned formally through educational or training events. The values that would motivate a person to know himself or herself in the emotional arena such as Self Actualization and Empathy do not occur until the third Phase, or fourth Cycle of Development.

As the development of Tools was the antecedent to the development of Instrumental Skills, so the Family and one's early social experiences are the condition out of which one's interpersonal skill potential grows. Bronowski in his book *The Ascent of Man* documents

141

that the initiation of human social organization as we now know it occurred between 8000 and 6000 B.C. It happened when nomadic tribes of primitive humans stopped wandering and became settled agricultural communities.

"The largest single step in the ascent of man is the change from nomad to village agriculture. . . . The turning-point to the spread of agriculture in the Old World was almost certainly the occurrence of two forms of wheat with a large, full head of seeds. Before 8000 B.C. wheat was not the luxuriant plant it is today; it was merely one of many wild grasses spread throughout the Middle East.

"By some genetic accident, the wild wheat crossed with the goat grass and formed a fertile hybrid . . . and produced Emmer with twenty-eight chromosones. That is what makes the emmer so much more plump. The hybrid was able to spread naturally, because its seeds are attached to the husk in such a way that they scatter in the wind."[7]

Bronowski goes on to point out that another incredible genetic accident occurred, as the emmer cross fertilized again with the goat grass to produce a very heavy forty-two chromosome derivative that we call bread wheat. But here came a strange ecological event that Bronowski states as follows:

"Yet there is something even stranger. Now we have a beautiful ear of wheat, but one which will never spread in the wind because the ear is too tight to break up. . . . Suddenly man and plant have come together. Man has a wheat that he lives by, but the wheat also thinks that man was made for him only so it can be propagated. For the bread wheats can only multiply with help, man must harvest and scatter the seeds; and the life of each, man and the plant, depends on the other."[8]

This strange historical act of interdependence created agricultural communities which in turn created the need of men and women to live and stay in one place. From this grew the city, the social organization of human beings, and the direct consequence of interpersonal interaction, whose high point is Intimacy. It was the creation of this environment that was to make the feeling emotional side of civilization a possibility. Why is this important?

The philosopher of art, Susan Langer has amply demonstrated that you cannot have feelings without images.[9] That is any internal images that we have through dreams or sudden recall have parallel feelings that go with them. In other words the feeling is the effect of an internal image on the body. For example if you are driving to work, and you suddenly remember that you left your lunch at home, you experience a feeling of annoyance or disappointment as soon as you have the image of your lunch sitting on the kitchen counter.[10]

And so once again the imagination is an integral part of the skill of Interpersonal communications. But now something very critical occurs—the imagination not only begins to integrate one's feelings in the formation of social skills, but it begins to integrate the Instrumental and Interpersonal dimension so as to radically alter the person's World View, as he or she moves from Phase II to Phase III. In order to understand this we will need to revisit Imaginal Skills as a developmental stage in the maturation of the imagination.

Until the the fourth Cycle and specifically Phase IIIA, imaginal skills are really the part the imagination plays in the development of Instrumental and Interpersonal Skills. Once the Interpersonal dimension begins to flower it begins to reintegrate the personality causing the imagination to have a whole new role in the person's life.

IMAGINAL
SKILLS
REVISITED

Strange as it may seem, it is as if the Psyche, that internal universe, is beginning to assert itself into the external interpersonal world. The overall effect is the Genesis Effect, which is to cause the person to be motivated by creatively acting on, rather than reacting to, the world. DIAGRAM VI.2 will enable us to make some valuable connections.

see Diagram II.1

see also Diagram VI.3

As the Diagram indicates the Imaginal Skills are first of all central to all skill development. Secondly they are a part of the Instrumental Skills (the top circle) which are derived historically from the Tool/Body connection. They are also, as the Diagram indicates, a part of the Interpersonal Skills. Thirdly we note that the Imaginal Skills are indicated by two circles, moving to the right of the Diagram.

The second Circle represents the Imaginal Skills as a separate and unique entity that moves beyond their simply being a dimension of the other two skills. They are the basic ability to recognize the independent authoritative value of one's own inner psychic uniqueness and capability. It is therefore a critical stage in a human being's own spiritual growth. Its major function at this stage in life with the person coming alive in this new and unique way is to integrate the following.

1. To integrate and enable the person to transcend the preservation and pro-creation dimensions of the imagination. The preservation side is simply that all human beings have internal images that are set off at any point of threat, causing the defensive action of anger. It is

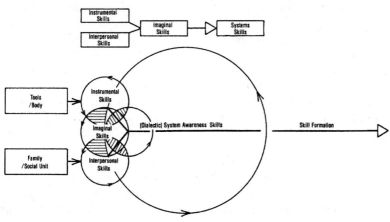

**THE DEVELOPMENT OF SKILLS I.
IN DIALECTICAL FORMATION**

Diagram 6:2
**THE
DEVELOPMENT
OF SKILLS**
The diagram illustrates the dialectical relationship among the four skills. It further illustrates how the integration of the Instrumental and Interpersonal through the Imaginal Skills results in an expansion of consciousness, and in the development of Systems Skills.

the revivifying of the value of Self Preservation and is probably more of a masculine value, although it is a part of everyone's psyche. The critical skill which is both imaginal and interpersonal is therefore: the ability to express anger creatively, without fear, at a moment's notice, with productive consequences for all concerned. It is a basic ingredient of Self Actualization, Equality, Autonomy and all the Phase IIIA values.

The pro-creation side has to do with the fact that all human beings have a physical sexual side which is activated by images of sexual fantasy. These are often only felt as one becomes sexually stimulated at the sight of an attractive man or woman. The key imaginal skill here is to not be afraid of such feelings, and to be able to discuss these in an adult responsible manner with any mature person of the opposite sex, without becoming inappropriately physically involved. The pro-creation aspect of life is however an anticipation of the full creative potential that an individual has in all areas of his or her life.

Growth beyond this Cycle is not going to be possible in an integrated way without this occurring. The reason is that each of us has a masculine and feminine side, whether we be male or female, so that what is really happening here is the integration of these two into our lives. This then leads naturally to the next integration.

2. To enable the person to discover his or her own unique gifts and identity as a man or as a woman. This of course includes the recognition that masculine and feminine psychology is different, and that each calls for different demands on the person. This includes facing one's limitations in life, relative to gifts and potential. For some unfortunate persons this includes coming to grips with physical and psychosocial disabilities that most of us do not have to contend with.

see Body Politics, chapter 3 and Kelsey, Appendix

An obvious example of these disabilities is homosexuality. It is very often a condition that does not make heterosexual relations possible for some. This is a severe limitation that is not only physical but also social since it brings with it severe negative social discrimination.

It is not any more of a moral problem than it is for anyone else that has to live his or her life by creative value commitment. Religiously homosexuality is not a sin, it is a genetic condition. The moral issues revolve around what a person does with it relative to life style. The same moral issues exist for the single, celibate and married person.

3. To enable the person to seek authority and moral decision making from within, as conscience, rather than from external authority. This is simply a restatement of the difference between the first two Phases and the last two Phases of Development.

THE BEGINNING OF A PERSONALITY REVOLUTION

We discovered in working with hundreds of cases that persons at this fourth Cycle experience a sudden expansion of consciousness, unequaled by any other growth movement in their lives. This occurs when there is a minimum integration of the Instrumental and Interpersonal Skills with the new Imaginal Skills dimension. This expansion includes a new awareness and minimum skill development as

144

outlined in the three points directly above. The minimum skills have to include the minimums described from each Cycle in the last chapter.

In the Instrumental area they include: minimal Instrumental Skills of pain tolerance, rote learning, language, mathematics, and the minimal requirements of one's profession. Since, as we have noted, these skills are body related they must additionally include minimal skills of diet, physical health and exercise. In the area of spirituality this must additionally include minimal knowledge of one's religion such as history and scripture, and minimal disciplines in the areas of meditation and relaxation techniques.

Minimal Interpersonal Skills include the ability to enable cooperation and care to occur in personal relationships rather than isolation, and the ability to express one's feelings creatively, including anger and sexual fantasy. Finally it includes the growing ability to separate empathy, as reflecting back another's feeling, from sympathy, which involves getting caught into another's feelings.

When this all coincides with a minimal development in the Imaginal Skills in the three areas indicated above an alteration in perception occurs that changes the world of complexity into a vision of simplicity. It is a spiritual conversion that happens to anyone who matures in an integrated way at this point no matter what his or her religious persuasion. It also results in the development of System perspective and System skills.

This experience of simplicity is best explained by looking at DIAGRAM VI.3 which is a slightly different version of Diagram VI.2.

IMAGINAL INTEGRATION

The Diagram illustrates the fact that early in our lives we learn many skills, and in fact accumulate a great complexity of instrumental and social data. When the Instrumental and Interpersonal Skills form a dialectic through the Imaginal Skills at the fourth Cycle of Development, a reintegration of all the skills occurs at a new level. This causes an expanded awareness internally of one's capabilities in the world.

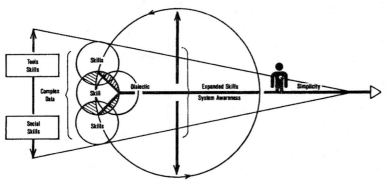

THE DEVELOPMENT OF SKILLS II.
IN SPIRITUAL FORMATION

Diagram 6:3
SKILLS AND THE DEVELOPMENT OF SIMPLICITY
The diagram illustrates the relationship between the development of a whole complexity of skills as we grow and mature, and "simplicity" as a revolution in consciousness that occurs through the integration of these skills through the imaginal and internal component of our lives.

One reason for this is that the Self's image of itself in the world is largely reflected through its confidence relative to the gifts and skills that it has. Once this integration occurs through the imaginal dimension all the past is rewritten in a new and different way. Past potentialities and skills suddenly come to the fore and are immediately usable. This is in fact what really happened to Julia and Bryan in our example at the beginning of the chapter.

Julia was unable to use her interpersonal skills to support Bryan, and Bryan was not moving ahead because he had not finished his education—his instrumental completion skills. The simple brainstorming technique we used is a specific method of expanding and learning to use one's imagination. It is an Imaginal Skill.

They also happened to be at a precise developmental level that made their rapid growth together possible. Consequently the use of this Imaginal Skill integrated the Instrumental and Interpersonal dimension of this couple. This released the creative energy needed to allow them to move ahead and complete their education and work creatively toward changing their living environment. We note that in their case, their ability to cooperate supplied the missing skills that each needed.

SIMPLICITY AND SPIRITUAL GROWTH

see Contemplation and Discernment, chapter 2

The Diagram above also illustrates that at the same time there is also an expansion of awareness internally of one's Self that enables a person to see the world more wholistically, resulting in the spiritual consequence of Simplicity. Simplicity recognizes that the parts are many, but the whole is One. In other words Simplicity is the consequence of the inversion of complexity such that the consciousness of the person alters and he or she perceives the world entirely differently.

It is this experience that describes the movement of a person from the fourth Cycle (The Interpersonal Cycle) to the fifth Cycle (The Communal/Collaborative Cycle). This is an additional expansion of consciousness beyond what Julia and Bryan experienced.

see The Vows and Organizational Dynamics, chapter 9

In the religious traditions, Simplicity relates to the vow of poverty which was beautifully expanded in meaning by Saint Francis of Assisi. Interestingly enough the Benedictine monks still refer to this vow as Simplicity. The concept of Poverty as a religious discipline means in its crudest sense the giving up of, or the non-preoccupation with, material possessions. But its real spiritual significance is far deeper.[11]

The connection he made was to recognize that the key to spiritual enlightenment was in the skill and virtue of Detachment. Francis recognized as did the eastern mystics like Buddha that attachment to any desire or need prevents growth.

The attachment to material possessions is only one example, and often screens out of people's consciousness the real meaning of detachment. The concept is that anyone can become obsessively attached to an object of desire for a number of reasons. Common examples are power and the need to constantly achieve and succeed in the expansion of one's business, overeating, addiction to alcohol, addiction to sexually promiscuious experiences from a variety of sexual orientations, and even the attachment to a person such as a smothering relationship with a child. The reasons for these symptoms of attachment are many, such as the belief that these things make me feel worthwhile, enable me to succeed, or even help me survive.

All these things are in fact an expression of the Taboo side of personality, which will be dealt with in more depth in the next chapter. They are mentioned here as a way of explaining detachment, which is the skill to separate out one's self from these obsessions. The insight called Religious Poverty was that in doing this the virtue of Simplicity as we have explained it becomes possible. What must be said in addition that Saint Francis was not able to say is that Detachment as Simplicity only results in this conscientizing experience at a certain level of human maturity and integration. *see Manna and Taboo chapter 4, and Contingency, chapter 7*

The diagram also illustrates that System awareness is an expanded awareness (larger circle) which is a consequence of a new integration (dialectic) of all the previous skills, resulting in the development of System Skills. System Skills involve the ability to see and understand how all the parts of any complex organization of data or of an institution relate to the functioning of the whole. These skills also include being able to make decisions based on a knowledge of the whole organization rather than on its parts.

SYSTEM SKILLS
see Leadership and System Skills, chapter 8

System Skills, then, are a peculiar blend of imagination, interpersonal sensitivity, and instrumental competence, which enable a person to see all the parts of a system or an institution as they relate to the whole. System Skills are not management skills, although they require good management skills. System Skills basically become possible only after the System perspective occurs—after the complexity becomes simple. Why? Because the person with this perspective suddenly sees the whole first and the parts second—the person sees the simple unity of it all.

Additionally System Skills involve the ability to design and plan change once the perspective is clear. More than any of the other skills, one encounters here the need to have minimally integrated skills from the other three areas. Let us look at another example to illustrate.

Don was the Chief Executive of a chemical manufacturing company. He had been trained as a research chemist and had invented a new non-corrosive paint that did not have the problems lead based paints have, such as lead poisoning. As a result the company made money and he was moved from the laboratory to a fairly high management position.

He had excellent instrumental skills as a professional research chemist. These were in the ACT area. VISION wise he wanted to accept the position and hoped one day to become Vice-President of the company. His office was full of flow charts explaining how the whole company worked—it was a system picture. But he was a very stressed person.

His whole training as a chemist had been related to breaking up things into their component parts, and then working with the chemical parts to discover new applications. His imaginal capacity was therefore related more to categorizing and assessing data, not in coming up with new unthought of ideas. His whole life had really been very rational in its orientation. When he got into management he suddenly found himself in a world of not only technical problems but complex human problems for which he was not equipped. The Vision and the Act areas were separated in his case by a lack of skills which he suddenly needed but which he had no training or background for. This is not an untypical story.

Since the skills needed were first of all interpersonal, and take training and time, he was unable to cope with the job and finally had to resign. One thing that the personnel division learned was that integrated skill assessment is needed for a person who is going to be in a lead position that requires comprehensive skills, and particularly for a position that requires System Skills.

Don did eventually recover his sense of dignity. Through counseling and training he was able to learn how to report and identify feelings. We eventually introduced him to a series of training seminars in group dynamics, which is a skill area absolutely essential for management personnel. It is only through training in group dynamics that a person can learn the skills that bridge the interpersonal with the system dimension. These particular skills turned out to be the Choice area connection that enabled his imagination to move beyond assessing data to seeing new possibilities.

Interestingly enough he did eventually, some two years later, end up in a significant leadership position. He noted the following in a conversation: "You know when I was first in management I used to worry about all the guys in the shop, or how my secretary felt today. Everyone's problem was my problem—you know? Then something happened. Like this last week one of the employees that I have known for years came in. I knew he had been drinking on the job. He sat in my office and just gave me hell for about fifteen minutes. I don't even know what he was yelling about. A year ago I would have gotten an instant ulcer worrying about him. I was really calm, I mean calm inside. I just said to him, 'You can feed me all the garbage you want, but I really don't have to eat it!' I then asked him what he was going to do about his drinking problem, because it wasn't just a problem for him and me, but for his family and the whole division he was working in. Do you know, I don't know what happened but he changed after that—he has been reliable ever since."

We discussed the event at some length, and discovered that he simply viewed the world more wholistically and simply than he had before. All the management skills and other training that he had had previously suddenly took on a new perspective and were able to be used in a whole new way. The skills were the same but his inner vision of the world had been rewritten.

Simply put his new vision with its hope and perspective and his ability to detach from the employees' problems conveyed a healing power that altered that individual. In this sense although this was in no conventional way a religious event, it was in fact deeply spiritual, in that not only had he transcended himself in his own development, but this was now carrying over in a productive and creative way to others. What explanation is there for this? We do not know all the answers but over the years another phenomenon has come to light, as we examined many similar cases—we call it the "Onion Effect."

The "Onion Effect" refers to a phenomenon that is illustrated by DIA-GRAM VI.4 that resembles the cross section of an onion.

The Diagram illustrates the Seven Cycles of Human and Spiritual Development. The series of ellipses are the fields of awareness of each individual Cycle, as we saw and described them in the last chapter. The line of of the seven Cycles represents the normal psychological view of development, where time is linear. That is to say one can only get to Cycle Four after having completed the minimum tasks at Cycles One, Two and Three. As such this is an hierarchical view of the maturation process.

Spiritual integration implies that the person is conscious of the larger field of awareness, indicated by the circle at the end of each Cycle in the Diagram, that encompasses all the possibilities up to that Cycle of Development. For example a person who was integrated spiritually at Cycle Six or Seven would be able to imagine how the person at Cycle One or Two felt in a given situation.

Some readers might wonder about, or even object to, the word spiritual being used in this manner. When one speaks of spiritual integration this normally implies a particular religious orientation. I am using the word intentionally much more widely to include the wholistic expression of the development of the psyche—one's inner spirit.

Traditionally psychological counseling has as its goal to enable individuals and families suffering from emotionally related difficulties to cope with their problems in order that they can be productive members of society. Productive here means emotionally stable such that they enhance cooperation rather than isolation in their local family and community. Some counselors even claim that what they do is value free—this claim will be shown to be false in the next chapter.

see Values and Ethics, chapter 9

Spiritual Direction, Pastoral Counseling and Pastoral Care, which all overlap, have traditionally had as their goal to treat the whole per-

CONSCIOUSNESS AND SPIRITUAL DEVELOPMENT

Diagram 6:4
THE ONION EFFECT
Each ellipse represents a Cycle of development, whereas the fuller circle related to it indicates its wider field of consciousness. As such each Cycle has the possibility of expanded consciousness the more it integrates in all the former Cycles.

son as gifted by God, and endowed with a special God given potential. The whole person includes the physical body, the imaginal and emotional components, and the moral behavior of the person as they relate to the larger community.

In more general terms it implies that the person is living by a certain set of values in his or her life that cause resurrection and integration in that life rather than a destructive life style. It is in this sense that I am using the word spiritual, because it is at this level that *it is applicable to anyone no matter what his or her particular religious persuasion.* I am also asserting that from my own bias, integration is the ability to see the world more wholistically as one matures, and to act with the consequential behavior that comes with that consciousness.

TRANSCENDING TIME

The following two diagrams are illustrations, at an individual and group level, of time being transcended through the Cycles of Human and Spiritual Development. The linear model that we referred to in the last paragraph is based on time as sequenced as we normally experience it in the everyday world. This is how the left side of the brain perceives reality. We designate this T1.

When time is transcended so that normal development processes or the left brain perception of time is altered in any way, we speak of time as T2. T2 represents the right brain's perception of the world, as in the world of dreams and quantum physics. In this sector time is relative.

Let us illustrate this from our first example from our paint Executive Don in his interview with the employee who had a drinking problem. We remember that it was Don's presence that seemed to change the man. What was it about his presence that caused the alteration?

The example involves the dialectical relationship of three values: Security and Care/Nurture as they lead to Human Dignity. In the linear understanding of time as T1, Human Dignity is a value from the fifth Cycle of Development, whereas Security and Care/Nurture are second Cycle values. DIAGRAM VI.5 helps us understand how Don actually transcended time.

Diagram VI:5 In the psychological model, which is linear in nature, represented by the seven ellipses, Human Dignity could not be the consequence of the other two values. The consequence would have to be a second Cycle value such as Self Worth.

In the spiritual model where time is relative (T2) Don is operating from a greater field of awareness than his employee who is in Cycle Two mode of awareness—the first shaded area. The person counseled is enabled to transcend time, and the whole world of Cycle Five becomes present to him in a moment, the second shaded area, allowing him also to transcend time and experience another level of development.

Don transcended time by confronting the employee in a way that did not threaten his Security. In fact he asked him what he was going to do to improve his life to better his work. He did not say, "I will fire you if you don't shape up." He, from the experience and point of view of the employee, Cared for him, by being the first person to really confront him in a non-threatening way.

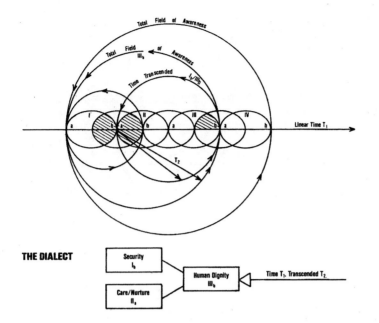

THE DIALECT

Security
I$_b$

Care/Nurture
II$_a$

Human Dignity
III$_b$

Time T$_1$, Transcended T$_2$.

Total Field of Awareness

Linear Time T$_1$

Diagram 6:5
THE INDIVIDUAL TRANSCENDING TIME
The diagram posits the example of a person at a third phase of development (Cycle Six) talking to a person at Cycle Two (see shaded areas). Because of the (dialectical) interpersonal interaction of the values, the person at Cycle Two begins to behave at the Cycle Six level. Normally it might take him or her years to experience such a level of development—as such he or she has in fact transcended time.

This however came out of Don's own new level of development where he had a wholistic perspective, seeing life in clearer and simpler perspective. As such he brought a third Phase value of Human Dignity to the person, with all the hope of a more global Phase, and enabled the person to see new possibilities.

It was spiritual, although Don did not view himself that way, because it did cause resurrection, healing, and a new life orientation for the employee. Now let us take a group example, where the same phenomenon can occur as the values of several persons intermingle to form a group value or faith center.

DIAGRAM VI.6. illustrates how a single group of persons can operate in two entirely different ways by choosing to live out their reality on two different sets of values.

GROUP TRANSCENDENCE: DEVELOPMENT AND REGRESSION (T1/T2)

The example involves a community of persons, or a small administration. Any one person could have the value clusters illustrated in the Diagram and still function with a narrow field of consciousness. A person with Cycle Six (IIIa/IIIb) awareness, as in cluster 2, may only have the narrow focus of that ellipse of development, and not be aware of the larger field of awareness. A person at a prior Cycle of Development, with a total field awareness, could be a more integrated person. Spiritual integration, then, is in part an awareness of the larger field of consciousness, no matter what Cycle the person is at. Developmental psychology does not, for the most part, address this issue of the wider field of awareness.

The diagram addresses the issue of administrative and small community alignment. That is to say, it illustrates what can occur in a group of persons who have a mixture of value priorities. If the group is able to define its priorities and live out their values according to cluster 2, even although some persons are operating with cluster 1 values,

151

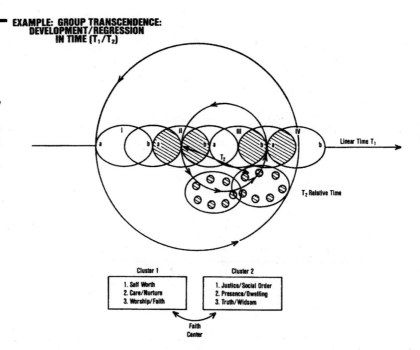

Diagram 6:6
A GROUP OF PERSONS TRANSCENDING TIME
The diagram illustrates how a group of persons with a certain value mix will begin to behave at a different level of consciousness. They transcend time—forward or backward—in Cycles of development.

EXAMPLE: GROUP TRANSCENDENCE: DEVELOPMENT/REGRESSION IN TIME (T_1/T_2)

Linear Time T_1

T_2 Relative Time

Cluster 1	Cluster 2
1. Self Worth	1. Justice/Social Order
2. Care/Nurture	2. Presence/Dwelling
3. Worship/Faith	3. Truth/Widsom

Faith Center

the group can transcend linear time (T1) and actually function at Cycle Six. The reverse is also possible. The purpose of the Diagram is to illustrate that attention to value priorities of individuals in a group can greatly enhance the group's development, rather than retard it.

A mini example of this dynamic was in our example of Julia and Bryan. When they were alienated from each other, when I first knew them they were living as isolated individuals. As a couple their values were not unlike the first two values in cluster 1 in the Diagram. When they started to work together they started living at at least another Cycle higher emphasizing Achievement, Education, Service, Self Actualization and Empathy. The complexity of group alignment and its implication for management will be covered in more detail in chapter VIII.

CONCLUSIONS AND INSIGHTS

We will now review some of the conclusions of the chapter and what came out of working with these issues with hundreds of individuals over the last 10 years.

1. That the other side of values is the skills that enable a value or a cluster of values to be actualized. Although a composite of values do not guarantee that the value will be a priority with a person, such as care for example, it is however true that the value will not be able to be actualized without the skills.

2. That skills represent the Manna side of development at each Cycle of Development. Further that there is a movement both at the value and the skill level from internalized values that become partially unconscious until we call them up, to a new set of values and skills that we aspire to in the future.

The internalized skills and values are called ACT skills and values, *see Diagram VI.1* and the future aspired to set are called VISION values and skills. These two intersect in the present in the so called CHOICE area. This is the area where I learn to recognize my limitations and known potential in the ACT area, and begin to work toward my VISION through my present CHOICES.

This movement is the grist of human and spiritual formation, and has its parallel in the Cycles of Development, where a person's present concentration of energy is called the CHOICE area. Values before this are the ACT area, and those following are called the VISION area.

What is interesting is that in working with 1000 profiles with individuals we have found that values that are not being taken care of in the Act area can lead to a person acting out his or her worst self. Bryan in our example discovered that an important value for him was Care/ Nurture, which he was not getting from his wife when they first came to see me. This made his already difficult behavior worse because this was in his ACT area, and it was not being taken care of.

3. That in order for the skills to become a (Manna) source of integration, all four skills need to be developed in a minimal way especially in the adult stages of a person's life cycle. We noted that the imagination must be well integrated at each Cycle for the Instrumental and Interpersonal skills to develop. We also noted that exceptional development and the experience of Simplicity and System awareness occurs only when this happens.

What we have also discovered is that particularly for the adult, spiritual growth may be retarded, not because a lot of skills are absent, but because a particular skill is absent that affects all the others. We noted this in the example of Bryan and Julia as a couple. It can also occur at the individual level. An example might be helpful.

John was a successful single man of thirty-two years of age who was a creative writer and who practiced regular physical exercise, diet and meditation. He, however, had bouts of high anxiety due to the pressure of his job, coupled with physical deterioration beginning with heavy smoking. He considered himself normally to be a non-smoker, but would smoke a pack or two a day for about two weeks during this anxiety period. He felt smoking was bad for anyone's health—and so additionally he ended up feeling guilty.

We began with a little biofeedback training. I asked him to keep a daily diary of what happened to him when this occurred. Additionally I asked him to take the temperature of his finger tip each time he started smoking. What John discovered was that when he started to get under pressure, he immediately bought a pack of cigarettes.

After he smoked the first cigarette his finger temperature dropped between 10 and 15 degrees Fahrenheit. He noticed immediately that his shoulder and neck muscles began to ache and his muscles became more tight in those areas. Additionally he started to drink more coffee, and his friends reported that he was becoming more and more authoriatarian and less able to listen to them. This evidence soon changed John's life style. Why?

When we looked into it John soon discovered that the stress was always increased by the smoking. In his internal images, his brain was concluding that cigarettes reduce anxiety. But when he smoked the internal side of his nature was clearly concluding that something was really wrong and actually put the body into a flight-fight reaction both in reduction of temperature, by restricting the blood vessels, and through muscle tension. This in turn carried over into the interpersonal area and started to reduce his capacity to listen as the habit became more controlling.

We could analyze this forever, but the bottom line is that it was the actual lighting of the cigarette that significantly increased the stress reaction. We know this because when he refused to do this later he was easily able to live with the anxiety. He did this by imagining to himself that he was relaxed and at a beach each time he felt the need to smoke, and the feeling and need went away. Clearly the two critical skills used were Imaginal, in his specific use of the imagination, and Instrumental in his recording the physical daily data.

Its consequence was to set off a whole chain reaction of new living skills, and did in his case lead eventually to a more global perspective on reality. The lesson here is for counselors and Spiritual Directors to realize that very often the correct diagnosis and minimal work can shift a person's consciousness and growth pattern significantly.

4. That when the skills develop in an unintegrated or incomplete way unconscious immoral or destructive decision making can and does occur. This happened in the early experience of Don the paint company chemist and executive. When he was first in a management position he made personal decisions about people based on the technical requirement of the job only. This alienated so many people that he finally had to be asked to resign.

During the adult cycle of a person's life, particularly in executive positions where there is considerable pressure, we find that when this occurs there is a marked absence or deficiency in one of the skill areas. We were able to monitor this by having instrumentation that not only told individuals what their values were, but gave them the percentages of skills relative to the values that they had chosen. We found that when a young person, or a person at an early Cycle, looked at his or her values the Instrumental Skill percentages were usually high and the Systems Skills low.

This was expected since it reflected the developmental cycle, where one would normally take care of one's Instrumental Skills during one's early educational and professional life. We also found that executives who were over thirty-five years of age normally had low percentages in the Instrumental area, since they had learned most of those skills earlier in their professional life. But when there was an imbalance in any of the other areas serious problems often resulted.

Lack of Imaginal Skills would disenable persons to take creative risks, and lead them to continue to manage operations as they had al-

154

ways been managed. Lack of systems skills is particularly a problem in complex and international settings. The person will tend to become increasingly distressed and burn out or leave. Insufficient interpersonal skills in management causes the person to unconsciously use the system against an individual and cause interminable emotional problems with personnel.

The point I am making is that integrated skill development for prospective leadership and for a person's overall spiritual growth is essential. We will return to this subject later as we deal with corporate management issues in chapter VIII.

5. That skill integration combined with particular value combinations enable persons and groups to transcend linear time, through the phenomenon of the "Onion Effect."

The "Onion Effect" and its relationship to the relativity of time, and the whole question of what does integrated spiritual development mean, and, even more importantly, how does it occur, now needs to be addressed.

What we have at this point is a lot of the component parts, but we need to look at time in more depth and its relationship to creativity, anxiety and faith. This we will do in the next chapter as we also look at the Taboo areas and the "Oscillation Effect." Let us now move to Chapter VII: The Unity of Time: Faith and the Oscillation Effect.

Chapter 6:
Time Traveling: Simplicity and the Onion Effect

NOTES

1. Jackson (1980), p. 238.
2. Neumann (1954), p. 416.
3. Elgin (1982), pp. xvi–xvii. In the journey each of us is called to make, there is a going inward and a returning outward. Elgin describes his journey to the East (India) as inward and his return to the West (U.S.A.) as outward. There is ebb and flow, a going backward and going forward, a cycle.
4. Wadsworth (1971).
5. Fowler (1981), p. 25.
6. Campbell (1971). The healing power of imagery is also stressed by Jung. To revisit our images is to own them and feel at home with them. They are uniquely "ours."
7. Bronowski (1973), pp. 64–65.
8. *Ibid.*, p. 68.
9. Langer (1957).
10. The self develops not merely in an interior sense but also in its finding expression and response in the external world. This is the unity of the internal and external universes mediated by values.
11. Friars Minor of the Franciscan Province of Santa Barbara (1962), p. 163: "Poverty . . . is the foundation and guardian of all the virtues." This is a reminder of the Buddhist theory of detachment from one's expectations, without which there can be no peace, no kingdom of God, no transformation.

THE UNITY OF TIME:
FAITH AND THE OSCILLATION EFFECT

Our very notion of personal identity—the self, the soul—is closely bound up with memory and enduring experiences. It is not sufficient to proclaim "I exist," at this instant. To be an individual implies a continuity of experience together with some linking feature, such as memory.

Paul Davies.[1]

What are those most sacred hopes, those most compelling goals and purposes in your life? These are the questions of faith. They aim to help us get in touch with the dynamic, patterned process by which we find life meaningful. They aim to help us reflect on the centers of value and power that sustain our lives. The persons, causes and institutions we really love and trust, the images of good and evil, of possibility and probability to which we are committed—these form the pattern of our faith.

James Fowler.[2]

PURPOSE To view reality through the eyes of time as relative, where "Being" rather than "Becoming," as in the developmental perspective, is the focus.

CONTENT The chapter begins by looking at the quality of a person's life through the relationship of time to the activity of work and the experience of play and leisure. Time is then examined through the eyes of the existentialist framework, where future and past become present in the "now." The consequences of this on the structures of human awareness as experienced through anxiety, guilt, reconcilliation and faith are examined. Finally the chapter returns to the concept of time and posits the concept of "The Oscillation Effect."

LINKAGE The last four chapters have been examining human and spiritual growth from a developmental perspective that viewed time as being primarily a sequence of events, often related to the physical aging process. The last chapter showed how even within this perspective time is not as rigid and objective as it appears to be. This chapter extends this theme by showing how in mysticism and existentialism time is simply another dimension of space that can be transcended, particularly through the spiritual and faith dimension. Our focus up until this point has been on the individual and the individual in relationship to others. In Part III of the book, we will look at the influence of the Corporate and Institutional dimension and its influence on human and spiritual development.

At the heart of the structures of human awareness is the concept of the sanctification of time. It is central to spiritual and human development. When we change our perception of time, we change our perception of the world we live in. All through history the perception of time has been central to philosophy, theology and the sciences.

In the last two chapters we looked at time as linear (T1) resulting in a developmental view of the human being's growth process. In the Onion Effect we began to look into another point of view (T2) where time becomes relative. In this chapter we are going to look at time from this point of view as described by Existentialism and the Mystics.

Next we will explore the Taboo area of human personality as we look at the concepts of failure, guilt and anxiety on the one hand, and their positive opposites of power and creativity on the other hand.

This will lead us inevitably to a dilemma of how we are to view time. When we view it developmentally it gives us valuable information that it seems we cannot deny about the human condition. On the other hand, as we shall see the existential and mystical dimensions introduce us to another way of viewing time that also gives rise to equally important but different information. Which are we to believe? Our answer will be both, in what we will call the Oscillation Effect. Let us begin by an examination of the Existentialist view of time.

The root of the word Existentialism is from *ex-sistere*, meaning to stand out and to emerge. It is basically concerned with what is real, what is reality. And often as the existentialists point out, what is true is not what is real. It is the the science of "Ontology" (*ontos* is Greek for "Being") or more appropriately "Being-in-the World." It is a combination of the idea of Being and Becoming as being a unified experience of reality.

It is a philosophy that refuses to split reality into subject and object and sees them as one. The existentialist would claim that Piaget and Kohlberg, in emphasizing the rational side of the human, and Erikson by emphasizing the emotional side, probably speak the truth, but fail to see the reality that is a whole that is greater than these individual parts or perspectives.

The existential view of life engages persons by asking the questions: *see Harrison and* What is the nature of reality? What does it mean to be human, and *Prendergast, Appendix* what makes human life meaningful?

Instead of looking at life through the eyes of development through time as stages of physical and emotional maturation, they ask us to freeze time and go down into the depth of a person's being, to look at what Peter Koestenbaum calls the Deep Structures.[2a] The archetypal deep structure is that of Being. One approach to Being is through the dimension of time. It is through the eyes of time says Evelyn Underhill that we see "the very stuff of reality."[3]

One practical way to look at time this way is to recognize how it relates to specific activities and relationships we all have every day of our lives. Simply put we work, we maintain ourselves through sleeping, eating and hygiene, and we relax and play to recreate ourselves. But underlying this is the depth reality of Being, Doing and Becoming.

These three have always been the recurring themes of spiritual growth. The external expectations of the world of Work (Doing) and the time it consumes are always in tension with the time required for play and the internal need for "Being Myself."

It is in the realm of Being that I can experience contemplation and intimacy, whereas it is in the realm of Doing that I may efficiently assert myself as a productive human being. What is required is the correct balance which is unique for each person. It is this harmony of presence as Being and action as Doing that enables a person to Become his or her best self. This Becoming is not the Becoming that occurs as I grow older and change with the passage of earthly time, but the Becoming of internal quality alteration as I become more integrated and whole.

Too much work can negate my Being values, converting Being and Doing into obsessive Having. On the other hand, if I can maintain the appropriate balance between the two, both Being and Doing are affirmed resulting in my Becoming more creative, liberated, and even resurrected. DIAGRAM VII.1 will illustrate this a little further for us.

The basic reasoning here is that anything that I own I have to Maintain (center of Diagram). This is the condition of Having. If I own property, a car, or a business, this means that "I have" these things to Maintain. Maintenance is an extension of Doing.

But what has been fascinating to observe is that in our modern age, the stress of working, that is Doing, causes persons to often be obsessed with their role, as an executive, a bishop or a rock star. Maintaining the role can be more stressful than maintaining property. Owning things and and owning a role are both components of the Doing side of life.

Diagram 7:1 **BEING & DOING**

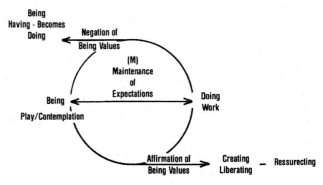

158

Doing, then, has an essential maintenance dimension to it which is a negative drain of energy. Doing something, like working physically to repair my house or my car, is physically draining energy. But this does not compare to the drainage of energy that is involved in maintaining other people.

When I maintain a role, what I am really doing is living up to others' external expectations; this can prevent me from "Being" me. When I listen to other persons' problems, such as an irritable employee or someone I am counseling, or even visiting a sick friend, I am being drained of emotional energy. This is the consequence of the necessity of Doing things to live, and of Having responsibilities.

Additionally we found that in the same way Doing and Having are split up into components of Work and Maintenance; we needed to split Play up into play as Recreation and play as Play/Freesence. As work relates to Doing, so Play is to "Being." Becoming as we have said is the consequence of the right positive relationship between the two.

Play basically is a non-duty obligation activity which has no particular productive outcome that is necessarily planned. Creativity is often very productive, but what is created is much more often a surprise. Work on the other hand is the opposite, and is characterized by duty, obligation and necessary specific productive outcomes, such as my finishing this book. For the reader who wishes to pursue this further I have written more extensively on this in other publications (Hall, 1973, 1982).

Play/Freesence was a word that we invented 15 years ago to convey the old Greek idea of leisure. Freesence is Free-essence. The concept is that it is a high form of play that takes as many skills as one's professional work. Examples are sailing, contemplation as an ascetical discipline and photography.

The basic idea is that of detachment and the religious understanding *see Simplicity and Spiritual* of poverty explored in the last chapter—namely that as one balances *Growth, chapter 6* the play or Being areas with the stress of the Work or the Doing and Having areas, so one becomes detached, and Being and Becoming are set in motion. This is the alteration of Deep Structures.

Returning to the Diagram we see that when persons become over worked, or over identified with their work, their role, or their ownership of anything, the Doing aspect becomes out of balance and narcissism returns once again, in a new form of possession called Having. We talk about it this strongly because at this level the very "Being" of a person is actually negated.

On the other hand when the work is in balance with the kind of quality play we have mentioned, the person is spiritually Detached from having to own and have anything, and the Being side is released, and experienced as liberation, creativity and—in religious terms—resurrection.

Six years ago when we took the list of 125 values we found that we could easily categorize them into Work or Doing values such as Work/Confidence or Administration, Maintenance values such as Security or Health, and Play values such as Play, Art and Intimacy. This was built into our computerized value inventories. The information that it yielded has been helpful to hundreds of persons since then.

Basically what we discovered was that when a person's values priorities did not reflect a sound work/play balance, his or her life was predictably stressful. We also found that the balance is different for everyone, but that there were limits for everyone. We found that when the percentage of values chosen and prioritized by persons in the work and maintenance area exceeded the play value by more than 20%, people would most often complain of stress.

In real numbers we used another instrument called the IF-System to actually measure the hours of time spent in these areas over a 10 day period. We found that when persons had less than 2.5 hours of play a day over an average of 10 days not only were they stressed, but the Play/Freesence area became non-active. This in turn affected their ability to be creative at work or at home. The average of 2.5 hours implies that it could have been zero some days and very significant on other days, such as a weekend or a day off.

We also discovered that the Play/Freesence area is something that does not occur until adulthood, unless the person is functioning with a priority on the values within Cycles Four through Seven. When this is the case we find that when a man or a woman had less than 3.5 hours of Play/Freesence a day his or her ability for intimacy, creativity and meaning making significantly diminished. In other words detachment that enables the balance of time at work and play to occur in a harmonious manner enhances the Deep Structure of "Being" and quality "Becoming." Critical to the existential position is the place that anxiety plays in a person's "Becoming" and how this relates to the value of life, and to value choices that one makes in order to create a life that is meaningful.[4] Again time and how we understand it is at the center. But before time is the condition that stands behind all the deep structures called Contingency.

CONTINGENCY, TIME, ANXIETY AND GROWTH

Persons are born into the world as finite human beings. That is each is born with natural limitations. The primary and most basic limitation is that we are born into physical bodies which will eventually stop functioning. Additionally we may become ill at some point and risk death. We can be killed by a range of natural disasters. In order to grow and survive we have to make choices and plan, and we have to act on those choices in order for our plans to come to fruition. But the reality is that as many times as we might succeed in what we are doing, we also have the potential for failing. This whole state of affairs is called the state of "Contingency."

Within the existential framework Anxiety is caused, or is the natural consequence of our consciousness about this state called "Contingency." Life and staying alive is "contingent" upon many things from being fed, to not becoming ill, to not being hit by a car or truck when I am looking the other way. Contingency is the initial and beginning state of every "Being" who is born aware of his or her vulnerability and the inevitable fact of his or her eventual bodily death.[5] DIAGRAM VII.2 will help to explain this reality further.

160

ANXIETY AND CHOICE

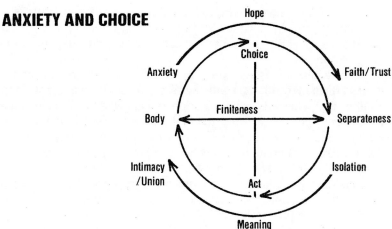

The Diagram extends this concept of "Contingency" by pointing out its natural expression through the person as he or she tries to live and express himself or herself in the world. First we are born in a physical form (Body) and have to cope with loneliness (Separateness). This introduces us to a natural state of Anxiety with which we have to cope through the choices we make, and how we act on those choices. When we make choices with courage, by having Faith and Trust in ourselves and others, we experience Hope, and overcome our feelings of Isolation and Separateness. This is experienced as Meaning making with the promise of Intimacy and Union with others and even with God.

Modern writers such as Yalom, Bugental, May, Koestenbaum and my own earlier works treat this material in detail for the interested reader.[6] I will only make a few comments with reference to the development of the Self, from the existential point of view, as compared to our previous discussion.

see The Inner Connection, chapter 2; The Self, Interim Reflection; and Body Politics, chapter 3

The Self as we have previously talked about it transcends sexuality in that it is more than a physical reality. On the other hand any human growth process is initiated by our experience of the body—that is, simple reality, as the Diagram indicates. This experience develops a little differently for men than for women as we noted earlier. This means that we are all vulnerable when we are born into the world.

It is this vulnerability that causes the normal feeling of anxiety. The dynamic side of this approach, the becoming side, is that the anxiety faces us with the necessity of having to choose life, or choose death. That is, every choice brings us isolation and separation, if it is a poor choice, and care and comfort in our early years if we make other kinds of choices.

From the existential viewpoint this choice is limited by the environment and the particular set of contingencies that I am born into. From a developmental perspective this is another clear reason why development through the Cycles occurs—it is a part of the very make up of our being human.

Choice as the Diagram indicates is not the same thing as Act. Choice here is an activity of the imagination whereby the person is able to

161

imagine various alternatives about the future. If, for example, I am graduating from high school and considering career options, what I am able to consider relative to my future is going to depend on my imagination.

If I have had successful experiences in the past that have been positively affirmed by others, I will have some recognition of my skills and abilities that will feed my imagination and allow me to fantasize about a number of possible futures that I might consider. On the other hand if I have had several negative experiences, and a low sense of my own Self Worth, my imagination may be negative, and not able to generate any positive dreams for the future.

Act is simply choosing one option and acting upon it. For some people just thinking about alternatives is very anxiety provoking. For others that is a simple matter, but they get anxious at the point of doing something about it. This is particularly true if one's ability in the past to make productive choices and act on them has been very negative. For example I have counseled many students who have failed an examination in a given subject, and were so anxious that when they went to take it for a second time, they were unable to remember anything. They were unable to act. On the other hand when persons can overcome this anxiety, and Act successfully, by writing the exam, they experience a new sense of themselves.

see Harrison and Prendergast, Appendix Meaning then comes to persons as they are able to make productive choices in their life that enhance cooperation rather than alienation from other people. In other words creativity and intimacy lie behind all meaning in human life. We create only by having the freedom to choose, and we gain perspective on reality only as we can relate to others with care and intimacy. Evelyn Underhill has pointed out in her study of the Mystics that for her the singular quality that makes human beings human is their ultimate ability, unlike all other creatures, to relate intimately to the Divine. She summarizes this idea with much that we have discussed above in the following challenging assertion.

"Over and over again—as Being and Becoming, as Eternity and Time, as Transcendence and Immanence, Reality and Appearance, the One and the Many—these two dominant ideas, demands, imperious instincts of man's self will appear; the warp and woof of his completed universe. On the one hand is his intuition of a remote, unchanging Somewhat calling him: on the other there is his longing for and a clear intuition of an intimate, adorable Somewhat companioning him. Man's true Real, his only adequate God, must be great enough to embrace this sublime paradox."[7]

We are now going to examine Time in more detail through a series of diagrams, illustrating its particular relationship to memory and imagination, anxiety, and guilt.

TIME, MEMORY AND IMAGINATION The Self as pure being-in-the-world is the center of a person's awareness, where all time and experience are in the present. As such the past is experienced as Memory and the future as Imagination. Imagination here is being used selectively to describe a future action. In fact Memory consists of stored images in the brain. Imagination here is

162

*At the center of the circle we
see the "Self" in the present
moment. For each of us as we
focus on the present moment,
we travel through time into
the past as we remember
things (memory), and we
enter into a number of
possible futures as we
imagine (imagination) the
future.*

used to connote the ability to develop new images that speculate on future possibilities for me, as illustrated in DIAGRAM VII.3.

Successful action in the past creates confidence for an imaginative awareness of creative alternatives which in turn generates possible new choices. When these choices are acted on with positive results in one's life this leads to an increased sense of hope and confidence about the future. Interpersonal cooperation and community occur rather than loneliness.

I remember that when my daughter was six years of age she was having a particularly difficult time with her friends. Her school work was unsatisfactory, and she was spending more time at home alone, which was not at all like her. She had additionally received a bicycle for her birthday some two weeks before, but it had not as yet been taken out of the house.

Finally I asked her if anything was bothering her. She replied "Nothing is the matter, but none of my friends like me!" "Why do you think that?" I replied. "Well, they all have bicycles and go everywhere on them, and I can't go with them." I reminded her that I had told her that I would teach her to ride the bicycle, but she had told me she wanted to wait for a week or so. Finally she admitted that she was afraid to try to ride, because she might not be able to learn, and then her friends really would think she was stupid.

The next day which was a Sunday, very early in the morning, when no one was around we went over to her school playground for a training session. She would ride and I would run beside her with my hand on the seat so that the bicycle would not tip. She would continually remonstrate that she would never be able to do it on her own, and that she was not going to try because she would fail. But I kept insisting that she get on the bicycle.

Finally, I told her that we were going to cycle down the playground and then turn and come back without stopping. "Only this time," I said, "I am going to hold you up from behind the bicycle where you can't see me." "You make sure that you hold on," she said. Well off we went. I ran along beside her as before, talking all the time, but halfway down the playground, holding my breath, I let go, but kept running and talking to her. "When do you want me to turn?" she said. "Whenever you want to," I replied. "You make the decision; after all you have been cycling without me for half of the playground!" At this point I ran past her. Her smile is something I will always remember. Her confidence grew so much that both her school work and her popularity with her friends changed overnight.

For the existentialist the power to act and create one's own life is critical to what reality is all about. A philosopher journalist like Jean-Paul Sartre felt that one literally did not exist until one had made a choice and acted on it.[7a] Acting on a choice that is successful empowers a person to be confident not only in his or her future choices but in his or her interpersonal interactions, as did my daughter in the above story. Choosing is the literal creation of Beingness by each of us.

ANXIETY AND THE DIMINISHED SELF

What happens when the choices that we make turn out to have negative consequences, or what happens if the environment is restrictive and does not allow us the freedom we need to choose in the first place? DIAGRAM VII.4, will take us further into an examination of these questions.

When someone evaluates a past action as a failure feelings of shame and guilt are a natural consequence. This evokes negative mental images concerning future choices, which further results in anxiety. Anxiety, then, is felt as apprehension about the future. The final consequences is that both the guilt and the anxiety lead to inertia and increased inability to make choices in the present.

One writer, Anton Boison, who was the father of modern Pastoral Counseling, noted that the failure to act is the key to all Human and

Diagram 7:4
THE SELF (MYSELF) UNDER ATTACK
The diagram shows the Self in the middle of time as it considers a past failure in its memory. When this happens we have negative images about our ability to make productive choices (in the future). We feel less valuable and often isolated as a consequence.

ANXIETY & THE DIMINISHED SELF

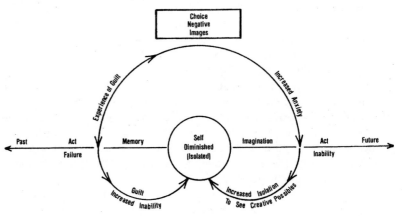

164

Spiritual growth. He notes that the term "personal failure" for him denoted a "sense of inner disharmony which extends from the 'divine discontent' which is a pre-condition of effort and of growth, to enable the person to compensate for the possibility of the loss of that which makes life worth living to the individual."[8]

Clearly the anxiety that occurs from the need to make right choices in our lives and to create something for ourselves in the world, as well as simply exist, is normal, and a part of everyone's makeup.

Since we can never make perfect choices because life is so full of contingencies, failure is always inevitable, and so therefore is its natural consequence Guilt. What Boison is indicating is that these feelings are *see Manna and Taboo,* what motivate persons to change. This is all a part of what we have *chapter 4 and Contingency,* termed earlier in the book the "Manna" side of life. Here anxiety and *chapter 7* guilt are a normal part of everyday living.

My daughter in the above example was actually feeling guilty and anxious about rejection from her friends, before she learned to ride her bicycle. In fact, however, she was not rejected by them; rather she had, in her perception, failed by not learning to ride her bicycle. My point is that these are all natural feelings and a part of what motivates us to be responsible, to risk and to live.

What we want to investigate now is the experience of exaggerated anxiety and guilt as a part of what we have continually referred to as the "Taboo" side of our nature. What happens when a person makes a choice that leads to circumstances that threaten his or her whole meaning system, or in Boison's terms, that which makes life worth living? We will begin with a concrete example.

John was a 30 year old man who had been married to Margery for **GUILT,** seven years. They were good friends with another couple of approx- **ANXIETY** imately the same age. They all went to a local church together, usually **AND THE** to the Eucharist each Sunday, and had lunch together afterward. John **DEMONIC** was attracted to the other man's wife Joyce, but never ever mentioned **SIDE** it, feeling that such attraction was natural. One day Joyce's husband **OF FAITH** George was killed in a car accident, in a city some three hundred miles away.

John agreed to take Joyce up to the mortuary where her husband was and help with the funeral arrangements. Margery stayed at home and looked after both sets of children while they were gone, which was approximately three days, over a weekend.

After the funeral John and Joyce stayed overnight in a local hotel, and in the mutual grief they both had a few too many drinks, and ended up sleeping together, and comforting each other physically. John came to see me a week later in a deep depression about what he had done. He had told his wife and she was making life miserable for him. His wife blamed him and felt that he had taken advantage of a friend at a time of tragic loss.

John's depression was increasing to the point that he was missing several days of work, and literally beginning to become disfunctional, just sitting in a chair at home for long periods of time without moving.

After several weeks of counseling the following came to light. John believed very much in marriage, and loved his wife. He felt that Intimacy and Loyalty were the two values that were more important to him than anything. Margery agreed. Margery's point, and he agreed with this, was that they had taken life vows together in church for better or for worse, and therefore divorce was out of the question. But in fact John had broken the vows. They appeared deadlocked and trapped in their own and each other's anger.

All that she would say for the first two sessions was: "I cannot believe you could do this to me; maybe it is my turn now?" The conclusion was a shouting match and more depression on John's part. There was no movement until one day I suggested that the real problem was not adultery on John's part but idolatry on both of their parts! DIAGRAM VII.5, which is an extension of the Diagram above, will help us to understand the situation further.

In the Diagram it is a perceived failure that sets everything into motion. Any Failure is in the Past, since it has already been acted on. This is Boison's feeling of disharmony or "Divine discontent." But this was not a natural discontent, as in the case of my daughter's growing problem, but something much deeper and potentially destructive. The smaller half circle in the middle of the Diagram is the natural experience of day to day failure, anxiety and guilt. The wider half circle that overarches this is the exaggerated or "demonic" experience of failure. The initiating act of failure, in this case John's physical experience with Margery after the funeral, challenged John and Margery's joint Valued Faith Center. Their faith in each other was based on the values of Family, Intimacy and Loyalty.

I accused them of idolatry. What idolatry means is simply that a narrow set of values or even an object like a car or a job is given ultimate significance; it is as if it is turned into a God. A Valued Faith Center is

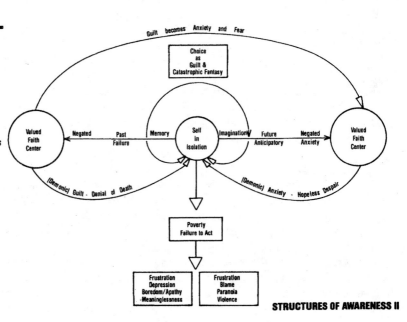

Diagram 7:5
FAITH AND THE DEMONIC SIDE
Once again we see the self (myself) in the center circle traveling into the past by remembering a failure—this time it involves acting against those values I hold as very important priorities in my life. I move against my faith Center causing exaggerated (Demonic) anxiety and guilt.

STRUCTURES OF AWARENESS II

166

a cluster of values that contains the total source of the person's meaning. Therefore when one's Faith Center cannot deal with a situation, creating alienation and isolation rather than meaningful community, it is simply inadequate. What any religion tries to do is to point to what the minimum adequate value system is that constitutes a faith center.

In the Diagram Poverty or the inability to act is the ultimate conse- see *Simplicity and Spiritual Growth, chapter 6* quence of the experience of the failure of idolatry or the apparent breakdown on one's value center. Poverty here is demonic or destructive poverty. What the Diagram is illustrating is what occurs when a person experiences a failure in his or her life. But unlike our earlier Diagram the failure here is of one's central value system.

In the Christian configuration, the Faith Center must be a cluster of values that brings about reconcilliation or forgiveness no matter what the circumstance. Since this did not occur their value system was inadequate. As it turned out the critical missing value was Limitation/ Celebration, or the ability to realize we are never perfect, and that we can keep learning from our mistakes no matter how poor the mistakes.

Where did John's depression come from? Guilt, anxiety and fear which are the consequence of the rejection of a valued faith center become exaggerated or demonic when the values under attack are central to the meaning system of the person, or in this case the couple.

When this happens the guilt is further exacerbated by fear of what will happen and denial. This is the root of the "Taboo" area—denial. John at first was unwilling to admit that he was really at fault. His wife was unwilling to admit anybody can be vulnerable in a situation such as this. But underlying all of this was the fact that as far as John was concerned he had acted against his own value system. Doing this is the act of failure that leads to the experience of Guilt. Guilt always occurs when I act on values that I feel contravene the value priorities I feel are sacred. In the early Cycles of Development (1–3) these values often reside outside of myself, so that I feel guilty when I do not come up to others' expectations, such as those of my parents, or in this case my wife.

Later on in Cycles 4–7 it is the breaking of personally owned values that are the cause of guilt. Now guilt automatically produces the feeling of anxiety, which is fear of the future, a fear of what will happen to me because of what I have done. Persons in this state will talk about being a total failure, and often start thinking about death and serious illness occurring to them, as an unconscious extension of their guilt and anxiety.

As present anxiety expands into anticipatory anxiety, one becomes anxious about anxiety itself. When this happens one's future valued faith center appears meaningless and non-existent. Despair and hopelessness are all pervasive. When this happens the imagination becomes catastrophic and all future choices appear negative.

John recognized that he had broken the rules, contravening his own ultimate values so guilt followed, plus the anxiety of what the consequences might be. This can cause very severe anxiety which we call demonic anxiety. When this happens the stored images constituting memory begin to reshape the imaginal capacity of the person so that it becomes catastrophic. In other words all the images that are generated are negative. In mental health terms this is the basis of psychosis and neurosis. The consequence is that the future is negated and all hope with it—this is possession at its worst. Its root cause is an inadequate Faith Center, and its behavioral consequence is the inability to make choices in the present.

We call this condition Poverty. It is the inability to act in productive ways. We acknowledge that this may not always be self induced. It could be a social condition imposed upon a person in which productive choices in such matters as employment are impossible, invoking the same process, destroying one's Faith Center, and causing profound feelings of anxiety and guilt.

In the present moment the person is unable to act and feels angry and frustrated. A prolonged experience can then lead to feelings of depression, boredom, apathy and even total meaninglessness as the Self becomes more and more isolated.

When the reality of poverty is imposed socially, for example through economic poverty, then self-blame, paranoia and even violence may follow. At the personal level such feelings may result from an inadequate Faith Center whose values cannot transcend the failure, making forgiveness and alleviation of the guilt and anxiety impossible. This would be the condition of idolatry, or giving exaggerated impor-. tance to a set of finite values. What about the other side of this dismal picture? For this we need to look at Faith and time in a different light.

STRUCTURES OF AWARENESS: VALUES, FAITH AND TIME
see Conclusion, chapter 1

Behaviorally a value is an important priority in my life that I choose and act on (see Chapter I). It becomes clear that existentialism see itself as primarily concerned about values. Its basic premise is that we choose and create our own lives, and it is in the choosing that we create the value priorities that we live by.

Secondly existentialism claims to bridge the subjective/objective chasm created by traditional psychology and much of traditional philosophy. This too can be put in value terms. Values theory was traditionally set into two camps that are still very evident in some religious and educational circles.

The objective camp is usually very rational and cognitive in orientation and states basically that values are a set of norms and rules that are given, that we must live by. When I mention values in a seminar, someone will usually ask me what values I am talking about. Do I mean Christian values, or liberal values, or democratic values? The concept is that there are a set of givens that everyone must agree to, and they are the values everyone should abide by, such as the Ten Commandments.

In the subjective camp as in some modern psychology, the orientation is exactly opposite. Values are the consequences of my choices and my own personal and private priorities. In this extreme all values are relative and related to individual choice.

The existential position, and in this case the opinion of this author, is not one or the other. Such a split is false—values are priorities that are inherently given, in that they potentially exist in all persons. All *see Value Lists and* 125 values are potentially present in each of us as possibilities. Also it *Definitions, Appendix* is obviously true that history and the traditions of ethics and religion can point in a constructive way to life giving, rather than destructive choices that should be made in anyone's life.

On the other hand modern psychology and spirituality confirm that each person needs to choose certain value priorities at given points in his or her life if creative growth is to occur. It is essential, for example, for a person to have chosen and internalized the values of Security and Self Worth at given stages in his or her life. At other levels integrated persons must elect by conscience, using their intelligence to decide what values they are going to live by, and in what priority order. With all this in mind let us look at the relationship between values and our Centers of Faith.

James Fowler has very adequately presented the concept of Faith as **VALUES AND** something that is intrinsic to everyone's life no matter what his or her **FAITH** religious or philosophical orientation. For Fowler *Faith is a shared center of values and power around which we tell our stories.*[9] He further adds that our Faith alters depending on the Cycle of Development that we are in. What does this all mean?

Very often persons confuse values and faith with a credal belief system. But to say one believes in God or the Virginity of the Virgin Mary is not the same as having Faith. It is the same parts and whole problem we spoke about earlier. First of all Faith is faith in someone. It is always *see Defining the Corporate* relational. Faith is not belief in a set of rules or norms, but an act of *Culture, chapter 10* trust or allegiance to someone. To have Faith in God means to have a personal living relationship with him. The Creeds, rules and norms that are insisted on are the external expression of the values that we hold in common—they constitute an essential part of our covenant together.

Now I can say I put my faith or trust in the President, or in my wife. That means that I trust they are going to be faithful to me, and I am going to trust them to make some decisions that affect my life. That is I trust them because I have a covenant relationship, a commitment relationship with them. What this means is that we have a common set or cluster of values that we mutually believe in that enables us to trust each other—that is what the basis of Faith is all about.

Some people are going to want to ask what this has to do with religious faith? Surely Faith is not a secular issue that has nothing to do with religion? Of course not. The connection is that in modern western religion such as Christianity and Judaism and even Islam, God is a person to whom one relates and whom one trusts and with whom one has a covenant relationship. Faith, then, is the values that stand behind the covenant relationship that one has with another person or with God. To believe in Jesus Christ really means to be energized by the same value clusters that he was energized by, as an aspect of our personal relationship to him.

How do we know it is really a Faith experience? We know because this kind of value center empowers and stimulates us to action. It also becomes the center of our story telling. Basically Faith in the religious sense is being stimulated by values that are ultimate for us. They are the most important thing in our lives.

Take for example a young couple who are about to get married. They are excited about the wedding next Saturday, and can talk about nothing else, other than the house they are going to buy, and the exciting things they are going to do on their honeymoon. All their stories are about their wedding and their marriage. The values have to do with Care, Intimacy, Family, Education and Successful Work. At this point these are their ultimate values, not God or religion—this is where their story-telling is, and where they are empowered and excited. This is their faith. Faith, then, is always triadic as shown here.[10]

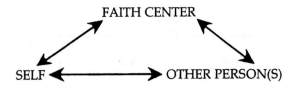

FAITH CENTER

SELF ←——————→ OTHER PERSON(S)

The young couple are getting married in a common faith context. The Self of the young woman or of the young man relates to the partner through a common Faith Center—that is a common set of values and stories. This brings us to a very critical question: *Given life is full of Contingency and difficult choices that we all have to make, what values must we choose that will guarantee to help us and bring us through any difficulties that we might encounter?* DIAGRAM VII.6 will begin to ground all this for us.

This is an extension of DIAGRAM VII.3. The Self stands in the present with Memory in the past and Imagination as the future, as in the other diagrams. Meaningful and creative choices require that the per-

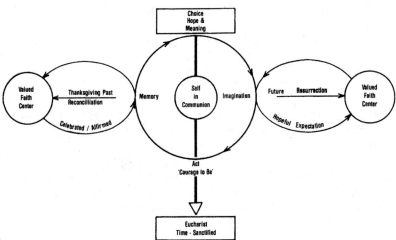

Diagram 7:6
THE SELF IN COMMUNION AND HARMONY WITH THE WORLD
Again the Self is at the center traveling into the past and into the future. Confronted by any failure or disappointment, one feels at one and in harmony with life when one's Faith Center— one's values—are adequate. The future becomes transformed and we experience a new aliveness— a resurrection.

170

son have the "courage to be" or to act in the face of one's natural experience of anxiety. When this occurs the person finds himself or herself in communion rather than in isolation from others. This is the basic tenet of Faith, namely, that it is a communal experience as in the triadic effect above.

In the case of John and Margery the real Faith element was their willingness and ability to stay in relationship and work things out. The value of Loyalty was an essential part of this. Secondly the value of Limitation/Acceptance, or acceptance of each other's vulnerability, was what caused the final healing.

Their Faith Center only became an Ultimate Faith Center when they were able to see these values come to fruition. For when this happened they were able to let go of their disappointment and imposition of guilt and allow John to experience forgiveness, and each of them to experience reconciliation.[11]

When one's Faith Center contains values that enable any difficult event in one's life or any failure to be transcended, then thanksgiving and reconciliation can occur. In the Diagram this is experienced as Celebration as the persons involved feel affirmed through the forgiveness. This then moves into the future, not as anxiety, but as Hopeful Expectation, as the imagination is developed positively rather than catastrophically. The future is renewed, as the value center becomes a real and ultimate center of faith as it did for John and Margery. The consequence was a piece of resurrection for them as they felt new life come into their marriage.

Let us return for a moment to Diagram VII.6. What the Diagram illustrates is that when we are able to continue to celebrate our limitations and feel affirmed, catastrophic images are recreated into positive images. This is at the heart of the Genesis Effect. Once again the person **THE RESURRECTION SIDE** is able to make hopeful choices as the demonic anxiety is transformed into optimistic expectation—an experience of resurrection.

The initiation point is Failure, but behind this lies the existential condition of Human Limitation. We are limited by the very environments we are born into, the opportunities available to us, our intelligence and physical health and so on. Given all this it is an easy thing to put the blame for all our problems on these external factors, as John and Margery initially tried to do. This is the root of all evil—denial.

From the religious perspective, and particularly the Christian one, Christ confronted all these external contingencies and showed that even these could be overcome. He confronted all the political, social and religious ills of his day, and was as a consequence confronted with the ultimate human limitation—the death of the body. The message of his death and bodily resurrection was the defeat of the final limitation—death itself. But the far deeper message was that "resurrection" is a life principle that goes on every day in our lives until the day we face physical death as he did.

In the Eucharist, the Christian celebrates weekly through a ritual of breaking of bread and sharing in a common cup of wine, the remembrance of Christ's last meal with his friends, which was followed by his death through crucifixtion the following day, his burial and finally the stories of his bodily "Resurrection."

The original Jewish concept of remembrance in this ritualized way is that when the community does this, God becomes transcendentally and really present. That is, as we remember his great acts such as Resurrection, he who is not limited by linear time (T1) becomes present to us by transcending the space/time continuum (T2.) This whole process, then, may be seen as the Sanctification of Time through the forgiveness of past acts, and the conversion of anxiety about the future into hopefulness.

The ritual of the Eucharist is focally symbolic of the Christian's ongoing sacramental life, where Christ overcomes our failures and brings about reconciliation for all persons. This then moves into the future as Resurrection and Hopeful Expectation, on a daily basis.

There was a resurrection side for John, Margery and Joyce although it was a very delicate matter. First of all John and Margery relooked at their values and added the dimension of limitation which they celebrated, by admitting what had happened. They then talked jointly about it with Joyce.

The three then covenanted to keep their feelings out in the open to avoid compromising situations. John and Margery interestingly made a covenant together in church, that if they did commit an indiscretion they would tell the other person about it immediately, and not allow it to destroy or harm the love they had together. This was in effect adding the value of Limitation/Celebration to their Faith Center—it was for them the essential reconciliation and resurrecting component that had been missing.

THE OSCILLATION EFFECT

We have now looked in depth at two major ways of viewing time: time as linear (T1) in the Developmental models, and time as relative (T2) as in the Existential and Mystical models. Each seems to have its own truth, each giving rise to unique and useful information not accessible by the other.

It is as if one operates more on the vertical plane of Becoming through time within the space/time continuum, while the other emphasizes Beingness and transcends and stands outside of linear time. They are the vertical and horizontal planes of what overall constitutes reality, which is a whole.

see The Information Age, chapter 2 For us limited human beings it is difficult to see the whole, and we needfully have to revert back to each model at different times in order to gather the information that each can uniquely give us. This the paradox that is One single reality. We call this backward and forward action of retrieving information *The Oscillation Effect*.

The philosopher Rousseau in a mystical experience noted that he suddenly realized that the continuity of time is in effect a series of minute individual moments.[11a] Both the continuity and the deep structure of the moment are aspects of reality.

The existential view of Faith and Ethics as an essential Faith Center

172

that each person needs is an invaluable insight that carries over into many areas of life. For example what are the essential values needed to maintain a faithful marriage? What are the essential values needed by priests or counselors for them to carry out their task in life under any contingencies? What are the bottom line values for an Executive, a Surgeon or a Lawyer?

Such information gives the professional counselor or anyone who is interested access to the relationship between their values, anxiety and creativity that the developmental approach does not have access to.

On the other hand Faith is undoubtedly developmental as we have already illustrated in the last several chapters. The fact that there are stages of development gives rise to information about the changing nature of a person's values and Faith Center at different times in his or her life. This is information not accessible to the purely existential approach.

The following represents conclusions relative to the various integrations that are possible from all the chapters in PART II of the book on Personal Genesis.

PERSONAL GENESIS: CONCLUSIONS AND INTEGRATIONS

The existential position leads us to the following discernment question: what values and priorities do I need to live my life by to insure a meaningful existence no matter what contingencies I will encounter? The developmental approach poses the question: what tasks do I need to complete—what values do I need to actualize that will insure that my maximum potential as a gifted person can be fulfilled as I grow and mature through the different stages of my life?

1. INTEGRATIONS IN FAITH AND DEVELOPMENT

The Mystics pose the additional religious question: how do I discern how my gifts, potentials and inherent values fit into the overall plan of God's creation—what is my moral and ethical obligation as a human being at this particular point in history? Let us look at these issues. When we look at the triangulation of everyday faith we can see that these approaches need not be in conflict. DIAGRAM VII.7. represents a person's growing in consciousness, as we outlined in chapters III, IV and V. At any given Cycle of Development a person is living by a given Faith Center. That is, he or she is energized by a certain cluster of values which are priorities at at a given Cycle.

In the picture the person in the middle is sharing his or her values with other persons—this is the interpersonal nature of a Faith Center. They are values that I share with others, that "We" are empowered by, and around which we tell our stories. As the Diagram indicates, such a value cluster could enable me to grow or to regress.

The Diagram indicates the process by which persons transcend their development from Cycle to Cycle. Briefly as the persons integrate their values between the stages they become aware of new future possibilities. In the existential mode this would be as follows: as their imagi-

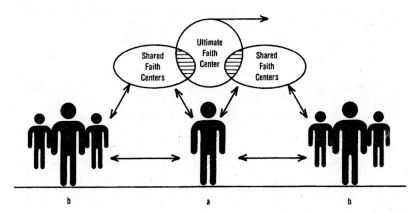

nation and hopeful expectations of the future are increased, they have increased internal images of what is possible, and each image has its own values counterpart, and its own skills requirements.

When this growth in consciousness occurs there is an internal rewriting of one's past images of Faith. Developmentally the past is simply viewed differently. But it is only with the aid of the existential point of view that we can appreciate what happens.

Since in its perspective all time is in the "Now" and the past is memory as stored images, these internal images are actually expanded in quality and information, so that one's whole past is actually rewritten. Past sins and failures are, or can be, literally wiped clean. The overall effect is a new consciousness and a new Faith orientation.

The piece that is still missing is the Ultimate Faith Center in the Diagram. This is meant to imply a cluster of values that in fact causes integrated development. In existential terms it is a value cluster that addresses any of life contingencies, as illustrated in the example of John, Joyce and Margery.

That is to say a forward movement in the Cycles implies that at some level this Ultimate Faith Center is at work encouraging a person to grow and live in the world in an entirely different manner than before. What has not been addressed, and is not addressed by Fowler in his *Stages of Faith*, is the question of evil, and the fact that an Ultimate Faith Center could move a person toward destruction rather than growth.

2. VALUES, CENTERS OF FAITH AND THE OSCILLATION EFFECT

We have noted in these chapters that values are the mediators of the Genesis Effect, and stand behind the world views and leadership styles of each of the Cycles of Development. The instrumentation that we developed and tested out with over a thousand persons was designed to enable a person to see where his or her center of energy was, or what his or her Choice area was relative to a particular Cycle of Development. This of course was based on the idea that persons develop for the most part in a linear way as they grow older with time. But we also discovered a contradiction!

By taking all the values that a person chose, no matter what the

174

Cycle of Development, and calculating their mathematical value based on how many times a person chose a value, we were able to see what the priority order of the Goals and Objectives were. What one would expect to find is that a person's top priorities were from one's Cycle of Development, which after all is where one's focus of energy is. And predictably this was the case most of the time. But very often, particularly when a person was in a change or crisis period, this was not the case.

We found that sometimes people transcended ordinary development, or would regress suddenly. The Oscillation Effect can help to explain how this occurs. Bill was an executive with a profile that had most of his values in the Intrapersonal Cycle 4. This is the Cycle that emphasizes work as Service, and stresses personal development through values like Self Actualization, Autonomy, Health and Empathy. His first six values (125 value list in the Appendix) in the Goal area and his first five values in the Means Objective area were as follows. These are not listed in priority order and are not therefore numbered.

Goals	Means
Self Interest/Control	Safety/Survival
Security	Economics/Profit
Self Worth	Limitation/Acceptance
Service/Vocation	Search/Meaning
Human Dignity	Limitation/Celebration
Contemplation	

When I first saw him he was very stressed, and obsessed with making money in Real Estate Development. The consequence was a minor heart attack which forced him to reconsider his lifestyle. He did in fact make a radical lifestyle change which included a change of job and an entirely different attitude toward people and his religion. Diagram VII.8 illustrates the two situations, both from the same overall set of values and both indicating Cycle Four on his profile.

The figure in the middle is Bill. The two clusters represent his center of shared values or Faith Center. In the first cluster the values are prioritized primarily out of the first Phase of Development up until Phase IIA and illustrate a very narcissistic orientation. They are all from the top of the above value list. At the time he was very stressed because of problems with his business, and very authoritarian in the way he related to his employees, his wife and two teenagers.

The Diagram shows him relating to individuals and buildings, through his faith orientation. Now a part of his stress was the fact that he felt that he was not living the values he believed in. The consequence was guilt and anxiety leading to physical stress and a minor heart attack. He also felt during this period that he had no power over his life. Everything was controlled from the outside through the pressure of his business.

In the second cluster the same values are operating, but the ones

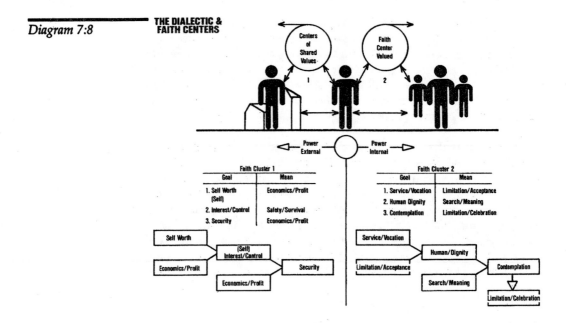

illustrated are now the values from the bottom of our list. These are now at the top of the priority list beginning with Service and Limitation/Acceptance. The values from the first cluster are not shown; if they were, they would appear at the bottom in the second cluster.

These show Bill after the heart attack having for the first time in his life chosen a job that he liked, which was to manage a Farm that he had owned for years, and had been in the family for two generations. For him this was his first love and what he truly felt called to as a life vocation. It was Service/Vocation, but it paid less money.

He had to accept the limitations of less money and a new monitoring of his health through diet and exercise—the consequence was a new sense of Human Dignity. Working with the earth was a matter of ecology for him, and related to his whole view of creation—it was meaningful and consequented in a serious contemplative attitude toward life in general. He felt that God was calling him to what he was doing through the very Celebration of his Limitations.

Bill's values from a strictly developmental point of view appeared according to our instrumentation in Cycle 4, but on the other hand he was able to ignore this and prioritize his values so as to chart whatever lifestyle he wanted, which is the existentialist's dream. What he chose in the first place was to regress to the first or second Cycle, and he almost died in the process. Confronted with death and not denying his condition, he radically changed his values, which meant a total change in behavior and skills. His attitude towards himself and his family changed and he started living at a fourth or fifth Cycle of Development.

Admittedly such an experience is rare, but clearly it is possible. In fact history is replete with such examples. Bernard of Clairvaux was a

176

nobleman's son who left home and became a Benedictine monk who gave counsel to the great Kings of twelfth century Europe. Gandhi was a graduate from a London Law school ready to practice in south Africa, and was thrown off of a train because he was dark skinned. Overnight he converted from law as a vocation to global justice as his life work. Alain Gerbault, one of the world's first circumnavigators, was a Davis Cup Tennis champion in the 1920's who left French society to live out his life alone on his 39 foot cutter the Firecrest. He died in French Polynesia after confronting the local governor and attempting to defend the rights of the local native population.[12]

Classically the name for such a sustained value alteration, a rearranging of one's priorities, is called Conversion. Many would object to me using the word Conversion this way, stating that it is only applicable to a religious experience that causes sustained behavioral change.

A. Minimal development and integration into one's life, especially in the first two Phases of Development of the goal area values, such as Self Preservation, Security, Family and Self Worth, Work and Self Confidence.

B. Minimal Integration of the four skills, so that a sound rather than a distorted conscience is developed.

C. The development of productive values dialectics as Faith Centers at each cycle to insure higher levels of integrated development, rather than a movement toward the various forms of narcissism possible at each Cycle.

D. Minimal appropriate balance of Being, Doing and Becoming as reflected through the balance of Work and Play in a person's life. This should be effected through a process of detachment reflected in the Work/Play activities.

E. Minimal attention to the balance between the masculine and feminine in one's life, with sufficient awareness of the difference between male and female psychology.

F. Recognition of the unity of the subject/object relationship in each and every value component, and that a split between these two is false and destructive. That is every value has the two dimensions of its applicability to one's self and its applicability to others.

Care/Nurture implies the willingness to be cared for, but also the necessity to also care for and nurture others. This is especially applicable in the justice/human dignity areas. Justice for one's self must also be reflected in an active stance toward justice issues in one's life.

MANNA DIMENSIONS NEEDED FOR PERSONAL GROWTH
see Manna and Taboo, chapter 4 and Skills throughout chapter 5

I would agree but add that the basis of a religious experience, when it is truly that, is the reorientation toward higher levels of integration on the part of the person by consciously choosing and committing himself or herself to a new set of value priorities.

Whenever this happens Conversion is in effect. Others like James Fowler feel that a case can be made that conversion occurs at each and every stage of development in a person's life, since people are in fact changing their values when they do this.[12a]

I think this is a valid point of view, but this would suggest that psychological growth and spiritual integration are the same process or at least very similar. As we saw in the Onion Effect in the last chapter this is not the case. Conversion as I have explained it is only applied to the integrated development of a person which brings us to our next point.

3. INTEGRATED DEVELOPMENT: MANNA, TABOO AND TRANSFORMATION

Finally, integrated development, which is the development of the human to his or her potential heights, is a process that involves the continual integration of the inner world of the psyche/soul with the outer world of human endeavor and external expectation.

As such each Cycle of Development is of itself its own expression of a Deep Structure which needs minimal integration for the person to grow in a healthy manner. This includes the Manna and Taboo dimensions at each of the Cycles. The Manna dimension is the positive growth factors that are required for minimal integrated development.

The Taboo component is equally important and basically involves the pursuit of self knowledge. It includes the components listed with each of the Cycles, but is particularly emphasized in Cycle four and following.

see Conclusions, chapter 10

In conclusion the following is a list of assumptions needed to be considered for the maximixing of personal creative and spiritual development:

-That life needs to be lived to the "hilt" and that death be placed in perspective as but one of its natural components, so that life lived fully produces resurrection and re-creation for everyone you touch.

-That we need to live faithfully committed to our chosen values, risking and learning from our necessary mistakes and to learn what faith really is.

-That, no matter how hurtful, we must persist in discovering creative ways to enhance interpersonal exchange.

-That it is necessary to treasure rather than fear the psyche through feedom of expression, rather than a system of controls.

TABOO DIMENSIONS NEEDED FOR PERSONAL GROWTH

A. The ability to face one's particular physical and emotional limitations at different stages in one's life cycle.

B. The ability to face contingency factors in one's life through the development of realism and pain tolerance, by being able to cope with anxiety and guilt, converting catastrophic images into ones of hopeful expectation.

178

C. The ability to discover ways of discovering adequate centers of value and faith to deal with all of life's contingencies in both the personal and the professional arenas of one's life. This would include investigating global and religious value systems in a responsible manner.

D. The ability to insure the proper balance in one's life of work and play, and of the four skills, to avoid distortions in one's view of the world. At Cycle Four and following this would include assuring that one had minimal institutional and intimate support systems. This last point will be addressed again in PART III.

E. The ability to live a creative and resurrected life which requires constant willingness to face anxiety, avoid systems of denial, and make risk orientated choices that we act on, that inevitably will lead to failure at times, as well as success.

-That, in the final analysis, creativity is communal, and requires interdependent exchange and respect of all persons.
-That creativity is purposeful and is rooted in the Creator, and it is integral to life and meaning.
-That in the last analysis creativity is relational and is the consequence of the harmony of harmonies.

Having said all these things about human and spiritual development, we now have to say that in our experience this is only one half of the story. Almost all theories of human and spiritual development have avoided what we consider to be the interconnection between the human being and the institutional dimension of society. This final piece is what we call the *Corporate Genesis,* in the final part of the book, PART III.

Chapter 7:
The Unity of Time: Faith and the Oscillation Effect

1. Davies (1983), pp. 119–120. Time and space have the qualities of elasticity. Time-warp and space-warp are realities which render the present moment of great importance. In the present, I can remake my past and begin a creative future.
2. Fowler (1981), pp. 3–4.
2a. Koestenbaum (1978).
3. Underhill (1955), p. 29.
4. See Yalom (1980) on anxiety, freedom and responsibility and on the nature of guilt.
5. See Ryckman (1978), p. 355 where he discusses Rollo May's theories. May defines anxiety as a response "to the immanent threat of non-being," unlike Freud who reduced it to an "unpleasant feeling" resulting from a conflict within. Yalom (1980) also relates anxiety to an increasing consciousness of contingency.

179

6. Hall (1973, 1976, & 1982), Yalom (1980), Bugental (1965 & 1976), May (1977), and Koestenbaum (1978).

7. Underhill (1955), p. 41.

7a. Sartre (1953).

8. Boison (1936), pp. 147–148.

9. Fowler (1981).

10. *Ibid.*, p. 33: "Lasting human associations at every level exhibit this triadic form, though often our covenants are tacit and taken for granted rather than explicit." The concept of a "Faith Center" is secular as well as religious.

11. The theological concept of "option fundamentale" approximates Fowler's concept of an ultimate faith center. In this framework sin in the "mortal" sense is a choice made contrary to a person's own faith center. Thus the significance of reconciliation and atonement (at-one-ment).

11a. Clark (1969), p.274.

12. Gerbault (1981).

12a. Fowler (1981).

PART III

The Corporate Genesis

We like to think that each of us possesses freedom individually. We are thus reluctant to give up a part of that freedom in order to create an integrated society. Durkheim offers the opposite view. He argues that freedom is the social creation of the body politic and that each of us draws his or her individual liberty from that social body.

William Ouchi[1]

Now the earth can certainly clasp me in her giant arms. She can swell me with her life, or take me back into her dust. But her enchantments can no longer do me harm, since she has become for me, over and above herself, the body of him which is and him who is coming. The divine milieu.

Teilhard de Chardin[2]

This third and last part of the book relates to our final discussion of the *Genesis Effect* which we began in chapter I. There we discussed this phenomenon as the circular effect of the human being's internal images on the external world of nature.

History is really the story of how the internal images of this strange creature with reflective consciousness have slowly tamed, sometimes desecrated the external environment by recreating it to suit himself or herself. These internal images monitored by the values inherent in language became the external form of modern civilization—its cities, its societies, its arts and sciences, its philosophies, its theologies, its values.

Spiritual development has always been seen in in the western traditions of Judaism and Christianity, and to some extent Islam, as rooted in community. That is Human and Spiritual growth is tied to the very nature and structure of society through the values that filter through to us from its institutions.

Specifically our institutions are value laden and affect how we work, how we feel and how we grow spiritually every day. Why? Because they are in fact projected images from someone's or some group's value and faith center—it is as simple as that. Consequently it is very important for us to know what those values and those influences are, not just to protect ourselves, but so that we can responsibly learn to create the kind of institutions that will enhance integrated Human and Spiritual development.

Do we have all the answers on how to do all these things? Absolutely not, but we do have information that can help us to make less mistakes. There are some things we can do, and some things we need to know about values and the Corporate Genesis that can be helpful.

The next four chapters, Boundary, Document, Retrieve and The Ethics of It All, are about some of the things we have learned about values from working and consulting with a wide range of institutions. The Institutions were Religious, Educational, High Tech, International, and all equally interesting.

What we learned was that Human and Spiritual development is not an individual matter, but something that can only be understood as one begins to relate the person to the institution. Both are symbiotically related in the their mutual growth process. One is but the mirror of the other. What we learned, we feel will be helpful to anyone working in administration, executive leadership or consulting and counseling.

There are, however, some assumptions and themes that will be present in the next three chapters that we should be aware of. These assumptions are a part of the methodology of how the chapters are written, and of how the author views institutions.

The concept of the Omega point that Teilhard de Chardin refers to in all his works, and which is alluded to in his book *The Divine Milieu*, which the quotation above is from, is that it is the end point of consciousness to which all humankind is moving. For him this is a religious phenomenon where the consciousness of all humanity will be at one with God's purpose at that time. He sees a level of consciousness in all things, of which humanity is the high point. Global communications and institutional networks and structures are a part of this high sphere of consciousness.

Compare chapters 3, 4 and 5.

His most basic assumption is that all of life is developmental, and as such it is purposeful. Further for him that purpose is value laden and related to the whole of human meaning. Likewise in the next three chapters an inherent assumption is that, in the same way that the individual's life is developmental, so is the life of an institution. Further it is assumed that these two are intricately related, and cannot be separated.

The following Diagram will take us a step further in putting the content of the last part of the book in perspective.

WORD AS CREATION

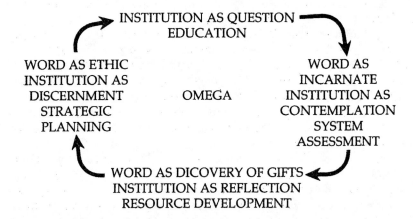

INSTITUTION AS QUESTION
EDUCATION

WORD AS ETHIC
INSTITUTION AS
DISCERNMENT
STRATEGIC
PLANNING

OMEGA

WORD AS
INCARNATE
INSTITUTION AS
CONTEMPLATION
SYSTEM
ASSESSMENT

WORD AS DICOVERY OF GIFTS
INSTITUTION AS REFLECTION
RESOURCE DEVELOPMENT

Here the assumption is that the Institution is a Question and not just an answer. If a Corporation manufactured a successful product in 1929, such as a slide rule for doing mathematical calculations, it would not survive in the present unless it discovered, by asking significant Questions, a new product like the pocket calculator.

This means that an Institution to survive beyond a few years has to have a purpose, and has to go through its own cycles of development. But since most of the Institutions in society outside of the Church and Goverment are new, this is an area where there is not a lot of information. It is here that a study of religious organizations can be helpful. This will occur in chapter VIII, along with some educational material to help us understand something of System Dynamics.

Organizational Development has its own language to help us understand the system just as theology, psychology and all the other disciplines have. This is a part of the Genesis Effect—the specialized use of language. This is also the special role of Education to help us understand all these different languages.

I find that when I am in a new consultation this is where I have to begin. I have to listen to the client to learn their language about their system. Then I have to teach them about some of the language of values and organizational development. In Chapter VIII we are going to be working with all the elements at the top of the Diagram. We will be discussing Word as Creation, as we look at the language and purpose of the Organization. This is a process of Education about Systems, to give us a minimal understanding of this field. Also we are going to be talking about Institution as Question—the concept of an Institution as a living entity with its own values that help shape and form the human condition.

INSTITUTION AS CONTEMPLATION

The concept here is that once one has a minimal common language to understand a system, how does one learn to understand a given Institution in sufficient depth to shape it in such a way that it is not only efficient, but humanizing also? To Contemplate is to look at something with an intimate and caring eye. The theology here is Incarnational. In Christian theology Christ was Incarnated, made like one of us, so that we would know that God understood the human condition and its reality, as we do. Assessment is a process of looking at an Institution and its personnel in a depth way through various processes, in order to "See" or Contemplate its Incarnate reality.

The Organizational component here is in depth quality Assessment of a system. It is quality information retrieval. Quality assessment and information retrieval is the collection of value based data as well as other kinds of information, in order to do strategic Planning. Quality Information retrieval as Document Analysis and its relationship to the development of Corporate Culture will be the subject of Chapter IX. Chapter X will look at the Information retrieval process in more depth.

INSTITUTION AS REFLECTION

Chapter X will look at the retrieval of Quality Information as it relates to the development of a system, and move into the Reflection mode. In consulting and giving spiritual guidance to something as complex as an Institution, no one has all the answers. It does in fact take a Contemplative and Reflective stance where often Wisdom must come from another source. This is where the reality of evil enters in, and will also be a part of chapter X.

This is why we talk here about Institution as Reflection. Theologically it is only as we face the issues of good and evil, and Reflect in depth on our own reality, that we come in touch with what we really have to offer—our Gifts. In consultation this evolves as an Assessment leads a system to see and appreciate what its real resources are. Theologically gifts are not just skills but they are the coincidence between my skills, as value based, and how I am called to actualize them within a given purpose in society.

see Skills, chapter 6

I have had endless experiences within consultations of individuals with a multitude of skills who decide that they do not want to use them, but are called, so they say, to do other things. This is of course

185

all right as long as this does not become a burden on others. More often than not, what is really going on is that the person has been very successful in educational ventures, and skill building, but has never related these to his or her own God given gifts and therefore values. The very separation of skills from values is in itself destructive to human and spiritual integration. The relationship of Human and Spiritual integration to Organizational Development and renewal will be the subject of chapter X.

INSTITUTION AS DISCERNMENT
see Scientific World View, chapter 2; Discernment Questions, chapter 4; and Appendix

Institution as discernment is really the subject matter of chapters IV through XI. Discernment really has two dimensions to it: the collection and retrieval of information as we have just been discussing it, and a decided plan of action. When we act on all the data we have collected and reflected on, inevitably we are in the domain of Ethics. In an Organizational consultation it is necessary to collect sound information for sound strategic planning. But there is another dimension to consider also.

This other dimension is the Ethical dimension that will be addressed in chapter XI. When we are involved in Quality Information Retrieval, we are always involved in values, our values, and how they will affect others. At the institutional level many many people will be affected. This is usually true of anyone involved in any of the professions that this book addresses, such as Counseling, Spiritual Direction, Organizational Consultation, and anything to do with the development of human being.

We begin in the next chapter, BOUNDARY, by looking at the question of "Limited Design Criteria" and Organizational Development. The emphasis will be on the value component and how it might inform us about human growth and purpose.

NOTES

Part III:
The Corporate Genesis

1. Ouchi (1984), p. 228.
2. de Chardin (1960), pp. 154–155.

BOUNDARY

We have observed few, if any, bold new company directions that have come from goal precision or rational analysis. While it is true that the good companies have superb analytical skills, we believe that their major decisions are shaped more by their values than by their dexterity with numbers. The top performers create a broad, uplifting, shared culture, a coherent framework within which charged-up people search for appropriate adaptations.

Thomas Peters and Robert Waterman, Jr.[1]

For when asceticism was carried out of monastic cells into everyday life, and began to dominate worldly morality, it did its part in building the tremendous cosmos of the modern economic order. This order is now bound to the technical and economic conditions of machine production which to-day determine the lives of all the individuals who are born into this mechanism.

Max Weber[2]

The Vitality Curve [of an institution] is a stylized slice of life, a conceptual framework for understanding "how life is." With it, it is possible to demonstrate the development and decline of social reality. With it, it is possible to uncover the pattern of development and decline, and to learn from them.

Lawrence Cada, S.M. et al.[3]

PURPOSE

To explore and examine the nature of institutions—the corporate nature of society and its effect on human and spiritual development.

CONTENT

The chapter begins by relating the four skills to the development of organizational psychology in recent history.

Central to the focus of this chapter is the idea that institutions are developmental, like human beings, and are value driven like human beings. As such several developmental formats are reviewed, in order to begin to look at the dynamic interaction and boundaries between human and institutional value systems.

LINKAGE

The previous chapters focused on development through an examination of the individual. The organizational dimension as such was focused through an examination of leadership styles. This chapter extends this focus into an examination of the nature of "Corporateness" through small groups and institutional development. Values are of central importance to the individual and in the corporate setting—in the next chapter this will be particularly illustrated through the examination of Corporate Document Analysis.

A number of years ago I initiated and developed an organizational and educational research corporation in the mid-western United States. I was at that time a recent immigrant to the country and was still learning about the culture. The corporation lasted for about ten years, at which time it had finished its work, and it was closed down. They were the hardest and most growthful years of my life.

The experiences of those years were extremely varied. When I first went to the area where I was working. I had never owned a house before. Within one year of buying my first house which was owned 90% by the bank a group of us decided to initiate this new business. One of the things we decided to do was to apply for a large grant from a local foundation to help us with our research.

Feeling the bite of success in this new entrepreneurial culture that I truly loved, I sold everything that I had and moved into a larger and very prestigious house, with four acres, and enough space for a library and office to get the operation going. Several weeks later we did receive a large grant, to be shared with a local University, from the foundation, that was a great help in getting the business started.

It was around Christmas time, and my wife and I were invited to a neighborhood party. One of the neighbors turned out to be one of the officers of the foundation from which we had received the grant. He commented later that evening, as we stood with our backs to the lounge fire and looked at the snow falling, "You know, I said to the board when we were considering your grant, 'He must be all right having bought a house in this neighborhood. I am sure that he will live up to our expectations.' "

What I discovered was that I had chosen half consciously to run my business on the values of Image, Prestige, Efficiency and Success. This is what I was portraying to the foundation and others, and this is what they expected of me. I soon discovered that I had betrayed my own deeper Faith Value Center, and had to live with the consequences. But my mistakes and my schooling in life continued.

I hired best friends to help me with my business, and found you cannot be a father and a mother and a business person at the same time—it's difficult to fire family members! I found you cannot be a founder and creator, and public relations officer, marketing manager and bookkeeper at the same time and live to tell the tale. I found that you cannot design your company by choosing the values first, setting up, as we thought we had, a system of participative management, if the cultural environment, the internal resources and the leadership maturity are not all congruent with one another.

The above is not as it may seem a confession of faults; rather it is a description of learning mistakes that hundreds that I know and have

188

talked to have also made. In fact my basic premise is that we learn most of what we know by our mistakes, but what we need to additionally learn is how not to make unnecessary serious mistakes that can be damaging to ourselves and others.

Much of what I now have to offer to my students, those who ask my advice, or ask for consultation, is a little from the successes that I have had, but much from what I have learned from my mistakes. But also much of what I have learned I have done so by reflecting on those mistakes with wise advisors, friends and teachers. Nothing I learned was learned alone or in a vacuum. Additionally much of what I and others learned this way is now available in abundance in the recent and emerging field of organizational psychology and development.

A great deal of sound literature is available in the field of organizational development which we are not going to cover in this text. However we will make reference to some seminal works that will enable the reader to pursue the material, referenced or covered briefly in this chapter, in more depth.

Returning to the experiences above, there are a number of specific things about organizations and how they develop that were learned which will be the subject matter of this chapter. The first is that the spiritual growth of a person cannot be dealt with individually; the interaction of that person with the basic institutions that make up his or her life has to be included. *The person is not so much an individual relating individually to others making choices in a totally free environment, as he or she is an individual as a system interrelating with other systems.*

Secondly all systems have a value core or center out of which comes all their behaviors, rules and management structures, and gives rise to what popularly is called the Corporate culture. An essential dimension of this is called "Limited Design Criteria" which is a measure of the relationship among freedom, creativity and structure in any given organization.

Thirdly this value core is developed through the history of the organization, is rooted in the images of the founder, and is expressed differently in various cultures and historical epochs, causing any institution to have its own life cycle. This information comes to us primarily out of research done on religious communities, but is applicable to any institutional form.

Lastly there is the relationship between values and external and internal boundaries in an organization. It is the understanding of these boundaries that will lead us into the practical implications of value methods for organizational assessment and strategic planning.

The entrance into the world of organizational development through persons is via a study of leadership. As we noted earlier in chapters IV and V, leadership is a consequence, not so much of personal power and authority only, but also of the values and world view of the leader as he or she reflects a particular Cycle of Development. It is also the consequence of the integration of the necessary skills at that Cycle.

In previous literature I have stated (Hall, 1979) that there is a his-

ORGANIZATIONS, PERSONS AND SKILLS

torical relationship between leadership development in large institutions and the development of skills. Before the 1850's leadership was for the most part connected with aristocracy or the ruling classes. There was a merchant class but it grew significantly during the American, French and English (Industrial) Revolutions. Leadership was viewed as something that was literally bred into someone, or God given. The idea that leadership could be learned was a new and novel idea.

see Quality Information, chapter 2 At the turn of the century as mechanization began to change the old order, and Industrial power began to usurp the property of Kings and Queens, out of the old older's ashes grew a need for a new efficient order. In the west, as Max Weber has shown in the quotation at the beginning of the chapter, this grew out of the religious fervor that had itself created the scientific and Industrial Revolution that got it all started in the first place.

Out of this grew the concept of Scientific Management. Basically it implied that management and leadership were similar if not the same, and that any talented person could be trained to carry out its functions, if he or she, usually he, had the intellect, stamina and will. It meant learning accounting and standard business, sales and marketing techniques that were being transferred from the learning of the great entrepreneurs like Rockefeller, J.P. Morgan, Parsons and Thomas Watson, Sr.

MANAGEMENT, INSTRUMENTAL AND INTERPERSONAL SKILLS

see Instrumental Skills, chapter 6

This period went from just before the turn of the century until after World War II. In terms of skills it was an emphasis on Instrumental Business skills. It was an emphasis on the rational side as referred to by Peters and Waterman in the first quotation at the front of the chapter from their book *In Search of Excellence*.[4] It was an emphasis on rational analytical skills that stressed a standard tiered hierarchical management design that was used by the first business tycoons, but which has literally been around since Moses appointed Judges in Israel.

The growing awareness of the nature of the human person that was coming through sociology and psychology caused a parallel jump in our understanding of the interrelationship between mental health, motivation and and small groups development.

It was the beginning of the group dynamic movement, that has given rise to new system and family interaction theory, and opened up the organizational field into the arena of Human Relations Training.

see chapter 6 for explanation of skills It has meant the introduction and acceptance, to a large degree, of the importance of Interpersonal skills. To be an efficient and productive manager of a bank, the Bishop of a Diocese or even an effective member of a high-tech research team means having minimal interpersonal skills. And what "minimal" means is considerable, compared to what it meant 20 years ago. It assumes not only minimal human sensitivity but minimal skills and awareness of methods of conflict management.

190

The high tech, high touch revolution of the last five years appears to be causing new trends away from the large Corporate centrally controlled organizations of the entrepreneurial period, to smaller interdependent units. There is still a lot of discussion about this, but it is clear that individuals are preferring smaller and more intimate and creative work spaces, at least in the economically advanced countries. Whatever one might think about where this trend is moving relative to large Corporations, it is clear that even within these systems, there are developing a variety of smaller more flexible units.

THE IMAGINAL SKILL CONNECTION *see Imaginal Skills, chapter 6*

Examples of this are the Matrix form of management where the units of an organization are still broken up into the standard areas of research, marketing, sales, and whatever other units are required. Each group will have a manager in charge as before, but in addition many other groups may be set up with personnel from the formal groups, setting up a complex matrix of interdisciplinary resource events. This process maximizes the creativity, flexibility and learning of the individual members. These are some of the elements in the Quality circle which is such an integral part of Japanese management. It is basically a structure that enables and enhances individual imaginal development.

The efficiency and workability of these different methods and trends depends on a number of factors. My point is only to stress that this is a clear trend and movement toward the development of the Imaginal skills in management circles. Similarly as we noted earlier, you cannot develop the interpersonal emotional side without this having an effect on individual Imaginal development. It would appear that this is happening as a global management trend. Since it is fairly new one should not expect that such movement and its methods will always produce the desired results.

As we also noted in chapter VI, in advanced and exceptional cases the integration of Instrumental, Interpersonal and Imaginal skills leads to System awareness, and therefore the possibility of management skills being converted into System skills. Is this beginning to happen too, or is this only a trend for the future? The answer I believe is yes, to both points. Its effect on Western Civilization is likely to be radical in transforming our society into something quite different than is presently experienced. Why?

LEADERSHIP AND SYSTEMS SKILLS *see System Skills, chapter 6*

If System skills were to become a part of management expectation, the consequence for healthy organizations and leaders would be to create the following:

1. Organizations whose management design follows from their values rather than from other external purposes.

2. Organizations whose management design would bring about efficient development of the Corporations' product goals, while maximizing the possibility of human and spiritual growth of its members through creative management design.

3. Organizations which in the future would move toward a concern

about the overall societal and natural global environment and issues of human justice in a non-judgmental manner when dealing with cultures and groups that have significantly different ideological orientations.

see Simplicity and Spiritual Growth, chapter 6 4. Organizational leadership, in its integrated rather than demonic form, would as a consequence begin to view the world through the eyes of Simplicity. No matter what the religious viewpoint of such persons this could constitute a major global spiritual revolution.[5]

The basic assumption behind all of this is that there is a direct connection between spiritual growth and organizational structure and management design. At this point we need to look closer at Organizational Structure and Values.

LIMITED DESIGN CRITERIA, VALUES AND THE ORGANIZATION

see Leadership Level, chapter 4 and Leadership throughout chapter 5

Organizational structures can of course take many forms. But in the same way that leadership styles fall into seven general styles depending on the values in each Cycle of Development, so management design also is affected by the value orientation.

For example, the Institutional leadership style of Efficient Management is going to lead to a management design which is highly structured, hierarchical, and beauracratic in nature. Leadership and power will be in delegated tiers of command. On the other hand if the organization is struggling for survival with Phase One values, the leadership style is going to be very Autocratic, and the Institutional design is going to be monarchical with all the decisions, from wall color to financial investment, through one person.

In addition to this there are many different types of organizations: religious and non-profit organizations, where often many of the workers are volunteers, profit organizations that range in size from a small family business to the Corporate Giants, Military and Government organizations. It is not my intention to discuss any of these but simply to acknowledge the large range of possibilities. But whatever the form that they take they are all affected by the factor of *Limited Design Criteria*, which in turn is a direct behavioral arm of the systems values. First what do we mean by Limited Design Criteria?

Limited Design Criteria is the concept that the more rules, regulations and structures you have in an organization the the more oppressed and less creative is the membership. The concept, however, also states that the absence of rules, regulations and structure leads to maximum individual freedom and the self destruction of the organization. *Limited Design Criteria, then, is really a question: what rules, regulations and structures does any given institution need in order to maximize* see Diagram VII.4 *the effective completion of its goals and objectives, on the one hand, and the maximum humanization of its membership on the other hand?*

The goals and objectives of an organization, as of an individual human being, flow directly from the values that the organization operates on. But an organization is a complex system. In order to see the value connection we are going to have to look at different ways of understanding the organization as a system.

The earliest and most common model of an organization is the closed system model. This was the traditional model for centuries up until the last 30 years. Basically it is an in house hierarchical model that places leadership at the top, normally in the form of one person, with a pyramid of military command going from the president to vice presidents, down to department heads, first and second line supervisors, and finally to the parking lot attendant.

We see it in government, in the military and in the church. In terms of the Cycles of Development it is typical of all organizational models in the first three Cycles of Development. Authority is external to individuals, and is given by appointment. Loyalty to the system is stressed, and the world is seen only through the glasses of its own institutional perspective—it is a closed system.

In recent years the open system concept has developed, beginning with interim models like the matrix system mentioned earlier. There are many models which vary according to their value orientation and Cycle of Development. They are all the models from the fourth to the seventh Cycle.

The general approach is that the system consists of several different interacting elements which are kept in harmony and balance by management leadership whose job it is is to insure efficient coordination, accountability and effective goal completion of given ends and tasks.

Of the various models available Goodstein and Cook, in an article called "An Organizational Development Primer," cited the following model that they felt was more comprehensive than most.[6] The model is represented by three concentric circles. The middle circle represents the values from which the structure flows as is represented in DIAGRAM VIII.1.

They had the following to say about it: "A more complete model is offered by Jones (1981) in his 'Organizational Universe Model.' Typical organizational values, including respect and dignity in the treatment of people, cooperation, functional openness, interdependence, authenticity, and profitability, are placed at the core of a set of concentric circles. The next ring, goals, considers how the values are articulated or operationalized. For example, if one of the values is respect for people, courtesy in all interpersonal interactions might be the operationalized goal. When people are treated discourteously, it can be assumed either that the value of respect is not authentic, or that the relationship between courteous behavior and respect is not clear to members of the organization or not explicit enough to guide their behavior."[6a]

The next circle in the series of concentric circles is what Jones called the informal structures through which the values and goals are operationalized. These include Accountability as a formal system of individual evaluation and feedback; Rewards given to individuals for quantity and quality performance; Reporting relationships or lines of authority; Decision making processes by which problems are identified and solved; Communication patterns—both formal and informal; and Norms which are formal and informal rules of human conduct within the organization.

193

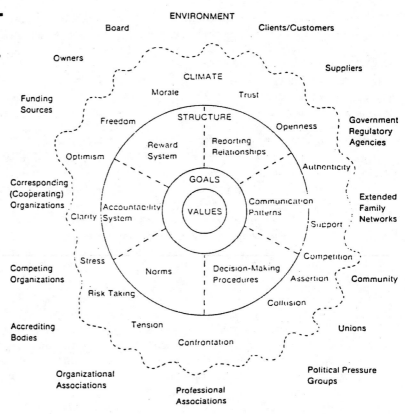

Diagram 8:1
THE ORGANIZATIONAL UNIVERSE MODEL

All of this leads to the next circle which is the Climate and its elements. The climate is the general feeling and sense of moral cohesion or lack of cohesion that results from all the other elements. The elements of the climate include such things as ability of leaders to take risks, competition, stress and tension, clarity, trust, moral support and authenticity. The final concentric circle includes all the external forces and relationships that members of the organization participate in or have to cope with. Examples are such entities as Unions, Accrediting Bodies, Suppliers and so on.

The Jones model is helpful, because it in effect pulls together from a wide range of literature all the basic elements of an organization and what is required for its development.

BOUNDARIES AND CONSULCUBE

Another work that is particularly helpful as an overview of organizational structures, written for the consultant, is a very comprehensive work titled *Consultation: A Comprehensive Approach to Organizational Development*, by Blake and Mouton.[7] It is a very practical work and provides a clear framework for contextualing problems. The organization is divided into Units of Change, Focal Issues that enable the system to grow or cause problems, and common Kinds of Intervention that are used to cope with problem issues. DIAGRAM VIII.2 from their work will enable us to understand this further.

194

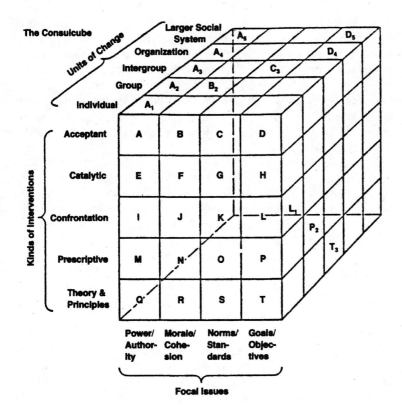

The Consulcube

Units of Change

Larger Social System — A_5 — D_5
Organization — A_4 — D_4
Intergroup — A_3 — C_3
Group — A_2 — B_2
Individual — A_1

Kinds of Interventions

	Power/ Author- ity	Morale/ Cohe- sion	Norms/ Stan- dards	Goals/ Objec- tives
Acceptant	A	B	C	D
Catalytic	E	F	G	H
Confrontation	I	J	K	L
Prescriptive	M	N	O	P
Theory & Principles	Q	R	S	T

L_1 P_2 T_3

Focal Issues

UNITS OF CHANGE. This side of the cube helps us to understand the organization as a series of *Boundaries*. An example will serve to illustrate the point.

I was asked by the Vice-President of a Corporation that produced and developed equipment for chemical analysis to meet the President. They were growing very rapidly and had about 200 employees, and were experiencing conflicts between competing research teams in the Chemical and Electrical Engineering Divisions.

In the first meeting they gave me a lot of information about the overall organization. He told me he was a religious man who was interested in a value analysis of the Corporation. His stated goal was to enable the Corporation to be guided by certain values, and his central concern was the inability of different groups to cooperate. Additionally he spoke a great deal about the future developments and his interest in building the type of environment that would complement the environment of the local community, and in that sense contribute to the local society. Finally he complained bitterly about his administrative team and the fact that one or two persons, especially his chief financial officer, had a questionable value system.

We can see from this description that all the Units of Change in the Diagram were mentioned. I was dealing with the President as an Individual, who in turn said he was concerned about the goals of the whole Organization. At the same time he had interest in the Larger Social System relative to its impact on the community.

Additionally he noted concern about small groups as they related and cooperated with each other—the Intergroup. Finally he was interested in the disagreements evident in his own advisory council. How I have found that very often in doing consultation work, the most important first step is to find out which of these several Boundary systems is actually the one that one is being asked to deal with. Listening to his words I would have concluded that it was intergroup relationships, or the values of the whole organization. In fact it turned out quite differently.

The second meeting was to be over lunch at eleven thirty on a Monday morning. Before we started eating the President had drunk three double vodka martinis, and he drank another three through the meal. He told me that he wanted to hire me, and the first job that I had was to help him fire his finance officer who obviously had the wrong values, in that he disagreed with his policies. Needless to say I did not work on the consultation. In this case the critical boundary point and central Unit of Change was the President himself; all else would have been irrelevant if change was in fact to occur. He was the one that needed to make some changes—on himself—which he was not willing to do.

FOCAL ISSUES. At the bottom of the Diagram we see the four focal issues always evident in an organization, and all necessary for a system's well being and functioning. All four of them are related to, and flow directly from, the values of the system or its leadership. They are as follows.

see Leadership Level, chapter 4 and Leadership, chapter 5 1. Power/Authority. The focus of power in a system is going to be located in one or more of the units of change described above. For example if 51% of the stock of a company is suddenly bought up by a foreign Corporation it will be the Larger Social System that is exerting considerable influence. In the case of the example above the Power/Authority issue was focused in the Individual—the President of the Company. Relative to the Cycles of Development he was operating out of the second or even the first Cycle, and was as a consequence exhibiting Autocratic behavior, to myself and his employees.

2. The Goals and Objectives of an Organization are respectively the long and short term expectation of what the Individual, Group, InterGroup, Organization or Larger Social System expects to accomplish in a given period of time. It is the key to organizational focus, direction and vision. Very specifically they are the organization's expression of its long and short term values.

3. Norms and Standards. These are the written and unwritten rules of behavior of the system at the various levels from the individual to the larger social system. For example there may be written rules that each employee receive medical benefits, and that all executives have degrees in engineering and wear a suit and tie to the office. There may be unwritten rules and norm behavior such as celebrating everyone's

birthday by having a bonus for each individual on his or her birthday, or going home early each Friday.

I have seen and experienced unwritten norms in organizations that expect unlimited overtime with remuneration, if one expects promotion, that engineers are better than persons with degrees in psychology or business, that women are not good executive material, that marriage interferes with loyalty, and that manners and courtesy are essential to service and a good work environment. The point is that whether they be written or unwritten, they operate at each level of change, and they reflect specific value clusters within the organizational environment.

4. Morale/Cohesion. This is the same as what was referred to earlier as Climate. It is really the atmosphere at each unit of change brought about by the norms, rules and standards as they are reflected in the individual's behavior within groups in the system.

KINDS OF INTERVENTION. Blake and Mouton are suggesting that the way to approach a problem in any organization is first to know what the basic unit is you are dealing with, such as the example above, where the basic unit turned out to be the Individual or the President of the company. Secondly one tries to locate what the focal issue is relative to one of the four categories explained directly above. They then suggest that that having been done, any given unit, with its given focal issue, will be able to be dealt with by one of five different types of interventions.

1. ACCEPTANT. The concept here is of accepting what the client says in an empathetic manner to build trust and security with the person in a non-judgmental manner. The method is therapeutic and can enable a client to sort out issues from emotional content, in order to make better objective decisions.

2. CATALYTIC. This is a method of assisting the client in a quality information assessment process. The purpose is to collect information to enable the client to have a clearer and perhaps different perception of the organization in order to bring about change. The information acts as a catalyst as it interacts dialectically with the client population.

3. CONFRONTATION. This is a process of challenging the value assumptions that a client has that may be causing distortions in the organization. This can easily flow from the CATALYTIC mode above, as a consequence of information collected. In my example above I had to confront the client on his drinking habits and his use of me to do something for him that was inappropriate.

4. PRESCRIPTION. This is basically an approach where a problem is solved by a prescribed formula based on assessment information. It is an approach that views assessment and diagnosis as the essential beginning ingredients to the solution which is then prescribed. For ex-

ample in one organization I worked with which was a specialized counseling agency of 50 persons, the focal issue was the poor Moral Cohesion and Climate.

An assessment revealed that 20% of the personnel had very severe personal problems. The fact of the matter was that they were attracting persons who had the same mental health difficulties as their clients. The consequence was that they were facing collapse due to a growing negative reputation with several funding agencies. The prescription involved changing their hiring practices, and requiring some testing and specialized interviewing, before they accepted a candidate's application. Within a year their major problems in this area were solved.

5. THEORIES AND PRINCIPLES. This is basically an educational approach where information about a particular problem, or the nature and structures of organizational behavior, enables the client to see and understand his or her problems in a new light. This method favors assessment and diagnosis as in the other methods, but additionally assumes the role of training personnel internal to the organization to be preferable to the consultant being directly involved.

Blake and Mouton are the first to point out that all these pieces are a way of diagnosing an organization. They are presented here as a way of understanding systems, as a way of seeing how the various parts and boundaries are a part of a much larger whole. Clearly the various interventions, focal issues and units of change constantly interrelate with one another.

What is interesting about all the recent approaches to organizational development is the acknowledgment of the centrality of values. What is equally interesting is that none of the approaches are developmental! In this sense they lack from the existentialist viewpoint an element of reality. They are primarily designed for problem solving and for increasing the productivity and efficiency of the system. As a consequence each of the approaches has been concerned with the short, rather than the long term picture. In fact organizations like people go through developmental stages.

GROUP DYNAMICS The one place where developmental issues are cleary acknowledged and written on in depth is in the studies of small group dynamics within the area of Human Relations Training. Although this is only one area in the total study of organizational behavior it is a very central one.

This is particularly true in the light of recent developments in Matrix Management Systems, Quality Circles, and multiple small group interrelationships. In the new advancing High Technology companies, which often place their primary resources into research and development teams, group dynamics must be a part of the essential technology if they are to be successful at what they are doing.

The study of small group interaction by psychologists and sociologists has been in effect for at least fifty years. It was the pioneering work of the National Training Laboratories and the Center for Group

Dynamic Training at the Massachusetts Institute of Technology that did much to advance its acceptance beyond the area of group therapy and psychotherapy into the general market place of education, business and religious organizations.

As a consequence of this group dynamics has become a central part of organizational development work, especially that sector that stresses Human Relations Training. Within this area much has been written on the developmental aspects of the small group. Generally speaking all groups go through several stages of development. They begin with a stage of initial anxiety, and move to stages of emotional exchange and leadership dependence, conflict recognition and resolution, to a final stage of interdependence. One of the founding fathers of the modern Group Development movement, Leland Bradford, puts it this way:

"Group behavior is affected by the dynamic interaction of many factors, making possible varied approaches to understanding the behavior and the development of groups. One approach assumes there are phases or major problem areas in the continuing life of a group. Each problem area, when adequately resolved, creates an improvement in internal group functioning and consequent productivity. These Phases are:

- Initial group formation and initial movement
- Confronting a difficult problem
- Overcoming the problem with cooperative problem solving
- Group reorganization of structure and function

Groups seem to go through these phases over and over again, each time, hopefully, at a slightly deeper level. In a sense a group reforms each time it meets."[8]

Irvin D. Yalom, an existentialist writing about groups in a book on *The Theory and Practice of Group Psychotherapy*, points out the unusual advantages and attributes of the developed group as Bradford explains it above.[9] He notes that the small group of seven to ten persons, when developed dynamically, has the advantage of teaching a person, whatever the setting, things that cannot be taught in a large group setting such as a classroom, or on an individual basis such as having direct contact with a single supervisor.

GROUP DEVELOPMENT AND THE CURATIVE FACTORS

Although he is addressing the development of the therapeutic groups in counseling, what he has to say in fact applies to any group setting. There are, however, several conditions that must be met to make significant group development occur. First the group is limited in its development by its size. An optimal size is between five and ten persons. Secondly the group has to meet regularly, usually once a week, and everyone has to be at each meeting, within the limits of necessary exceptions.

Yalom lists a number of issues that he calls "Curative Factors" that can result from such a group as it develops to becoming a cohesive whole. They are as follows.

1. Installation of Hope. Let us consider the issue of problem solving. In a group setting three things can occur: support to keep trying, encounter with another person who has solved a similar problem, and the possibility of the synergetic effect and solution as more than one person bring their expertise to the situation. When this happens once or twice in a group, the group becomes a Hopeful place to be.

2. Universality. This is the experience through group sharing—we all have common problems. As the group develops in levels of trust, its members discover that emotional and interpersonal difficulties are common to all of us.

3. Imparting of Information. The sharing of certain kinds of information, especially emotional information, or discussing a particularly difficult personnel issue is much more helpful and efficient in a small group setting.

4. Altruism. This is close to number one above. It is close to calling a group to look at its long term value based goals, relative to the hopeful side of life at difficult times. This requires not only the developed trust in a group but the right type of enabling leadership that prevents a group from being overwhelmed by its problems, or a particular person's problems. It keeps the parts in perspective with the long term whole.

5. The Corrective Recapitulation of the Family Group. Yalom notes that in any group, the deeper the trust level, the more unconscious will be the association of some in the group with their family of origin.
If the family or origin was healthy, this will be productive, but if it was one that had difficulties this could be carried over into the group, no matter if it is a therapeutic group or a Quality Circle. For example, there may be dependencies built up in the group that duplicate parent-child relationships, rather than the adult to adult ones that are called for. The sensitive trained leader can watch for this and work with it so that it does not get in the way of the tasks at hand.

6. Development of Socializing Techniques. This is a very helpful factor that can enable a group to cope with difficult or embarrassing problems that are to difficult to deal with on a one to one basis. The withdrawn person who does not speak a great deal can be helped to be more outgoing simply through the regular supportive social contact of a group. Very often in settings where the administrative group has persons who are elected because of their technical expertise, such persons may lack the social skills they need in a management setting to be successful.

7. Imitative Behavior. This is very often a part of the last item. Issues from manners and dress to behaving in a manner that engenders

confidence and efficiency can be learned through helpful role models, which an individual can admire, respect and imitate.

8. Interpersonal Learning. This is an extension of items 6 and 7, and includes helping persons to express anger creatively, engage in conflict resolution, and confront and make persons accountable in creative and affirming ways.

9. Group Cohesiveness. This is the result of the development of trust in a group as outlined above. It would be the same as what Bradford calls "cooperative problem solving." It is the result of consistent group development.

10. Catharsis. This occurs at different levels depending on the goal of a group. It is the sudden insight that comes personally around a personal issue or a problem to be solved, through high levels of interaction in a very Cohesive Group.

11. Existential Factors. The basic conditions that arise out of the existential framework, raised in a an earlier chapter, such as loneliness, the tragedy of death or illness, and the ability to make very critical choices and decisions, are often better handled within the context of a trusting Cohesive group.

One place where there has been significant research on the development of whole organizations is in the religious field, and in particular on the development of Western Religious Life. There is a specific reason for this, and that is the very communal nature of Christian theology, through its Judaic roots, and as particularly expressed by Saint Paul in his first letter to the Christians in Corinth. In the twelfth chapter and in the twelfth to fifteenth verses he says the following:

INSTITUTIONAL LIFE CYCLES

"The body is one and has many members, but all the members, many though they are, are one body; and so it is with Christ. It was in one Spirit that all of us, whether Jew or Greek, slave or free, were baptized into one body. All of us have been given to drink of the one Spirit. Now the body is not one member, it is many. If the foot should say, 'Because I am not a hand I do not belong to the body,' would it then no longer belong to the body?"[10]

The early Christian Community began full of optimism and idealism, envisioning itself as symbolic of a new Kingdom of Hope on earth. It was a commune system that had built in social services and desire to feed the hungry and cure the sick. It was orginally a network of fairly small groups compared to modern churches. The concept was that the individual was symbiotically linked and nurtured by the group, it being the primary unit of development not the individual.

In addition the equality of the parts as expressed above was connected to the unique skills and talents of each individual. Persons were seen as unique, each having a unique set of Gifts. In modern language the Gifts would be a combination of Values and Skills. The two were not separated. Not only this but a Gift was first of all seen as God given, much like the idea that we all have in a seeded fashion the 125 values we referred to in earlier chapters. The gifts to be nurtured meant nurturing the skills around the values that are life giving to the community.

I often meet and counsel people with many Degrees, and skills, which are not related to what they feel they want to do. I have counseled several persons working in church and agency settings because early on in their work they would tell the director of the agency or the minister how things should be done, rather than trying to discover what the community needed, and end up by being asked to leave. This is a very common occurrence with some persons. Obviously such problems can be very complicated.

But it often surprises persons when I will say: "You are not having a career or psychological problem but a spiritual problem." "What do you mean?" will be the reply. I point out that they have Skills, and Values, but the two are not working together, and so the result is that they have no Gifts—and it is Gifts that one needs to be employed successfully! One person I spoke to said that her skills were in Word Processing, but her value of Empathy and Care led her to believe she was "called" to do counseling. "Do you have counseling skills?" I asked naively. "No!" she replied. Strange as this may seem this is not an unusual situation. Gifts are the Skills derived from one's values that are needed, usable and requested by the community, whether it be a Church or IBM.

The various parts of the body are essential, necessary and invaluable to the functioning of the whole. As such each member of the organization, in this case the early Church, with his or her particular talents and skills was seen as essential to the overall Unity of the total Institutional structure at a local and global level. Initially the local leader Bishop was to maintain the unity of the local cell or body, and represent it to the Church as a whole. It was a matrix of small groups, represented by the local leader whose primary duty was to preside or enable the brethren to celebrate their life together.

One of the primary organs of renewal in the Christian Church down through the ages has been Religious Communities, such as the early Monasteries that did so much to urbanize and develop the European continent. Many of these institutions like the Order of Friars Minor (the Franciscans), the Benedictines, the Jesuits and the Ursulines have been in existence for centuries. The Benedictines have been around for nearly 1500 years. Obviously they are different from the modern industrial organization like IBM not only in purpose but in longevity.

A team of religious sociologists wrote a book called *Shaping the Coming Age of Religious Life*, in which they studied the life Cycles of several religious congregations over a long period of history, only to discover that those which survived went through predictable cycles of development. They studied both historical and sociological models.[11]

In their historical study they found different forms of religious life appeared in times of major societal transition. This in turn created special needs for the society as a whole over long periods of time. For example with the fall of Rome and the emergence of medieval Europe and new urban centers came the rise of Monasticism. With the fall of medieval Europe and the rise of the industrial revolution came the Teaching orders, that coincided with missionary and colonial expansion. It was these communities that initiated hospitals and schools in response to the needs of the new immigrant populations of the new world.

Their sociological studies showed that each of the systems that survived went through a series of life cycles that they termed the "Vitality Curve." The vitality curve refers to the natural rise and fall of an institution relative to its usefulness and success in society historically. The following quotation is that same one that is at the beginning of the chapter. "The Vitality Curve is a stylized slice of life, a conceptual framework for understanding 'how life is.' With it, it is possible to demonstrate the development and decline of social reality. With it, it is possible to uncover the pattern of development and decline, and to learn from them."[11a]

They additionally noticed that each institution went through a series of predictable stages, changes and crises. My point is to illustrate that this life cycle phenomenon is true of any institutional form no matter what its purpose. DIAGRAM VIII.3 is an expansion and adaptation of their work.

First we have the *Foundation Period*. The founder of the Institution could be Saint Francis with the Order of the Friars Minor, or Thomas Watson, Jr. of IBM. This period is characterized by the vision of the founder and his or her values that connect with the needs of the times, and engender the support of an intitiating group or community. This period usually is limited within the lifetime of the founder. The central crises are those common to institutions relative to leadership direction. Very often the one who founds a system is not the right person to manage it and see that it has continuity.

The *Expansion Period* is that time when in business terms the product

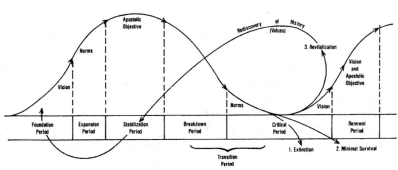

Diagram 8:3
THE ORGANIZATIONAL LIFE CYCLE
The diagram illustrates how institutions go through natural life cycles over a period of fifty to one hundred years. The life cycle is linked to the values of the founder of the organization, beginning with the Foundation Period.

203

becomes a felt need in society. In the religious system it is a time when the vision and charism of the founder becomes a sign of hope for others in the society. During this time the Norms of the organizational structure are put into place. It is a time of excitement and geographical expansion. It is also a time when the values of the founder are interpreted and institutionalized, and very often documented. This may last for one or two generations.

The *Stabilization Period* marks the high point of service in the form of apostolic or missionary expansion in the religious domain, and of product development and financial stability and profitability in the industrial sector. It is felt that this period lasts from fifty to one hundred years. It is the time for maximization or organizational structures and *see Cycle 3, chapter 5* goal identity. Value wise it is the institutional period of Cycle 3, with the emphasis on conformity, unity and loyalty.

Next comes the *Breakdown Period*, marked by a natural alteration in societal and cultural values and needs that change with time and history. As we noted earlier in the book persons change when they have to, but institutions do not naturally change. Therefore the *Breakdown Period* is inevitable. It is primarily a crisis of belief or value confusion, marked by denial that anything is really changing. Loss of creativity, loyalty and numbers is a natural consequence. This can lead within a short period of time to the *Critical Period* and extinction of the system.

The *Critical Period*, is a time of crisis of the very viability of the institution—as to whether it should close down, continue on a minimal basis, or try to renew itself. The critical factor here is courageous leadership that has the pain tolerance to make some very difficult, often rapid intuitive decisions.

In the *Renewal Period*, sometimes the system can be revived or revitalized. For a Religious Congregation this means a return to an examination of the values of the Founder of the community. All Religious Congregations have a Rule of life or a set of Constitutions which describe the philosophy of the Founder, and his or her own aspirations, as they are reflected through the Structures of Government.

These are the value based management structures of the Congregation. Theoretically renewal involves a return to this initial value base of the Founder in order that these original values can be re-visioned relative to the needs of the times. When this occurs the cycle starts all over again.

In other kinds of institutions another dynamic is often introduced. In the religious community the Founder is really giving a unique interpretation to the call of Christ relative to a specific service or need or lifestyle that he or she is envisioned with. In other religious settings such as a diocese with a new Bishop or a parish, with a new minister or priest, that person becomes a new instant founder!

We might ask what about other institutions such as an Industrial Corporation manufacturing computer parts—will they experience the same cyclical effect? I think so, although they do not have the longevity of the religious system. On the other hand, technology and culture is moving so fast today that the life cycle process is moving quicker.

As a product is developed and becomes successful through the founding vision of let us say some inventive electrical engineer, so it will only become marketed as a founding Corporation is put in place. Many highly successful Corporations fail in the expansion period because of insufficient management skills on the part of the founder. Once the system has stabilized the product, whatever it is, it is only going to sustain the system until the cultural and product needs in society change.

Revitalization may mean a return to the original inspiration of the founder, or it may mean starting all over again. But either way, for the for profit Corporation, starting over means having a new exciting innovative product, much like the one that initiated the system in the first place. Now such a product will only be present if the research and development for such an entity was already in place—and that takes us back to the values that initiated the Corporation in the first place. What we are now facing is a lot of questions about what all this information can tell us. Let us try to pull this together by looking at the subject of Boundaries.

We have noted that all organizations arise out of a central value system, that they are developmental, and that they all go through predictable life cycles, if they last that long. What is the connection between the internal components of an institution, its boundaries, the values of the system and these developmental cycles that we have been discussing? The following four conclusions are a summary of the connections and integration that we have noted in our research and consultation.

INTEGRATIONS: THE QUESTION OF BOUNDARIES

1. Every organization runs, lives and survives on the initiating values of the founder or founding group. Peters and Waterman, Jr. put it this way:

"Let us suppose that we are asked for one all-purpose bit of advice for management, one truth that we were able to distill from the excellent companies' research. We might be tempted to reply, "Figure out your value system. Decide what your company stands for. What does your enterprise do that gives everyone the most pride? Put yourself out ten or twenty years into the future: what would you look back to with the greatest satisfaction?"[12]

2. Every organization that is not founded on minimally adequate value centers, or in Fowler's language Faith Centers,[12a] will not survive the Vitality Curve, or natural organizational life cycle. Very specific examples of this will be given in the next two chapters as we examine issues around the development of a value based corporate culture. In the same way that an individual and family need a minimally adequate value system, so does a large Corporate entity.

We have encountered a number of religious systems, Religious Congregations and specific parishes that assumed their value systems were adequate because they were based on commonly accepted Christian norms. Several of them self destructed because they failed to realize that it was not their religion that was the problem, but their inadequate interpretation of it. I have encountered the same problem with organizations which have excellent products, but insufficient values in the service and management areas.

3. Human and Spiritual growth are interconnected with system or organizational growth. This is a factor that comes through the religious traditions, as reflected in Saint Paul's analogy of the community with the Body.

Saint Paul's concept of the Body is I believe true for any organization. It is in fact the very heart of the *Genesis Effect*. Namely that the organization in that it is derived from human values is in fact a projection of the founder's or founding group's internal images of reality. When those images are inadequate the system will eventually fail. We will take a look at the specific institutional connections that cause growth in the individual in chapter X.

see The Oscillation Effect, chapters 3 and 7

4. Finally since the values are at the heart of the organizational structure it follows in our experience that there is a direct relationship between the Cycles of Development and development of an institution. This was described in the last chapter as the Oscillation Effect. On the one hand institutions in our experience go through the Cycles of Development up to the point where they are reinforced by the external environment; on the other hand the institution appears to have a wide range of values reflecting several Cycles at the same time. These constitute two different Boundary Systems.

Boundary System 1. Most institutions that reach the Stabilization period will often experience the first three Cycles, much as an individual growing up will. When an institution is founded this is a hard

see Diagram III.1 and IV.1

survival period, much like the first Cycle of Development. That is, say the values are going to be survival and security values. As the founder tries to get things started the initial personnel are bound to be dependent upon her or him—this is the period of Benevolent Leadership as in Cycle Two. In the Stabilization Period the institution usually moves to a formal organizational structure as in Cycle Three.

In the Breakdown Period some institutional leaders revert to Cycle One. A few transcend these Cycles and enable the institution to renew itself. This as we shall see is due primarily to the adequacy of their value center. The limited Design criterion we mentioned earlier is also directly related to these Cycles. The rules and structures are more closed in the first three Cycles and more individually controlled as the system moves toward Cycle One. The opposite occurs in Cycle Four with a movement toward creative balance in Cycle Five.

It does not make much sense to talk about an institution functioning beyond the third Cycle. The reason is that Cycles Four and up are primarily expressions of small group development and interaction. What you have in the later Cycles are individual groups functioning at these levels networking with other groups within a total system whole—a matrix system. I have only seen administrative units go beyond Cycle Three, but not a total system. In fact for a total system to operate this

206

way would be destructive! You would have all chiefs and no Indians! This is I believe due to the very nature of the Oscillation Effect and the presence of the second boundary system.

Boundary System 2. In this system we view the total organization at any given moment. Time as in the existential model becomes a series of individual moments. Past and future are one not only in individual consciousness but in the group's consciousness, as different sub-groups represent different Cycles of Development. In Paul's terms the group is a unified Body which if integrated can cause exceptional growth, or negative growth if the opposite is true.

This integration effect, as with the individual, depends on the integration in a healthy way of the four skill areas. In fact exceptional growth toward simplicity and system awareness can only occur through the support of such a body-politic, in my opinion.

Additionally there is considerable evidence that exceptional healing in the field of family therapy and psychotherapy can occur in the small group setting. Recent work by groups such as the Shalem Institute in Washington with group Spiritual Direction and the overall experience of the Monastic and communal contemplative movement support this concept.[12b] It is also far more practical from an economical standpoint. As such it would appear that the central ethical purpose of institutions at a global level is to further human integrated consciousness. This is not to negate the value of any individual product or service that any institution or organization might have, but to put this in a wider and more essential ethical framework. Clearly consciousness is the high point of evolution on this planet, and the development of the organization as a complex projection of internal human images is the means by which this process can be developed further.

To gain clarity on this view of the boundary system let us look at DIAGRAM VIII.4.

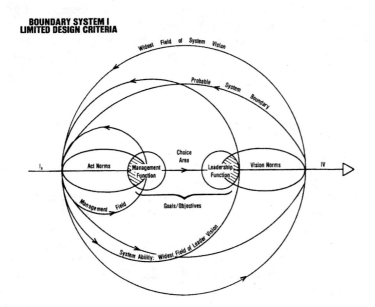

BOUNDARY SYSTEM I
LIMITED DESIGN CRITERIA

Diagram 8:4
INSTITUTIONAL BOUNDARIES
The diagram illustrates how the different functions and roles within an institution are functioning within different value boundaries.

The Diagram shows the field of values consciousness within an institutional setting. This is a boundary system. The boundaries are as follows:

1. The lower boundary is the Act Norms or the most basic behaviors and rules that will enable this community of persons to function together. It is characterized by the earlier Cycles of Development.

2. The upper boundary is the Vision Norms which are those behaviors and aspirations that describe the future of the community or organization. It is characterized by the later Cycles of Development.

Limited Design Criterion is assuring sufficient rules and structure that will most enable the system to develop its value based Goals and Objectives. Too much structure, or insufficient attention to the Management and Leadership functions as they relate to the value based boundaries and fields of respective awareness, will make this impossible.

The Diagram illustrates the different fields of awareness open to the developed Leader, and the functions appropriate to each field. We note a management or supervisory function needed to develop communal identity; an organizing, planning and education function that would be needed for building the organization through its goals and objectives; and we note the developmental function related to the systems vision and strategic planning.

CONCLUSIONS

The last 10 years we have worked to develop methods of assessment that would identify and address all in specific terms the institutional Boundaries and what specific value center an organization would need to grow and develop.

Strangely enough our first inroad to this process was the computerized value analysis of Documents—this gave us surprising information about the Genesis Effect, and a specific method of identifying system Boundaries, that eventually led to a new approach to the development of System Faith Centers, Corporate Culture and Strategic Planning. We will begin to look at these applications starting with the next chapter: DOCUMENT.

NOTES

Chapter 8:
Boundary

1. Peters and Waterman (1982), p. 51.
2. Weber (1976), p. 181. Weber surrounds his own main thesis with qualifications, and his claim that "Puritanism provided the vital spark which ignited the sequence of change creating industrial capitalism" must be read with his qualifications in mind. That there is a link between the inventive and productive drive let loose in the industrial revolution and the Christian demythologizing and liberating of nature for exploration and exploitation is historically clear.
3. Cada *et al.* (1979), p. 77.

4. Peters and Waterman (1982).

5. It would be demonic if the higher values and skills developed internally by corporations and their leadership enabled them to maintain products, contracts, controlling roles, etc. which are phase one in expression and intent.

6. Leonard Goodstein and Phyliss Cooke. "An Organizational Development Primer." Pfeiffer & Goodstein (1984), pp. 207–215.

6a. *Ibid.*, p. 208.

7. Blake and Mouton (1983). Other sources are French and Bell (1978), Ouchi (1984), Ouchi (1981), Dyer (1983), Ruch and Goodman (1983), Deal and Kennedy (1982).

8. Bradford (1978), p. 4.

9. Yalom (1975).

10. New American Bible, I Corinthians 12:12.

11. Cada *et al.* (1979).

11a. See note 3 above.

12. Peters and Waterman (1982), p. 279.

12a. Fowler (1981).

12b. Shalem Institute for Spiritual Formation at Washington Cathedral in Washington.

DOCUMENT:
THE BEGINNING OF CONVERGENCE

Through the Dark Ages which proceeded from the barbarization of Western Europe, it was the Church and its monks who preserved the remnants of ancient civilization and Christianity itself with its systematic thought and its ethics.

The remedy was supplied by St Benedict, the father of the later Western monasticism, in two ways. His rule was an ordered and practical code of laws for the working of a monastery, and it adapted monasticism to Western ideas and Western needs.

The Shorter Cambridge Medieval History[1]

The thought of mixing practical business matters with pie-in-the-sky concerns may seem strange, but popular beliefs aside, philosophy and business are the most compatible of bedfellows.

A philosophy can help an organization to maintain its sense of uniqueness by stating explicitly what is and isn't important. It also offers efficiency in planning and coordination between people who share in this common culture. But more than a vague notion of company right-and-wrong, there needs to be a carefully thought-out philosophy, preferably one available to all employees in booklet form.

William Ouchi[2]

PURPOSE   To see how research on the analysis of institutional documents revealed that values are the basis and core of Corporate Culture.

CONTENT   The chapter begins by illustrating how historical documents like the Rule of Saint Benedict carried the values of one historical epoch to the next. The rest of the chapter looks at the method, purpose and importance of document analysis.

LINKAGE   The last chapter examined the nature of institutions and the fact that they are developmental and value driven. This chapter illustrates the value connection by looking at the phenomena of Document analysis and its relationship to the "Genesis Effect."

I have stated consistently from the beginning of this book that religion, science and the behavioral sciences need to learn from, and to cooperate with, each other. It might seem strange, but it was nevertheless true, that significant learning about day to day business organization occurred through the discovery of a method to analyze the Constitutions and Rule of a Religious Congregation. The method was value based Document analysis.

We discussed at the begining of the book the concept of the Genesis Effect, and the relationship between inner images and external expressions of those images through the arts and technology. The mediator of this is values inherent in human communication—communication through spoken and written language. It was God's Word in the book of Genesis that caused the creation to come into being.

This chapter is on Document analysis. Document analysis became a very important bridge process in helping us to identify critical methods for the overall quality assessment of institutions. On its own it is a very limited venture, but combined with other processes it became a critical piece of a larger picture. As a consequence this chapter is a bridge to the next chapter called Retrieve which examines the larger picture of Systems Assessment and Strategic Planning. At this point let us look at Document in a little more depth.

In the quotation at the beginning of the chapter it was the Benedictine Rule that brought order to the monastic movement that was the very continuity for civilization as the old Roman Empire in the west collapsed and a new order emerged. From this philosophical and very basic management document called the Rule emerged the concept of what Dom Gregory Dix has termed the Sanctification of Time.[2a]

In a consistent orderly manner the Monks conducted the "Opus Dei" (God's work)—the seven fold daily round of psalms, scripture and prayer in self built monastic enclosures that were self run farming facilities of superb ecological balance, to provide for their every needs.

They were bright, dedicated, value driven persons, who discovered new farming techniques, invented the first clock to tell them when to pray, invented new devices for cloth making, and attracted thousands to settle in and around their property. They were seen by many as the Kingdom of God manifest on earth. The consequence was that many large European cities are the direct descendants of these early Monastic settlements, which not only farmed and made cloth, but initiated the institutions of Education and Medicine that we take for granted today.

The second quotation by William Ouchi reinforces the growing awareness in modern business of the centrality of values and a sound philosophical point of view to the success of any business enterprise.

Peters and Waterman in their book: *In Search of Excellence: Lessons from America's Best Run Companies*, conclude their study by saying "Every excellent company we studied is clear on what it stands for, and takes the process of value shaping seriously. In fact, we wonder whether it is possible to be an excellent company without clarity on values, and without having the right sort of values."[3]

This is not a new idea even in business, but it is new in its overall and general level of acceptance. Thomas Watson, Sr. who in February of 1924 got the board of the Computing-Tabulating Recording Company (CTR) to rename itself International Business Machines (IBM), and became its first Chief Executive, built that company on a set of workable and very specific values. The values pivoted on Service and Loyalty and were supported by Creativity through Research, Cooperation and Teamwork.

The values were integrated within themselves in that Service and Loyalty were to both the employees and the customer. IBM until this day will always rather move a person laterally rather than fire him or her if he or she did not work out in a given job or project.

see Diagram VIII.3

Research insured ongoing flexibility relative to the Vitality Curve, and cooperation built community and placed loyalty to the company before the success of any given individual. This was later partly codified in a book on the company's values and beliefs, written by Thomas Watson, Jr. titled: *A Business and Its Beliefs*.[4]

We can make three conclusions from all of this. One, not only does an organization need a well spelled out philosophy to be excellent, but as Ouchi and Saint Benedict before him demonstrate, it needs to be written down in the form of a document. Two, behind every philos-

see Values and Faith, chapter 7

ophy stand a certain set of values, what we called in the last chapter the Value or Faith Center. Third, the philosophy and the values have to be "the right sort of values" and philosophy, since different values lead to different ethical outcomes.

In the late 1970's we began to ask the question: what would happen if we did an value analysis of a document? My son Martin and I in the last year of his High School decided to analyze the speech patterns of Reagan and Carter in the Presidential campaign. It was nothing complex but a simple dry run experiment.

We collected some newspaper clippings of their speeches and their debate on television, paralleled their arguments through other media events such as domestic and foreign policy, and analyzed the values in each section.

We did this by first reading the values, and the number of repetitions of the value, from the list of 125 values. Then we added values when necessary that were present by virtue of a hidden but obvious meaning. The values were then analyzed by placing them in priority order, and in each Cycle of Development, as explained in the earlier chapters. Now that we know the results of the election and some of the policies of the new administration it is interesting to go back to that study.

The overall results were as follows. Carter's speeches reflected an emphasis on Cycle Five values with an emphasis on World Peace, Justice, Human Dignity and Rights. They also reflected an absence or lack of foundational values in the admistrative area. This led us to raise the discernment questions: would his message be understood by the average person? *see Cycle Five, Communal Collaborative Cycle, chapter 5*

The question was also raised: would the admirable position he was taking be appreciated by enough of the voting public? Finally the question was raised: does the lack of administrative values suggest a reason why he is having difficulty getting some of his strategies past Congress, and is this what will continue to happen should he be elected?

President Reagan's values on the other hand reflected the first three Cycles with a heavy emphasis on the first Phase of development, with a marked absence of values in the visionary area. The priorities were first of all on Self Preservation, Security and Care/Nurture, as an expression and concern for the unemployed, high interest rates, and for National Security. *see Cycle One, chapter 4 and Cycle Two and Three, chapter 5*

National security was reflected in concerns about Iran, Central America, Russian domination, and American patriotism and pride. His Cycle Three values reflected an emphasis on patriotism. It was interesting that he placed a much higher emphasis on administration, even although he was saying in his speeches that he would cut back on government. This also raised some interesting discernment questions and reflections.

At the reflective level it seemed to us that Reagan's direct appeal was to people with Phase One needs relative to inflation and unemployment. This, plus his emphasis on National Security as an extension of personal security and patriotism, could win him the election, since the majority of people are not into fifth Cycle values of Justice and Dignity at a more global level. Secondly his emphasis on administration would suggest that he would be more successful at getting his projects through Congress.

The questions raised were as follows. Since the values that he was verbalizing, Self Preservation and Security, were so well received at the personal level, would they not backfire at the international foreign policy level? Since the speech patterns showed very few vision values this was a question that was raised twice.

The question was raised about the possibility, therefore, of significant and even unreal military spending, and a possible pro-conflict attitude toward the perceived enemy. Finally doubt was seeded in our mind as to his real ability or will to reduce government, since his values seemed to suggest the opposite.

Some of the projections and questions obviously were well anticipated. Others some will still argue about. You the reader can make your own judgment. We recognize that this little experiment was very limited, and may not have even represented the person as much as the person and his speech writers combined with party policy.

What it taught us in a very concrete way was that simple Document analysis using a value base gives new and often unanticipated information and questions relative to a given subject matter or situation. Even if the questions could have been anticipated it gave us a more specific focus and understanding of what we were seeing in the election. This led in the years that followed to a specific computerized program designed to analyze documents and raise Discernment Questions.

DOCUMENT

In 1978 a group of fellow associates with myself and Benjamin Tonna, a sociologist who had specialized in Documentation, decided to develop a formal method for document analysis. The opportunity came through the vision and foresight of Father Francis George, who was the Vicar General of the Congregation of the Missionary Oblates of Mary Immacualate. He is a philosopher particularly interested in Founderology: the study of the relationship and influence of the founder of an organization on its long term development.

The consequence was that in 1978 a friend and fellow professional Father Ronald Carignan, OMI together with an international team did an analysis of the new (released in 1982) Oblate Constitutions and Rule. What made the event unique was that the venture was not done with any agenda other than to explore the documents and see what would be learned. Not only this, it was done with persons representing three language groups: French, English and Spanish. Not only this but the analysis was to include a cross cultural historical study by comparing the new draft document with the original 1826 Constitution and Rule, the 1926 and 1961 versions. Since the Congregation was founded by Bishop Eugene de Mazenod in France, and the Congregation is international, we considered it to be a cross cultural study.

The major contribution of the study was to allow Ronald Carignan and me to establish a set of Assumptions about the values based analysis of Documents, that later on through the work of Barrara led the way for the process to become computerized. The Assumptions were further refined over the years into the following format.

BASIC ASSUMPTIONS IN DOCUMENT ANALYSIS

1. Major philosophical and theological documents of an historical institution should contain a coherent value system—historically and internally.

By historical here is meant any document that was written before the majority of the present population of the company or congregation was present. In an international Corporation and Religious Communities this would also include any documentation that was initiated in another country.

2. There should be a balance between Primary Goal Values and Means Objective Values.

see Goals and Means, chapter 3

3. There should be an appropriate balance and relationship between ACT, CHOICE and VISION Values.

214

4. ACT Values should be clearly represented as bottom line Values on the one hand and be open to development and new expression on the other. *see Integration of Skills, chapter 6*

5. The CHOICE area Values should be appropriate and complete enough to promote integral human development and growth.

6. The VISION Values should be sufficient and suitable enough to give direction and motivation to the development of the CHOICE area values.

7. The overall values system should be broad enough to integrate members at different stages of Value development.

8. The document, within the historical period it was written, should reflect and be consonant with recent historical changes in society. When the document is related to a religious institution it should also be consonant with recent historical changes in the Church.

9. When appropriate the document should reflect minimal Values necessary for the integration of the institution into an international setting.

10. The document should favor Values that grow out of and reflect the original philosophy and charism of the organization.

see Body Politics, chapter 3, and Kelsey, Appendix

11. When appropriate the Values should reflect Values that are particular to a male or a female setting.

12. When a comparative analysis of historical documents is carried out, a new revision should reflect continuity in the basic Values related to ACT, CHOICE and VISION areas. They should also reflect changes in local and world society, and when appropriate in the Church during that period of time.

13. In organizations where legal prescriptions are a part of the document they should, by and large, relate to the ACT area Values. Examples of this have been the inclusion of Professional Codes of Ethics and State Licensing requirements in Psychological and Health Care Agencies, and Canonical prescriptions within the Constitutions and Rules of Religious Communities.

14. The documents should reflect Values priorities consonant with ethical and where appropriate the theological convictions and life style of the organization. What these are, are more self evident in some organizations than others. As has been stated previously the idea that any organization or consultant can be value free is nonsense. For a Christian organization it means that the document must reflect a resurrection or gospel orientation. For professional Health Care Agencies *see Faith Center chapter 7b and Ethics in chapter 9*

the documents should reflect minimal ethical standards. However sometimes such norms are not available in which case the organization needs to be enabled to develop such standards through new documents.

<table>
<tr><td>THE PROCESS</td><td>The process for the actual analysis was similar to the one described above when my son and I analyzed the presidential campaign speeches. First a team is assembled from the organization that wishes to analyze its documents. The process is done in all the languages represented by the system if it is an international group. The reason for this is that the values transcend the language and make this possible.</td></tr>
</table>

see Kelsey, Appendix   Over the past several years such analyses have been computer managed to facilitate the rapid processing of a lot of data. This has led to research processes whereby the values and their definitions were standardized in several languages. A value cannot be translated from one language to another; a team in the original language has to first understand the images, experiences and meaning of a particular value and then name it in their own language.

The team now takes the document and analyzes the values, by team consensus, for every paragraph in all the documents. Sets of paragraphs are then grouped for comparisons. For example chapters and separate books or documents may be compared. Sections on executive leadership will be compared with sections on supervision, government and promotional practices. In fact over the years we have found that the number of comparisons is innumerable and varies with the document and the purposes for analyzing the document.

Once the paragraphs to be compared are established the values from those sections are fed into the computer and profiles are derived that give the Cycles of Development, Skills, Time Quality Dimensions, Leadership Levels, Faith and Ethical orientation and relevant discernment questions for each section analyzed. The profiles are then compared and analyzed based on the original assumptions that Ron Carignan, Hall and Ledig and I developed above. Let us conclude with some of the results.

TOWARD CONVERGENCE: WHAT DOCUMENT ANALYSIS HAS OFFERED

Since 1978 we have analyzed many Religious, Health Care, Social Agency and Corporate Philosophy documents. Interestingly enough the original assumptions have stood up no matter what the orientation of the institution. An additional factor and gift to us was that the original document analyzed, The Constitutions and Rules of the Congregation of the Missionary Oblates, turned out to be a remarkably coherent and congruent document. The final 1982 document is an unusually balanced and healthy statement—this is an observation after seeing the analysis of dozens of other documents.

Another factor that has aided this development is the rediscovery of what we stated earlier about the Benedictine Rule. The Constitutions and Rules of Religious Congregations are more comprehensive than the philosophical documents of other organizations, because they include the total life perspective, both of the organization and of the individuals that live within it.

They include sections on individual education (Formation), life style and vocation relative to work (Ministry). At the same time they also have sections on management (Government) at the local, international and top executive levels, mission goals and future vision. They even have sections on aging and human dignity and development. *Consequently they are an invaluable resource relative to the understanding of Documentation and the development of Corporate Culture in any organizations, including international business corporations.*

THE VOWS AND ORGANIZATIONAL DYNAMICS

The importance of organizational documents and their analysis became particularly evident as we began to see that the central focus of Religious Life relative to its structures for exceptional Human and Spiritual growth—what are called the Vows—have general application to human and organizational development. Let me explain by first of all looking at these vows in more depth. The vows are a commitment by a professional "Religious" person to Chastity, Obedience and Poverty. Historically and originally there was only one vow—Simplicity—from which the three vows grew into their present form. Each vow has in fact a range of interpretations relative to its meaning depending on the consciousness of the individual. Maggie Ross in talking about the vow of Chastity reflects on this idea as follows.

"In its most primitive interpretation, chastity has meant for the married person to remain monogamous, and for the celibate to refrain from any sexual activity in relationships."[5] First, we note that this is the most primitive interpretation, but at the other end of the scale: "There is in Chastity and its motivation, its signification of single-hearted love, a kind of knowledge—a gnosis if you will, but a true gnosis—of the freedom that comes with this purifying fire that transforms eros, crucified, yes, but resurrected too, and resurrected in the fullest sense of the new creation which reproduces itself now."[6]

The first thing she points out is that the vow does not apply to Religious only but to everyone. It represents an intrinsic truth. The second point she makes is that there is a very wide range of experience of its possible meaning.

In a similar manner Obedience can mean being willing to be led in order to be of service, at one end of the scale of consciousness, and at the other it can mean living by and being obedient to a transcendent set of values that transforms obedience into an expression of servant leadership. *see Cycle Five Leadership, chapter 5*

Poverty can mean giving up material possessions and living in common by pooling resources to be of maximum service, at one end of the scale, or as we indicated in the chapter on skills, it can mean detachment, simplicity and global justice. An example of the high end is indicated in this quotation from the Rule of The Society of Saint Francis: "Poverty is the refusal to exploit or manage the natural world to suit one's own ends. It recognizes the beauty, the sanctity, the goodness of things. It values them too highly to reject or depise them, for it receives them as the work of God; yet it seeks not to possess them but to use them for God's glory, for the welfare of man and of the universe itself.'"[7]

The more we studied documents religious and non-religious alike we saw these themes emerge. Not many business executives would understand these vows as they have been described. But with some translation they would, and they have.

The bottom line for Chastity is that it represents human and spiritual identity. In the documents it is represented by clusters of values relative to the human person and his or her identity and dignity at each Cycle of Development. Obedience is directly related to the concept of Leadership and appears similarly in different forms at each Cycle. Poverty in the first Cycle represents human misery, economic and human deprivation; as a vow and as it is expressed in the later Cycles it becomes a way of life that liberates people from those conditions—it becomes human ethics and justice. All these factors are of central importance to any organization.

The response at this point by some may legitimately be—so what? Why is it it important to relate the vows to ordinary organizational life? Is that not taking the integration of religion and business a little too far? I must admit at one time I wondered myself, until we noticed, through a number of documents, that there was a dynamic relationship between these units—they were not separate entities but they were dynamically related through the Cycles of Development. In fact they were dialectically related much as we have described the value dialectics in previous chapters. Let us see how this works.

THE DIALECTICS OF ORGANIZATIONAL GROWTH—AN EXAMPLE

The following dynamics were drawn from several documents, although one or two like the Oblate one contained the whole process in various sections. Beginning with the first two Cycles, Obedience as Leadership is perceived as Hierarchical, usually in one person, and the institution is viewed as being in a constant state of survival. Chastity as Human Identity is seen as giving up one's life including sexuality for the institution. Poverty is the dialectical consequence which is seen as giving up personal ownership in order to Work and do the Service the institution provides, as follows:

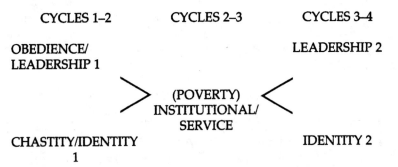

CYCLES 1–2	CYCLES 2–3	CYCLES 3–4
OBEDIENCE/ LEADERSHIP 1		LEADERSHIP 2
	(POVERTY) INSTITUTIONAL/ SERVICE	
CHASTITY/IDENTITY 1		IDENTITY 2

see Leadership Level, chapter 4 and Leadership throughout Chapter 5

In the first dialectic leadership is very hierarchical and makes it an institutional rule, through the documents, written, or unwritten, that celibacy is necessary for service. Crudely put the job is so demanding that the obligations of a family will interfere in making sure the institution is successful.

218

This example is of the historical Religious Community. But the Army, no matter what country you were fighting for, demanded this of all its soldiers in World War II. I have counseled Corporate Industrial Executives who have told me that they don't care what their top leaders do in their private lives, but they expect them to stay single—because they demand first priority dedication, and a family would have to come second!

When the values of a document were congruent relative to the Assumptions we listed above, the dialectic moved forward, so that the purpose of the organization was to give service. Religious service might mean running hospitals; this could be the same with a medical facility. Service could also mean producing good business machines as in the IBM example. Now the dialectic could go backward to producing products that are destructive to the environment and people like the heroin industry. However in this example we are sticking to the process observed in integrated documents.

Two possibilities occurred at this point—either the leadership style changed or the individual's identity changed. *Basically what we saw and observed in a number of different Documents was that the dialectic between the leadership and the identity component was symbiotically related, such that Human and Spiritual growth is the direct consequence of the dialectic between an institutional reinforcement in interaction with the experience of an individual or group of individuals.*

Before Cycle Four it occurs when the individual leader changes and leads the institution to change. After Cycle Four it occurs as a group of leaders in community or as a team bring about systematic organizational alteration. The consequence is as follows:

CYCLE 3	CYCLES 3–4	CYCLES 4–5	CYCLES 5–6

OBEDIENCE/LEADERSHIP 2   LEADERSHIP 3
Negotiated Management

SERVICE   > (POVERTY) VALUED/SERVICE
                                     Dignified Community
CHASTITY/IDENTITY 2   IDENTITY 3
Autonomous Gifted Person
(Limited Lover)

Cycle Three represents the end of the first Dialectic where the high point was institutional service; this connects institutionally with the individual experience of Service at Cycle Four, where leadership becomes Laissez-Faire and management starts to move from the Efficient Management style to a negotiated Management Style.

This is the point in the Cycles of Development where Imaginal and Interpersonal skills develop, and the person begins to become autonomous, and in tune with his or her unique gifts. In the religious celibate setting the person begins to come to grips with the lonely side of celibate love. We appreciate the "limited lover."

The dialectic leads once again, in an integrated setting, to Poverty as Service which is self chosen at the individual level, and to an emphasis on efficient but dignified team work. Although this is the next natural growth period it is in our experience the most destructive if a system remains here too long. If the document primarily reflects this level of operation only it is a major problem. The reason is that this level reinforces over-independence which can lead to system and personal leadership regression. Often people will change jobs or even careers at this point if sound institutional structures are not in place. We will work with this in more detail in the next chapter.

The last dialectical movement that we have noted is as follows:

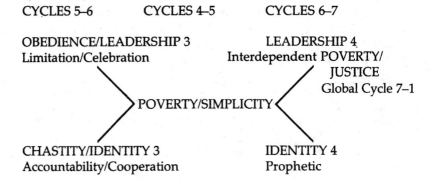

CYCLES 5–6   CYCLES 4–5   CYCLES 6–7

OBEDIENCE/LEADERSHIP 3   LEADERSHIP 4
Limitation/Celebration   Interdependent POVERTY/
                                        JUSTICE
                                        Global Cycle 7–1

POVERTY/SIMPLICITY

CHASTITY/IDENTITY 3   IDENTITY 4
Accountability/Cooperation   Prophetic

Once the Laissez-Faire level at Cycle Four has been transcended, Servant Leadership occurs characterized by its ability to lead from personal authority and the self knowledge that comes from the ability to literally celebrate and learn from one's limitations in a group setting. This level of leadership functioning simply demands an Identity, a level of chastity that Maggie Ross spoke of above. It is an intimate level where stress management and contemplative practice go hand in hand with a high degree of cooperation and accountability at the organizational level.

This causes the phenomenon of simplicity that we spoke of in an earlier chapter. In turn in a few documents, normally of long standing International Corporation and Congregations, this moves to the global level, where the leadership becomes Prophetic in its identity and the love inherent in the vow of chastity becomes global in its dimension, as the organization becomes realistically and practically involved in global issues of justice, ecology and technology.

CONCLUSIONS This journey into the analysis of documents raised more questions than it solved at first. Some of the initial results and questions were as follows:

1. When a document shows an absence or imbalance of values in the human identity (Chastity) area, leadership formation (Obedience) or Justice and Ethics (Poverty) it raised questions about the integration and completeness of the document. The question was: was this also reflected in the lived situation of day to day organizational behavior?

2. When a document had insufficient ACT area values this would indicate an insensitivity to the human condition and to organizational survival issues. Likewise an absence of VISION values would indicate insufficient attention to the future relative to the institution's ability to create a meaningful place for itself in the long run. The question again was: were these elements reflected in the day to day experience of the institution?

3. When the document reflected varying views and definitions through its value clusters of major issues such as leadership, organizational structure, goals, mission and marketing, this would lead, or could lead, to mixed messages and even polarity in the structure. Again the question is how is this reflected in actual organizational behavior.

In fact the first major question was: what is the relationship of data gathered from document analysis to actual organizational behavior? The second question became: what do you do when the organization has no documents, or its documents are incomplete? The information from Document analysis became invaluable to the answer to these questions, and led finally to the development of a number of different programs and processes designed to answer these questions—they were called Matrix Q, "Q" standing for quality, and "Matrix" for the idea of the convergence of quality information in a system of Organizational Assessment. RETRIEVE was at the center of this process and is the subject matter of the next chapter.

Chapter 9:
Document: The Beginning of Convergence

NOTES

1. Previte-Orton (1953), p. 283.
2. Ouchi (1981), p. 131.
2a. Dix (1945).
3. Peters and Waterman (1982), p. 280.
4. Watson quoted by Peters and Waterman (1982), pp. 279–280.
5. Ross (1983), p. 63.
6. *Ibid.*, p. 72.
7. The Society of St. Francis. *Manual of the Third Order of St. Francis.*
8. Much of the development of these later instruments is due to the work of Barbara Ledig (see article in Appendix), in cooperation with Dr. Irving Yabroff. Much of Ledig's work was based on one thousand personal interviews using an instrument called Interform (The Hall-Ledig Interview Format).

RETRIEVE:
FAITH, VALUES AND CORPORATE CULTURE

The leader is a representative of an institution, big or small. The bishop has his diocese, the bank executive, his or her bank. The leader, however, is also a person with his or her own values, gifts, and ministry. Every leader must struggle with the problem of how to satisfy the institution's needs without compromising his or her own values and gifts. This is an age-old problem. David slew Goliath successfully but did not confront his real problem until he had led Israel and remained uncorrupted.

Brian P. Hall[1]

In total over a period of about six months, we developed profiles of nearly eighty companies. Here's what we found:

Of all the companies surveyed, only about one-third (twenty-five to be precise) had clearly articulated beliefs.

Of this third, a surprising two-thirds had qualitative beliefs, or values, such as "IBM means service." The other third had financially orientated goals that were widely understood.

Of the eighteen companies with qualitative beliefs, all were uniformly outstanding performers; we could find no correlations of any relevance among the other companies—some did okay, some poorly, most had their ups and downs. We characterized the consistently high performers as strong cultures.

Terrence Deal and Allan Kennedy[2]

PURPOSE To examine in detail through case studies the dynamic relationship between persons and the Corporate Culture of an institution as an expression of the "Genesis Effect," and to look at the consequences for spiritual growth.

CONTENT The chapter begins with a discussion of information retrieval and computerized assessment as a methodology for discernment, strategic planning and organizational development. The concept under discussion is that human and spiritual development cannot be separated from organizational renewal. The problem of evil is discussed as well as practical suggestions for healthy individual growth through organizational development.

LINKAGE This chapter links the last two chapters on values and organizational development to the spiritual development of the individual person and leader in the Corporate setting. This then leads us to the final chapter that will examine some of the ethical implications of this work and the "Genesis Effect."

We have finally arrived back at Chapter I and the concept of Genesis and the retrieval of information. This chapter is about Retrieve, an overall method and approach to quality information retrieval. As a civilization we have become expert at the gathering of all kinds of information, especially statistical, factual and technical information. This is all very important.

The question that we have tried to address through research and the development of instrumentation is: how does one collect comprehensive quality information on an institution or a network of institutions such that the results are specific enough to lead directly and naturally into Strategic Planning?

This chapter will only outline that process briefly, since our main intention will be to share some of the experiences and the insights that we gained.

Six years ago I moved to the University of Santa Clara. Working with local team we called Omega associates,[1a] and my European counterpart Benjamin Tonna, we became heavily involved in the concept of quality information retrieval utilizing the value system we had developed.

Benjamin Tonna's idea was that if we could analyze the information he had retrieved from the study of overseas missions in his years as Executive Director of SEDOS (an international documentation center in Rome), and all the information we had gained through the study of organizations, we could discover a system of quality information retrieval. The resulting system was international in scope in that it transcends language and culture, in that it is multilingual and value based.

Our first program, which took approximately five years to develop, is called DISCERN. This involves a personal questionnaire that gives a computer printout of approximately twelve pages that analyzes the value patterns of an individual. It gives profile information and raises specific discernment questions relative to a person's faith and spiritual development. It gives a person the information that was covered in Chapters III, IV and V.

Sharing this at a conference in Rome led the Oblates of Mary Immaculate through their Vicar General, Father Francis George, to ask us to do a cross cultural, historical analysis of their Constitutions and Rules. This was referred to in detail in the last chapter.

Since that time, taking the original DISCERN program we developed a new computer scored instrument and program called DOCUMENT. The analysis revealed continuing philosophical and theological trends and internal inconsistencies in the many documents that we examined. To our surprise the analysis also projected, through discernment questions, management problems within an institution or system.

223

As our research continued we soon discovered that we could take a composite of the individual value inventories and come up with group profiles of an institution's or administration's members. We called this CONVERGE.

CONVERGE, as a separate computer program, in turn revealed new information that we, again, had not anticipated. For example, when there were clusters of groups with different values at different leadership levels, tensions and polarities were made evident.

This became particularly useful in working with research and small administrative teams where tensions often run high, and where appropriate team alignment was necessary. The process was also very helpful in working with the issues of house and work team alignments in religious communities, who were looking for more effective processes to improve the quality of their members' lives.

RETRIEVE is the high point of our work. It came about through our work with several International Communities and Corporations. We were asked to do a total system assessment in order to retrieve information for strategic planning in three areas: personnel and leadership development, human and financial resources, and management structures. The purpose was to retrieve information specific enough that they could discern what changes they needed to make in order to survive the next half century.

They had already collected through their own internal resources all the hard data they needed which was made accessible to us. By hard data is understood statistical data such as the number of new personnel, number of persons leaving, number of persons in particular ministry or language groups, etc. The difficulty they were having was that this type of information does not lead with sufficient clarity to Strategic Planning. After all it is simply descriptive of what is.

Philosophically we had always thought it was the quality element which could supply this link. What we did was to design interview formats which could also be used as a questionnaire when an interview was not possible. The questions were directed at specific issues of the quality of a person's life relative to day to day experience. For example, questions included such things as:

1. What is the quality of your present living situation?
2. What is the quality of your working situation?
3. What has been the quality of your experience with leadership in the last four years?
4. What is your experience and understanding of team loyalty?
5. What do you understand to be the most important goal of this organization, relative to your personal experience?
6. What is your experience of the present quality of your leadership?

In doing such interviewing with close to one thousand people in the last five years we (Hall and Ledig) came to recognize a series of anticipated responses that can be made to each question. Not only this, but each anticipated response reflected a particular value orientation.

224

For example, one response to the first question above might be that their experience with their living situation is very negative and they are isolated and have no support. Values that this would probably reflect are ones of Self Preservation and Self Worth. Another response might be that their quality of living is very good and they feel well supported and they are working more creatively now than they ever have. This would reflect values such as Creativity, Friendship, and Peer Support.

We were able to write a data based computer program that correlated all the responses by percentage for a given population, and correlated the underlying values giving rise to a separate discernment profile, and also made cross correlations between questions by using the underlying value matrix. We called this new program: RETRIEVE. This led to a final composite program called MATRIX Q.

What *"Matrix Q"* actually is, is not simply the interview form (RETRIEVE) or questionnaire (DISCERN) as illustrated in the previous paragraphs, but a composite of the individual inventories (DISCERN), the group program (CONVERGE), the Document analysis (DOCUMENT), and the latter interview or questionnaire process (RETRIEVE).

This information, being all computer programed, was finally dovetailed with the hard statistical data, giving rise to the final information package—*MATRIX Q*. It was given this title because it was a matrix of quality information and hard data that was intended to give rise to a quality assessment of an institution.

What has been interesting is that the results of such a study have led to very specific suggestions for Strategic Planning, since it flushed out the discrepancies between what was actually happening in the lived situation, and what the system aspires to as reflected by its documents and internal resources.

The most critical part of all of this was the discovery that *MATRIX Q* was a total method of systems quality assessment. In religious terms this is a process of "Communal Discernment." That means among other things: *that the total Corporate reality is involved, and that this process causes conscientization and change as it is done.*

It is not a matter of doing an assessment and then decoding the information in order to figure out what Strategic Planning needs to be carried out. *It is a matter of doing a Discernment process in such a way that the group changes, and it in the process comes to a common mind resulting in a Strategic Plan of action for the organization.*

For the religious group Communal Discernment assumes the added dimensions of prayerful reflection, and the common faith conviction that this final consequence when done in an integrated manner results in a Strategic Plan that is at one with the Lord's plans of Salvation for the created order.

Further we found that the information was reversible. Namely we found Document analysis led us to discover a process of developing and documenting the "Corporate Culture" of any organization. From the values we were able to derive the goals and objectives and task expectations inherent in the same values.

Not only this but we found that this reverse process is really necessary for all organizations to involve themselves in no matter how far along the road of efficiency and success they are, to insure that their value and Faith Centers are really what they expect them to be. Let us begin to look at this a little closer through the eyes of a particular experience.

AN ILLUSTRATION: BUSINESS AS USUAL OR THEOLOGY?

This experience in many ways is typical of much of the Discernment work and organizational consultation that I and my team of associates do all the time. But on the other hand this particular experience has some elements that I have only experienced half a dozen times in the last few years. It is an experience that includes the phenomenon of evil.

Dr. M. Scott Peck, a psychiatrist who wrote the book *People of the Lie: The Hope for Healing Human Evil*, notes that psychiatrists and modern psychologists are not supposed to talk about evil.[3] Minimally, he noted, they find it difficult to cope with professionally. This is certainly understandable. His encounter with it was in a therapeutic setting, and in the incident at Mylai. What we are going to explore here is an overall consultative experience, where this occurred as a small but significant part of a consultation with a small administrative group.

One of my convictions that came from this experience was that since the 1960's many Corporate entities are experiencing the value and potency of small group interaction. Quality Circles, Research and Development Teams, and small Governing Administrative Teams like the one we are going to examine are examples of where this phenomenon can occur. It is here, in these new potentially intimate and creative entities, that lies enormous potential for interdependent growth in the Corporate World, and the equal propensity for the destructive experience of evil.

THE EXPERIENCE OF ONE ADMINISTRATIVE GROUP

The event was with a group of 10 administrators over a three day weekend. The majority of persons in the group were women and they were all seasoned executives. One person in the group was a male. This was a part of an ongoing consultation with a corporate group that owned and ran medical facilities and auxiliary residential care facilities in Canada and the United States. They had extensive documents which we had analyzed.

The President of the group and her assistant were both present. They were older than most of the other members of the group and had been in their present position for fifteen years. In fact the President was only one year away from retirement.

The identified purpose of the weekend was to examine data they had collected, to look at their own personal values, and to strategize for the next twelve months, at which time it was expected that much of the group would be changed, due to the retirement of the President—Margaret.

As we looked at the data, which was all hard statistical data, on trends and financial planning, we became aware of how it would be

226

impossible to make any sense out of it until the goals of the group were clear.

The group in its present composition had been together for about three years, and were continually complaining about lack of clarity about goals. One person would continually want to talk about the present fiscal situation, another would want to talk about the need to do long term planning, while others would take up all the time with a discussion about a particularly difficult individual.

From our point of view the underlying issue was the lack of sharing and coherence in the group around its commonly held values. Once they were established, we stated (myself and one other associate), everything else would begin to fall into place. Everyone had filled out our Inventories and had received personal copies of "Discern" which is the value profile that gives each individual his or her values, the Cycle of Development, and all the information that follows that we looked at in Chapters IV–VII.

We spent a day working on this, and some pleasant sharing went on that began to build up the team spirit. During this period as is normal we got involved in discussion and counsel around executive stress, time management, and the need for everyone to have his or her own support groups and trusted people that one can delegate things to. This was done in groups of two.

Later in the day we introduced the instrument "Converge" which is simply the composite group profile. It gives the same information as an individual value analysis, except it gives a detailed breakdown of leadership style differences, and lists relative to the group's experience the prioritized value based Goals and Objectives of the group, based on the list of 125 Values.

The idea was that now that we were familiar with our own personal values, we would move to a consensus of group values. At this point the group became significantly more tense, but it was difficult for us to see where it was coming from, since all said they were willing to proceed. After the coffee break the group seemed more relaxed, but Margaret was missing—she had a headache and left the message that she would be back in the morning!

Margaret was central to the group, naturally, because after all she was the President. I decided to go to her room and speak to her privately. What followed became the key that opened the door to the whole consultation.

We spoke privately for about one hour. She told me of how she had been President for fifteen years, and that when she had begun the organization was less than half the size of what it was now. She was in her early sixties, and she had never been married. As is the case when we get older, more of our friends and loved ones become ill or die— she had recently lost her brother and a good friend. What became evident as she talked was her anger, and her lack of interest in anything other than her work.

Additionally she kept remarking how difficult it was to succeed in what she was doing. Finally she stopped and said: "Well, what do you

PRIVATE IMAGES AND INFORMATION

227

think about this silly old woman?" I replied that I did not think she was silly, but I did think she was angry, lonely and disappointed in something or someone. To me she seemed successful. "Why," I asked, "do you feel that somehow you have failed, or am I misunderstanding you?" She responded in a gush of energy and tears.

"Oh, the organization is going well," she remarked. "It's successful, but I am out there all on my own, and not one of them appreciates what I have to go through." "What do you mean?" I asked.

Angrily she raised her voice and said: "I have only got one more bloody year before my time is up. All the changes I have made over the last five years have alienated half my friends. I even had to fire someone I knew and worked with for years—the man had a family, which is more than I have." She then laughed angrily. "I even dreamed about it when I was napping before you knocked on my door." "What do you mean? I asked.

"I dreamt I was in a prison cell. It was large and very dark, and outside I could hear her, I mean them, accusing me." "Who is the 'her'?" I asked. Margaret then went on to tell me that an old school friend she never had got on well with was the Director of one of their largest facilities. The facility was failing and it was due apparently to her friend's insensitivity to the staff and the board members.

Margaret had gotten the information from two board members who were also old friends of hers, but who had sworn her to secrecy relative to the personal information that they were telling her about the Director. The information included the fact that the Director was blaming Margaret for everything, stating that Margaret had never liked her or supported her. She had further urged that the board bring a law suit against Margaret—which in fact did not materialize.

Superficially it would appear that Margaret was confusing her responsibility with that of her own executive board, and that she should have shared it with them, instead of taking all the responsibility on her own shoulders. But this she refused to do based on the fact that information had been shared with her in confidence.

BOUNDARIES AND CONFIDENTIALITY

As we talked more in depth a number of things came to light. First several issues were bearing down on her, each different but all having similar feelings and consequences. When this happens very often the right side of the brain does not always differentiate between the causes. The result can be an experience of being overwhelmed by negative feelings, and even internal images or nightmarish dreams. In this case its symptoms were of loneliness, rejection and fear of failure and disapproval, all of which were perfectly natural given the circumstances.

Margaret's one love had become her work, and she had for years failed to relax or play enough. She was in terms of our earlier discussions very "Doing" orientated. She was denying her need for friendship and the need for personal support, except with her family and one personal friend. She had lost the friend and a brother, through death, in the last year. Loss and the grief it brings is very often experienced as anger at the abandonment it brings due partly to the frustration of not being able to do anything about it.

In addition to this she was about to retire in a year from her life's work. She did not want the praise of having done a good job so much as she wanted to know that people liked her for what she was. She wanted to be affirmed for her "Being" rather than her "Doing." So in addition to the actual loss she had experienced there was this future loss of the job, and possible loss of all her friends that she worked with. "Is this realistic?" we might ask.

Normally we might expect a person to rise above it all, but to discover that someone she had known for years and was supervising disliked her, and even hated her, was too much. Finally, to put the icing on the cake, she was given this information in confidence so that she could tell no one about it, except to someone like myself, who was also sworn to confidentiality.

The composite experiences of loss of loved ones, separation due to disapproval, and impending retirement gave rise to the legitimate feelings of disapproval, rejection and abandonment with their natural consequence of despair. The dream simply summed up all her feelings of trappedness, anger and fear of what others would do, say, and feel about her in the future. The suggestion earlier on the Consultant's part that the group now needed to discuss its goals and values and come to a consensus simply brought all this to a head.

Margaret was in addition caught in a Boundary bind. On the one hand she needed the support of the administrative group at both the business and the informal level, and yet at the same time she was stuck with information that she felt was given to her in confidentiality.

CROSSING
THE
BOUNDARIES
AND THE
EXPERIENCE
OF EVIL

What she did agree to do was to share her feelings of loss relative to the two deaths, and her worry about retirement. Why? Because the team was already aware she was not at her best and were in fact concerned. Whenever a person has strong feelings in a group, most people pick this up, although very often they are not able to articulate what it is they are sensing.

The group was asked to sit in an open circle facing in to each other. After they were briefed on the situation we asked Margaret to state some of the personal issues that she was feeling. First she spoke for a minute or so on the fact that she had experienced some personal loss in her life that had unsettled her somewhat.

She then began to talk about her fear of retirement, but was immediately cut off by the one man in the group, Mark, who blurted out: "Everytime we begin to get somewhere like working on the group's values and goals, you, Margaret, or someone else comes in with all this feeling stuff and gets us off the subject again!" The group went deathly silent.

I finally broke the silence: "Mark, I wonder if you heard what Margaret said, and if you did I wonder if you could imagine what she felt when you said what you did." He looked at me angrily but a little less than he had been, and said, "Yes, but then I am always misunderstood!" Normally, when I am my best psychological self, I would have responded by asking what the others felt, or for someone to explain what was going on, or for someone to clarify the situation for us. But this time something different was occurring.

The feelings were intense, much more intense than I expected. I remained quiet for a moment and then suddenly became aware of a presence in the group, unrelated to anyone who was sitting there. If you were to ask me if I saw it or felt it, or imagined it, I could not tell you, except to say that others reported to me after that they had experienced the same phenomenon. It was as if there was a blackness or darkness in the middle of the circle.

My only explanation is that it was like a black hole, a negative flow of energy that was affecting everyone in the room. I was perplexed and afraid and surprised myself by speaking: "What I believe we are experiencing is the presence of evil!" The group became absolutely silent, and as I spoke the entity or energy left, and the feelings of anger in the room disappeared.

THE FRAMEWORK FOR DISCERNMENT

It is not my intention here to wax theological or explain this occurrence, which I am now finding to be present in a number of consultations. What happened led to some very positive outcomes. After a period of quiet one of the other women, Terry, asked the question: "What does this all mean, and in particular what does it mean for us?"

From this and other similar experiences we were able to make some practical suggestions. The first was to recognize that this was a negative experience that the group was being confronted with. The experience as such was raising discernment questions through the experience. To know the questions one had to know what the experience meant. The experience of Evil is present in our experience when at least the following four elements are all present at the same time in a small group:

1. There is an absence of light. What I mean by this is there is an absence of disclosure. One or more persons in the group are failing to disclose information that the group absolutely needs to do its job. This does not imply in any way that people have to bare all their feelings and give private information to the group. This is in fact even more destructive. It means that certain information has to be given at a feeling level often, in a small group setting, for the group to be able to function well with dignity.

2. That one or more persons experience that the best they have to offer is turned against them. This is a critical experience. Margaret trusted the group, told the necessary information about her fears, and was rejected for doing so. But what is equally important is, as we later found out, Mark had exactly the same experience. The group as it had been operating was causing him to look for another job. He was not feeling that he was a useful member of the group. When he did state what he felt, he was also rejected.

230

3. That persons feel that they are losing Meaning. The overall consequence of the presence of evil is a general loss of meaning on the part of the majority of the group. This is more than momentary confusion, it is the feeling afterward in one's personal life that life is losing some of its purpose and meaning. This is accompanied by feelings of disappointment in the future, anger and frustration.

4. The group loses its sense of Direction—it begins to become Goalless. The last component, that is simultaneously present with the other three, is that the group loses its sense of direction relative to its overall and specific goals and objectives. At the heart of this condition is the fact that it is not the goals and objectives that are at issue but the values that lie behind them. Put in other language the Faith Center of the group is not focused enough. The Faith Center practically speaking is the consensus values that motivate and empower the group in this component that is being eroded.

Most organizations are in effect a network of small groups, and as such have the potential of high creativity, and of falling into the kind of boundary problems indicated in the above experience. Basically we have come to realize that each small group in an institution is experiencing the following dialectic:

PRACTICAL OUTCOMES: BOUNDARIES, POLICY AND CULTURE

Traditionally in the hierarchical organization you only have two components—the Institution to be led, and the individual leader. Within the pyramid of authority each person was an individual in authority and under authority. This is still the case to some degree or other in all institutions. After all, as we have constantly noted in the book, the leadership style has to line up with the requirements of the situation, to be workable.

More and more the team situation as described above is becoming acceptable and preferable. This means that more and more groups operate as teams of equals in more collaborative styles. This will require, as was indicated in chapter VI, specialized skills to cope with the new situation.

see Skills, chapters 4 and 6

Additionally one now has the dialectical effect indicated above. Namely the individual as an equal with other individuals finds himself or herself in a small group framework, guiding and leading the institution.

In the example we have been discussing the President, Margaret, was trying to come up to the expectations of the institution without sharing it with the rest of the administrators. But since they did in fact have authority it really became a matter of partial or incomplete sharing—causing incomplete disclosure as in item one above.

see Time, Being, and Doing, chapter 7 Secondly in the small group where there is more loyalty and more intimacy, and the feelings and expectations are of a higher quality, the emotional drainage is significantly increased. The example above is an indication of this. As a consequence the "Doing" can become stressful as was indicated in an earlier chapter, and can become "Having" a role as was starting to occur with Margaret. Therefore in such a situation the individual's personal values and quality of life have to be more carefully guarded. This is where the above dialectic occurs.

see discussion of Being & Doing in chapter 7 In other words unlike the past the individual's life cannot be so easily separated from his or her work. Why? Because in the new reality the stakes are higher; the harmony between "Being" and "Doing" must be worked with much more closely. Hence in the above example it was seen as appropriate to begin the consultation by helping the administrators with their individual values and lifestyle.

But this is only a part of it, because left like that, it would contribute to the imbalance that is required to deal with such a situation as the one described. That is to say only helping Margaret as a way of supporting the leadership would not have been sufficient in the long run, because the group is like the Body and functions as a whole. She was not a leader apart, but a part of the whole. Let us look at the dialectic once again:

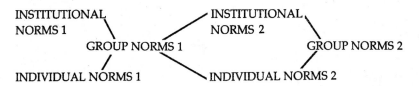

INSTITUTIONAL NORMS 1   INSTITUTIONAL NORMS 2

GROUP NORMS 1   GROUP NORMS 2

INDIVIDUAL NORMS 1   INDIVIDUAL NORMS 2

The situation as we have described it is conveyed by the dialectic with the Institutional and Individual Norms 1, leading to the Group Norms 1, which in our experience led to the negative situation reported. Basically it was one that gave insufficient support to the individual, not by intention but by virtue of the structure of the group.

Norms here means the formal and informal rules of behavior, like Margaret assuming she should not expect support. The second half of the dialectic indicates what did happen. Basically we discovered that in order for a group to recreate itself and avoid the experience we described, which in my experience occurs frequently, the group has to:

see Onion Effect, chapter 6 1. Come to a consensus on its own group values in a constructive dialectical relationship as described in the "Onion Effect" in chapter VI. Convert these values into a Corporate Document that can be favorably compared with other documentation if there is any, as a description of the small group's own Corporate Culture.

2. Develop a Covenant Statement, which is a Policy statement for the internal working of the group only—not policy in the sense of an organizational wide statement. This is a way in which the groups

come to a consensus on minimal norms for individual health, and to maximize the health and productivity of the group at the same time. This would include dealing with issues of confidentiality as cited in the example.

3. Convert the Norms into a Policy for the group. Most groups, especially group administrations, are so overwhelmed by their tasks that they never get below the task to view the values that motivate them. A total system analysis or the analysis of documents will tell you what the value boundaries of an organization are, but they will not tell you the values of the local group—what the lived situation is.

What Margaret and the others discovered was that the small group has its own life and value orientation which is often separate from the individual on the one hand, affecting his or her personal life, and the Institution's need on the other hand. It has its own dynamic if you wish. The first thing we did was to use the group values to develop the group's Corporate Culture.

The group's Corporate Culture is discovered by working on its Value Center, or in religious terms: the group's Faith Center. It is normally done in reference to an administrative group or a small community in a religious setting. The process is helpful with persons in executive positions, working in small administrative group settings, in helping them clarify roles and decision making policy. This process assumes that each person has taken the individual inventory DISCERN, as the above group had. From this was derived the group profile CONVERGE.

CORPORATE CULTURE DEVELOPMENT AND FAITH CENTER ANALYSIS

The group begins the Covenant process by looking at the Primary Goals and Means Objectives and the way they are prioritized. The Values here are not Value Descriptors as in the individual DISCERN profiles but are values from the list of 125 values. As such their meaning is more specific. See the APPENDIX for a full list of values and their definitions.

The group was now led to discuss and examine the priorities and to come to consensus on their order. The client, in this case our administrative group of ten persons, was led to see the relationship between the goals and means objectives, and to discern whether or not the priorities that they had chosen were growthful or regressive. It is understood that a dialectical relationship between Goals and Means exists as follows:

see Values and Dialectics, chapter 1

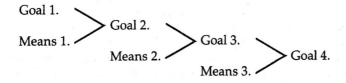

That is to say the first Goal the group has is actualized by the first Means value, which in turn results in the second Goal. Often a group's priorities can lead to negative or frustrating consequences for the group and individuals in the group. Therefore, the purpose of the exercise is to enable the group to choose a practical and a life giving ordering of their values. Let us illustrate the process with an example from our group's common set of values. Their first five priorities from the 125 list were as follows. This is how they were prioritized in the instrument CONVERGE.

Goals

1. Work/Labor
2. Self Worth
3. Service/Vocation
4. Integration/Wholeness
5. Equality/Liberation

Means

1. Intimacy
2. Community/Support
3. Achievement/Success
4. Independence
5. Education/Certification

The first four dialectics would be as follows:

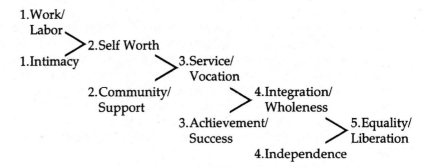

Very often clients will prioritize their values in an unworkable combination, which they try to live out, leading them into frustration and unhappiness. Work and Intimacy would not lead to a greater sense of Self Worth; it would lead to a lot of internal confusion.

In our example the need for intimacy and support by Margaret was confusing the work environment with personal needs. This led her to talk to the board members out of her intimacy side, and caused her to get isolated on her work side. Since this was the first dialectic the other values became neutralized.

We noted also that the first two goals came from the second and third Cycles of Development which is a hierarchical style of management. The means values of Intimacy and Community/Support are from the fifth Cycle which is collaborative in style, which at the very least gives confusing and mixed levels.

Margaret was saying she wanted to be collaborative, but then her style was to withdraw and make the decisions herself, which basically was a Benevolent hierarchical approach. Such an approach is all right if the situation calls for it, which was not the case in this situation.

Interestingly when we analyzed their management document and national policy statement the same value conflict came out, although with some different values. There was a conflict in the document which was very hierarchical when it talked about regional leadership, and collaborative when it talked about the national leadership, like Margaret. When all this came to light it removed a lot of the guilt, and the group was able to take charge of its own life, by concretely deciding how they wanted their values to be prioritized. They reprioritized the same values as follows:

Goals	Means
1. Work/Labor	1. Community/Support
2. Service/Vocation	2. Achievement /Success
3. Equality/Liberation	3. Education/Certification
4. Integration/Wholeness	4. Independence
5. Self Worth	5. Intimacy

We now placed them in their dialectical relationships to see if they were workable or not, as follows:

This dialectic was workable for the group as follows: When an individual has a satisfactory Work experience due to the support of peers at Work (Community/Support), then this will affect what he or she does at Work positively—it becomes meaningful as a vocation (Service/Vocation). As the group Achieves and Succeeds at what it is doing the Work becomes energizing and humanizing. In the case of our group where each of the administrators worked a region, alone for the most part, Achievement/Success with the support of the group did in fact result in the experience of Equality and Liberation.

Because they were alone in the field and very independent in what they were doing, they covenanted with each other through a policy they developed for the group, to balance this with individual educational programs, that would improve the health and professional competence of each individual (Integration/Wholeness).

Finally this new sense of self that each person had, plus the Independence of the job, ideally would increase the sense of Self Worth that each administrator could have. The Self Worth marked by the two ** in the dialectic circles around to the beginning again and becomes -

**SELF WORTH, the foundation for the Work and the community that was supporting the whole effort.

DEFINING THE CORPORATE CULTURE: A PROCESS

In working with the dialectics you are increasing the imaginal capacity of the group, and exercising various life plans for the group and for the individuals within it. Often it is quite obvious what a dialectic should be. At other times a dialectic is clearly unworkable. Sometimes what is workable is unclear, until the person has tried out some new Confirmatory behaviors in his or her life. Remember: the basic purpose is to enable group leadership to discern and make less mistakes than is necessary; perfection is not for mere mortals.

This process is not meant to work magic but rather to set up a minimally reinforcing environment through the small administrative group that enables them to be maximally productive at the institutional and at the personal level. *In other words maximum Human and Spiritual development only occurs as it connects harmoniously with the community within which it works out its life. This community more often than not is a network of communities making up what we normally call an institution or organization.*

The final steps in the process for the group involves defining the first five goals and the first four means values, and placing the final paragraphs into a coherent document. Our group after working with the process for a few months changed the value of Self Worth, realizing that what they really intended by the word was something less personal and much more global like Human Dignity, which they defined as follows.

"Human Dignity is the experience of being totally accepted by another person. This transcends the experience of frustration, guilt and failure, consequenting in an experience of wholeness and integration. Human Dignity also means being physically touched and accepted by concrete expresions of help and support when one is tired and frustrated. It is the experience of transcending, accepting and even celebrating one's physical and emotional limitations."

The definition was enhanced by supportive quotations from their organizational documents. As a group works on a process this way they are changing and being conscientized as they do it. They are literally making the Word flesh. Finally the value definitions, with their supporting quotations, were arranged in the order that they flow in the dialect, with interconnecting sentences or paragraphs to form a cohesive statement. When this is done in a religious setting, supporting statements from the Bible, Rules and Constitutions or other authoritative documents are added.

see Values and Faith, chapter 7 and Integrations, chapter 8

What the group now has is its Faith Center statement, or its statement of Corporate Culture. This of course should be related to the statement of values in its basic documents. If there are no basic documents, this becomes the beginning of that documentation. Once this task was completed it was a relatively simple task to derive from this document policy for the group and goals and objectives for the short and long term future.

One aspect of this, and perhaps the most useful and practical for many administrative groups, is the derivation of Directional and Relational Norms.

The *Relational Norms* are the minimal expected behaviors of the group at the interpersonal level. It is the expression of personal ideas, and feelings that lead to a more communal expression of values and management of conflicts and differences.[3] The composite of these give rise to a supportive Climate within the group. These norms become an objective measure of the group's Climate.

The Directional Norms are related to the goals of the group, and include such processes as problem identification, evaluation and decision making.[4] What the group wants to accomplish in a year would be termed Long Term Goals. What they want to accomplish in the next month would be termed Immediate Objectives. The reason for such a methodology is to arrive at the Norms through our values, which places the group in charge of its declared values for the future, rather than simply reacting to the needs of the given moment.

For an example, let us imagine that we are working with a group administration of five persons in a Social Agency. We will use the same values as in the above examples, as follows:

Goals	Means
1. Family/Belonging	1. Support/Peer
2. Work/Labor	2. Achievement/Success
3. Service/Vocation	3. Education/Certification
4. Integration/Wholeness	4. Independence
5. Equality/Liberation	5. Intimacy

Dialectically they appear as follows:

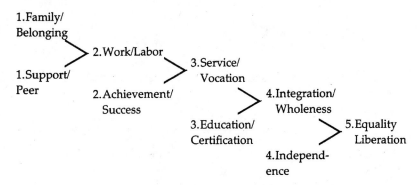

In order to derive the Norms we simply take the first dialectic which is as follows:

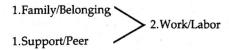

237

The group now brainstorms the specific in time and measurable behaviors that they feel should result from this dialectic. By measurable, it is understood that the behavior is described in sufficient detail, and that it becomes obvious to the group when it has or has not been acted upon. The following represents some examples of Relational Norms from the dialectic.

SOME RELATIONAL NORMS

- We will meet each week for one hour, at 9 o'clock on Monday morning, to share our feelings and expectations about the coming week, and to ascertain if anyone needs special help or support in a given area. Each person will be expected to share his or her thoughts.

- When a person is having difficulty in his or her work or undergoing stress of some sort, this should be reported to the group, so that others do not misunderstand someone's anger or frustration. When the source of frustration is outside the work environment, details of the event should only be shared very minimally. The purpose is to avoid unnecessary maintenance of misunderstood feelings.

- Minimal sharing of positive and negative feelings is expected at all group meetings.

Once this is accomplished the process is repeated with the other dialectics. As such the second dialectic would be:

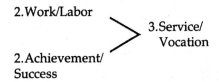

2.Work/Labor

3.Service/ Vocation

2.Achievement/ Success

The following represents some examples from the Directional Norms of this dialectic.

SOME DIRECTIONAL NORMS

- To reduce the overall overhead of the agency by 20% in the next fiscal year.
- To have each department head report on his or her plans for reduced overhead, in writing, in one month.
- To have each member of the administrative team submit an action plan in writing for increasing the client load, at the next meeting.
- To have a written statement of the agency overhead costs in the last fiscal year for each member of the administrative group two days before the next meeting.

When a complete Relational and Directional Norm list is completed, the Norms are grouped into common clusters, prioritized and written into a Policy Statement for the group. Such a statement would become part of a personnel manual.

When the Directional and Relational norms are placed into a formal statement where the members of the group agree to hold each other mutually accountable, you have what we term the "Covenant Statement." It normally includes minimal expectations for personal development, educational development and role accountability relative to one's specific job assignment.

In an earlier work I note (Hall, 1982) that in addition to any of the norms that comes from our specific values, when an administrative group moves beyond the fourth Cycle, an additional set of support factors is essential if the individual is going to be able to function in a healthy manner. These factors are also mentioned in chapter V relative to these Cycles of Development. They are as follows.

CONCLUSIONS: SUPPORT NORMS FOR LEADERSHIP DEVELOPMENT

1. Minimal personal integration. This begins with a relative balance of the four skills mentioned in chapter VI and a minimal knowledge of one's self as reflected through acceptance of one's limitations.

This means in other terms that the Taboo and Manna sides of one's life have to be taken care of sufficiently. This means that in times of pressure, such as the example of Margaret above, one knows one's self sufficiently to cope or ask for help. This personal integration beyond *see Time, chapter 7* the fourth Cycle in particular must include a sound Work/Play or Being/Doing balance, with sufficient skills in stress reduction.

2. Minimal work Integration. Beyond the fourth Cycle, and particularly in participative models of management, anything the executive or anyone else at that level does must be able to be delegated within 24 hours. Basically this relates to our earlier discussion in chapter VI of detachment, poverty and simplicity. When one has a pressure orientated job, where certain things cannot be delegated, then detachment from stress is inevitably impossible.

What is very important to note for this integration and the two that follow is that they are only possible when they are supported by small group policy and the system as a whole.

In my experience this is a chronic problem with Bishops, Clergy and Medical Doctors. Both these professions often convince themselves that they have an ethic or a theology that only allows them in their role to carry out certain duties. This is of course an individual spiritual problem. However, I believe it is exacerbated often by the attitude of the local institutional support structures that makes delegation impossible, expecting perfection on the part of the professional that too often leads to emotional difficulties. A key to its prevention is in the next two integrations.

3. The Intimacy Integration. Basically this is another component of detachment, and implies that each person, no matter what his or her

state in life, needs a peer that he or she can share anything with. Intimacy here does not refer to genital intimacy, but to someone, preferably of the opposite sex, who is not someone I work with, with whom I can share all my hopes and fears, good and bad things, and who shares likewise with me. The intimacy integration does not have to be with someone of the opposite sex, but this is helpful at certain Cycles to insure the appropriate inner masculine/feminine integration.

If one is celibate and lives in an institutional environment that does not trust a person to have such a friend then one's Cycle of Development is automatically limited. Jesus had very close friends; so did Francis of Assisi and Gandhi. In studying many great people personally and by studying dozens of bibliographies we have discovered that this is absolutely essential if integrated spiritual development is to occur.

Traditionally we have assumed that such a relationship would occur in marriage. This of course is the ideal, not the reality unfortunately, as national divorce statistics demonstrate.

But, even when it is the case, a married person may need another person in addition to provide this. This should be understood by couples as the role that a good friend would play. This would be appropriate intimacy, not genital in nature, and would be a natural policy in any marriage to maximize the growth of both partners, at a certain point in their spiritual development.

4. Peer Integration. This has been written about extensively by Caplan and Richards.[4] This is something that can only be arranged by a leadership group as a part of quality leadership development. Peer Integration is the pairing of leaders from different institutions, or areas within a single institution, so as to enable them to give one another peer advice and support in an ongoing, pre-arranged, regularly scheduled way. It is something that requires short term formal training, and it is something that has to be arranged to some degree by the sponsoring institution. Caplan puts its benefits this way:

"Peer consultation is a process of borrowing and lending. From this process of interchange of ideas, abilities, knowledge, conceptualizing skills and workable schemes comes a mutual enrichment which enable both parties to face their respective tasks with increased enthusiasm."[5]

5. Grass Roots Integration. This applies primarily to the later Cycles of Development, where the person is integrated sufficiently to talk to persons at different levels of value development, such that the other person feels completely "at home." It is like the last integration something that is pre-arranged and regular in occurrence. It is a meeting of peers at the human level.

In conclusion this chapter has tried to illustrate in a number of different ways that in the long run Human, Spiritual and Organizational development are all connected into one evolutionary spiral initiated in history and in ourselves by the *Genesis Effect*.

Our journey has taken us from the depths of the Psyche in the early chapters, to documents, through the passages of good and evil, to information and discernment in individual and organizational settings. What is the purpose of it all? Was it simply to investigate a phenomenon, share some research, come up with some practical suggestions? Yes, it was all these things but it was also a search that was driven by the very values that we have explored. Behind all of this there is also "The Ethics of It All" which is the title of the last brief chapter.

Chapter 10:
Retrieve, Faith, Values and Corporate Culture

NOTES

1a. Persons involved were Diane Snow, Irving Yabroff, Barbara Ledig, J. Keke, S. B. Robinson, and O. Harari.
1. Hall (1982), p. 2.
2. Deal and Kennedy (1982), p. 7.
3. Peck (1983).
4. Caplan *et al.* (1972).
5. Caplan and Killilea (1972), p. 270.

11

CONCLUSIONS:
THE ETHICS OF IT ALL

We have gone deeply into these new perspectives: the progress of the universe, and in particular the human universe, does not take place in competition with God, nor does it squander energies that we rightly owe to him. The greater man becomes, the more humanity becomes united, with consciousness of, and master of, its potentialities, the more beautiful creation will be, the more perfect adoration will become, and the more Christ will find, for mystical extensions, a body worthy of resurrection.

Teilhard de Chardin[1]

Then God said: "Let us make man in our image, after our likeness. Let them have dominion over the fish of the sea, the birds of the air, and the cattle, and over all the wild animals and all the creatures that crawl upon the ground."

God created man in his image:
in the divine image he created him;
male and female he created them.

God blessed them, saying: "Be fertile and multiply; fill the earth and subdue it. Have dominion over the fish of the sea, and all living things that move on the earth."

Genesis 1:26–28[2]

PURPOSE To summarize the book by relating values to ethics, and to make the argument that the "Genesis Effect" is ultimately an ethical reality, that calls each of us forth "to be" ultimately responsible for our own potential and for the created order.

CONTENT The chapter begins by relating the values and the stages of development to various ethical stances, and moves to some practical suggestions for analyzing a situation in ethical terms. Finally the developmental reality is related to the "Genesis Effect" and its call to us to view the global reality with concern, and to take responsibility for it.

LINKAGE This final chapter links all the previous chapters on human, organizational and spiritual development to the ethical reality that undergirds them all: "The Genesis Effect."

The purpose of this concluding chapter is to briefly look at the relationship of the Genesis Effect and values to Ethical Issues. My intention is not to be comprehensive in any way, but rather to make some
necessary remarks, and reference other works that we have drawn on
for further reading.

I have taught courses in values and professional ethics to students
from counseling psychology, pastoral counseling, Marriage and Family Counseling, Education and the Health professions at the University of Santa Clara for several years. Many of the students additionally
came from the fields of law and business.

Very often the graduate student population gets involved in these
fields out of their own experiences, positive and negative. Psychology
students may come into the program unconsciously wanting to work
on their own questions or difficulties. Pastoral students are often looking for meaning and spiritual guidance. A person interested in Marriage counseling may have experienced divorce and needs to convert
the pain into a positive meaningful career.

This is by no means all negative, for after all education is a search
for knowledge and understanding. On the other hand they are being
trained as professionals who are going to help others with problems.
This led us to require all the students to look at their own values using
the DISCERN instrumentation that was developed at the University,
to look at their Faith Centers. Additionally if they were health care
professionals they were asked to define the value of healing; if they
were in counseling they define healing and family. Law students
would define Law and Ethics, and Religious professionals the word
Ministry.

The intention was to aid them in coming to grips with the basic existential question: *What values, in what priority focus, and by what definition, are necessary for you to have in your profession in order to help you
cope with any contingencies that you may face in working with a patient or
client?*

The work was done within the context of a discussion about values,
ethics and legal issues. The work was also done in small groups and
the results shared with the whole class in order to expand the consciousness of everyone's issues.

Basically what I have discovered over a period of time is that the
ethical and moral developmental issues only connect and make real
sense for persons after they have examined their own values, in some
depth. Then the ethical dimension comes alive for them, and the issues become exciting. When it is done the other way around it is difficult for them to get a handle on what they are doing, while they are
in the middle of, let us say, an ethical dilemma in a counseling situation.

What we did to bridge the gap was first to suggest that the values in their Cycles are the atomic parts of everyday life, connecting the inner and outer world—the Genesis Effect. What values are was clear to them particularly as they worked with them relative to their own value centers. We then suggested that taking the developmental view, once you could see what cycle your major energy focus was coming from, you could then line this up with Kohlberg's levels of moral development.[3] His six stages more or less parallel the first three Phases of Value development.

In this way the person could now understand the relationship between values, as chosen priorities, and moral development, as the rational choice as to what is a right and what is a wrong choice, morally, at a given stage of development. This was used as a simple translation process and as a way of diagnosing a specific problem that the student might encounter.

The next bridge we introduced was the idea of Ethics. Moral Theory or Ethics is the science of the systematized principles of morally correct conduct and good ends. Traditionally the study of Ethics has included the study of various philosophical and religious views on the subject. This I commend.

Practically in the context I found myself I found it helpful to illustrate different Ethics Principles by reviewing the various Ethical Philosophies that lie behind Kohlberg's six stages. Having done this the connection between an Ethical Philosophy and the values was obvious. Not only this but the student was then able to use the philosophies of Ethics, Moral Development theory and values to analyze particular cases—which was very exciting. A very helpful resource in this regard is a book by Edward Stevens titled: *Business Ethics*.[4]

Stevens shows the relationship between Kohlberg's stages of Moral Development and different Ethical theories that are prevalent in Business. Very basically the first two Cycles of Development that we have discussed would lead to the Survival ethics of Social Darwinism, Machiavellianisn and Rational Self Interest. These can be best explored by referring to his work. My interest here is to point out that the survival cycles lead to survival Ethical orientations.

Social Darwinism regards those who survive economically to be superior because of the inherent laws of business, which parallel the laws of physical evolution and survival. Machiavellianism sees the bruter reality of the survival world we live in and separates its values from the world of family and friends in order to preserve some of the higher values. Rational Self Interest recognizes the blatant survival reality that each of us has to live with in order to survive. Clearly since we are all equal, if we each look out for number one, everyone will do all right.

see chapter 5 The middle Cycles, Cycles Three and Four, relate to a Legalistic Ethics and Ethical Relativism. In the third Cycle rules and law are viewed as universal Ethical Principles. At its most negative form the rules of a Corporation or a Church, as in a local congregation, are viewed as ethical principles applicable to all people. In terms of an earlier discussion this is idolatry, in that a finite reality is raised to an infinite status.

In Cycle Four the movement is toward Ethical Relativism where all points of view are valid. This particular stance has been very prevalent in some forms of psychotherapy, where the therapist claimed to be value free, and simply affirming of the stance of the client, being careful not to impose his or her own views or values. It is sophisticated, in that at least it is recognized that different persons do have valid and different points of view.

All these systems, notes Stevens, have the flaw of seeing the world through limited vision, an eye that is basically limited to the world view of the particular Cycle, to use our language, but not the global world that would account for everyone's perspective. Each of these Ethical views, he points out, assumes a particular view of reality that does not stand the test of time and the scrutiny of pyschology and philosophy.

In the final analysis for Stevens it is the later Cycles of Development that at least begin to hold up by not assuming they have all the answers. At the later Cycles the question of paradox is a part of the reality. Stevens really ends with questions through persons like Illich and Schumacher who in criticizing Western society begin to lead us to ask the paradoxical questions we need to ask, so that in Fowler's terms we will discover a Universal Faith and Ethic.[5]

What Stevens is pointing out is that at the developmental level of the person, within the context of linear time, any Ethic that is based on inadequate levels of consciousness will in the long run be based on an inadequate center of values. He is also pointing out that the environment of business will often through its own world view impose an inappropriate, or unethical framework on individuals in a given institution or Corporation.

Going back to the existential view of an earlier chapter, and adding the dimension of non-linear right brain time, we are confronted with the ethical question in a way that transcends all the Cycles: what cluster of values, what precise centers of value and faith do I need to carry me through all the contingencies of life? The above process was made real to the student population by having them bring in experiences and dilemmas that we would examine. Let me illustrate from a personal simple example.

Several years ago I was exercising over-rigorously and caused a hernia. Naturally my doctor suggested that I go into the hospital for a couple of days and get it taken care of. He recommended a surgeon and I went in for an appointment.

PAIN OR PLEASURE: AN EXAMPLE

In the meantime in talking to a friend, Dr. Daniel Duggan,[6] who did work in biofeedback, I decided that I would like to have the operation without any general anesthetics. That is to say I did not wish to use any medication that would render me unconscious during the operation. My view was that the introduction of several chemicals into the body was unnecessary for such a simple procedure. Dan then talked me through a relaxation and imaging procedure, where we went through the total surgical operation, anticipating all complications, and possible pain.

At first the surgeon was angry at my insistence at no medication and suggested that I go to someone else. He stated: "Look, when I have you or any other patient on the table, I want to do my job, and I don't want interference from amateur patients who may get sick on me or move at the wrong time. I want you to be a piece of meat that I can operate on—and that means medication!" I said that if he wished I would go to someone else.

He then reconsidered on the basis that he, I, and the anesthesiologist would have a discussion about it. The specialist in anesthesiology came immediately, and my doctor asked me to explain the situation, which I did.

The anesthesiologist smiled and said: "Well, isn't that refreshing. Do you know, the stuff that we use has about 24 different chemical components to it. In fact," he waxed on eloquently, to the disturbance of the surgeon, "I would never recommend that stuff if you can avoid it. After all it is only there because most people are afraid to wake up and see what happens, and the doctor, understandably, wants the control."

Enthused, I added that for such a simple operation I would also like to leave the hospital the same day, or at the latest the very next morning. The surgeon smiled, and very much to his credit agreed to go along with the procedure, as long as I had another training session with Dan.

The operation was a success. I in fact felt no pain and was able to watch the skilled surgeon at work. I must say that he was as pleased as I was. The surgeon did win on one point. The next morning as I had planned, with the help of my wife I got out of bed, walked three steps, and fainted—and woke up to a smiling wife and Doctor! I left two days after the operation as he had originally suggested.

We role played the interview with the anesthesiologist, the surgeon and myself in class. We brainstormed the values of myself and the surgeon as we appeared in the role play, and converted them in Kohlberg's stages and the ethics that lie behind them. The results were mixed but will serve to illustrate our method. The top six values were as follows:

Surgeon	Patient
1. Security	1. Integration/Wholeness
2. Self Preservation	2. Self Directedness
3. Care/Nurture	3. Being Self
4. Decision/Initiation	4. Independence
5. Human Dignity	5. Self Worth

The remarks that came out of the discussion were as follows. The priorities of the surgeon, as listed above, reflected his initial attitude, where his values are directly from the first two Cycles. Translated into a World View this would be an alien world that needs controlling.

246

This would translate into Kohlberg's Pre-Conventional level where what is right and wrong is based on avoidance of punishment as a physical criterion. That is to say right action relates to what is physically satisfying. The Philosophical Ethic would be in Stevens' analysis Rational Self Interest. In other words his initial concern was physical and professional control and safety. This they felt was, however, understandable.

As they continued the analysis they felt that in the overall picture, in terms of what he eventually did, the values were exactly reversed, placing Human Dignity first as respecting my position to his own risk. Decision/Initiation was second by virtue of the fact that he actually acted on it. This translated into Kohlberg's Post-Conventional Conscience stage where he finally appendaged himself to a faith center or professional Code of Ethics, which was critical of the norm, in Stevens' terms.[7]

I, the Patient, on the other hand began with a set of values in Kohlberg's Post-Conventional level, and in a Cycle of Development that emphasizes Independence and Self Direction. My conscience orientation was clearly well thought out in terms of what I felt wholeness and Integration meant relative to my body and my inner mind and images. Philosophically I was obviously critical of the medical profession for the purpose of a more wholistic view of the person.

The students also pointed out that in the long run my values also reversed, and Self Worth came first. This combined with what they felt was the second value, Self Directedness, which in the later experience made me unrealistically over-confident.

Ironically this is Kohlberg's Conventional level, where philosophically Law and Code are the Ethic. What I was doing was rebelling against these in the personalized form of the Surgeon and not listening at the point I should have. I was in the Conventional Level by virtue of my rebellion against it.

Conscientization to the issues by converting the values into their moral and ethical framework is one place where personal ethical growth can occur. We mentioned earlier that denial and non-affirmation of our values is critical at the individual level. One place that the individual is confronted with these issues is in the human relations professions such as health care and counseling. A few remarks about these professions would be in order at this point.

ETHICS AND THE ETHICAL PROFESSIONS

All professions have ethical responsibilities. However I want to direct these remarks to those professions which find themselves in ethical counseling as a part of their profession. This includes the health care professions, those in psychotherapy, marriage and family counseling, spiritual directors, pastors and pastoral counselors, and consultants in organizational development. Equally included would be all the related professions dealing with education, law, social services and justice issues.

Most of these professions have Codes of Ethics and documents that one can turn to. In recent years we have analyzed several documents relating to the medical and law professions, and found them often lacking in an integrated values system. Often they would emphasize administration, be lacking in values of human dignity and be remarkably lacking in imaginal skill related values.

In a couple of cases the values in the documents were sound, but the document was not available for anyone to read. In one health institution the administration and its management style were at some distance from the intention of the document, causing considerable conflict between the administration and the health care professionals.

Documents do not insure that the institution is operating ethically or soundly, no matter how sound the documents are. Documents are critically important only when they are living documents. I have known several executives in educational institutions who have shared beautiful value base documents that they had, that they wrote themselves without any consultation with anyone else. This is of course primarily a personal statement, valuable perhaps but limited.

Two points need to be stressed: Documents that are in existence that contain Ethical Codes, values and expectations need to be analyzed for consistency, integration and wholeness.

The question must always be raised: is the Value and Faith Center of the individual or the system adequate to the task, and will it reinforce the possibility of improved Human and Spiritual growth for each person in the organization?

Secondly when there are no documents or Codes of Ethics then this presents the group with an opportunity to develop them. Documents need to be written in such a way that they involve everyone in the organization to be fully utilized and helpful.

PROFESSIONAL CODES OF ETHICS
In looking at State requirements for the various professions, and the Codes of Ethics of organizations such as the American Psychological Association, or the American Association for Pastoral Counselors, we find that all these documents are very limited and not for the most part integrated or wholistic in any way. There is a reason for this—they were not intended to be. The same can be applied to Canon Law and its applications to religious documents.

Such codes are normally in the second and third Cycle of Development and occasionally rise to the fourth Cycle. They are there—as is most law—as minimal prescriptions. In an earlier chapter we talked about the ACT area of one's life or an organization, or a document; well this is the area that these codes relate to, and should not be expected to do much more than this—indeed they do not. Perhaps as people's awareness grows in this area such documents will be expanded.

SCIENCE AND RIGHTS
It has been a popular theme in some circles to see medicine and psychotherapy as value free, purely descriptive sciences. Ashley and O'Rourke have the following to say in regard to psychotherapy:
"Perhaps the biggest issue in psychotherapy is whether the therapist is permitted to change the value system of the client. The common answer is that the therapist should not change this system, but should

248

try to adjust the patient to the system. This answer is somewhat disingenuous. As the existentialist psychoanalysts point out, distortions in the patient's value system often underlie the disorder."[8]

The fact of the matter is that any method of counseling or psychotherapy, any approach to the medical sciences or any philosophy of business has its own value base, and therefore its own bias and point of view. Nothing, as Ashley and O'Rourke later point out, is value free where human beings are involved. Humans are value run, and so therefore are their businesses, and their psychotherapy practices and their hospitals, and even their societies.

Gerald Corey, Marrianne Corey and Patrick Callanan, in another helpful book, *Issues and Ethics in the Helping Professions*, make the point that the ethical issues in these relationships come down to two factors: the professional's responsibility and the client's rights.[9] This is very much reflected in the various State Licensing Laws and the Professional Codes of Ethics.

On the one hand they will talk about training requirements and the need to see and treat the client with dignity, which has to do with professional responsibility. On the other hand they will talk about the client's right to know what a diagnosis says and is, what the fees are, and what the goals and intentions of the practitioner are.

There are many specific issues that have to be dealt with, but a central one is the values of the professional person. Corey, Corey and Callanan state that "the question of values permeates the therapeutic process. . . . We ask you to consider the possible impact of your values on your client, the effect your client's values will have on you, and the conflicts that may arise when you and your client have different values." They go on to say:

"Perhaps the most fundamental question we can raise about values in the therapeutic process is whether it is possible for counselors to keep their values out of their counseling sessions. In our view, it is neither possible nor desirable for counselors to be scrupulously neutral with respect to values in the counseling relationship."[10]

What they are saying in relationship to counseling applies to all the helping professions, and to any professional who helps another person.

A friend and fellow psychologist once said to me: "You know, last week was my turn to be unpopular—I just got so mad." I naturally asked him what he meant. He went on to say that in his counseling practice, he had counseled several families in the process of divorce, ten to be exact, all of whom had high stress problems, and problems with alcohol.

ETHICS AND THE WIDER COMMUNITY

"But the thing that finally got to me," he noted, "was that they were all working for the same company." He noted how the company was resistant to any suggestions, and how difficult it was to push his point and suggest an in-house educational program on alcohol and stress. He finally added: "Of course, what I am really trying to do is get to the leadership and raise some questions about policy and values."

Corey, Corey and Callanan have this additionally to say about the issue of the counselor and the community at large:

"Working with people who come to them for counseling is only one way in which professionals can use their skills to promote mental and emotional health. It can be easy to neglect the fact that aspirations and difficulties of clients intertwine with those of many other people in their lives and, ultimately, with those of the community at large."[11]

This reintroduces us to the same issue that Part III of the book dealt with, namely that human and spiritual growth is ultimately a wider issue, one of organizational interface and ultimately the interface with global society. The same issue presents itself at the ethical level as the above example illustrates. How close really are the Global issues? Developmentally they are very close, as close as Cycle One, and the issues of personal growth and survival.

ETHICS, THE INDIVIDUAL AND THE WORLD AT LARGE

see Phase I Synopsis, chapter 3

Personal Human and Spiritual development, we have noted, only occurs as the individual experiences integration at the value and skill level. Basically the goal values in the first Two Phases from Self Preservation to Work cover those elements that are basically necessary for any human being to be human.

Benjamin Tonna in a book titled *Gospel for the Cities* asks the question: "What are the essential elements and conditions to allow human beings to live in a human way?" He notes that in the United Nations conference on the environment in 1973 the question was raised: what can the fundamentals of human rights be reduced to? The answer was a basic set of human needs. He notes those needs as follows:

"To give them a sharper focus, all these needs can be fitted into four categories: (a) employment—in response to the need to 'be independent,' to have a personal role in 'shared life'; (b) housing—not only in the response to the need for protection against the physical environment (cold, rain, sun) but also as a base of privacy; (c) public utilities and services—in response to the need for food, medical care, hygiene, education, communication; (d) community—in response to the social needs of public order, training, civil, cultural and religious life."[12]

see Cycle 7, chapter 5

The Philosopher and Ethician John Rawls places this polarity of human need into a Cycle Seven set of two Ethical Principles, in a book called: *A Theory of Social Justice*. The first one he calls the Just Savings Principle.

His First Principle reflects all the values in the first two Phases of Development, and reflects basic human needs. The Second Principle reflects values in the later Phases which can be the development of the highest of human and spiritual possibilities.

JOHN RAWLS' PRINCIPLES OF ETHICS

First Principle
Each person is to have an equal right to the most extensive total system of equal basic liberties compatible with a similar system of liberty for all.

Second Principle
Social and economic inequalities are to be arranged so that they are both:
a) to the greatest benefit of the least advantaged, consistent with the just savings principle, and
b) attached to offices and positions open to all under conditions of fair equality and opportunity.[13]

In terms of our study it is the responsibility of corporate society and particularly through its institutions and especially through its religious, social and legal institutions to insure the framework that will permit and encourage individuals to seek out those values which we described as Faith Centers that will enable them to maximize their creative God given potential. Often such a burden does fall on the leadership at the last three Cycles—but even persons at these Cycles are helpless without the supportive community that enables them to be its voice.

The bottom line is we are responsible for the choices that we make within the limits and boundaries of our consciousness. Beyond Cycle Four our choices are in fact limitless, relative to maximizing our own gifts and potential in the cultural milieu we find ourselves in.

What we have said about Taboo and narcissism should make us aware that human beings on the whole try to avoid the painful and will often deny the obvious, and are very often fearful of their inner life. To affirm life and the integration of the inner and outer connection I call the *Genesis Effect* is a basic ethical presupposition upon which this book is based. This ethical perspective would suggest that love of life and affirmation of our "within" is an important aspect of our responsibility.

From the religious perspective, as the existential situation is very oppressive due to personal illness or the social conditions, the fact of choices within that limited arena are nevertheless present, no matter how unfair that seems to be.

As a friend has often remarked to me speaking of very difficult and oppressive situations: "What we need to do is figure out what the next best thing to do is, no matter how limited it might be."

This brings us to the global dimension. This oddly enough is where Genesis begins and ends, and where the Cycles of Development begin and end. For the fact is that the most deprived of persons and the experience of survival is actually what the critical global issues are really about.

Gerald and Pat Mische in their wonderful book *Toward a Human World Order* point out that the three most central issues of our time are all global and are all survival orientated: World Hunger, the development of the Security State and threat of a Nuclear War, and the Problem of diminishing global food and energy resources.[14] This is a problem of

ETHICS AS A GLOBAL ISSUE

251

see *Needs and Global Harmony, chapter 3* Genesis in that the book of Genesis calls us to take authority over the world order—that is the primary Ethic of our day, since this world order is threatened in the above three ways.

The word religion in its original meaning means to make whole, or unify. What we need indicate according to the Misches is authentic religion where the inner development of the human being in his or her own spiritual journey correlates to the external changes needed in the world order. *This is an ethic of Genesis.*

At each Cycle of Development this would imply that really authentic religion, within whatever religious institutional setting, is only going to be healthy as the inner and the outer dimension become harmoniously balanced.

Ken Wilber in his book *A Sociable God* points out that the West has come through a long history of Institutional Religion in its experience of Christianity.[15] But he prophesies that the Church as we now know it will really become dynamic and increasingly salvific as it integrates more fully the contemplative depth approach to personal religion that is such a valuable asset of the East. I believe this is another way of getting at global issues of integration like those being addressed by Pat and Gerald Mische.

Put in another framework we need integrated persons at the Prophetic Cycle of Development who link this Cycle with the first Cycle, the survival level, so that Corporate development and individual development, within integrated leadership, can bring these realities together.

GENESIS REVISITED

It was not the primary purpose of this book to be a foundation for personal or business ethics. But that is a part of its contents. This is because this is simply a part of the nature of the beast, which is values and the Genesis Effect.

We began in the first chapter with a discussion of the book of Genesis, and we began this chapter with another quotation from the end of the first chapter of Genesis. The reason is that they are connected in content and purpose, and consequently make a fitting ending to this work.

The book of Genesis begins with God's primary act of creation: the creation through his spoken Word of the whole created order. This whole book has been about creation and creating human wholeness, through the experience of the Word as values.

At the end of the chapter of Genesis as quoted in the introduction to this chapter, God completes his creation with its high point: the conscious human being. In the quotation the reader will note that "man" is plural and refers to man and woman—"male and female he created them." For what purpose were they created?

They were created to look after the earth, to take responsibility for it. Also since men and women were made in God's image they were to be co-creators with God in the care and preservation of the created order. That mandate is The Ethics of It All.

Basically as we look at the development of the human being, our purpose is basically ethical in nature, namely to take responsibility for the created order. Theologically we cannot stop there no matter what our religious orientation.

We know from the very psychological nature of the person that meaning is absent when the ability to chart our own waters and the experience of intimacy rather than isolation are absent. We do not like to be trapped and we do not like to be lonely—it seems these existential factors were built into us from the beginning.

The ability to choose our life is at root the creative impulse in us. It is the Genesis factor. When we choose we see new alternatives, and acting on them is the act of creating something. This is the need in each of us to seek the Truth, and to Create, as the Creator did. We do it biologically and emotionally, we do it in the activity of our psyche, and we do it as we try to recreate the world through our art, our buildings and our love-making.

The opposite of loneliness is intimacy or union with each other. And not only this, but we even have this possibility with the Divine. The second meaning factor then is Love. This whole book has also been about Love. We have continually talked about integration, unifying ourselves through values, faith centers, skills, support systems and healthy organizations, and so on. This integrative element as it relates to creation is spoken to well by Teilhard de Chardin in the quotation above. Here is a part of it once again:

"The more humanity becomes united, with consciousness of, and master of, its potentialities, the more beautiful creation will be, the more perfect adoration will become, and the more Christ will find, for mystical extensions, a body worthy of resurrection."[16]

Purpose then as described in the Genesis Effect has to do with being Creators, being Lovers and being Responsible, or, if you will, being Ethical. Human love is the most important for the Mystic, and for that matter the author. Being Ethical is being a lover of the Divine, it is the ultimate purpose and possibility of being human, to be able to unite with Divine Energy.

Chapter 11:
Conclusions: The Ethics of It All

1. de Chardin (1957), pp. 153–154.
2. New American Bible, Genesis 1:26–28.
3. Kohlberg (1981).
4. Stevens (1979).
5. Illich (1971 and 1973), Schumacher (1973), and Fowler (1981).
6. Dr. Dan Duggan is the Director of the Human Support Department at El Camino Hospital in Mt. View, California, is certified in Biofeedback, and is on the faculty at the University of Santa Clara teaching graduate courses in Counseling Psychology.
7. Kohlberg (1981) and Stevens (1979).
8. Ashley and O'Rourke (1982), p. 344.
9. Corey, Corey and Callanan (1984).
10. Corey, Corey and Callanan (1984), p. 55.

11. *Ibid.*, p. 275.
12. Tonna (1978), p. 15.
13. Rawls (1971), p. 302.
14. Mische (1977).
15. Wilber 1983.
16. de Chardin (1960), p. 153.

APPENDIX A:
SPECIALIZED READINGS

VALUE LISTS

Short Value List

1. Self Preservation.
2. Wonder/Awe.
3. Safety/Survival.
4. Security.
5. Sensory Pleasure.
6. Property/Economics.
7. Family/Belonging.
8. Self Worth.
9. Belonging (Liked).
10. Care/Nurture.
11. Control/Duty.
12. Tradition.
13. Social Prestige.
14. Work/Confidence.
15. Worship.
16. Play.
17. Achievement/Success.
18. Administration/Management.
19. Institution.
20. Patriotism/Loyalty.
21. Education.
22. Workmanship/Technology.
23. Law/Duty.
24. Equality.
25. Actualization/Wholeness.
26. Service.
27. Autonomy.
28. Empathy/Generosity.
29. Law/Guide.
30. Personal Authority.
31. Adaptability.
32. Health/Well-Being.
33. Search.
34. New Order.
35. Dignity/Justice.
36. Art/Beauty.
37. Insight.
38. Contemplation.
39. Accountability.
40. Community/Support.
41. Detachment.
42. Corporate Mission.
43. Research/Knowledge.
44. Intimacy.
45. Wisdom.
46. Word/Prophet.
47. Community/Simplicity.
48. Transcendence/Ecority.
49. Convivial Technology.
50. Rights/World Order.

Copyright: Brian P. Hall. Nov. 1983.

List of 125 Values

1. Accountability/ Ethics
2. Achievement/ Success
3. Adaptability/ Flexibility
4. Administration/ Control
5. Affection/ Physical
6. Art/Beauty as Pure Value
7. (Self)Assertion/ Directedness
8. Being Liked
9. Being Self
10. Care/Nurture
11. Collaboration/ Subsidiarity
12. Commun- ications/ Information
13. Community/ Personalist
14. Community/ Supportive
15. (Self) Competence/ Confidence
16. Competition
17. Congruence
18. Construction/ New Order
19. Contemplation/ Asceticism
20. Control/Order/ Discipline
21. Convivial Technology
22. Cooperation/ Comple- mentarity
23. Corporation/ New Order
24. Courtesy/ Hospitality
25. Creativity/ Ideation
26. Criteria/ Rationality
27. Decision/ Initiation
28. Design/Pattern/ Order
29. Detachment/ Solitude
30. Detachment/ Transcendence
31. Dexterity/ Coordination
32. Discernment/ Communal
33. Duty/ Obligation
34. Economics/ Profit
35. Economics/ Success
36. Ecority/ Aesthetics
37. Education/ Certification
38. Education/ Knowledge/ Insight
39. Efficiency/ Planning
40. Empathy
41. Endurance/ Patience
42. Equality/ Liberation
43. Equilibrium
44. Equity/Rights
45. Evaluation/Self System
46. Expressiveness/ Freedom/Joy
47. Faith/Risk/ Vision
48. Family/ Belonging
49. Fantasy/Play
50. Food/Warmth/ Shelter
51. Friendship/ Belonging
52. Function/ Physical
53. Generosity/ Service
54. Growth/ Expansion
55. Health/Healing/ Harmony
56. Hierarchy/ Propriety/Order
57. Honor
58. Human Dignity
59. Human Rights/ World Social Order
60. Independence
61. Integration/ Wholeness
62. Inter- dependence
63. (Self) Interest/ Control

64. Intimacy

65. Intimacy/Solitude as Unitive
66. Justice/Global Distribution
67. Justice/Social Order
68. Knowledge/Discovery/Insight
69. Law/Guide

70. Law/Rule

71. Leisure/Freesence
72. Life/Self Actualization
73. Limitation/Acceptance
74. Limitation/Celebration

75. Loyalty/Fidelity

76. Macro-economics/World Order
77. Management

78. Membership/Institution

79. Minessence

80. Mission/Objectives

81. Mutual Responsibility/Accountability
82. Obedience/Duty
83. Obedience/Mutual Accountability
84. Ownership

85. Patriotism/Esteem
86. Personal Authority/Honesty
87. Physical Delight
88. Pioneerism/Innovation/Progress
89. Play/Recreation

90. Presence/Dwelling
91. (Self) Preservation
92. Prestige/Image

93. Productivity

94. Property/Control
95. Prophet/Vision

96. Relaxation

97. Research/Originality/Knowledge
98. Responsibility

99. Rights/Respect

100. Ritual Communication
101. Rule/Accountability

102. Safety/Survival

103. Search/Meaning/Hope
104. Security

105. Sensory Pleasure/Sexuality

106. Service/Vocation

107. Sharing/Listening/Trust

108. Simplicity/Play

109. Social Affirmation
110. Support/peer

111. Synergy

112. Technology/Science
113. Territory/Security
114. Tradition

115. Transcendence/Global Equality
116. Truth/Wisdom/Integrated Insight
117. Unity/Diversity

118. Unity/Uniformity

119. Wonder/Awe/Fate
120. Wonder/Curiosity/Nature
121. Word

122. Work/Labor

123. Workmanship/Craft/Art

124. Worship/Faith/Creed
125. (Self)Worth

Definitions of Descriptors and Values

Introduction   The following definitions are designed to be used with the 125 values as they appear in their respective stages and value clusters. Words that are cluster headings, termed Descriptors, are numbered 1–50. Words that are individual values appear under each Descriptor or cluster heading and are numbered 1–125.

These definitions are brief and are not intended to be comprehensive. They do provide a working guideline for persons seeking to understand the meaning of a value, and for persons using or doing research on the Hall-Tonna Inventory or one of its subsidiary programs such as HT-Document analysis.

Phase IA   1. (SELF) PRESERVATION: concern about physical survival and preservation of one's self.

63. (SELF) INTEREST/CONTROL: restraining one's feelings and controlling one's personal interests in order to survive physically in the world.

91. (SELF) PRESERVATION: doing what is necessary to protect one's self from physical harm or destruction in an alien world.

2. WONDER/AWE: overwhelming feelings of reverence, admiration and fear about the natural order.

119. WONDER/AWE/FATE: to be filled with marvel, amazement and fear when faced with the overwhelming grandeur and power of one's physical environment.

3. SAFETY/SURVIVAL: doing what is necessary to avoid the risk of personal injury or danger of loss in order to stay alive in adverse circumstances.

50. FOOD/WARMTH/SHELTER: personal concern about having adequate physical nourishment, warmth and comfort and a place of refuge from the elements.

52. FUNCTION/PHYSICAL: concern about the ability to perform minimal manipulations of the body to care for one's self and concern about the body's internal systems and their ability to function adequately.

102. SAFETY/SURVIVAL: concern about the ability to avoid personal injury, danger of loss and do what is necessary to protect one's self in adverse circumstances.

Phase IB   4. SECURITY: interest in being physically protected and defended.

104. SECURITY: finding a safe place or relationship where one experiences protection and is free from cares and anxieties.

87. PHYSICAL DELIGHT: the joy of experiencing all the senses of one's body.

5. SENSORY PLEASURE: experiencing physical pleasure through the senses.

5. AFFECTION/PHYSICAL: physical touching which expresses fondness of devotion.

258

105. SENSORY PLEASURE/SEXUALITY: gratifying one's sexual desires and experiencing one's sexual identity.
120. WONDER/CURIOSITY/NATURE: a sense of marvel and amazement about the physical world coupled with a desire to learn about it and explore it personally.

6. PROPERTY/ECONOMICS: the accumulation of property and material goods for security and power.
    34. ECONOMICS/PROFIT: accumulation of physical wealth to be secure and respected.
    94. PROPERTY/CONTROL: accumulating property and exercising personal direction over it for security and for meeting one's basic physical and emotional needs.
    113. TERRITORY/SECURITY: provision for physically defending property, a personal domain or nation state.

7. FAMILY/BELONGING: the relationship between parents and children **Phase IIA** that gives one the awareness of one's roots and physical and emotional connectedness.
    48. FAMILY/BELONGING: the people to whom one feels primary bonds of relationship and acceptance and the place of dwelling of one's parents.

8. SELF WORTH: having a favorable impression of one's self based on objective respect for one's own intrinsic value.
    125. SELF WORTH: the knowledge that when those I respect and esteem really know me, they will affirm that I am worthy of that respect.
    49. FANTASY/PLAY: the experience of personal worth through unrestrained imagination and personal amusement.

9. BELONGING (LIKED): to be regarded with favor by a group of significant others.
    8. BEING LIKED: to experience friendly feelings from one's peers.
    51. FRIENDSHIP/BELONGING: to have a group of persons with whom one can share on a day to day basis.
    110. SUPPORT/PEER: to have persons that are one's equals that sustain one in both joyful and difficult times.

10. CARE/NURTURE: to watch over and be responsible for others as they grow and develop and to receive the same treatment from others.
    10. CARE/NURTURE: to be physically and emotionally supported by family and friends throughout one's life from childhood through aging and to value doing the same for others.
    24. COURTESY/HOSPITALITY: offering polite and respectful treatment to others as well as treating guests and strangers in a friendly and generous manner. It also includes receiving the same treatment from others.
    41. ENDURANCE/PATIENCE: the ability to bear difficult and painful experiences, situations or persons with calm stability and perseverance.

11. CONTROL/DUTY: to exercise strong moral restraint to fulfill one's obligations towards family, friends and those in authority.
    20. CONTROL/ORDER/DISCIPLINE: providing restraint and direction to achieve methodological arrangements of persons or things according to the prescribed rules.
    43. EQUILIBRIUM: maintaining a peaceful social environment by averting upsets and avoiding conflicts.
    82. OBEDIENCE/DUTY: dutifully and submissively complying with moral and legal obligations established by parents and civic and religious authorities.
    99. RIGHTS/RESPECT: the moral principle of esteeming the worth (and property) of another as I expect others to esteem me (and mine).
    31. DEXTERITY/COORDINATION: sufficient harmonious interaction of mental and physical functions to perform basic instrumental skills.

12. TRADITION: handing down statements, beliefs, legends and customs from generation to generation and ritualizing them so as to preserve them and give them meaning.
    114. TRADITION: recognizing the importance of ritualizing family history, religious history and national history in one's life so as to enrich its meaning.

13. SOCIAL PRESTIGE: the reputation and influence that arises from success, achievement rank, and wealth.
    109. SOCIAL AFFIRMATION: personal respect and validation coming from the support and respect of one's peers which is necessary for one to grow and succeed.
    92. PRESTIGE/IMAGE: physical appearance which reflects success and achievement, gains the esteem of others and promotes success.

Phase IIB 14. WORK/CONFIDENCE: self-assurance about one's skills and ability to perform a job, be productive and make a living.
    122. WORK/LABOR: to have minimal skills and rights that allow one to produce a minimal living for one's self and one's family.
    15. (SELF) COMPETENCE/CONFIDENCE: realistic and objective confidence that one has the skills to achieve in the world of work and to feel that those skills are a positive contribution.

15. WORSHIP: religious ceremony of rendering honor and homage to God based on a commitment to commonly accepted beliefs and by regular acts of prayer and worship.
    124. WORSHIP/FAITH/CREED: reverence for and belief in God that is expressed and experienced through a commitment to doctrines and teachings of religious belief.

16. PLAY: non-dutiful, undirected, spontaneous exercise that satisfies the need to divert one's mind from duty toward fantasy, pleasure and amusement.
   89. PLAY/RECREATION: a pastime or diversion from the anxiety of day-to-day living for the purpose of undirected, spontaneous refreshment (which provides for a potential self to be experienced).

17. ACHIEVEMENT/SUCCESS: the ability to accomplish something noteworthy in the world of work and education and attain a desirable goal through one's personal efforts.
   2. ACHIEVEMENT/SUCCESS: accomplishing something noteworthy and admirable in the world of work or education.
   16. COMPETITION: to be energized by a sense of rivalry, to be first or most respected in a given arena; e.g. sports, education or work.
   39. EFFICIENCY/PLANNING: thinking about and designing acts and purposes in the best possible and least wasteful manner before implementing them.
   93. PRODUCTIVITY: to feel energized by generating and completing tasks and activities and achieving externally established goals and expectations.

18. ADMINISTRATION/MANAGEMENT: exercising executive functions in an institution, business, etc.
   4. ADMINISTRATION/CONTROL: having the authority to be in command to exercise specific management functions and tasks in a business or institution, e.g. finance, development, etc.
   35. ECONOMICS/SUCCESS: to attain favorable and prosperous financial results in business through effective control and efficient management of resources.
   77. MANAGEMENT: the control and direction of personnel in a business or institution for the purpose of optimal productivity and efficiency.
   12. COMMUNICATION/INFORMATION: effective and efficient transmission and flow of ideas and factual data within and between persons, departments and divisions of an organization.

19. INSTITUTION: concern for and devotion to an organization, establishment, or foundation which is committed to the promotion of a particular product or service.
   56. HIERARCHY/PROPRIETY/ORDER: the methodical, harmonious arrangement of persons and things ranked above one another in conformity to established standards of what is good and proper within an organization.
   78. MEMBERSHIP/INSTITUTION: the pride of belonging to and functioning as an integral part of an organization, foundation, establishment, etc.

98. RESPONSIBILITY: to be personally accountable for and in charge of a specific area or course of action in one's organization or group.

118. UNITY/UNIFORMITY: harmony and agreement in an institution that is established to achieve efficiency, order, loyalty and conformity to established norms.

20. PATRIOTISM/LOYALTY: devoted love for one's country and faithful support to those in authority.

    85. PATRIOTISM/ESTEEM: honor for one's country based on personal devotion, love and support.

    75. LOYALTY/FIDELITY: strict observance of promises and duties to those in authority and to those in close personal relationships.

    57. HONOR: high respect for the worth, merit or rank of those in authority; e.g. parents, superiors and national leaders.

21. EDUCATION: imparting or acquiring knowledge and skills by disciplining the mind through study and learning in a formal institution or training program.

    37. EDUCATION/CERTIFICATION: completing a formally prescribed process of learning and receiving documentation of that process.

    26. CRITERIA/RATIONALITY: the trained capacity to think logically and reasonably based on a formal body of information. The capacity to exercise reason before emotions.

22. WORKMANSHIP/TECHNOLOGY: the art or skill of executing quality work with simple and complex tools.

    123. WORKMANSHIP/ART/CRAFT: skills requiring manual dexterity that produce artifacts and modify or beautify person-made environment.

    84. OWNERSHIP: personal and legal possession of skills, decisions, and property that gives one a sense of personal authority.

    112. TECHNOLOGY/SCIENCE: systematic knowledge of the physical or natural world and practical applications of the knowledge through man-made devices and tools.

    28. DESIGN/PATTERN/ORDER: awareness of the natural arrangement of things plus the ability to create new arrangements through the initiation of arts, ideas or technology; e.g. architecture.

23. LAW/DUTY: following the rules established by government or other authorities as part of one's legal and moral obligation.

    70. LAW/RULE: governing one's conduct, action and procedures by the established legal system or code. Living one's life by the rules.

    101. RULE/ACCOUNTABILITY: the need to have each person openly explain or justify his/her behavior in relationship to the established codes of conduct, procedures, etc.

33. DUTY/OBLIGATION: closely following established customs and regulations out of dedication to one's peers and a sense of responsibility to institutional codes.

24. EQUALITY: experiencing one's self as having the same value and **Phase IIIA** worth as all other human beings in a way that liberates one for action.
    42. EQUALITY/LIBERATION: experiencing one's self as having the same value and rights as all other human beings in such a way that one is set free to be that self and free others to be themselves. This is the critical conscience of the value of being human.

25. ACTUALIZATION/WHOLENESS: experiencing the possibility of fulfilling one's potential and seeing this as related to the process of becoming emotionally and physically integrated and whole.
    61. INTEGRATION/WHOLENESS: the inner capacity to organize the personality (mind and body) into a coordinated, harmonious totality.
    72. LIFE/SELF ACTUALIZATION: the inner drive toward experiencing and expressing the totality of one's being through spiritual, psychological, physical and mental exercises which enhances the development of one's maximum potential.

26. SERVICE: the motivation to make a contribution to society through one's work.
    106. SERVICE/VOCATION: to be motivated to use one's unique gifts and skills to contribute to society through one's occupation, business, profession or calling.

27. AUTONOMY: the motivation to be independent and personally in control of one's life direction.
    60. INDEPENDENCE: thinking and acting for one's self in matters of opinion, conduct, etc., without being subject to external constraint or authority.
    27. DECISION/INITIATION: to feel that it is one's responsibility to begin a creative course of action, or to act on one's conscience without external prompting.
    7. (SELF) ASSERTION/DIRECTNESS: the will to put one's self forward boldly regarding a personal line of thought or action.

28. EMPATHY/GENEROSITY: reflecting on another's feelings, thoughts and attitudes with positive regard and acceptance.
    17. CONGRUENCE: the capacity to experience and express one's feelings and thoughts in such a way that what one experiences internally and communicates externally to others is the same.
    40. EMPATHY: reflecting and experiencing others' feelings and state of being through a quality of presence that has the con-

sequence of them seeing themselves with more clarity, without any words necessarily having been spoken.

107. SHARING/LISTENING/TRUST: the capacity to actively and accurately hear another's thoughts and feelings and to express one's own thoughts and feelings in a climate of mutual confidence in each other's integrity.

53. GENEROSITY/SERVICE: to share one's unique gifts and skills with others as a way of serving humanity without expecting reciprocation.

29. LAW/GUIDE: viewing principles and regulations that are established by governing authorities as a guideline for a personally active conscience.

69. LAW/GUIDE: seeing authoritative principles and regulations as a means for creating one's own criteria and moral conscience, and questioning those rules until they are clear and meaningful.

83. OBEDIENCE/MUTUAL ACCOUNTABILITY: being mutually and equally responsible for establishing and being subject to a common set of rules and guidelines in a group of persons.

30. PERSONAL/AUTHORITY: individual confidence in the right to have one's thoughts, feelings, words and actions respected.

44. EQUITY/RIGHTS: awareness of the moral and ethical claim of all persons, including one's self, to legal, social and economic equality and fairness plus a personal commitment to defend this claim.

86. PERSONAL AUTHORITY/HONESTY: the freedom to experience and express one's full range of feelings and thoughts in a straightforward, objective manner. This ability comes from a personal integration of thoughts and feelings and results in experiencing one's own integrity and power.

31. ADAPTABILITY: to express one's self fully in an effective, vivid manner coupled with the ability to receive the same expression from others.

46. EXPRESSIVENESS/FREEDOM/JOY: to share one's feelings and fantasies so openly and spontaneously that others are free to do the same.

3. ADAPTABILITY/FLEXIBILITY: to adjust one's self readily to changing conditions and to remain pliable during ongoing processes.

32. HEALTH/WELL-BEING: soundness of mind and body that flows from meeting one's basic physical and emotional needs.

55. HEALTH/HEALING/HARMONY: soundness of mind and body that flows from meeting one's emotional and physical needs through self-awareness and preventive discipline. This includes an understanding that commitment to maintaining one's inner rhythm and balance relates to positive feelings and fantasy.

96. RELAXATION: diversion from physical or mental work which reduces stress and provides a balance of work and play as a means of realizing one's potential.

73. LIMITATION/ACCEPTANCE: giving positive mental assent to the reality that one has boundaries and inabilities. This includes an objective self-awareness of one's strengths and potential as well as weakness and inability. The capacity for self-criticism.

33. SEARCH: a personal, creative exploration of one's gifts and talents along in order to discover one's meaningful place in society.

103. SEARCH/MEANING/HOPE: a personal exploration arising from an inner longing and curiosity to integrate one's feelings, imagination and objective knowledge in order to discover one's unique place in the world.

45. EVALUATION/SELF SYSTEM: appreciating an objective appraisal of one's self and being open to what others reflect back about one's self as necessary for self-awareness and personal growth.

34. NEW/ORDER: developing new and creative institutional forms that **Phase IIIB** maximize creative development and dignify persons.

18. CONSTRUCTION/NEW ORDER: to develop and initiate a new institution for the purpose of creatively enhancing society. This assumes technological, interpersonal and management skills.

35. DIGNITY/JUSTICE: commitment to the goal of providing every person with honor, respect and worth because he/she is fully human.

58. HUMAN DIGNITY: consciousness of the basic right of every human being to have respect and to have his/her basic needs met that will allow him/her the opportunity to develop his/her potential.

67. JUSTICE/SOCIAL ORDER: taking a course of action that addresses, confronts and helps correct conditions of human oppression in order to actualize the truth that every human being is of equal value.

36. ART/BEAUTY: appreciation for aesthetically appealing creations of color, shape and sound, both natural and person-made because they are deeply satisfying to the mind and senses.

6. ART/BEAUTY/AS PURE VALUE: experiencing and/or providing intense pleasure through that which is aesthetically appealing—both natural and person-made creations—simply for the mental and emotional stimulation and pleasure it provides.

100. RITUAL/COMMUNICATION: skills and use of liturgy and the arts as a communication medium for raising critical consciousness of such themes as world social conditions and awareness of the transcendent.

37. INSIGHT: intuitive understanding of an underlying truth about the nature of reality.
  9. BEING SELF: the capacity to own one's truth about one's self and the world with objective awareness of personal strengths and limitations plus the ability to act both independently and cooperatively when appropriate.
  68. KNOWLEDGE/DISCOVERY/INSIGHT: the pursuit of truth through patterned investigation. One is motivated by increased intuition and unconsciously-gained understandings of the wholeness of reality.

38. CONTEMPLATION: the art of reflection and thoughtful observation that consequences in intimacy and harmony with the nature of things.
  19. CONTEMPLATION/ASCETICISM: self discipline and the art of meditative prayer that prepares one for the intimacy with others and unity with the divine.
  90. PRESENCE/DWELLING: the ability to be with another person that comes from inner self-knowledge which is so contagious that another person is able to ponder the depths of who they are with awareness and clarity.
  47. FAITH/RISK/VISION: behavioral commitment to values that are considered life-giving even at risk to one's life.

39. ACCOUNTABILITY: being answerable to responsibilities and agreed-upon values and requiring the same from others.
  81. MUTUAL RESPONSIBILITY/ACCOUNTABILITY: the skills to maintain a reciprocal balance of tasks and assignments with others so that everyone is answerable for his/her own area of responsibility. This requires the ability to mobilize one's anger in creative and supportive ways so as to move relationships to increasing levels of cooperation.
  1. ACCOUNTABILITY/ETHICS: the ability that flows from one's personal awareness of one's own system of moral principles to enrich others by addressing their conduct in relationship to their value system. This assumes the capacity to understand another's level of ethical maturity.
  117. UNITY/DIVERSITY: recognizing and acting administratively on the belief that an organization is creatively enhanced by giving equal opportunity to persons from a variety of cultures, ethnic backgrounds and diverse training.

40. COMMUNITY SUPPORT: the recognition that when individuals are consistently upheld by a group the capacities of the group are greater than the capacities of isolated individuals.
  14. COMMUNITY/SUPPORTIVE: the recognition and will to create a group of peers for the purpose of ongoing mutual support and creative enhancement of each individual. It is the additional awareness of the need for such a group in the work environment and with peer professionals, to enable one to detach from external pressures that deter one from

acting with clarity on chosen values and ethical principles that might be otherwise compromised.

22. COOPERATION/COMPLEMENTARITY: the capacity to enable persons in a corporation or institution to work cooperatively with one another such that the unique skills and qualities of one individual supplement, support and enhance the skills and qualities of the others in the group.

41. DETACHMENT: commitment to the separation of one's self from one's responsibilities and anxieties in order to enrich the quality of one's life.

   29. DETACHMENT/SOLITUDE: the regular discipline of non-attachment that lead to quality relationships with others and with God.

   108. SIMPLICITY/PLAY: the capacity for deeply appreciating the world combined with a playful attitude towards organizations and systems that is energizing and positive. The ability to see simplicity in complexity and to be detached from the world as primarily material in nature. It can include the mutual sharing of property within a group.

42. CORPORATE MISSION: creating and designing organizations and institutions so that they dignify and enrich the persons within them while they creatively enhance society in general.

   23. CORPORATION/NEW ORDER: the skills, capacity and will to create new organizational styles or to improve present institutional forms in order to creatively enhance society.

   54. GROWTH/EXPANSION: the ability to enable an organization to develop and grow creatively. This assumes skills in management design and organizational development at a corporate level.

   80. MISSION/OBJECTIVES: the ability to establish organizational goals and execute long term planning that takes into consideration the needs of society and how the organization contributes to those needs.

   11. COLLABORATION/SUBSIDIARITY: the ability of an organizational leader to cooperate interdependently with all levels of management to insure full and appropriate delegation of responsibility.

   32. DISCERNMENT/COMMUNAL: the capacity or skill to enable a group or organization to come to consensus decisions relative to long term planning through prayerful reflection and honest interaction.

43. RESEARCH/KNOWLEDGE: systematic investigation and study of a given subject matter in order to understand the principles, meaning and truths of objective reality, and its practical ramification.

   38. EDUCATION/KNOWLEDGE/INSIGHT: the experience of ongoing learning as a means of gaining new facts, truths and principles. One is motivated by the occasional reward of new understanding that is gained intuitively.

267

25. CREATIVITY/IDEATION: the capacity for original thought and expression that brings new ideas and images into a practical and concrete reality in ways that did not previously exist.

88. PIONEERISM/INNOVATION/PROGRESS: introducing and originating creative ideas for positive change in social organizations and systems and providing the framework for actualizing them.

97. RESEARCH/ORIGINALITY/KNOWLEDGE: systematic investigation and contemplation of the nature of truths and principles about people and human experience for the purpose of creating new insights and awareness.

44. INTIMACY: awareness and acceptance of the full range of one's own thoughts and feelings, fantasies and realities and trusting those to another person in equal and mutually reciprocal ways on an ongoing basis.

64. INTIMACY: sharing one's full personhood—thoughts, feelings, fantasies and realities—mutually and freely with the total personhood of another on a regular basis.

71. LEISURE/FREESENCE: use of time in a way that requires as much skill and concentration as one's work but that totally detaches one from work so that the spontaneous self is free to emerge in a playful and contagious manner.

74. LIMITATION/CELEBRATION: the recognition that one's limits are the framework for exercising one's talents. The ability to laugh at one's own imperfections.

Phase IVA 45. WISDOM: knowledge of what is true or right coupled with just judgment as to action.

65. INTIMACY AND SOLITUDE AS UNITIVE: the experience of personal harmony that results from a combination of meditative practice and mutual openness and total acceptance of another person which leads to new levels of meaning and awareness of truth in unity with the divine.

116. TRUTH/WISDOM/INTEGRATED INSIGHT: intense pursuit and discovery of ultimate truth above all other activities which results in intimate knowledge of objective and subjective realities which converge into the capacity to clearly comprehend persons and systems and their inter-relationship.

46. WORD/PROPHET: the ability to comprehend a universal perspective of world order and justice and communicate it so lucidly that the oppressed become conscious of their oppression and life and hope are awakened in those who despair.

121. WORD: the ability to communicate universal truths so effectively that the hearer becomes conscious of their limitations such that life and hope are renewed in the individual hearer.

95. PROPHET/VISION: the ability to communicate the truth about global justice issues and human rights in such a lucid

manner that hearers are able to transcend their limited personal awareness and gain a new perspective on themselves and the needs of the disadvantaged.

    30. DETACHMENT/TRANSCENDENCE: exercising spiritual discipline and detachment so that one experiences a global and visionary perspective due to one's relationship to the divine.

47. COMMUNITY/SIMPLICITY: enriched quality of relationships within a group whose members are intensely committed to one another and to a common purpose so that personal creativity is maximized leading to a simplicity of life style which is authentic enough to have a far-reaching impact on society.

    13. COMMUNITY/PERSONALIST: sufficient depth and quality of commitment to a group, its members and its purpose that both independent creativity and interdependent cooperation are maximized simultaneously.

    111. SYNERGY: experiencing the relationships of persons within a group to be harmonious and energized so that the outcome of the group far surpasses its predicted ability based on the total abilities of its individual members.

    62. INTERDEPENDENCE: seeing and acting on the awareness that personal and inter-institutional cooperation are always preferable to individual decision-making.

48. TRANSCENDENCE/ECORITY: simultaneous awareness of the finite **Phase IVB** and the infinite as one comprehends the ecological balance of the world and the need to maintain beauty and harmony in the natural order coupled with the technological skills to enhance the natural beauty and ecological balance in the world.

    36. ECORITY/AESTHETICS: the capacity, skills and personal, organizational or conceptual influence to enable persons to take authority for the created order of the world and to enhance its beauty and balance through creative technology in ways that have world-wide influence.

    115. TRANSCENDENCE/GLOBAL EQUALITY: knowing the practical relationship between human oppression and creative ecological balance based on a simultaneous awareness of the finite and the infinite so that one can influence changes that promote greater human equality.

49. CONVIVIAL TECHNOLOGY: organizational or technological expertise combined with a concern for world social conditions that leads to the creation of life-enhancing organizations or technology that will improve world social conditions.

    21. CONVIVIAL TECHNOLOGY: the capacity to creatively apply technological expertise, both organizationally and with technical instruments, to develop means to improve social conditions in the world by improving means of distributing the basic necessities of life.

76. MACROECONOMICS/WORLD ORDER: the ability to manage and direct the use of financial resources at an institutional and interinstitutional level toward creating a more stable and equitable world economic order.
79. MINESSENCE: the capacity to miniaturize and simplify complex ideas or technological instruments (tools) into concrete and practical objectifications in a way that creatively alters the consciousness of the user.

50. RIGHTS/WORLD ORDER: commitment of personal and professional talents, skills and resources to improving the human condition in the world and promoting basic human rights.
66. JUSTICE/GLOBAL DISTRIBUTION: commitment to the fact that all persons have equal value but different gifts and abilities to contribute to society combined with the capacity to elicit interinstitutional and governmental collaboration that will help provide the basic life necessities for the poor in the world.
59. HUMAN RIGHTS/WORLD SOCIAL ORDER: committing one's talent, education, training and resources to creating the means for every person in the world to experience his/her basic right to such life-giving resources as food, habitat, employment, health and minimal practical education.

RESEARCH ON THE INSTRUMENTATION

Researching DISCERN

Jeanine Kelsey, M.A.
University of Santa Clara
Director of Research

Introduction The DISCERN program has undergone extensive research since 1982. Initial reliability and validity studies have been conducted on the instrument and the results have been positive and rewarding. Two articles in this appendix are reflections on that process. Dr. Oren Harari's article describes the philosophy and rationale underlying the research, its results and the implications for continuing and expanded research. This article informally describes the processes and outcomes of the research at this time.

DISCERN (also known as the Hall-Tonna Inventory) is a computer-scored individual discernment profile of values. It is also the source code that lies behind all of the *TRANSFORM* programs. Two additional programs have emerged from the original Inventory—CONVERGE AND DOCUMENT. CONVERGE measures all the values in a group and computes a group value profile. DOCUMENT is designed to perform value analyses on documents that reflect an organization's philosophy or founding statements.

Funding for reliability and field testing of these programs has been

270

provided by the Bannan Foundation of the University of Santa Clara. The research team was composed of Brian Hall, Dr. Oren Harari of the University of San Francisco, Dr. Irving Yabroff, and Jeanine Kelsey, M.A. Consultation in the early stages was provided by Dr. Maureen Hester of Holy Names College. Dr. Harari's expertise in research design plus his personal creativity and sensitivity to the desirability of quantifying an instrument based on qualitative dimensions provided the team with invaluable guidance through the research process. Dr. Yabroff has spent several years designing the computer programming for DISCERN. His intimate knowledge of the program design added to his personal expertise in statistics provided technical guidance for the more intuitive members of the research team—Hall and Kelsey. Several supporters of the project were available for on-the-spot consultations at critical periods at the University of Santa Clara. Dean JoAnn Vasquez of the Division of Counseling, Psychology and Education, Fr. Bob Schmitt, and Dr. Bill Yabroff have been available to the research team at various times throughout the project. Many others have donated their time. Graduate students in Dr. Hall's and Dr. Schmitt's classes, Holy Names Sisters (particularly Srs. Mary Pat LeRoy and Monique Theriault) and many others have contributed support, time and talent to the research processes, translations, and adaptations.

I. The Challenge

Reliability and validity studies on DISCERN have presented special challenges. Traditional strategies that are employed for statistical research designs are based on quantitative measures. Due to the fact that values are qualitative and, by their nature, reflect spiritual and intuitive dimensions, it has been necessary to address the research component of this study so that the result would be a creative blend of the qualitative nuances and subtleties of developmental value theory with the rigorous demands presented by sound empirical research.

In his article, Dr. Harari addresses the challenge of developing a network of empirically-derived data, logic, intuition and spiritual inferences all blended together. This permitted us to draw conclusions from the data that was both logically defensible and maintained the integrity of the underlying constructs and theory.

II. Standardization of the Language—Item Analysis

Prior to performing reliability and validity studies it was necessary to determine that the items in the inventory accurately reflected the values as they were defined in the theory. This procedure has been completed in English, French, German and Italian at this writing.

The purpose of the Item Analysis has been to standardize items in the inventory so that the statements reflect to the majority of people in a given culture the value it is intended to describe in its appropriate stage and phase according to its definition.

The size and composition requirements for groups participating in this procedure included the following: a group of 10–15 people composed of equal numbers of men and women with heterogeneous backgrounds regarding age, occupation, education, religion and socioeconomic status.

271

The process involved each group member having a copy of the statements. The statements were read aloud one at a time and 2 or 3 group members were invited to share a specific experience that this statement brought to mind. The research team referred to the definition of the value in that statement and determined whether or not the behavioral examples reflected the intended value in its appropriate stage and phase of development as well as the intent of the definition.

When a statement was not clear the definition and value was discussed with the group and the statement was reworded to fit the value and definition. A group consensus process was used to reword the statement to fit the language and the most common cultural interpretation.

III. The Content Validity Studies The question to be answered in designing content validity studies was—does the inventory measure what it was designed to measure? When a respondent selects a particular item, does it represent the same meaning to the respondent as it did to the designer?

Procedures to measure content validity were designed in a multiple choice/matching format. Statements in the inventory were divided into groups of 7. Values corresponding to the statements were randomized and arranged into groups of 10. Respondents were instructed to match the value with the statement that most closely described its meaning. This design maximized the chances of selecting a response that required thought and minimized the possibility of using the process of elimination to guess at a response.

Research subjects were selected on the basis of sampling as heterogeneous a population as possible including differences in marital status, socioeconomic differences, ages ranging from high school through elderly, sex differences and different religious and ethnic backgrounds. Participants met in 5 groups of approximately 10 persons each, totalling 68 participants. All participants were naive subjects with no previous training or education in value theory.

Standardized procedures were established in order to establish research controls and provide a basis for replication in ongoing research.

Criteria were established for minimally acceptable standards of content validity on the instrument. Two factors were considered—(1) minimum percent of correct responses to retain an individual item; (2) minimum percent of total items to accept the instrument as valid. The research team agreed on an 80% standard of acceptability for both factors.

Results of the content validity studies were quite satisfying. On total items, 83.5% scored over 80% accuracy. Specific items that scored under 80% will be examined in ongoing research to determine if the problem lay in the research design or with the clarity of the statement.

IV. The Reliability Studies The first task was to explore which reliability procedures were appropriate for this inventory—test-retest, equivalent forms, and split half. For a discussion of these three procedures see Dr. Harari's article

Test-retest reliability assesses the consistency of the instrument over time. Equivalent forms reliability compares two different forms of the same instrument. This procedure was rejected because there is only one form of the inventory to date. Split half reliability measures internal consistency by dividing the instrument in half. Traditionally the instrument can be divided either by odd and even items or by first half and second half.

Traditional methodology for split-half reliability was inappropriate for the design of this inventory. Therefore, we adapted the traditional methodology by creating an alternative design for split-half reliability. Since each value is represented in the instrument at least twice the items representing the values were divided in half and the inventory was split by value representations. A mathematical correction was calculated to allow for values that appeared in the inventory more than twice. Respondents' value selections were then correlated between the two halves created by this division.

A second consideration arose in determining which variables to measure. The inventory provides information on two different measures—developmental level of consciousness and priority value choices. There are only 8 stages and phases of development which provided a manageable number of variables to correlate with the expectation of receiving positive statistical results. Certainly lower correlation coefficients could be expected if they were calculated on 125 values or (a possible third variable) item selection. The inventory has a possible 385 item choices. In keeping with the philosophy of wanting to know as much as possible about the inventory and to establish rigorous standards for its acceptability, the decision was made to calculate correlation coefficients on all three variables—developmental levels, value choices and specific responses to specific items.

A third consideration was to determine criteria for research subjects. It is anticipated that DISCERN will be used by a cross-section of the population from high school age through senior adults across all socioeconomic classes and in various cultures. Research participants needed to reflect a cross-section of this population. In order to meet this criterion, research groups were composed of high school students and a sampling of adults that included differences in education, socioeconomic status, age, sex, marital status, and ethnic background.

A standardized and replicable format was established for reliability procedures. Research participants met in 5 groups of approximately 20 persons each. Respondents completed a demographic data sheet while individual responses were kept confidential. Explanatory information and instructions for participating in the research project were standardized and presented to different groups in a consistent manner. All research groups were conducted by the research director. Participants were naive subjects with no previous education in value theory.

A total sample of 104 individuals participated in the reliability studies. Test-retest studies were conducted 4 weeks apart with the same participants in the same setting. The statistical procedures used to correlate responses was the Coefficient Alpha Version I. Using specific values as raw scores, the test-retest correlation was .66, a very acceptable figure considering the number and heterogeneity of values in the inventory. Using developmental levels as raw scores, the test-retest correlation improved to .75. Using specific responses to specific items as raw scores, the test-retest correlation was a respectable .72.

The following table summarizes the reliability results:

| | Type of Scoring | | |
	Item Responses	Values	Dev. Level
Split-Half			
Version 1 alpha	.78	.73	.92
Version 2 alpha	.76	.66	.91
Test-Retest	.72	.66	.75

The results indicate a strong consistency in the pattern of data across the three types of raw score categories. Clearly, DISCERN is most consistent in assessing developmental level and somewhat less consistent, though still acceptable, in assessing specific values. Dr. Yabroff notes that the high consistency of developmental level is most critical to the purpose of the inventory. He also observes that the test-retest correlations being lower than split-half correlations is not surprising since test-retest measures are based on two administrations. This provides opportunity for more variation in scores with the opportunity for changes in the respondent over the time period that intervenes between test and retest.

V. Preliminary Conclusions on the Results of the Research   Part of the philosophical base for research on DISCERN (H-T Inventory) includes commitment to ongoing, long-term research that results in changes in the inventory as new data is gathered. For example, the validity studies that were performed prior to 1984 indicated that over 80% of the statements reflected clearly and accurately the value they were intended to reflect. However, possibly 25 statements in the inventory may not be clear to the reader. These statements will be addressed in future research and ongoing validity procedures will let us know if the problem was with the design of the research or with the design of the inventory and statements. As these statements are addressed and made more clear, it seems reasonable to expect that additional reliability studies will have even more positive results than these initial ones.

This commitment to the process of research as a long-term and ongoing affair underlies the conclusions we are making on the reliability studies to date. Based on the fact that over 80% of the statements in the inventory appear to be clear and accurately represent the intended value, we assume that the inventory is valid as a base from which to assess the outcomes of the reliability work.

We are also concluding that the initial test-retest and split-half outcomes are satisfactory for the inventory as it currently stands. This is particularly noteworthy since the coefficient alpha generally provides the lowest, most conservative estimate of reliability that can be expected.

The future will see us continuing to follow the research model and data base we began to establish in the processes described above. In addition to continuing to explore areas of the inventory that do not meet our standards of acceptability, we will concentrate on convergent and discriminant validities. That is, we will compare this inventory with others that we hypothesize it to correlate well with as well as those we expect it to correlate poorly with. Following this, we plan to be able to make predictions about how different populations will tend to score on the basis of a variety of demographic variables.

Ongoing research and the subsequent changes in the inventory and underlying theory provide a rich resource for students to develop and explore a particular field of interest as it relates to the value theory and to particular aspects of the inventory.

VI. Ongoing Research and Implications

"A Hybrid Left-Brain/Right-Brain Approach to Validity"

Oren Harari[1]
McLaren College of Business
University of San Francisco

Introduction

Validity refers to how much an instrument (e.g. an attitude scale, a personality inventory, an aptitude test) really measures what it purports to measure. The process of validation involves the methodology—i.e., the strategy, steps, and techniques—used to establish an instrument's validity. The validation of the Hall-Tonna Inventory of Values (H-T), often referred to as DISCERN in the text, involves much more than adherence to traditional methodology. It involves a fundamental and rather unique strategic base.

Essentially, the validation of the H-T reflects a hybrid of two modes of thinking, one that can be labeled as "left-brain" thinking, the other as "right-brain" thinking. Left-brain consciousness involves logic, sequential, linear, analytical thought, and an empirical quantitative orientation towards validation. Right-brain consciousness involves intuition, holistic simultaneous relational thinking, and a qualitative "feeling" approach to validation (see Ornstein, 1975; Restak, 1976; and Springer, 1981 for a discussion of right and left-brain properties). It is interesting that the two key players in the present validation process—the author of this article and Brian Hall—have each leaned towards and articulated a different mode of thinking. The author's approach to the process has been oriented more towards a left-brain mode, while Hall's approach has leaned more towards a right-brain mode. However, and this is critical, both men have understood, appreciated, and possessed enough of the other's mode of thinking to allow for effective communication, collaboration, and complementarity of thought and action. Hence there has existed a rather unique symbiosis of thinking, perhaps necessary to validate an instrument as complex and conceptual as the H-T. This "hybrid," if you will, has acted to synthesize the analytic and intuitive, the scientific and the spiritual, and the sequential and the gestalt during the validation process.

This paper is not a final report on the validity status of the H-T. As will be discussed, we view the validation of the H-T as an ongoing long-term affair. To that extent, this paper presents an update of the research efforts thus far. More important, however, this paper describes the validation *process* we have followed and will follow, along with the underlying assumptions, rationales and strategies.

Face Validity Any validation attempt of any instrument is difficult and time-consuming. For this reason, many instruments sold on the market have been inadequately validated. That is, the instruments may have "face validity" (the items "look" as if they measure what they say they do) but very often the more rigorous and appropriate validation methodologies are underutilized or simply not utilized at all. Hence, the instrument, while "appearing" valid, may really not be measuring what it purports to measure (cf. Friedman, 1983; Nicholls et al., 1983; Spence & Helmreich, 1983). Indeed, the American Psychological Association's committee on psychological tests (1974) has not recognized face validity as a legitimate validity. We wanted to pursue a solid validation process for the H-T, one that went beyond face validity. However, the inherent difficulties in carrying out this project were exacerbated by the fact that the H-T deals with constructs that are particularly hard to operationalize and measure. The H-T is comprised of a rich abstract domain: 125 hetergeneous values, many of them spiritual in nature. It is easier to validate an instrument assessing mechanical aptitude or attitudes toward birth control than an instrument assessing values such as "Convivial Technology," "Creativity/Ideation," or "Faith/Risk/Vision." Consider also that researchers have found it very difficult to operationalize and test humanistic theories such as Maslow's need-hierarchy. Yet the H-T, both as an instrument and in terms of its theoretical foundation, is much richer and has a much wider and more complex domain than does Maslow's theory. Hence, the difficulties inherent in any validation process become much more challenging in the case of the H-T.

Two Roads: Given these hurdles, it would have been easy to take one of the roads. **Two** One alternative I call the "pseudo-rigorous" approach. It is "pseudo-**Approaches** rigorous" because it merely appears rigorous on the surface. It focuses entirely on precision of instrumentation and operationalization, empirical rigor, measurement, and quantification. It is solely a left-brain approach that would ignore the right-brain content of many of the spiritual or holistic constructs tapped by the H-T. Hence, this approach looks rigorous but rests on a weak foundation. It tends to distort, sterilize, and trivialize the rich, subtle, and sophisticated constructs involved in the H-T. Using this approach, the theory underlying the H-T would be "fitted" (i.e., truncated, simplified) to existing methodological and statistical paradigms. For example, just as Maslow's notion of "self-actualization" has sometimes been opera-

276

tionalized as simply a need to have a challenging job, "Detachment/ Transcendence" in the H-T could conceivably be operationalized as the number of times a person meditates per week, or the extent of his or her training in meditative techniques. Such an operationalization, however, would be oversimplified and superficial. In reality, "Detachment/Transcendence" reflects an ongoing prayerful reflection and meditative practice that allows persons to detach themselves from their present reality and hence gain a new understanding of themselves and their behavior.

The second available alternative was what I call the "pro-humanism, anti-science" approach. This approach basically involves throwing up one's hands and concluding that empirical rigor is impossible under these circumstances. Because of the dangers involved in rigorous validation, discussed above, it is assumed that empiricism and scientific rigor simply cannot be applied in this "humanistic" context. The admonition, therefore, is to avoid using any semblance of rigorous validation because it is too mechanical, sterile, and "non-humanistic." In other words, the prevailing belief is: don't apply left-brain thinking to a right-brain problem. Stick to "face-validity," perhaps supplemented by some anecdotal or impressionistic evidence.

Neither of the above alternatives appealed to us. Yet it is interesting that these alternatives reflect an ongoing problem in applied psychology. Often, psychometrically-oriented researchers and humanistic-philosophical practitioners or theorists are like ships passing in the night. Each camp assumes that their underlying premises are mutually exclusive. A strict empiricist might find it impossible to confidently assess constructs such as "Art/Beauty as Pure Value" or "Wonder/Awe/Fate" in the H-T, or might operationalize them in such a way as to make them banal or sterile. A humanist-philosopher might state from the outset that, for these reasons, empiricism simply cannot or should not be used to assess these value constructs (see also Peck, 1983, for an interesting discussion of people's reluctance to apply the scientific method to study spiritual problems).

In the case of the H-T, we had an instrument that did tap humanistic and abstract constructs. Yet at the same time, we wanted to insure the validity of the H-T so that it could be used confidently for applied purposes (e.g., counseling, consulting) and for theory-building and ongoing research. Hence we decided on a hybrid of left and right brain approaches to validation, a weaving of "soft" humanism and "hard" empiricism. It was a compromise to the extent that neither alternative was fully adhered to. There was simultaneously a *rigor* in following a *general* model of accepted validation procedures, and a *slack* in following that model so as to maintain the integrity of the constructs and underlying theory. Our strategy was to develop a network of empirically-derived data, logic, intuition, and spiritual inferences all blended together. The purpose of the network was to allow us to draw conclusions that were both logically defensible *and* that "felt" right. In effect, this empirical-spiritual or logical-intuitive approach towards validation would involve steps that would allow us to make an analytically *and* emotionally justifiable conclusion that the H-T really assesses what it purports to assess.

Approaches to Validity The first step, of course, was to determine which validation strategy to use as a general model. The American Psychological Association's statement on educational and psychological tests (1974) and the Uniform Guidelines on equal employment selection (1978) recognize three types of legitimate validity: criterion-related, content, and construct. A comprehensive discussion of these validities is beyond the scope of the article (see Anastasi, 1976 or Cronbach, 1970 for a complete presentation). Suffice it to say that criterion-related and content validities were rejected as inappropriate. The criterion-related strategy would assess the relationship of the H-T with an external criterion via a correlation coefficient. Criterion-related validity is appropriate when one is attempting to predict performance on a specific, well-defined criterion variable, e.g., an employment test predicting job performance. This was not the case with the H-T. Moreover, we believed that the nature and predictive properties of the H-T were too rich and abstract to be summarized by one criterion or by a single validity coefficient. Content validation would determine the extent to which the H-T samples a specific domain of behavior that it purports to measure. This question, however, is not relevant for the H-T, because no specific domain of observable behavior or skills has been defined as a criterion. Content validation is used primarily for educational and employment tests. Hence, while the boundaries between content validity and the other two validities are often blurred (Dunnette & Borman, 1979), we believed that this approach was inappropriate for the validation of the H-T.

Construct Validation: The Model and the Emergent Hybrid From our perspective, construct validation was clearly the appropriate strategy. Construct validity has been called the validity which " . . . integrates criterion and content considerations in a common framework for testing rational hypotheses about theoretically-relevant relationships" (Messick, 1980, p. 1015). Construct validation involves compiling a mass of evidence to "prove" that an instrument truly measures the underlying constructs it purports to measure. The strategy establishes a network of data, theory, and logic to demonstrate validity. In their classic paper, Cronbach and Meehl (1955) called this network a "nomological net." This "net" consists of an interwoven set of hypothesized and empirically-tested relationships between the instrument and other measures. I will elaborate on this point later. The important thing to remember presently is that construct validation is an ongoing process based on the gradual amassing of observation, data, and theory.

In construct validation, no single psychometric measure, no single observation or no single conceptual thought provides the sole or ever-critical "proof" of validity. It is the gradually-developed network of measures, observations and bits of theory "glued" by logic that acts to clarify what the instrument is really assessing. Small wonder it is sometimes implied that construct validity is the ideal type of validity (see Cronbach, 1980; Messick, 1980; Tenopyr, 1977).

Our plan, therefore, was to utilize the construct validation approach as a general working model. However, our hybrid left-brain/right-brain approach would take the notion of construct validity one step further. We would permit "slack" in the model so as to allow for spiritual, humanistic, or intuitive inferences—the inclusions of right-brain thinking. Fundamentally, however, we would adhere to the general principles of the construct validation model so as to insure rigor and professional legitimacy; this represents left-brain thinking. I will now outline the steps that we have performed thus far in our validation process.

We began, of course, with a working document: the 15th version of **Validation** the H-T which had been developed over 20 years of research by Brian **Steps** Hall and his associates. A preliminary step was performed by Hall, **Undertaken** Kelsey and 15 research participants who spent two days focusing on **Thus Far** the basic theoretical structures underlying the inventory—the values and their definitions. Each value was addressed in its particular phase and stage of development. In addition, the definition of each value was read and reworded as necessary to be clear and adequate in its particular phase and stage of development. The purpose of this exercise was to assess the basic structural components underlying the inventory and to clarify the definitions. This group added five new values to the original list of 120 in order to gain greater developmental clarity to the value list. Following this the group came to consensus agreement that the underlying value structures were adequate and comprehensive and that the definitions were clear and understandable.

The next step was to insure that individuals completing the instrument would understand and interpret the items as the H-T developers intended. This is a particularly important issue in view of the highly abstract and global nature of the value constructs. The author, along with Brian Hall and two other members of his research team, Jeanine Kelsey and Barbara Ledig, first went through each item in the inventory and reworded it until both accuracy (the correct matching of item and value construct) and complete consensus (among the four researchers) was achieved. Even the instructions and format of the H-T were altered for the sake of clarity. In particular, certain sections were deleted, others were combined, others shortened and simplified, and the number of alternatives per item were reduced. This step achieved a leaner, clearer version of the H-T.

The next stage was to replicate this same process with individuals unfamiliar with the research paradigm and theoretical background of the H-T. Fifteen individuals volunteered to commit two weekends to this process. The individuals included students, business people, teachers, clergy, counselors and housewives. At the least, this group included a representative sample of the types of individuals who would ultimately use the H-T. The objective was to strengthen the H-T's clarity and to insure, once again, that naive individuals would achieve both accuracy (item to construct) and total consensus in their interpretation of the items. The group literally went over each item (including *each alternative*) one by one. Items and alternatives were discussed and, when necessary, reworded until both accuracy and consensus were attained. The author, acting as facilitator, would continually ask questions such as "What does this alternative mean to you? What sorts of behaviors does it suggest, i.e., what types of behaviors or attitudes would be elicited by someone who endorsed this alternative? Could the wording of this alternative be clearer or less ambiguous?" The discussions included philosophical ruminations as well as critical behavioral incidents. For example, the value of Detachment/Transcendence was discussed at length. It was defined to include qualities of prayerful reflection similar to transcendental meditation as well as more traditional Western concepts of prayerful reflection.

Hall, Kelsey and Ledig served as frames of reference, or standards. They utilized the standardized definitions of the values as their common reference point. They gave the group ongoing feedback as to how accurate it was in its interpretations of the items. The researchers were also critical in helping guide the group's efforts so that interpretations and rewordings reflected not only the construct but the complexity and richness of the construct. For example, in contrast to the value of Detachment/Transcendence, the value of Contemplation/Asceticism was addressed. This value reflects highly developed spiritual disciplines that have been developed and taught through generations and include the regular discipline of prayer, fasting and presence as one of one's highest priorities. Thus, it contains the component of Detachment/Transcendence but encompasses even more than that.

For each item and each alternative, differences of opinions were explored in depth until the twin criteria of accuracy and consensus (among group members *and* researchers) were attained. Finally, even the format and appearance of the H-T was further modified by consensus of the group and researchers for the purposes of greater clarity and user-friendliness.

Note the left-brain/right-brain hybrid in this process. First of all, the stages described thus far were essentially an empirical pretesting of the foundation, format and structure of the H-T. Indeed, the pretesting even permitted extensive rewording of items in terms of style, vocabulary and grammar both by researchers and by a sample of naive subjects. This empirical pretesting reflected left-brain strategy. At the same time, we eschewed the idea of a large sample completing a sterile questionnaire in favor of a small group of people working together intensely and intimately. Moreover, group processes were relatively unstructured within the boundaries established by the researchers. The discussions were freewheeling and uninhibited, touching upon a wide array of philosophical, spiritual, emotional and intuitive topics salient to the task. This dynamic represented more of the right-brain element of the process. It was a necessary element in order to insure that the integrity and richness of the underlying constructs were retained.

The next step in the validation process was primarily left-brain in structure: a preliminary assessment of the *reliability* of the H-T. I use the word "preliminary" deliberately. Since we considered the validation process as an ongoing, evolving process, we assumed that the H-T would be altered and revised on a regular basis. Hence, new reliability measurements would have to be taken with each change.

Reliability pertains to the consistency of the instrument. Validity asks the question: what does the instrument measure? Reliability asks the question: *whatever* the instrument measures, is it doing so *consistently*? Reliability, then, is a necessary precursor to validity, and thus becomes a critical element in the validation process.

There are three established models of reliability. "Test-retest reliability" assesses the consistency of the instrument's results over time. Individuals complete the instrument at one time, and their scores are correlated with their scores when they complete the instrument at a subsequent time. "Equivalent forms" reliability assesses the consistency across different forms of the same instrument. Individuals complete two "equivalent" forms of the instrument and the two sets of scores are correlated. "Internal consistency" reliability assesses the consistency across items within the same instrument. Generally, this is done in one of two ways. The instrument can be split in half (e.g., odd-numbered and even-numbered items; or first half and second half of the instrument) and responses in each half are correlated. The other approach is to actually compute the correlation of each item with every other item in the instrument. (See Ghiselli, 1964, for both theoretical background and specific equations.)

Since we did not feel that we had two equivalent forms of the H-T, the "equivalent forms" reliability was rejected. The other two reliability models were utilized, however. A sample of 89 individuals participated in the test-retest phase. This population included high school students as well as adults from diverse backgrounds. The time interval between test and retest was four weeks. Using specific values as raw scores, the test-retest correlation was .66, a very acceptable figure considering the number and heterogeneity of the values in the H-T. Using developmental levels as raw scores, the test-retest correlation improved to .75. Using specific responses to specific items as raw scores, the test-retest correlation was a respectable .72.

The internal consistency reliabilities were computed using two versions of Coefficient Alpha (see Kaplan & Saccuzzo, 1982, for rationale and formulae). Version I estimated split-half reliability when the variances for the two halves of the instrument are considered unequal. (If the variances of the two halves of the instrument are equal, the coefficient alpha and the traditional Spearman-Brown split-half reliability coefficient are equal. Hence, the use of alpha was a precautionary move on our part.) Version 2 was the more general model of coefficient alpha, one which averages the split-half reliability estimates obtained by dividing the test in all possible ways. Using the raw score categories described in the prior paragraph, the results can be summarized as follows:

Type of Scoring

	Item Responses	Values	Developmental Level
Version 1 alpha	.78	.73	.92
Version 2 alpha	.76	.66	.91
(For comparison, the test-retest results described earlier were:)			
Test-retest	.72	.66	.75

The results indicated a strong consistency in the pattern of data across the three types of raw score categories. Clearly, the H-T is most consistent in assessing developmental level and somewhat less consistent, though still acceptable, in assessing specific values. As Irving Yabroff, who performed the statistical analyses, notes, the high consistency of developmental level is most critical to the purpose of the H-T. Yabroff has also correctly noted that the fact that the test-retest correlations are lower than the coefficient alpha correlations is not surprising. Internal consistency measures are based on one administration of an instrument while test-retest measures are based on two administrations. There are at least two possible reasons why individuals' responses may change from time 1 to time 2. First, change may be due to unsystematic effects, e.g., differences in how a person feels when completing the inventory, or differences in the setting and administration of the instrument. Change may also be due to non-random effects, e.g., retention of items or familiarity with the instrument, or even real changes in the person's value orientation or developmental level between the time of the two administrations. We concluded that the preliminary test-retest and internal consistency reliabilities are satisfactory. This is particularly noteworthy since the coefficient alpha generally provides the lowest, most conservative estimate of reliability that can be expected (Cronbach, 1951; Allen & Yen, 1979).

As part of the ongoing validation efforts, another methodological step was undertaken to further double-check on the clarity and meaningfulness of the instrument content to respondents. A new sample of respondents was used in this step. The items on the H-T were randomized into clusters of 7 each. These 7 items were then put into a left hand column on a questionnaire while the adjacent right hand column consisted of the matching values randomly presented. (*Example below*)

Left column:

_____I am a person whose feelings and words usually correspond.

_____I am a person who values being a member of an organization.

_____I like to help develop new, creative institutions and systems.

_____A major concern for me is discovering new insights through study and observation.

_____I am a person who values history and tradition.

282

_____When I am in a group I prefer being supportive of and supported by my group.

_____I feel good when I am sexually and sensually satisfied.

Right column:
1. (Self) Competence/Confidence
2. Membership/Institution
3. Education/Knowledge/Insight
4. Congruence —expressing personal feelings, thoughts and actions that are consistent
5. Independence
6. Duty/Obligation
7. Sensory Pleasure/Sexuality

Each respondent matched each item with what he or she considered the value it illustrated. Actually, in order to prevent a "process-of-elimination" type of response, each left hand column had 7 items while the adjacent right hand column listed 10 values. Clusters consisted of no more than 7 items so as to prevent cognitive overload. Also, as a means of preventing overload and fatigue, each respondent was presented with clusters comprising items of only 1/3 of the entire inventory. In other words, a total of 68 new respondents participated in this step, but Group 1 (n-23) responded to the first third of the H-T, Group 2 (n-27) to the second third, and Group 3 (n-18) to the third third.

A criterion standard of 80% accuracy was set. That is, 80% of respondents to a given item had to correctly match the item and value in order for the item to "pass." The data indicated that 75% of the items did pass this test easily. We are now in the process of carefully investigating the 25% of the items that did not pass this test. We are also examining the distinct possibility that some to all of these items were in fact clear but that the matching value descriptions (right-hand column) were not. However, if we do have to modify any of these items so they can pass the 80% rule, we will naturally have to redo the reliability phases since the inventory will then be comprised of some different items. Again, that step would be entirely consistent with our ongoing *quasi-sequential, quasi-holistic* validation perspective. Moreover, we would expect an *increase* in reliability. If anywhere up to 25% of the present items are still potentially ambiguous to some respondents, then any reduction in ambiguity would increase the temporal and internal consistency of the instrument. This is an exciting possibility since the reliability coefficients are already satisfactory.

Ongoing Research and Implications

The future will see us following a general construct validation model. We will be gradually building the "nomological net" I discussed earlier. A wealth of specific hypotheses and potential relationships will be tested over the next few years so as to demonstrate the construct validity of the inventory and to improve its underlying theoretical base. We will be concentrating primarily on "convergent" and "discriminant" validities as defined by Campbell and Fiske (1959). Campbell and Fiske's model has been used as a framework for well-researched construct validation approaches. In its essence, convergent validity would answer the question: does the H-T correlate well with measures and indices that we hypothesize it to correlate with? Discriminant validity would answer the question: does the H-T correlate poorly with measures or indices that we hypothesize it to correlate poorly with? In establishing convergent and discriminant validities, one of our approaches will be what is sometimes called the "known-groups" or "contrasted groups" method (see Kerlinger, 1978). In this strategy, we will make predictions about how different groups with "known" characteristics *should* score on the H-T. For example, we might hypothesize that value priorities differ according to age groups, to socioeconomic level and to cultural background. Members of the clergy may reflect higher levels of consciousness than engineers. Women may tend to select values related to Care/Nurture while men may be more likely to select values related to Achievement/Success. Some key questions will include: What sorts of groups should score high (and low) on the different stages or developmental levels? What is the theoretical rationale for the predictions?

A variant of this approach is to take high and low scores on developmental levels and make predictions about differential behaviors or differential performance on various external behavioral or demographic indices. For example, we might predict that persons who register higher levels of development will be more likely to have experienced life in several different cultures and speak more than one language. Another means of assessing convergent and discriminant validities is by demonstrating hypothesized relationships between the H-T and scores on other measures. For example, we might predict that developmental levels should be differentially correlated with measures tapping self-esteem, work attitudes, and social/political attitudes. Or, more specifically, we might hypothesize that:

Stage I (Level I) has higher correlation with endorsement of McGregor's "Theory X," while higher stages (levels) have higher correlations with endorsement of "Theory Y."
Phase III correlates more with Kohlberg's Level III morality than with any other.
Phase III correlates more with agreement with Declaration of Independence than with the "small is beautiful" writings of Illich and Schumacher.
Attitudes toward the "job" or the "corporation" should be differentially correlated with Stages or Levels.
The H-T should be correlated higher with scales measuring values than with scales measuring other constructs, e.g., specific attitudes, personality, or aptitudes.

Another related way of demonstrating convergent and discriminant validity is by means of the multi-trait multi-method matrix (Campbell & Fiske, 1959). This strategy assesses the extent to which two or more measures (say, the H-T and peer ratings) are differentially and predictably measuring two or more traits or constructs (say, Developmental Levels I, II, III, IV, V, VI). Convergent validity is demonstrated when the measures agree on their assessment of each construct. For example, a high correlation among the two measures assessing each developmental level separately suggests convergent validity. Discriminant validity is demonstrated in various ways. One way is by demonstrating that the convergent validity correlations are higher than the correlations among the constructs when assessed by the same measure. For example, the correlation between the H-T and peer ratings when assessing Developmental Level I should be significantly higher than the correlation between Developmental Level I and II as measured by either the H-T or peer ratings alone. The reader is referred to Campbell & Fiske's (1959) classic paper for further details. We shall be using their approach as an important part of the validation model.

Finally, given our long-term perspective on this project, we hope to supplement the traditional cross-sectional data (i.e., results obtained at one point in time) with longitudinal data (i.e., testing and gathering data on the same individuals over a long period of time).

Note once again the hybrid left-brain/right-brain nature of our future work. On one hand, the general working model that we will follow is an established and rigorous approach to validation. That is the left-brain part of the paradigm. Simultaneously, however, some of the criteria or indices that will be correlated with H-T scores will be clinical types of inferences, global spiritual descriptions, and generalized assessments of mood or cognitive processes from the right-brain part of the paradigm. Moreover, the depth, heterogeneity, and richness of the value clusters will be maintained, despite the fact that by definition many of those values are complex, ambiguous, and highly conceptual. While we will use accepted methodological and psychometric steps as a frame of reference, we will be careful to avoid any moves that will simplify or distort the value constructs. Finally, we have adopted a holistic "timeless" perspective: we will be conducting different stages simultaneously; we will be making continual recalculations of statistics such as reliability coefficients; we will be continually modifying both the H-T and its underlying theoretical base; and we have set no particular deadline for a "final" validation statement.

BIBLIOGRAPHY

Allen, M.J. and Yen, W.M. *Introduction to Measurement Theory*. Monterey, Ca.: Brooks/Cole, 1979.

American Psychological Association (APA), *Standards for Educational and Psychological Tests*. Washington, D.C.: Author, 1974.

Anastasi, A. *Psychological Testing* (4th edition). New York: Macmillan, 1976.

Campbell, D.T., and Fiske, D.W. "Convergent and Discriminant Validation by the Multitrait-Multimethod Matrix." *Psychological Bulletin*, 1959, *56*, 81–105.

Cronbach, L.J. "Coefficient Alpha and the Internal Structure of Test." *Psychometrika*, 1951, *16*, 297–334.

Cronbach, L.J. "Validity on Parole: How Can We Go Straight?" *New Directions for Testing and Measurement*, 1980, *5*, 99–108.

Cronbach, L.J. *Essentials of Psychological Testing* (3rd edition). New York: Harper & Row, 1970.

Cronbach, L.J., and Meehl, P.E. "Construct Validity in Psychological Tests." *Psychological Bulletin*, 1955, *52*, 281–302.

Dunnette, M.D., and Borman, W.C. "Personnel Selection and Classification Systems." *Annual Review of Psychology*, 1979, *30*, 477–525.

Friedman, H.S. "On Shutting One's Eyes to Face Validity." *Pychological Bulletin*, 1983, *94*, 185–187.

Ghiselli, E.E. *Theory of Psychological Measurement.* New York: McGraw-Hill, 1964.

Illich, Ivan. *Toward a History of Needs.* New York: Pantheon Books, 1978.

Kaplan, R.M. and Saccuzzo, D.P. *Psychological Testing: Principles, Applications, and Issues.* Monterey, Ca.: Brooks/Cole, 1982.

Kerlinger, F.N. *Behavioral Research: A Conceptual Approach.* New York: Holt, Rinehart, & Winston, 1978.

Kohlberg, Lawrence. *The Philosophy of Moral Development.* San Francisco: Harper & Row, 1981.

McGregor, Douglas. *The Human Side of Enterprise.* New York: McGraw-Hill, 1960.

Messick, S. "Test Validity and the Ethics of Assessment." *American Psychologist*, 1980, *35*, 1012–1027.

Nicholls, J., Pearl, R.A., and Licht, B.G. "On the Validity of Inferences About Personality Constructs." *Psychological Bulletin*, 1983, *94*, 188–190.

Ornstein, R. *The Psychology of Consciousness.* San Francisco: Freeman, 1975.

Peck, M.S. *People of the Lie: The Hope for Healing Human Evil.* New York: Simon & Schuster, 1983.

Restak, R. "The Hemispheres of the Brain Have Minds of Their Own." *New York Times*, January 25, 1976.

Schumacher, E.F. *Small is Beautiful.* New York: Harper & Row, 1975.

Spence, J.T., and Helmreich, R.L. "Beyond Face Validity: A Solution." *Psychological Bulletin* 1983, *94*, 181–184.

Springer, S. *Left Brain, Right Brain.* San Francisco: Freeman, 1981.

Tenopyr, M.L. "Content-construct Confusion." *Personnel Psychology* 1977, *30*, 47–54.

"Uniform Guidelines on Employee Selection Procedures." *Federal Register*, 1978, *43*, 38296–38309.

NOTE
1. I would like to thank Brian Hall and Jeanine Kelsey for their helpful comments on an earlier draft of this paper. Their individual contributions throughout this validation process have been invaluable.

DEVELOPMENT OF THE SELF

In the early chapters the book builds on concepts based on the work of Jung, the psychoanalytical tradition, the views of the existentialists, and draws on recent developments acknowledging the differences in male-female psychology. The following three articles are here for the reader to explore these issues in more depth.

Barbara Ledig: Natural Valuing Systems: Value Development and Psychological Type

Jeanine Kelsey: Masculine-Feminine Development: A Value-Based Perspective

Mary Lou Harrison and Linda Prendergast: Existentialism and The Genesis Effect: A Synergetic Interaction

Natural Valuing Systems:
Value Development and Psychological Type

Barbara Ledig, M.A.
Omega Associates

The theory of value development as proposed by Brian Hall delineates a process within individual consciousness which is developmental in nature and is characterized by certain behaviors. These behaviors reflect priority value choices in terms of time and energy output. Carl G. Jung developed a theory of personality type which describes different orientations to reality and subsequent behavioral characteristics. The purpose of this paper is to explore the similar ways in which these two theories deal with behavior as the expression of an internal reality and with the interrelationship between this expression and the developmental process.

In this comparison I will use the Jungian theory of type in its fundamental approach to the functions of intuition, sensation, thinking and feeling as ways of perceiving and judging the environment. I will include the ideas of Jung on personality as a dynamic developmental process and the determinant of certain behavioral characteristics. I shall discuss different orientations to time and my own theory of an internal ordering which provides a means by which external images are given meaning in relationship to the images of internal reality.[1] The four functions will be dealt with in their relationship to motivation, self worth, value priorities and the development of skills.

The significance of the comparison of Jung's personality theory with Hall's value theory lies in the consideration of psychological/spiritual development as the integration of the four functions as understood by Jung on the one hand and the integration of skills associated with the four phases of development of Hall on the other. The concept of an internal ordering process came about as a result of examining the various ways in which different psychological orientations strive to create some connection between internal images and external reality so that a sense of harmony can exist between these two worlds. The ability to connect these images so that reality can be brought into a meaningful context provides a major basis for motivation and the extent to which this can be done successfully has a direct impact on self worth. Brian Hall refers to this connection between the inner and outer world as the Genesis Effect. The dynamics behind the Genesis Effect result in certain behavioral characteristics, abilities and motivational factors which differ in degree and intensity for different individuals. One way of clustering these differences is by their division into four major functions. The combinations of these functions result in a psychological type as described by Jung.

The Four Functions and the Genesis Effect The four functions are the means by which individuals perceive and judge the environment. One of the functions will be preferred over the others and will be the strongest function, referred to as the superior function. The other functions are referred to as the second, third and fourth functions and have the possibility of developing in strength as an individual grows and matures. This article will explore the developmental nature of the functions in relationship to the development of consciousness as it is viewed in *The Genesis Effect*.

The Perceiving Functions Intuition and sensation are the functions which are used to bring information into the field of awareness. They are called the perceiving functions and influence an individual's concept of time and reality.

Perceiving Through Intuition Intuition perceives first the totality of things before seeing the individual parts. Internal images are formed by connecting and relating disparate ideas and events leading to the development of images which have their own form and meaning. It is by nature wholistic in that the parts are seen in relationship to the whole.

The intuitive process experiences time as flowing backwards from future to present with the past holding importance only to the degree to which it connects to future reality. The present, likewise, is merely a connection to what the future may hold. This future experience of time influences the nature and quality of internal images which create the world view of the individual who perceives reality through intuition.

The intuitive way of knowing is an inner kind of knowing and is not dependent on any factual or external proof as is the trial-and-error method of the sensate function. Intuition knows through instantaneous insight into relationships and patterns between ideas, events and people. The experience is one of ownership and certainty, a sense of confidence in the validity of the inspiration. There is an awareness of the "I" who completed the task which results in a reinforcement of the ego. This is not to say that other types do not use intuition but that those in whom intuition is the superior function use it more easily as a way of interacting with the world. The very nature of this process results in an understanding of the symbolic representation of reality, of an understanding of symbols as the synthetic representation of a complex and universal truth sometimes referred to as an archetype.

The intuitive experience of time and reality leads to an internal structure of images based on future possibilities. Meaning is found in pursuing these possibilities through interconnecting and relating that which is experienced in the present to future reality. Much behavior is an expression of this quest for forward movement.

288

Since the future is often experienced as more real than the present the intuitive tends to move into it even against great odds. They have an unusual capacity for risk as the pull forward is stronger than practical reasoning. Each new event is seen with new connections, meaning and possibilities resulting in the flexibility and spontaneity necessary to allow opportunity for change or the consideration of new opinions. Planning ahead tends to stifle this spontaneity and ideally each new event is dealt with without the restrictions of facts or previously formed opinions.

The world view of intuition is one of myriads of connections, possibilities and events merged into a totality of future orientation. The expression of the images created by this orientation results in a stance to the environment which values vision and imagination. Innate to the intuitive process is the ability to use imaginal skills, those skills which are used in the creation of new ideas and images by relating disparate data and the system skills in seeing how the parts relate to the whole.

When intuition is found in an individual who is introverted it will be directed toward the inner world of ideas, thoughts and symbolic language. When it is found in an extroverted person it will be directed toward the outer world of people and things.

The dynamic value clusters represented by the Hall Value Theory which most naturally result from the intuitive way of being in the world and which provide the basis for motivation and meaning are those of Creativity/Ideation, Faith/Risk/Vision, Adaptability/Flexibility, Independence, and Knowledge/Discovery/Insight.

The other possibility for perceiving reality is through the function of sensation. Sensation perceives first the parts of things and then weaves them into a meaningful whole. It moves step by step through an experience, testing and evaluating based on what the senses perceive as being real through seeing, touching, feeling, smelling and experiencing.

The sensate experience of time is present oriented. The here and now is of primary importance. The sensate world is very connected to physical reality and basic internal images are more three dimensional and concrete than are those of the intuitive. Just as the intuitive finds expression through the world of insight and future possibilities the sensate finds expression through the world of physical reality. Fact and detail speak for themselves and create a picture of reality to which sensation can relate. It is a more tangible process than that of intuition in that it needs proof of the validity of things. Because this function is by nature closely connected to the senses it is in touch not with archetypal symbols but with the reservoir of human experience manifested in tradition, that is, the physical expression of values in history and the opinions of generally accepted authorities. This is the opposing pole of the same force which in the intuitive is expressed as an affinity for understanding archetypal symbols, a collective, archaic memory of times past. In their opposition intuition and sensation find a way to relate to a universal meaning system which is in harmony with their internal structures.

Behavioral For the sensate individual the concrete, not the abstract, is trusted as
Characteristics a valuable measuring stick of the worth of things. Since the present is
of Sensation the major area of focus much motivation lies in impacting and relating to the environment in a way that can be measured and evaluated. The degree to which a sense of achievement and of belonging can be accomplished will have a direct effect on the self worth of the individual. Planning is an important part of this process as it provides a means by which to move from the present to the future through the step by step process which is valued by sensation.

When sensation is found in a person who is introverted it will be directed to the sensation an experience from the environment creates. Those events which are capable of creating the strongest sensation will be reacted to most strongly. When sensation is extroverted energy will be focused on external things such as social interaction, recognition for achievements and tangible objects which convey an expression of an inner image.

Sensation is predisposed toward those values which involve doing versus being. The dynamic value clusters represented by the Hall Value Theory which are a result of the sensate orientation to reality are those of Efficiency/Planning, Social Affirmation, Tradition, Law/Rule, Membership/Institution.

The We have explored the concept of time and the internal images of the
Evaluating perceiving functions which result in certain behaviors and value prior-
Functions ities. I would like to now explore the judging functions as they relate to motivation, self worth, value priorities and skill development.

Once something has been perceived it is handed over to the judging or evaluating function so that some conclusion can be drawn about the perception. The judging functions, like the perceiving functions, affect an individual's orientation to time and reality. The two judging functions are the thinking function and the feeling function. These functions are opposites just as intuition and sensation are opposites.

Evaluating The thinking process is characterized by its focus on objective criteria
Through and rational thought. It is concerned with principles based on univer-
Thinking sally valid and proven points of view and builds a structure of measurement based on objective criteria which is valued for its constancy and externally proven validity. These complexes of criteria serve as a measure of worth by which all experience is evaluated. The process is systematic and insures a measure of constancy and continuity in building a thought system that is objective. A sense of worth is connected to the ability to maintain this objectivity.

The experience of time of the thinking function encompasses the past, present and future. Situations and events are important to the degree to which they can be linked to an historical past, experienced in the present as being related to a larger whole and having obvious implications for the future. Events have meaning as they are related to the larger process in this linear flow of time. Images are formed which reflect reality as a constant and ordered system.

This unique way of experiencing time and evaluating reality leads to the creation of an internal structure of measurement which is logical, analytical and impersonal. Motivation is found in striving to bring con- **of Thinking** flicting elements to resolution through their creative interaction so they can be in harmony with this structure. In the thinking process the tension which occurs due to the Genesis Effect results in behavioral characteristics stemming from a drive to bring unity to that which is in conflict and simplicity to that which is complex. **Behavioral Characteristics of Thinking**

Because of a three dimensional experience of time the thinking type has a need to be connected to the past as well as the present and future. Being able to make an impact on history carries its own reward and energy may be directed to such things as social reform, literary works or scientific discoveries. Life is experienced as flowing. Thinking persons want to know where it is flowing and what their position is in the flow. They may frequently assess their behavior, usually by some method of objective criteria such as codes of ethics or by seeking the opinion of others. Planning becomes important in that it is a means by which to stay connected with the ongoing process. The very nature of the thinking process is hierarchical in that it reasons by comparison and will organize life into a system of priorities, screening out the busy work and details in order to devote time and energy to more important issues. This is one means by which order is maintained. Another way is through the concept of shared responsibility. The thinking person respects those principles which provide the basis for order and consistency and wants others to do the same.

The world view of thinking is one of an ordered and constant system. When the thinking process is used as an evaluating function decisions are based on principles, objective criteria and rational thought rather than on subjective experience. That which is variable is considered unreliable. That which is selected to be integrated into personal experience gets woven into a new pattern through connecting and relating ideas and opinions and often results in the creation of a new thought or system of ideas, the function of the imaginal skills. Single, isolated events have no meaning unless they can be seen in relationship to the larger process. The workings of a system and knowledge of how the smaller parts relate to the whole, or system skills, are easy to understand.

When thinking is introverted focus will be more on the dynamics of the inner process as related to external facts or possibilities. When it is extroverted it will focus primarily on the laws and structures which have been created by established authorities.

Thinking is predisposed toward those values which involve doing versus being and the clusters most represented by this function are Criteria/Rationality, Objectivity, Mutual Responsibility/Accountability, Ethics and Knowledge/Discovery/Insight.

Evaluating Through Feeling The feeling function is perhaps the most difficult to give accurate description to as it is frequently confused with sensation (I feel a pain, etc.) or with intuition (I have a "feeling" that . . .). It is also confused with emotion. Feeling, however, may be expressed in many kinds of emotions. For example, the feeling of love may be expressed as the different emotions of affection, protectiveness, jealousy, and so on. The difference between the two is that emotion does not have the characteristic of wanting relationship with the object and feeling does. The type of relationship which is sought is one which is in tune with an inner core created through a series of experiences and the subsequent feeling reactions to the experiences. This core serves as an internal system of values by which new experience can be evaluated.

The experience of time of the feeling function is circular with the present being experienced in terms of the past and then being returned to the past in the form of memory. Events of the present are looked at in terms of the similarities they hold with the events of the personal past. In other words, personal experiences get coded into feelings. These feelings are accumulated over the years and are then decoded into an evaluation of present experience.

Behavioral Characteristics of Feeling When the feeling function is used as the evaluating function decisions are based on this subjectively derived internal valuing system. A sense of worth is related to the ability to be in tune with these inner feeling tones so that accurate and just evaluations can be made. There is therefore an emphasis on personal values and the the need to be fully one's self and to allow others to be themselves. The interpersonal skills are essential to this process and are those which are most accessible to the individual who chooses feeling as a way of evaluating experience. The need for relationship in the feeling process is a primary motivational factor. Images of ideal relationships which are in harmony with the internal feeling structure influence much of the behavior of the feeling person.

When feeling is introverted focus will be on the internal process and the feeling tones which intuition or sensation brings into the field of awareness. When it is extroverted the primary focus of energy will be on interaction with others and external events.

The values which result most naturally from the orientation to reality of the feeling function are those of Being Self, Expressiveness, Congruence, Empathy and Cooperation.

Valuing by Type and Phase As we look at the value priorities in the different psychological types we see that an experience of the primary goal values in Phase II and Phase III (those which tend to be experienced long term) will be colored by one's orientation to reality in terms of psychological type. I refer only to the values in these phases because Phase I values are primal needs and are non-specific in relationship to type or personality while values in Phase IV are more complex combinations of preceding values and occur only as a result of significant integration.

292

While a minimal experience of Family/Belonging is considered essential to all people it is related in a particular way to the sensate way of connecting to the world. Be it through the world of nature, of community or of respected institutions, the experience of the value of Self Worth is directly connected to the ability to belong and is a source of motivation and meaning. In contrast the intuitive, especially the thinking intuitive, is very independent. The inability to belong to the physical structures of family, of tradition, of institutions due to circumstances or misfortune does not hold the same trauma as it does for the sensate. It does not affect the meaning system and therefore the motivation of the intuitive who belongs to the world of insights and inspirations. Belonging, for the thinking person, is connected to one's relationship to a historical context. For the feeling person the ability to successfully experience oneself in relation to others is essential to a sense of worth and meaning. Motivation resides in the quest for ideal relationships. When values which affect the ability to do this are not within the experience of the feeling person disillusionment and despair may result. It is the absence of those values which are primary motivational factors in each particular type that is of particular concern. **Phase II: Primary Goal Values**

The person who uses the combination of intuition and thinking as a first and second function is often seen as the one most concerned with the value of (Self) Competence/Confidence. The Intuitive/ Thinker accumulates knowledge and skills at an untiring pace, always testing, evaluating and assessing his or her abilities to do and know many things. However, intuition, whether it is combined with thinking or feeling, focuses on the ability to discover new connections and possibilities. When it combines with feeling instead of thinking the focus is on possibilities in people rather than ideas. Although this is not usually defined as a need for competence it is the same dynamic that drives the sensate to be competent in conquering the environment, the thinking to be competent in creating and maintaining order, and feeling to feel competent in the ability to establish successful relationships. All of these behaviors stem from the same source, the need for congruence between an inner mode of ordering, with its respective images, and outer reality. It is a quest for harmony, experienced from four perspectives. The experience around the other values also reflects this quest for harmony. The degree to which it is possible to achieve this harmony determines the level of consciousness of the individual in terms of psychological/spiritual development and on the degree to which the second, third and fourth functions and their associated skills are integrated into the field of awareness. We can see how this happens by looking at the primary goal values in Phase III.

In Phase III the primary goal values become multiple as the goal value of Life/Self Actualization (Phase IIIA) will result in action which is expressed by the second, Service/Vocation. The nature of this value will be defined by the characteristics of the first, second and to some degree the third functions. For example, a person who perceives through **Phase III: Primary Goal Values** intuition may spend a lot of time and energy exploring possibilities and become increasingly adept at developing new ideas. This will lead to an experience of the value of (Self) Competence/Confidence. However, their ability to translate this into Service/Vocation or Life/Self Actualization and ultimately to Being Self and Human Dignity (Phase III values) will depend on their ability to evaluate them objectively (the function of thinking), to relate them to the human dimension (the function of feeling) and to ground them in practical and concrete action (the function of sensation). What I am proposing is that the degree to which Phase III values can be integrated is directly proportionate to the degree to which the second, third and fourth functions and their associated skills are integrated.

In Phase IIIB the value of Being Self will be lived out in a way particular to each individual personality type. The way in which it is expressed will be influenced by the qualities of the second and third function and will result in behaviors more complex than previously possible. For example, when intuition is directed toward new ideas via the second function of thinking, the third function will be feeling. Feeling will bring to intuition and thinking the ability to connect the behavior around this cluster to the human dimension. New ideas will then be seen in the context of their ability to enhance the human condition and expressed as the value of Human Dignity. Human Dignity and Being Self are actually a constellation of the values of Self Worth, Family/Belonging, (Self) Competence/Confidence, Life/Self Actualization and Service/Vocation. Through their synergistic interaction these values have combined to form new and more complex values equaling more than the sum of their parts. The individual way in which the value of Being Self is experienced is influenced by a person's psychological type and will determine the way in which the value of Human Dignity is given expression in the lived experience.

Values and Personality Integration   The way that one moves through the cycles of development will be influenced by the pre-existing complexes of values of each unique type. Phase I which is generally short lived speaks to extremely basic needs and lays the ground work for further development. It is at Phase II that we begin to see the clustering of values as related to particular psychological type orientation. A minimal experience of values in this phase, especially the primary values of Family/Belonging, Self Worth, (Self) Competence/Confidence, is essential. The other observation at this phase is that values around instrumentality are most easily learned by the sensate person. This is a phase in which belonging needs are extremely important and one which will probably be experienced most fully by the sensate personality on the first cycle through the developmental process. The intuitive will move through it more quickly yet less adeptly and thoroughly as their focus of energy is on the values in Phase III which have to do with new ideas and the pursuit of possibilities. However, because healthy development requires the minimal integration of all the skills and because one cannot survive long at Phase III without having successfully completed certain tasks which occur at Phase II the intuitive will cycle back to Phase II to complete this unfinished task before being able to successfully live out the values of the third phase in a meaningful way. The sensate will most likely complete the second phase more fully and then begin to integrate into their experience the values of Phase III. This is in keeping with the natural processes of these two functions: the intuitive function seeing the whole and then differentating the parts, the sensate function moving step by step to create a whole.

Another dimension is the integration of the functions from a Jungian perspective. As the second function becomes more developed the integration of the third function begins. When sensation occurs with feeling the third function will be thinking. Those values connected with the thinking process will begin to hold interest and to be energizing for the sensate in this period of life development. There will be a moving toward the integration of these values which will add new dimensions to those previously held. The cycling process does not leave behind other stages and phases but adds new dimensions to them. At midlife, the fourth function begins to come into play. In sensation, the fourth function is intuition. It is at this point in the life of the sensate that those values which we have assigned to the intuitive begin to come into awareness more fully. It is perhaps only at this point that a move from Phase IIIA/IIIB, or cycle five, the Communal ±/ Collaborative cycles can be possible. It is here that we see values in their dynamic combinations more complex in their content but simplified in their expression. An example of this follows.

The value of Tradition, an important value for sensation, may combine **One** with the value of Creativity/Ideation, a basic intuitive value, leading **Example** to the experience of Supportive Community. The thinking value of **of the** Criteria/Rationality and the feeling value of Empathy are dynamically **Cycling:** integrated into this complex to create the value of Community Per- **The** sonalist. This value is an expression of the integration of the four func- **Sensate** tions and the four phases of development with each of the functions **Function** starting from a different point and cycling in a different pattern. If sensation is accompanied by thinking, then feeling will be the third function. Those values generally attributed to thinking may have been fairly well actualized in healthy development and the focus will move to the feeling, or more personal, values of Phase IIIA. Once again, at midlife, the energy around intuitive values will begin to attract the attention of the sensates who will leave the completed tasks of their previous phases and move into cycle IV for the beginning of the midlife journey reexperiencing previous value clusters in a more complete yet simplified way. The other functions go through a similar process.

It is interesting to note that the Intrapersonal cycle, characterized by a new awareness of one's gifts and a questioning of the present status of things, is also the one in which there is the beginning of coming to terms with the third function, bringing new dimensions and new questions into the field of awareness. It is necessary to modify one's stance to the environment as life becomes more complex and new information is brought in. During the gradual integration of the third function, there is a synthesis which occurs between values as new skills are learned resulting in a new or third value different in quality from either of the previous two, such as (Self) Competence/Confidence and Life/Self Actualization combining to form the value of Being Self. Once the primary skills of the third function are minimally integrated into the totality of the person, the energy of the fourth begins to be increasingly available. It is at this point that Hall says one is pulled forward with a new life energy. For example, intuition brings to its opposite, sensation, the ability to see broader horizons and increased possibilities for the implementation of skills in the world. The dynamics of this are manifested in the characteristics of the Communal/Collaborative cycle in which energy is directed toward the new possibilities inherent in old institutional forms (intuition and sensation) and ethical choices are infused with personal meaning (thinking and feeling).

A New Information is continually changing as new input through the pre-
World ferred perceiving function of either intuition or sensation leads to new
View types of information which change the world view. As the new skills of the Communal/Collaborative cycle begin to create an expanded world view, as the inferior function becomes more and more one's friend, the vision of the Mystical cycle begins to appear. "I now see all of humanity and the physical/material world as a sacred gift in which I must be responsibly involved . . . . I find myself with a new perspective on the creative order . . . . It is as though I see it as God sees it" (*The Genesis Effect*, Chapter 5).

It is at this point that extreme care must be taken to balance the activities and focus of one's life. The most hidden part of the Self has lent energy and wisdom to the developmental process. An important aspect of this process has been the balance between work and play, or between doing and being, especially at Cycle V during the increasing integration of the third function and the beginning of the integration of the fourth function. As the fourth function increases in energy, it gives the potential for high levels of expression on the one hand, and severe distortion of focus on the other. At the Mystical cycle, it is coming into increased activity. Growth, at this cycle, "requires careful attention balancing involvement in organizational development based on humane values and time devoted to the kind of intimacy and solitude which are truly energizing" (*The Genesis Effect*, Chapter 5). This is the balance between Being (intuition and feeling) and Doing (sensation and thinking). It is the balance between the opposites. The superior function must always maintain its post, delicately balancing the input of the other functions, especially the less well developed inferior function which will always reside partially in darkness. This is the life task at this cycle. It must be taken seriously, or the world view of the physical/material world seen as a "sacred gift in which I must be responsibly involved" may be severely distorted. This could be manifested as an attitude of extreme control over others and the environment, the vision of rampant and uncontrolled possibilities with loss of focus, feelings of hatred for those who are different or for highly irrational mandates which hold negative control and power over others.

A continuous cycling through these phases and stages is a life long journey and one which requires commitment and dedication to the inner process. The expression of values at Phase IV is an uncommon experience known only to those few who successfully complete the journey. The process of integration is always individual and highly complex and no theory can encompass all of its dimensions. One can only hope to discover new ways to increase conscious participation in this journey so that the potential which resides within each individual can be more fully realized. The Developmental Value Theory of Brian Hall offers an objective and unique framework through which to view the human journey as it interrelates with the external structures of society. The theory of Psychological Type offers a way to understand this journey in terms of individual differences. Together they provide a powerful tool with which to creatively narrow the gap between personal expression and the creative use of this expression in the world.

BIBLIOGRAPHY

Assigioli, R. PSYCHOSYNTHESIS. The Viking Press, New York, 1971.

Colombo, B. Unpublished research.

Jung, C. G. COLLECTED WORKS. Bollingen Series, New York, Pantheon Books, 1953–54.

Jung, C. G. TIPI PSICOLOGICI. Universale Scientifica (translated by Cesare L. Musatti and Luigi Aurigemma). Editor Boringhieri, Torino, 1977.

Keirsey, D. and Bates, M. PLEASE UNDERSTAND ME; AN ESSAY ON TEMPERAMENT STYLES. Prometheus Nemesis Books, Del Mar, 1978.

Myers, I. B. GIFTS DIFFERING. Consulting Psychologists Press, Inc., Palo Alto, 1980.

Van der Hoop, J. H. CONSCIOUS ORIENTATION. Harcourt Brace, New York, 1939.

Vaughn, F. AWAKENING INTUITION. Anchor Books, Doubleday, New York, 1979.

Yabroff, W. Unpublished research.

[1] I have been influenced in this area by the writings of Humphrey Osgood and his concept of time in relationship to psychological type.

Masculine-Feminine Development: A Value-Based Perspective

Jeanine Kelsey, M.A.
University of Santa Clara
Director of Research

The development of men and women tends to differ as they grow through the cycles of development which are described in *The Genesis Effect*. Since values are internal images that people carry with them, they arise from the internalizations of people and things that begin to form during the first few months of life. (Mahler, 1975) And the way we experience "mother" (the primary caretaker in our society) and in-

297

ternalize that image initiates a process of development of values that we will carry throughout our life. One's early experience of "mother" forms the basic images and impressions of the nature of interpersonal relationships—the interpersonal values.

Later we internalize our image of "father" (our representation of the outside world). Another sequence of images is initiated that continues with us, evolving and continuing to develop as we experience more and more relationships "out there". These images and impressions of "father" are the basis for the values we form of the nature of institutions and systems in the external world.

Since each of us is a unique individual, our images of "mother" and "father" vary immeasurably from one person to another. From the values perspective these differences between us create fascinating opportunities for growth and creative expression of those images in unlimited ways. However, the things we have in common include the fact that we all carry with us certain internalized images of the world that began to form with our initial experience of "mother" (interpersonal values) and "father" (system values). The way these experiences are internalized forms the basis for subsequent value development in both men and women. And these images tend to take different courses for men and for women.

Sociologist Nancy Chodorow provides some understanding of the difference in the way men and women tend to develop as a result of their initial experience of "mother" and "father".

Given that for both sexes the primary caretaker in the first 3 months of life is typically female, the interpersonal dynamics of gender identity formation are different for boys and girls. Female identity formation takes place in a context of ongoing relationship since mothers tend to experience their daughter more like, and continuous with themselves. Correspondingly, girls, in identifying themselves as female, experience themselves as like their mothers, thus fusing the experience of *attachment* with the process of identity formation. In contrast, mothers experience their sons as a male opposite and boys, in defining themselves as masculine, separate their mothers from them selves, thus curtailing 'their primary love and sense of empathic tie.' Consequently male development entails a 'more empathic individuation and a more defensive firming of experienced ego boundaries'. For boys, but not girls, 'issues of *differentiation* have become intertwined with sexual issues.'

Consequently, relationships, and particularly issues of dependency, are experienced differently by women and men. For boys and men, separating and individuation are critically tied to gender identity since separation from the mother is essential for the development of masculinity. For girls and women, issues of femininity or feminine identity do not depend on the achievement of separation from the mother or on the progress of individuation. Since masculinity is defined through separation while femininity is defined through attachment, male gender identity is threatened by intimacy while female gender identity is threatened by separation. Thus males tend to have difficulty with relationships, while females tend to have problems with individuation. (Gilligan, p. 8)

These patterns are reflected in boys' and girls' play patterns in elementary school. Janet Lever's research on games boys and girls play concludes that after the boy establishes firm ego boundaries he continues to define himself as a separate individual by developing values of rationality and competition in order to experience achievement and success. These combine to provide the basis for his sense of self-competence and confidence. He plays with his enemies, competes with his friends and learns independence and organizational skills for coordinating the activities of large and diverse groups of people. Girls' play, on the other hand, reflects values of friendship and belonging, care and nurture, and cooperation. Girls tend to play in smaller, more intimate groups of the "best-friend dyad" and in private places. This fosters the development of the empathy and sensitivity which arises from close affiliation with a "particular other" rather than a "generalized other." (Gilligan, 1982)

Research on the value theory is paralleling the research of Chodorow and Lever. Data from the value-based inventories developed by Dr. Hall is consistent with patterns that these two researchers are describing. Value priorities for men and for women tend to differ as they mature through the phases and stages of consciousness. In the theory the four phases of development are divided into two stages—A and B. Values in Stage A of all the stages reflect primarily interpersonal values—a continuum of values arising from one's original images from one's experience of "mother", while values in Stage B emphasize system values arising from one's initial internalization of "father". Keeping this background in mind we will reflect on the world views of each stage and phase of development and explore the differing developmental paths for men and for women.

Phase I

In Phase I the world is seen as a hostile place over which an individual has no control. At this level of consciousness he or she tends to be passive and dependent, doing whatever seems necessary to protect himself or herself from interfacing directly with the world. These people are often attracted to powerful autocratic leaders such as Jim Jones and his Jamestown colony. Married women at this stage are often dependent on their husbands and passive in their roles outside the home. Single people are dependent on a job where they do exactly what they are told in a rote manner in order to survive and provide food and shelter for themselves and their families.

In Phase I it is a bit difficult to differentiate between those values which are typically masculine and ones that are typically feminine, but the tendency toward interpersonal values (reflecting attachment) in Stage A and system values (reflecting separation) in Stage B are illustrated in the following table.

299

Phase I Value Examples	
Stage A	*Stage B*
Self Preservation	Security
Wonder/Awe/Fate	Sensory Pleasure
Food/Warmth/Shelter	Territory/Security

Relationships between men and women at this level of development are based on mutual dependency and a need to rely on others to obtain the basic necessities in order to survive physically.

As Phase I values are actualized, they provide the structure for continued development of gender identity and ego boundaries. The way each individual resolves these issues creates the basis for the process of gender differentiation and value development which takes place in the second phase of development.

Phase II The Phase II world view is one in which the world is seen as a problem with which I must cope. Women in this phase of consciousness do a lot of caring for and nurturing of others. They become mothers, nurses, teachers, secretaries and so on. Men in this phase are often typified by the concepts in the book *The Organization Man*. They are businessmen, engineers and professionals who are intensely devoted to their company or to the organizations with which they are affiliated.

The roles that men and women live out at this phase are somewhat more mature expressions of the values that were reflected in Lever's study of boys' and girls' play patterns—women's value priorities reflect relationship and attachment while men focus on separation and individuation. Interestingly, the world view is the same for males and females at this stage, but society tends to place a higher value on the masculine priorities. This is evidenced in salary levels as well as prestige afforded to men compared to women.

Examples of the value priorities in the two stages at this phase of development are indicated in the example below. Note the patterns in these groupings. Values perceived as common to men fall into the "B" stage while those ascribed to women tend to fall into the "A" stage.

Phase II Value Examples	
Stage A	*Stage B*
Self Worth	Self Competence/Confidence
Family/Belonging	Work/Labor
Friendship/Belonging	Achievement/Success
Care/Nurture	Competition
Tradition	Patriotism/Esteem
Social Affirmation	Criteria/Rationality
Fantasy/Play	Play/Recreation

These value priorities are reflected in the nature of relationships of men and women at this phase. This is society's idealized image of the ideal man meeting the ideal woman, falling in love, establishing a career and raising a family of well-adjusted children, owning a home in the suburbs and living "happily ever after".

The transition into the Phase III level of consciousness provides a challenge for both men and women. The urge to self-actualize (Maslow) begins to stir in both men and women . . . to participate in the world from a sense of one's own competence and autonomy. Most of our society does not support this level of consciousness development with its related values in spite of the impact of humanistic psychology and the writings of futurists such as Toffler and others. The cultural taboos surrounding this transition are reinforced by the media, business and industry, religious institutions and family traditions. They all tend to reinforce the value priorities of "The Organization Man" and the "good woman". While the individual is experiencing new urges from within which creates anxiety, he or she also experiences stress from without by the pressures of the culture. Very often psychotherapy is the resource people turn to in order to successfully negotiate this transition in their development. Sometimes it is accomplished with the support of a trusted peer.

Phase III

In addition to the internal stress and the cultural taboos surrounding this growth, there are clear differences in the challenges men and women face in making this transition. Each must resolve different issues in order to become autonomous and self-actualizing. Society has reinforced the man for his ability to be rational and objective while women are affirmed for carrying the responsibility for feelings and relationships. According to Rubin, "thought, defined as the ultimate good, has been assigned to men; feeling, considered at best a problem, has fallen to women". (Rubin, 1983, p. 72)

Carol Gilligan describes this transition for women as follows:

The 'good woman' masks assertion in evasion, denying responsibility by claiming only to meet the needs of others, while the 'bad woman' forgoes or renounces the commitments that bind her in self-deception and betrayal. It is precisely this dilemma—the conflict between compassion and autonomy, between virtue and power—which the feminine voice struggles to resolve in its efforts to reclaim the lost self and to solve (this) problem in such a way that no one is hurt. (Gilligan, 1982, p. 71)

Levinson describes the transition for men at this stage as a de-illusioning process. The man tends to carry the illusions that he has already achieved his own autonomy; that his personal relationships are ideal and satisfying to himself and his significant others; and that he is a stable, fully integrated individual. His transition involves tumultous struggles within the self and with the external world. He must experience his own feelings—his need for attachment as well as for

301

separateness; his need to experience and integrate his feminine qualities and integrate those qualities with his masculinity; his youth with the reality of his aging; and his powerful forces of destructiveness as well as his creativity.

The Phase III world view, then, becomes awareness that the world is a project in which I may participate. At this level of consciousness the individual begins to create out of one's own style of thinking, expressing one's self, making one's own decisions and being able to acknowledge reality without necessarily adjusting to the status quo or a specific social milieu—an internal locus of control. Businessmen may begin to conceive new and creative organizational systems. Engineers may develop new technology to better serve humanity. Administrators may develop more humane organizations. Professionals may specialize in an area that is of personal interest.

What, then, happens to mothers, nurses, and teachers? They may become administrators, establish their own business, begin a new career that allows them to achieve as well as to nurture. (Sheehy) As a man and woman face the challenge of moving into the third phase of consciousness they discover that society perpetuates the "rational man/hysterical woman concept" while at the same time they each come face-to-face with their own unresolved internal issues, their weaknesses and limitations as well as their strengths and personal authority.

Value patterns that emerge in Stages A and B in Phase III continue to reflect the masculine and feminine patterns, but they begin to reflect the integrations that each is experiencing.

Phase III Value Examples

Stage A	Stage B
Equality/Liberation	Construction/New Order
Actualization/Wholeness	Human Dignity
Service/Vocation	Justice/Social Order
Autonomy	Being Self
Personal Authority/Honesty	Faith/Risk/Vision
Health/Healing/Harmony	Mutual Responsibility/Accountability
Search/ Meaning/Hope	Research/Knowledge Intimacy

Core ingredients in a relationship at this phase include self-acceptance, and equal caring about one's self and one's partner, autonomy rather than symbiosis, and commitment to ongoing growth and change which includes romance and fun. (Koestenbaum) This relationship is based on reality and choices rather than on need and romanticized illusions . . . providing the basis for intimacy as each partner lives out his or her strengths and limitations and accepts the strengths and limitations of the partner.

Ongoing growth through the tumult of Phase III leads the individual **Phase IV**
to the fourth phase of consciousness. There is very little formal research on this phase of development. The assumption is that as we
successfully resolve the conflicts and polarities of the third phase, add
high levels of skill integration and spiritual maturity, we are able to
see and address issues of global complexity with a simple clarity. In
this way we transcend our own needs and limitations and bring our
talents and strengths to bear on issues of global magnitude, such as
justice and world poverty. This level of consciousness is implied from
studies of the mystics and other individuals whose lives have had positive and productive global impact. Examples of individuals who reflect this level of consciousness include Mother Teresa, Jonas Salk, and
Gandhi.

At this stage of consciousness an individual tends to transcend one's
own sexuality, having integrated the masculine and feminine polarities within every man and woman. In fact, the challenge is to experience integrated development of all the aspects of one's life . . . young/
old, destruction/creation, attachment/separation, as well as mascu-
line/feminine. The integrated world view here is that the world is
again a mystery, but over which we feel compelled and drawn to care
and in which one can be simple and playful. Disintegrated development can be manifested in destructive ways as was graphically illustrated by Hitler.

Values at this stage continue to reflect stronger masculine tenden-
cies in the "B" Stage and stronger feminine qualities in the "A" Stage.
This is evidenced in the following examples.

Phase IV Value Examples	
Stage A	*Stage B*
Intimacy & Solitude as Uni-	Ecority/Aesthetics
tive	Transcendence/Global
Truth/Wisdom/Integrated	Equality
Insight	Convivial Technology
Prophet/Vision	Macroeconomics/World
Detachment/Transcendence	Order
Community/Simplicity	Minessence
Interdependence	Justice/Global
	Distribution

Relationships at this phase include distance, relativity, freedom and
flexibility that spring from a deep transcendental union of a man and
woman, each of whose consciousness has been highly developed.

Ongoing empirical research is being conducted to explore the devel- **Conclusions and**
opmental processes of men and women. This research will reflect de- **Implications**
velopmental patterns from populations in the U.S. as well as from
other countries. It will explore the value development and priorities

of men and women in various occupations, with dissimilar religious affiliations, of differing socioeconomic statuses and having varying levels of education.

These results will be compared to other studies of masculine and feminine development in psychology, sociology and anthropology, history, etc. This will provide a base of cross-cultural and cross-disciplinary data to continue to explore the interesting and complex differences in men and women from the value perspective.

REFERENCES

Auel, Jean M. *The Clan of the Cave Bear*. Toronto: Bantam Books, 1980.

Bardwick, Judith M. *Psychology of Women*. New York: Harper & Row, 1971.

Bolen, Jean Shinoda. *Goddesses in Everywoman. A New Psychology of Women*. San Francisco: Harper & Row, 1984.

Chodorow, Nancy. "Family Structure and Feminine Personality." In M.A. Rosaldo and L. Lampere, eds. *Woman, Culture and Society*. Stanford: Stanford University Press, 1974.

———*The Reproduction of Mothering*, Berkeley: University of California Press, 1978.

Claremont de Castillejo, Irene. *Knowing Woman*. New York: Harper & Row; 1973.

Cox, Sue. *Female Psychology: The Emerging Self*. Chicago: Science Research Associates, 1976.

Dinnerstein, Dorothy. *The Mermaid and the Minotaur—Sexual Arrangements and Human Malaise*. New York: Harper & Row, 1977.

Edward, Joyce, Ruskin, Turrini. *Separation-Individuation: Theory and Application*. New York: Gardner Press, 1981.

Erikson, Erik H. *Childhood and Society*. New York: W. W. Norton, 1950.

Friday, Nancy. *My Mother/My Self*. New York: Dell Books, 1978.

Fromm, Erich. *Escape from Freedom*. New York: Avon Books, 1941.

Gerstein, Martin, Pappen-Daniel. *Understanding Adulthood*. Fullerton, Ca.: California Personnel and Guidance Association, 1981.

Gilligan, Carol. *In a Different Voice*. Cambridge: Harvard University Press, 1982.

Gould, Roger L. *Transformations: Growth and Change in Adult Life*. New York: Simon & Schuster, 1978.

Koestenbaum, Peter. *Existential Sexuality: Choosing to Love*. Englewood Cliffs: Prentice-Hall, 1974.

Kohlberg, Lawrence. *The Philosophy of Moral Development*. San Francisco: Harper & Row, 1981.

Lever, Janet. "Sex Differences in the Games Children Play." *Social Problems* 23 1976: 418–487.

Levinson, Daniel. *The Seasons of a Man's Life*. New York: Alfred A. Knopf, 1978.

Maccoby, Eleanor, ed. *The Development of Sex Differences*. Stanford: Stanford University Press. 1966.

Mahler, Margaret. *Essays in Honor of Margaret S. Mahler: Separation-Individuation*. New York: International University Press, 1971.

———*On Human Symbiosis: The Vicissitudes of Individuation*. New York: Lane Medical Library, 1968

———*The Psychological Birth of the Human Infant*. New York: Basic Books, 1975.

Margolis, Maxine. *Mothers and Such: Views of American Women and Why They Changed.* Berkeley: University of California Press, 1984.

Maslow, Abraham. *Toward a Psychology of Being.* New York: D. Van Nostrand Co., 1968.

Miller, Jean Baker. *Toward a New Psychology of Women.* Boston: Beacon Press, 1976.

Murphy, J.M. and Gilligan C. "Moral Development in Late Adolescence and Adulthood A Critique and Reconstruction of Kohlberg's Theory. *Human Development* 23 (1980) 77–104.

O'Leary, Virginia E. *Toward Understanding Women.* Monterey, Ca.: Brooks/Cole, 1977.

Rubin, Lillian B. *Intimate Strangers: Men and Women Together.* New York: Harper & Row, 1983.

Scarf, Maggie. *Unfinished Business.* New York: Doubleday and Co., Inc., 1980.

Sebald, Hans. *Momism: The Silent Disease of America.* Chicago: Nelson Hall Co., 1976.

Sheehy, Gail. *Passages.* New York: Dutton, 1976.

Spencer, Anita. *Mothers Are People, Too: A Contemporary Analysis of Motherhood.* New York: Paulist Press. 1982.

Stack, Carol B. *All Our Kin.* New York: Harper & Row, 1974.

Vaillant, George. *Adaptation to Life.* Boston: Little, Brown and Co., 1977.

Whyte, Wm. Hollingswood. *The Organization Man.* Garden City, N.Y.: Doubleday, 1956.

Existentialism and the Genesis Effect:
A Synergetic Interaction

Mary Lou Harrison, M.Ed. and Linda Prendergast, M.A.
Omega Associates

The interplay between the Genesis Effect and the existential perspective results in a powerful way of working with people to facilitate change and growth. *The Genesis Effect* describes the connection of internal images with external reality and gives a practical method of retrieving information about the value structure and meaning system of the individual. Existential psychotherapy nurtures the inner being to achieve a harmony between our internal awareness and outer experience. How many of us have tried to "be" something that doesn't fit who we are and have been uncomfortable? Western culture has encouraged this inauthenticity by its emphasis on objective outer reality and its neglect of our inner vision. The result is a loss of vitality when we sever our experience of life from its inner source. J.F.T. Bugental, an existential therapist, describes this loss:

There are so many unchangeable, external obstacles to our full aliveness: chance, illness, death, and the intrusions of social, political, and economic forces. We all face such losses and fight against them however we can. But the losses we bring on ourselves because we did not know in time what was possible or what we most dearly wanted for ourselves, these are the most anguish-filled, the most bitter to contemplate (Bugental, 1976, pp. 1–2).

A main purpose of *The Genesis Effect* is to encourage this inner awareness of our needs, wants, dreams, our being and to offer a practical methodology for identifying the inner value clusters that energize us. In that way the reality we experience isn't sterile and flat, but fluid and vitally nourishing as the inner vision creates our reality in continual interaction with it, in transformation and renewal.

Working with the value model of the Genesis Effect involves information retrieval from developmental theory as well as from existential thought. This paper will explore the existential side of information retrieval through the roots of existentialism, the central ideas of the existential perspective, the uses of existential thought in therapy, and finally the contribution of value clarification as a practical approach to existential therapy. Without the value model the existential viewpoint leaves us with an existential crisis of an overwhelming number of alternatives for direction and behavior. The value dialectics take existential therapy beyond just a philosophical and spiritual journey to a practical road-map for growth.

Roots of Existentialism Existentialism as a movement and a labeled force did not really begin until the 1841 Berlin lectures of the German philosopher F.W.J. Schelling. Within his audience listened Kierkegaard, now often referred to as the foreparent of existentialism. But the substance of existentialism has been around since the beginning of conscious thought: the search for meaning, the conflict of intimacy and unity versus isolation and separateness, and the role of anxiety in helping man deal either creatively or destructively with the direction of his life. For primitive beings, the options may have been fewer, but very clearly the result of choices could end in survival versus non-survival.

Throughout history religion has attempted to help people understand and deal with their existential reality. Repeatedly in the Bible man is confronted with choice: " . . . I have set before you life and death . . . therefore choose life that you . . . may live." (Deuteronomy 30:19) The Bible helps people make choices which connect inner images with external reality. For example, Moses turns aside to see the burning bush and hears God call, a call from the internal realm of consciousness. This call becomes objectified as Moses changes his behavior from keeping flocks to leading the children of Israel out of Egypt. Later in the Bible we have accounts of Jesus confronting the contingency of the individual and bringing meaning and unity to life. Nietzsche says, "He who has a why to live for can bear almost any how." (Leslie, 1965, p. 47)

The Existential Perspective Some of the more recent identified existential philosophers include Sartre, Frankl, Oden, Bugental, Yalom, and Koestenbaum. Each has a unique perspective, and taken together they define current existential thought. The philosophical basis of existentialism is the crucial tenet that we are all born to die, and that this contingency of life creates existential anxiety—a normal and very necessary condition if growth is to take place. In existentialism, the present is the only field of awareness. Past is seen as memory and guilt; the future is seen as

imagination and anxiety. The very crux of our existence is our limitations: *our limited being* since death is inevitable, *our limited choice and
action* since we can actualize only a few of the alternatives available to
us, and *our isolation* since we come into this world alone and go out
the same way. The existential position is that in the midst of this mortal condition of contingency and limitation, each of us makes decisions
moment by moment that lead to either vitality or withdrawal. The way
we deal with our contingency, the way we go about making choices
in our lives that lead to intimacy and meaning or to separation and
meaninglessness, dictate a way of being or non-being, a condition of
authenticity or inauthenticity, a life of creativity or stagnation.

It is important to remember that we have both a freedom to make
choices in our lives and a responsibility to do so in a manner that leads
to intimacy, creativity, vitality, and authenticity. Freedom is really
freedom to choose, knowing that we cannot predict the outcome and
cannot know all the determining factors. But, again, with that freedom
comes responsibility—accepting that I am the doer, rather than taking
the stance of being done-to. We may be "put" into various situations,
but it is the choices we make in any given situation that determine a
condition of meaning or meaninglessness in our lives. This tenet is illustrated in the "Structures of Awareness and Anxiety" and the "Dim-
inshed Self" diagrams by Brian Hall, which show clearly the difference
between choice grounded in hope and meaning versus choice coming
out of negative images. (*Genesis Effect,* chapter VII.)

Perhaps one of the most useful aspects of the existential perspective
is its humanistic orientation, focusing not on pathology alone, but giving a wider scope of patterns both pathological and creatively healthy.
The existential approach is one that each person can use in a way that
is meaningful and useful in a personal context. It also sees science,
humanities, and religion as expressions of our needs and as ways of
bringing meaningfulness into our world. Frankl talks of the tremendous culture that existed among the stench of death in the concentration camps. He maintains that humor, music, art, and religious faith
acted as the glue that held the survivors together despite the depths
of the desecration of life. Bugental maintains that the existentialist
view restores our divinity by recognizing that we are not merely organisms or mechanisms. Rather, living from the center of our existence, we can experience and acknowledge the possibilities open to us
if we are courageous enough to be conscious and alive in the choices
we make. We are always making choices, even if the choice is to do
nothing. By taking the risk of making a conscious choice, a determined
choice, we act in authentic, vital, life-giving ways.

Awareness is thus a key focus of existentialism—awareness of the
state of contingency we live in, of our finiteness, of our limitations,
and of our responsibility to create the meaning and values in our lives
through our choices. Choosing is a continual demand of our existence,
and some of our choices result negatively, leading to guilt. Guilt comes
from the knowledge of our past choices while anxiety is directed toward our concern for future choices. When we have a decision to
make, and must in some way act, we relate to our future in terms of

unknown possibilities and feel anxious. At the same time, we are relating to the past, to memories of times when our choices lead to negative consequences and we experience guilt. We'd like to somehow change the past and also predetermine the future. Both are impossible.

Consequently, we need to clarify values to help us understand our choices and meaning in life. By identifying clearly our own individual values—which are simply our internal images externalized through our behavior—we can effectively and meaningfully make choices which are life-giving.

Value<——— Past<——— SELF———> Future———> Value Threats
Negation
           Guilt   Anxiety

Figure 1

As shown in Figure 1, guilt occurs when we are aware that we have not lived up to the often unrealistic ideal image we have of ourselves. An event that results in guilt is usually an event that denies or conflicts with something we hold as a value. The experiences of guilt and anxiety are normal consequences of awareness according to the existentialists and can be incentives for growth.

Existentialism and Therapy The existential framework emphasizes that conflict arises from an individual's confrontation with the givens of existence, not from the Freudian concept of suppressed instinctual strivings nor from the neo-Freudian view of conflict with significant adults and the environment. The method to explore these givens is personal reflection on the ultimate issues of death, freedom, existential isolation, and meaninglessness, which all involve an inherent existential conflict: I become aware of the inevitability of my own death, but I want to continue living; I am responsible for my own freedom in the absence of external structure, yet I desperately want ground and structure; I am aware of my essential isolation from others and from the world, and yet I wish for protection and to be part of a larger whole; and as a human being I seek meaning in a world that has no absolute meaning (Yalom, 1980, pp. 8–9). Existential therapy, then, refers to these concerns and to the fears and defense mechanisms arising from them. Although people grow developmentally through stages, this position cuts beneath the individual life history when one inquires about the deepest and most fundamental sources of dread in the present moment.

This humanistic approach to therapy holds that each of us is more than the sum of our parts. It also holds that we exist in interpersonal relationships, have potential in that area, and that a central fact of human existence is our awareness of which we are not always conscious but which is present, nonetheless. In addition, we participate in our experience through choices which influence our level of awareness and provide the potential for change. Choices give an indication of our orientation to life, for they are somewhat intentional and are made in an effort to give us a balance between rest and disequilibrium.

308

Characteristics of existential therapy include that it really cares about people, it values meaning much more than procedure, and it looks for human ways to validate us and our existence. It focuses its attention on our experiences, and maintains that all knowledge is relative, with infinite possibility and potential for change—including that tomorrow we may die. Therefore today's experiences are of prime importance. This approach does not deny the contributions of other views, but tries to supplement them and give them a setting within a broader conception of human experience.

Therapy in the existential framework examines the issues of non-being, death awareness, and anxiety. Non-being occurs when we live in ways that do not go in accord with life, so the purpose of psychotherapy is to help people see the ways that they are avoiding being, trying instead to exist in a state of non-being through resistances.

Existential anxiety comes from the threat of non-being and neurotic anxiety. In other words, when we try desperately to avoid the things in life we are most afraid of, like rejection or failure, we end up avoiding life itself. An example of this is a woman who is manic-depressive and has attempted suicide several times. She is also an alcoholic, and apparently goes into periods of agoraphobia. Her background is complex and includes an extremely overpowering mother. Everytime this woman seems to be getting her life in order, when things are going quite well, she goes into a panic mode. She retreats to her home and her bottle, eventually attempts suicide, but always calls someone at the last minute to bail her out. It appears that she is so afraid of failing, so uncomfortable with the realities of life, and so aware of the eventuality of death, that she actualizes her self into non-being in an attempt to avoid the pain of life. As with Frankl's paradoxical intention, that which she is most afraid of happening and tries desperately to avoid, becomes reality.

Our being is not only given to us, but it is demanded of us. It is our responsibility, and we are faced with answering to what we have made of ourselves. We stand in judgment of ourselves. Consequently we face anxiety of self-rejection or condemnation. Guilt anxiety " . . . can drive us toward complete self-rejection, to the feeling of being condemned—not to an eternal punishment but to despair of having lost our destiny." (Tillich, 1952, p. 53) An example is a woman in her sixties who is sad and constricted. She grieves for what she has lost in life, the opportunities she let slip past her, and despairs now in a state of low self-esteem. Despair is the ultimate situation: without hope. The person who feels despair also feels great pain from not being able to affirm herself. In a sense, all human life is a continuous effort, often through non-being, to avoid despair.

Ironically, while the boundary between physical death and life is clear, the concepts of life and death merge together psychologically. So, while death destroys people physically, the idea of death when accepted authentically saves them. Yalom contrasts forgetfulness of being, an inauthentic state when we're caught up in the trivialities of everyday life, with mindfulness of being, an authentic awareness of our fragility and responsibility. He cites examples of how certain experiences jolt us into confrontation with death which can lead to profound personal change. In one patient disabling interpersonal phobias miraculously dissolved after she developed cancer. When asked about this she responded, "Cancer cures psychoneurosis". (Yalom, 1980, p. 160) Yalom's hope is that therapists be able to use this therapeutic potential without waiting for the chance events of accidents, illness, or death of loved ones.

Death is a primary source of anxiety and a major life task is to deal with the terrifying fears of extinction. Coping with these fears involves shaping defenses against death awareness from which may come the two main sources of psychopathology, the idea of specialness or personal inviolability, and the belief in the existence of a personal ultimate rescuer (Yalom, 1980). Although we all know consciously that in terms of the basic boundaries of existence we're no different than anyone else, deep down we believe the rules of mortality don't apply to us. The denial of illness is a function of the belief in our own inviolability. Likewise the belief in an ultimate rescuer serves to restrict personality as we look to someone else to save us or make decisions for us instead of creating our own uniqueness.

We are always faced with our contingency. We can never predict with complete assurance, therefore anxiety is a normal condition. Anxiety is recognizing that I don't know all that I think I need to know in order to protect all that I love and to keep what I fear from becoming a reality.

Anxiety can take two forms: existential and neurotic. When we accept our contingent situation, our responsibility for choice, and recognize the potential for tragedy, we will experience existential anxiety. When we try to reduce or deny our existential anxiety or to convince ourselves that we have assured a certainty in life, we open ourselves up to neurotic anxiety. Tragedy is a part of living. Denying that fact, destroying or repressing that inevitability, brings us an existence of non-being filled with neurotic anxiety. On the other hand, existential joy is possible when we open ourselves to the realization of possible failure or tragedy and appreciate each moment, rather than aborting our joy out of fear of losing it. What we cherish, love, and hope for is ours if we are brave enough to open ourselves to the world in an authentic, being way. Getting lost in music or a beautiful painting, opening ourselves to the grandeur and wonder of nature, loving someone fully, all of these offer opportunities for existential joy. Neurotic anxiety wipes out possibilities; authenticity encourages them.

The task in therapy is not to escape from anxiety, but to face and integrate the natural anxiety of the human condition as part of growth. The therapist doesn't need to provide any unique experiences, but rather help the client recognize the universality of the existential situation. The concept of authenticity provides the substance and meaning for the journey of therapy. We have an inward vision, a sense of our own being that enables us to experience the times when life pulses strongly through us and the times when it drains away toward a kind of death (see Bugental, 1976). Therapy, rather than a matter of healing an "illness", can be a joint venture where both therapist and client have to acknowledge the natural resistances to accepting the givens of existence. Then it is possible for both to accept the responsibility for creating their own life with meaning and vitality. This journey is continuous, since at each moment we face the need to choose again, to live with the question, "What does it mean to be alive?"

Existentialism reveals that for full aliveness we need to acknowledge and accept our limitations, our guilt, our anxiety, our isolation and within this state of contingency responsibly create a life of meaning. **Contribution of the Value Theory to Existential Therapy** The value theory and instrumentation described in *The Genesis Effect* provide guidance to do this. Each Phase of the Consciousness Tract (I–IV) describes a world view within which to define meaning in the present moment while at the same time the progression of Phases maps out a wider journey. This model thus combines the existentialists' emphasis on the present moment with the developmentalists' emphasis on the stages of life's journey. Awareness of values and their relationship through dialectics as reflected in behavior offers concrete perspective for creating and defining our individual meaning systems (*The Genesis Effect*, chapter 5).

Hall's Model of Value Theory, taking the Four Phases of Consciousness, divides the value structure for each person into three areas of energy: act, choice, and vision. The act area is comprised of those values which have been internalized as part of our "repertoire" and are free-flowing and instinctual through integration. The values in the act area (for example the act area values of Family and Self Worth for the person who is in Phase II B / III A) are still very much a part of the individual's value structure. The act area values represent needs that the individual has been able to meet and integrate into his or her life. Should these needs not be met for some reason, such as illness or crisis, the person will flip back to the act phase and expend energy meeting basic needs by acting upon those values. This is, existentially, an attempt to find meaning in the face of contingency and limitations. The choice area consists of values which represent the energy expended in our everyday behavior—the priorities that we are working on, so to speak. The vision area is comprised of those values beginning to become energized, the values toward which we are moving in our future integration.

Through the value theory, an individual can choose the values to respond to the existential realities in a meaningful way. For example, the response to the fact of our limited being may be with the values of (Self) Preservation and Safety/Survival in Phase I, as the concern is to preserve the human body. In Phase II the fact of limited being may be authentically confronted by seeking more Education, Achievement/Success, and Self Competence/Confidence. By Phase III a person may give high priority to the values of Life/Self Actualization and Being Self by making the most of life within the recognized contingency. In Phase IV the limitations of mortal existence may be viewed from the perspective of Transcendence/Global Congruence with an awareness of the infinite and finite at the same moment of consciousness.

Taking the limitation of choice and action, a person in Phase I may be unaware of the possibilities of choice and find significance in the value of Wonder/Awe/Fate, in a life determined by outside forces. An individual in Phase II may define the limitations in terms of Duty/ Obligation or may seek more choices through Education or Work/ Labor. It is not until the Phase III world view that one can fully generate one's own meaning and fully face the limitation of death, choice, and action. The values here may be Limitation/Celebration and (Self)Directedness. In Phase IV the individual limits can be confronted with the value of Interdependence and Synergy as consciousness becomes a "we" perspective rather than "I".

Each phase of development thus requires a different therapeutic approach as individuals confront the existential realities from vastly different perspectives. Use of the value theory provides concrete guidance for approaching the issues at each level of consciousness.

It is important to realize that the result of an interactive linkage of the value theory and existentialism is a continuous thread that operates like a mobius strip. Not only do values come out of a response to existential reality, but at the same time values create an existential reality. As one works through the Hall-Tonna Inventory with an individual, his or her value structure and meaning system becomes apparent. In working through the dialectic, as it appears in the Hall-Tonna Inventory, one begins to get a clear picture of where this individual is existentially. If, for instance, the dialectic shows a value goal of Family/ Belonging paired with the value means of Competition, existentially this individual may be experiencing guilt, anxiety, and a confusion of meaning in life. On the other hand, Family/Belonging paired with Care/Nurture might result in intimacy and meaning. By using the Hall-Tonna process to look at the value choices, priorities, and dialectics or interplay, we are able to identify the way in which choosing and acting out our values determines our existential state—how we move toward intimacy, choice, hope and meaning or toward separation, anxiety, hopelessness, and meaninglessness. Here we see the value theory as a way of retrieving specific existential information, a way of assessing and understanding what is going on for the individual. The ways in which the individual chooses and acts upon values create a unique existential reality for each person.

The other side of this, while at the same time a continuation of the one thread, is that values are chosen in response to existential reality. As discussed earlier, it is easy to see that the values an individual chooses often come out of the existential reality of contingencies, limitations, and anxieties. If one is faced with a life-threatening disease, the value of Self Preservation is likely to come strongly into play.

The interplay of values responding to existential reality and existential reality resulting from values is a fluid dynamic continually in force. Value assessment gives a picture of the client's present life situation. Then a path of growth is mapped out by modifying the value dialectics. Later an evaluation of the changes results in another assessment leading to more decisions about present and future priorities. In doing therapy, whether from a value approach or an existential framework, it is helpful to see how each affects the other. This perspective does not just give aid to the therapist in planning therapy strategy. By helping the client examine his or her value structure and meaning system in an existential framework, many pieces of a puzzle are often unlocked and the client is then able to see his or her own life-picture.

Not only does the Genesis Effect contribute to the individual, it offers perspective on the issues of cultural and global concern. The lack of a unified and coherent world view that seems to be a central factor in mental illness of individuals is evident on a larger scale. In an age of "future shock", with its drastic and rapid change, depersonalization, congestion, injustice, and threats of poverty and nuclear war, we can see signs of a collective mental illness shared by most of Western culture where the view of reality is fragmented and mind is split from body. Life can seem absurd and meaningless.

Through the application of value theory to discover what is important to us now and what values we are working toward, we can shape a vision of the future. Without the dream, the internal images, life is dead. Many contemporary problems stem from a lack of vision, an absence of hope. With a practical vision, "development can be a setting for salvation which leads to resurrection" yet change without a vision "can reduce a bewildered individual to a defensive self-centeredness, to . . . the agony of a lived destruction of life" (Illich, 1969, p. 99). This process is individual and collective.

The restoration of balance and flexibility in our economies, technologies, and social institutions will be possible only if it goes hand in hand with a profound change of values. Contrary to conventional beliefs, value systems and ethics are not peripheral to science and technology but constitute their very basis and driving force. Hence the shift to a balanced social and economic system will require a corresponding shift of values—from self-assertion and competition to cooperation and social justice, from expansion to conservation, from material acquisition to inner growth. Those who have begun to make this shift have discovered that it is not restrictive but, on the contrary, liberating and enriching. As Walter Weisskoph writes in his book *Alienation and Economics*, the crucial dimensions of scarcity in human life are not economic but existential. They are related to our needs for leisure and contemplation, peace of mind, love, community, and self-realization, which are all satisfied to much greater degrees by the new system of values (Capra, 1982, p. 397).

Working with values therefore has implications for each of us individually and offers direction in making future choices on a global scale as we take responsibility for the forces of evolution and cultural development. This global influence begins with individuals and small groups as we recognize the failings and limits inherent in being human and help people deal with past guilt and use anxiety over the future in positive actualizing ways that lead to meaning and unity. Life is not easy. It is full of pitfalls and unknowns around the next bend. But somehow we must help people balance their need for security with the need to reach out and take a risk. For it is only through risking that we live, that we grow, that we move toward unity with God and our fellow human beings.

Living is a courageous act. Our existential reality is ever present. On a plaque set before the stone presidents at Mount Rushmore is a quote from Theodore Roosevelt:

Far better to dare mighty acts though checkered with failure, than to cast your lot with those poor souls who neither suffer much nor enjoy much. For they choose to dwell in the gray twilight of those who know neither victory nor defeat.

By choosing to face the existential issues of anxiety, limitation, and separation, and respond to these with value analysis and information retrieval, individually and collectively we can create new dreams and visions for authenticity and transformation.

BIBLIOGRAPHY

Bugental, James F.T. *The Search for Authenticity*. New York: Holt, Rinehart & Winston, Inc., 1965.

Bugental, James F.T. *The Search for Existential Identity*. San Francisco: Jossey-Bass Publishers, 1976.

Capra, Fritjof. *The Turning Point*. New York: Simon & Schuster, 1982.

Clinebell, Howard. *Contemporary Growth Therapies*. Nashville: Abingdon, 1981.

de Saint-Exupery, Antoine. *The Wisdom of the Sands*. New York: Harcourt, Brace and Company, 1950.

Fabry, Joseph B. *The Pursuit of Meaning: Logotherapy Applied to Life*. Boston: Beacon Press, 1968.

Frankl, Viktor E. *Man's Search for Meaning*. New York: Simon & Schuster, 1959.

Frankl, Viktor. *The Doctors and the Soul*. New York: Vintage Books, 1955, 1965.

Hall, Brian P. *The Development of Consciousness: A Confluent Theory of Values*. New York: Paulist Press, 1976.

Hall, Brian P. *Value Clarification as Learning Process: A Sourcebook of Learning Theory*. New York: Paulist Press, 1973.

Howe, Ruel L. *Man's Need and God's Action*. Greenwich, Conn.: The Seabury Press, 1953.

Illich, Ivan. *Celebration of Awareness*. New York: Doubleday & Company, 1969.

Koestenbaum, Peter. *The New Image of the Person*. Westport, Conn: Greenwood Press, 1978.

Leech, Kenneth. *Soul Friend*. San Francisco: Harper & Row, 1977.

Leslie, Robert E. *Jesus and Logotherapy*. New York, Nashville: Abingdon Press, 1965.

May, Herbert G., and Metzger, Bruce M., editors, *The New Oxford Annotated Bible With The Apocrypha*. New York: Oxford University Press, 1962.

May, Rollo. *The Meaning of Anxiety*. New York: Washington Square Press, Pocket Books, 1950, 1977.

Needleham, Jacob, translator, *Being-in-the-World: Selected Papers of Ludwig Binswanger*. New York: Harper Torchbooks.

Oden, Thomas C. *The Structures of Awareness*. Nashville: Abingdon Press, 1969.

Reeves, Clement. *The Psychology of Rollo May*. San Francisco: Jossey-Bass Publishers, 1977.

Roberts, David E. *Psychotherapy and a Christian View of Man.* New York: Charles Scribner's Sons, 1950.

Tillich, Paul. *The Courage To Be.* New Haven and London: Yale University Press, 1952.

Toffler, Alvin. *Future Schock.* New York: Random House, 1970.

Tournier, Paul. *The Meaning of Persons.* New York: Harper and Row, 1957.

Wyssm, Dieter. *Depth Psychology: A Critical History.* New York: W.W. Norton and Company, Inc., 1966.

Yalom, Irvin D. *Existential Psychotherapy.* New York: Basic Books, Inc., 1980.

READINGS IN DISCERNMENT

A basic concept in this book is that religion and psychology are not separate but part of a single whole. As such the concept of discernment is seen as central to the spiritual traditions. Discernment in Judeo-Christian tradition is based on the literature of the Old and New Testaments as is Islam to a limited extent. The following three articles are offered for the reader to explore further the ideas of discernment.

Joseph A. Grassi: The Bible and the Discernment of Spirits: The Old Testament

Joseph A. Grassi: Discernment of Spirits: The New Testament View

Robert L. Schmitt, S.J.: Discernment

The Bible and the Discernment of Spirits: The Old Testament

Joseph A. Grassi
University of Santa Clara

By "discernment of spirits" in the Old Testament is meant the ability to know whether God is really speaking through some person who claims to be God's prophet or spokesman with a special message for the people. This was of utmost importance: to know something was God's will—that it was right and true—meant that all God's power was at work in it. Consequently God would bring the plan or situation to its final outcome no matter what obstacles might be in the way.

For biblical writers, the supreme rule for discernment of spirits was *truth.* Truth belonged to the very essence of God. In fact, it was as truth or fidelity that God revealed his name to Moses. (Exodus 34:6) Therefore, anyone who claimed to speak in God's name had to reflect the truth of God himself. The book of Deuteronomy prescribed that this criterion be applied to any case where a prophet claimed to speak in God's name:

If you say to yourselves, "How can we recognize an oracle which the Lord has spoken?", know that, even though a prophet speaks in the name of the Lord, if his oracle is not fulfilled or verified, it is an oracle which the Lord did not speak. The prophet has spoken it presumptuously, and you have no fear of him. (18:21–22)

This matter was considered so important that a true prophet should be obeyed as God's own voice and a false prophet risked even a death penalty. (18:19–20)

A story from the bible illustrates how this truth standard was applied to a very practical situation where there was a disagreement between prophets. The king of Aram (Syria) had taken away an Israelite town, Ramoth Gilead during the 9th century B.C. The king of Israel (the northern divided kingdom) asked Jehoshaphat, the king of Judah (who was visiting him at the time), to cooperate in a campaign to liberate Ramoth Gilead from the Syrians. However, Jehoshaphat, a pious king, was concerned to find out the will of God in this important matter. He said to the king of Israel, "Seek the Word of the Lord at once." (1 Kings 22:5) The king of Israel gathered together 400 prophets who unanimously declared that God had delivered up Ramoth Gilead to them. (22:6) However, King Jehoshaphat was concerned lest the king of Israel might have selected "yes men" to provide the answer he desired. Here we note that conflict of interest is a ground of suspicion for any spokesman of God in those days as well as today. Since the king provided the court prophets with food and support, it would be to their interest to please him with their pronouncements.

The king of Judah, Jehoshaphat, suspected this might be the case and said, "Is there no other prophet of the Lord here whom we can consult?" The king of Israel replied, "There is one other through whom we might consult the Lord, Michaiah, son of Imlah; but I hate him because he prophesies not good but evil about me." (22:7–8) This answer illustrates a corollary to the criterion of truth: a real prophet is willing to risk making enemies by being critical when necessary of government and authority. A prophet who is never critical is not a prophet at all. Perhaps this is why many genuine holy people tend to make others uncomfortable. They are open and honest, not playing the role of "gentlemen" in the sense of refraining from saying what might offend others.

In the biblical story, only Micaiah, in contrast to the 400 others, proclaimed the unpopular truth that the Israelites would suffer a terrible defeat if they engaged in a war that God did not want. True prophets often find themselves with an unpopular message they must deliver simply because they are convinced it is true. The false prophets in our story became so angry that one of them, Zedekiah, came up to Micaiah and slapped him in the face, saying that the Spirit of God could not have spoken through him. (22:24) The king of Israel ordered Micaiah thrown into prison and given only small quantities of bread and water until he (the king) returned triumphantly from battle. Here again, the willingness to bear insults and suffering is another sign of a true prophet. The outcome of the biblical story shows how Micaiah proved himself to be a true prophet of God. In the ensuing battle, the king of Israel was shot by a chance arrow, even though he had gone disguised into the battle with the Syrians.

As in the case of Micaiah, the ability to suffer and the willingness to take an unpopular stand are characteristic of true prophets and leaders. They are so convinced of the truth that they are willing to place their own life and reputation at stake. Although the bible does not declare every war to be unjust, the true prophet (like Micaiah) is willing to take a stand against kings and governments who rely on military power and alliances to accomplish their goals rather than seeking what God—a God of peace—really wants.

Another prophet, Jeremiah, was faced with a terrible struggle with the king and the military just before the fall of Jerusalem (587 B.C.). The king of Babylon, the mightiest nation on earth, was urging Jerusalem to peacefully surrender and become a vassal rather than presuming on God's power to deliver them. Jeremiah was ready to appear even as a fool to convince the people that God did not want them to fight. In obedience to God's word, Jeremiah refused to take a wife and have children because the government's trust in the military would ultimately lead to exile in Babylonia. (Jeremiah 16:1–14) Jeremiah was even threatened with death by the religious institutional leaders because he dared to say that the Temple would be destroyed if they continued to trust in a military solution. (16:11) His stand was similar to that of Jesus who shocked his countrymen by not announcing that the Roman oppressors would be crushed. Instead he declared that the Temple of God would be destroyed if they did not deal with the oppression within their own country.

Jeremiah was scourged and placed in stocks by order of the priest Pashur who was in charge of the Temple. (20:1–2) The prophet was so discouraged and worn out by this reaction that he was seriously tempted to give up his prophetic vocation. (20:7–18) Only after long hours of prayer did he receive the strength to continue in his resolve. Later he was thrown into a dungeon (37:15) and finally into a cistern to die (38:6), but he never ceased to proclaim the unpopular message of peace.

A second criterion, closely connected to the first, was fidelity to the covenant. God's covenant represented his own inner nature of justice, and explained how he wanted people to conduct their lives in view of this justice. The covenant took the form of the ten commandments and all the laws and commands of God found in the bible. However, the essential characteristic of true prophets was that they understood and proclaimed the very heart of this covenant which was justice for the poor and oppressed.

The following are some examples of this core of the covenant. Isaiah expressed it very simply and directly in these words:

Put away your misdeeds from before my eyes; cease doing evil; learn to do good. Make justice your aim: redress the wronged, hear the orphan's plea, defend the widow. (1:16–17)

Isaiah considered this commitment to justice so important that without it all worship of God was a worthless sham and insult to him:

317

When you come in to visit me, who asks these things of you? Trample my course no more! Bring no more worthless offerings; your incense is loathsome to me. (1:12–13)

Jeremiah warned that God's continued presence in the Temple was conditioned upon justice to the needy. The prophet condemned those false prophets who claimed that God's dwelling in the Temple was a guaranteed source of spiritual and material security. He wrote,

Put not your trust in the deceitful words, 'This is the temple of the Lord! The temple of the Lord! The temple of the Lord!' Only if you thoroughly reform your ways and your deeds; if each of you deals justly with his neighbor; if you no longer oppress the resident alien, the orphan, and the widow; if you no longer shed innocent blood in this place, or follow strange gods to your own harm, will I remain with you in this place, in the land which I gave your fathers long ago and forever. (7:4–7)

This text demonstrates that there can never be a divorce between "spirituality" and practice, especially justice. To worship God with silence in the matter of justice is not to worship God at all. Ezekiel the prophet gives great attention to the spirit and the inner dimensions of religion. Yet he could not separate "the spiritual life" from a life of justice. According to Ezekiel, the person who really lives is one who, oppresses no one, gives back the pledge received for a debt, commits no robbery; if he gives food to the hungry and clothes the naked; if he does not lend at interest nor exact usury; if he holds off from evildoing, judges fairly between a man and his opponent; if he lives by my statutes and is careful to observe my ordinances, that man is virtuous— he shall surely live, says the Lord God. (18:9)

Such insistence on worship of a God of justice often brought prophets into open conflict with "institutional religion." By this, I mean priests, ministers, or religious leaders who claim to mediate God's blessings independently of any commitment to justice for the poor and oppressed. Amos the shepherd prophet was a striking example of a prophet who came into conflict with such leaders. Amaziah, the priest at Bethel, a central shrine in Israel asked the king to expel Amos because the prophet's message was a direct condemnation of a sanctuary worship that was divorced from the concerns of the oppressed. God announced through Amos that he even hated worship, prayer and liturgical song that was unconnected with the plight of the needy:

I hate, I spurn your feasts, I take no pleasure in your solemnities. . . . Away with your noisy songs! I will not listen to the melodies of your harps. But if you would offer me holocausts, then let justice surge like water, and goodness like an unfailing stream. (5:21–24)

Amos was convinced that the earth and its resources belonged to God and should be shared equally by all. To go to God in worship without taking responsibility for extremes in poverty and riches is the worst kind of hypocrisy:

Hear this, you who trample upon the needy and destroy the poor of the land! "When will the new moon be over," you ask, "that we may sell our grain, and the sabbath, that we may display the wheat? We will diminish the ephah, add to the shekel, and fix our scales for cheating! We will buy the lowly man for silver, and the poor man for a pair of sandals; even the refuse of the wheat we will sell." (8:4–6)

It is important to note that the biblical prophets never appeal to the rich for charity or generosity to relieve oppression and hunger. It is a matter of pure justice, since the bible teaches that the earth and its resources are a gift from God that are *lent* to human beings for the benefit not of a few, but of all equally. To make sure that this was accomplished, no land could ever be sold permanently to others outside the family or clan. It could only be sold for a maximum of fifty years, since every fiftieth year was a jubilee year in which all land had to return to its original owners. It is interesting that the American Liberty Bell inscription, "Proclaim liberty in the land," is taken from the biblical description of the jubilee year:

This fiftieth year you shall make sacred by proclaiming liberty in the land for all its inhabitants. It shall be a jubilee for you, when every one of you shall return to his own property, every one to his own family estate. (Leviticus 25:10)

The reasoning behind the Jubilee year is that there is no such thing as an absolute right to private property. The land belonged to the God of all people who wanted it used by his tenants for the benefit of all: "The land shall not be sold in perpetuity; for the land is mine, and you are but aliens who have become my tenants." (Leviticus 25:23)

From this second criterion of fidelity to the covenant we can draw some conclusions about the signs of any genuine spiritual or religious leader: to be a religious person means to worship a God of justice and to make definite commitments in the area of social justice. Religion simply cannot be taught or practiced as a spiritual or interior matter without reference to political and social problems. These matters are not optional or electives but an essential part of worship of a God whose very essence is justice itself.

On the other hand a prophet or religious leader is not a mere "activist." The great prophets of the Old Testament always brought out that real exterior change in society could only be realized through a deep trust in the interior Spirit of God and by an inner conversion. For example, the prophet Jeremiah insisted that God wished to establish a new covenant among his people that would consist in the law of God written in their hearts rather than on stone tablets. This inner teacher would do away with the dependence on external authorities:

But this is the covenant which I will make with the house of Israel after those days, says the Lord. I will place my law within them, and write it upon their hearts. No longer will they have need to teach their kinsmen how to know the Lord. (31:32–33)

Ezekiel declared that true righteousness would be made possible only by an inner conversion effected by the Spirit of God:

I will give you a new heart and place a new spirit within you, taking from your bodies your stony hearts and giving you natural hearts. (36:26)

In summary, we can draw up the following list of rules of discernment for true leaders, based on the prophets in the Old Testament. The supreme rule is truth and fidelity to the covenant, but this can be broken down into the following norms:

1. Conflict of interest immediately places a shadow of doubt on anything a person says or does. Words or actions that would not be said or done except for money, prestige or some kind of personal advantage do not come ultimately from God. Truth is spoken for its own sake.

2. This truth is not a statement from the mind, but from the whole person, whose life and reputation are behind what is proclaimed. When this type of truth is present, leaders are willing to suffer and even die for the sake of the values and truths they talk about because they are true to the very core of their being. Their lives are simply not worth living if they cannot express them in word and action.

3. A true leader has no interest in winning popularity contests by telling people what they want to know and hear. Such leaders are positive and encouraging, but at the same time openly and honestly critical of themselves and the political and religious institutions under which they live.

4. A genuine prophet simply cannot refrain from speaking and acting in response to human oppression in any way that it exists. Religion cannot be silent about matters of politics and social justice. These are matters concerning the land, property, resources and their use, which according to biblical teaching can never be regarded as the private and absolute rights of a few people or corporations.

5. Real leaders are people of deep prayer and spirituality. They know they are facing a humanly impossible task, so they trust on deep interior resources made possible by the Spirit of God.

In addition to the prophetic rules of discernment based on truth and justice, there is also a second and even more profound biblical criterion based on God's very essence which is that of love and mercy. On one occasion Moses begged God for the privilege of actually seeing his glory. However, God replied that no human being could actually see his face and continue to live. (Exodus 33:21) Moses continued to insist, so God told him he would pass by while Moses was hidden in a rock hollow. In that way he could glimpse some portion of God's glory and still remain alive.

The biblical account describes that God passed by Moses and covered him with his hand, while pronouncing and revealing his great name Lord (Yahweh). God said,

The Lord, the Lord, a merciful and gracious God, slow to anger and rich in kindness and fidelity, continuing his kindness for a thousand generations, and forgiving wickedness and crime and sin. (34.:5)

The quality described by the words kindness and mercy is God's covenant love or *hesed* in Hebrew. It is a deep personal love based on responsible relationship. A special characteristic of this love is that it flows from a keen ability to listen to his people and understand them, especially in their weakness and suffering. The Hebrews used the word "listening heart" to describe this type of compassionate love. It was this deep quality that prompted God to intervene in the history of his people when they were in desperate need as slaves of the Pharaoh in Egypt. God appeared to Moses in a burning bush on Sinai and said,

I have witnessed the affliction of my people in Egypt and have heard their cry of complaint against their slave drivers so I know well what they are suffering. (Exodus 3:7)

Notice the emphasis on God's sensitivity in this text: he *sees* their affliction, *hears* their cries of suffering and *knows* in a very deep sense what they are going through.

Since this divine sensitivity is so important, the greatest quality a human being can have is the same "listening heart" when it comes to relationships with people. This was most especially important for kings and human leaders. This is illustrated by the stories of the young King Solomon as an exemplar of the wisdom tradition of the bible. The story is told that one night Solomon had a dream in which God told him he would grant anything that was asked of him. (1 Kings 3:4–15) The first concern of Solomon was his responsibility as a leader of his people. This was the way in which he had been chosen to serve God. So he responded, "Give your servant, therefore, an understanding heart to judge your people and to distinguish right from wrong. For who is able to govern this vast people of yours?" (3:9)

In the text, the words "understanding heart" are literally in Hebrew a "listening heart." God was very pleased with Solomon's request because he had not chosen a long life, riches, or victories over his enemies. God said to him, "I do as you requested. I give you a heart so wise and understanding that there has never been anyone like you up to now, and after you there will come no one to equal you."

The bible relates this story to teach us the roots and meaning of Wisdom. It is a gift from God, since it makes us like God himself in the unique divine listening and compassionate quality. In imitation of

King Solomon, it must be asked for in prayer. The prophet Isaiah describes the ideal future ruler in this way: "The spirit of the Lord shall rest upon him: a spirit of wisdom and of understanding." (11:1)

After the story of Solomon's dream, the bible describes how this wisdom was put into practical life by the ability to make good decisions in matters affecting others. Two harlots were brought before King Solomon. The two women had lived together and each had a newborn child. During the night, one of the children died, and each of the women claimed that the live child was hers. They looked to the king for a decision in what seemed an impossible case since there were no other witnesses. However, the "listening heart" of Solomon enabled him to have a deep sensitivity for the feelings of the true mother of the child and decide whose child was really alive. (3:16–38) At the end of the story the author notes that all of Israel heard of this decision and were in awe because "they saw that the king had in him the wisdom of God for giving judgment."

The bible goes on to show that when a person has this "wisdom of God," he or she has a broad openness and sensitivity not only to human beings but to all of plants, animals, and nature. The biblical author notes this of Solomon: "He uttered three thousand proverbs and his songs numbered a thousand and five. He discussed plants, from the cedar on Lebanon to the hyssop growing out of the wall, and he spoke about beasts, birds, reptiles and fishes." (5:12–13) These words illustrate the observing and listening quality of wisdom. The proverbs and songs mentioned in the text were actually artistic and poetic ways to describe this wisdom and pass it on to others. The bible points out that this wisdom is the only really effective way to reach out to others and profoundly influence the world. The author of 1 Kings writes, "Men came to hear Solomon's wisdom from all nations, sent by all the kings of the earth who had heard of his wisdom." (5:14)

To especially highlight these effects of Wisdom, the author devotes an entire chapter (10) to the story of the Queen of Sheba who came thousands of miles to hear the wisdom of Solomon. She was amazed by what she saw and heard. She exclaimed that she had not believed the reports she had heard, but now she knew that his wisdom and prosperity exceeded everything she had heard. She blessed God who had given Solomon wisdom, judgment and justice to rule over Israel.

Although it is helpful to enumerate "rules of discernment" there is really only one supreme "rule", which is not really a rule at all. It is the gift of wisdom—the gift of a listening heart." Dr. Brian Hall has well described this supreme quality of human leadership in his book, *Shepherds and Lovers* (Paulist Press). It is explained in a very simple way by Jesus himself who describes the Good Samaritan as (literally) one whose insides or heart went out in compassion to a suffering human being lying by the road even though he was a complete stranger. (Luke 10:33)

BIBLIOGRAPHY

Blekinsopp, Joseph, *The Men Who Spoke Out* (London: Dalton, 1969)

Clements, R.E., *Prophecy and Covenant* (Naperville, Ill.: Allenson, 1965)

Heschel, A., *The Prophets* (N.Y.: Harper & Row, 1963)

Kraeling, Emil, *The Prophets* (Chicago: Rand McNally, 1969)

Lindblom, Johannes, *Prophecy in Ancient Israel* (Phila.: Fortress, 1965)

Maly, Eugene, *Prophets of Salvation* (Herder, 1969)

Mowvley, Harry, *Reading the Old Testament Prophets Today* (Atlanta: John Knox, 1979)

Rad, Gerhard, *The Message of the Prophets* (N.Y.: Harpers, 1977, 1965)

Reid, David P., *What Are They Saying About the Prophets?* (N.Y.: Paulist, 1980)

Scott, R.B.Y., *The Relevance of the Prophets* (N.Y.: Macmillan, 1968)

Wilson, Robert R., *Prophecy and Society in Ancient Israel* (Phila.: Fortress, 1980)

Wisdom

Brueggemann, Walter A., *In Man We Trust: The Neglected Side of Biblical Faith* (Atlanta: John Knox, 1972)

Crenshaw, James L., Ed. *Studies in Ancient Israelite Wisdom*, (N.Y.: Ktav, 1976)

Murphy, Roland, *Seven Books of Wisdom* (Milwaukee: Bruce, 1960)

Rad, Gerhard von, *Wisdom in Israel*, James Martin, trans. (Nashville: Abingdon, 1972)

Scott, R.B.Y., *The Way of Wisdom in the Old Testament* (N.Y. Macmillan, 1971)

Discernment of Spirits:
The New Testament View

Joseph A. Grassi
University of Santa Clara

In today's world, many areas exist where it is very difficult to distinguish between good and evil. Relatively few people would be willing to choose undisguised evil, a frightful monster. Consequently, those who do promote evil carefully disguise it under appearance of good so that people without careful discernment will choose what is apparently good for themselves and for others. Governments may appeal to citizens to support their efforts of economic exploitation and expansion by appealing to patriotism as a virtue rewarded by God. Advertisers may try to sell their products by presenting an unneeded luxury as an essential requirement of life itself. Actually we need no outside source of influence. We even convince ourselves that something is good by considering only good aspects and ignoring the examination of areas which could be harmful to ourselves or others.

The New Testament church was faced with a similar problem. The way they dealt with it can serve as a very useful model for modern day men and women faced with difficult choices. Then as today, there were leaders and teachers who presented conflicting and attractive views of what it meant to be a Christian. In doing so, they claimed that they were led by "the Spirit." So it became quite important to establish definite criteria to discern or separate what was really from the Holy Spirit, or the tradition from Jesus.

Our methodology here will be to survey the New Testament, examining each significant document where criteria for discernment are given, and let the material speak for itself. In doing so we will try to see the criteria in the light of the historical situation and problems that gave rise to their formulation. We will limit ourselves to those sources which deal with *orthopraxis*, how a Christian should act and live, rather than those which deal with *orthodoxis* which concern doctrinal beliefs.

The Gospel of Mark

The gospel of Mark is especially directed to the Christian living in a Greek world. The Greeks liked to think of a holy person as a man or woman of personal power and gifts, such as healing or prophecy. Christians were tempted to use this model: they were the followers of Jesus, a powerful healer and exorcist who had now given his powers to them so they could continue his work. The image was that of a superstar messiah and superstar Christians, his followers. Mark quotes Jesus' saying that "false messiahs and false prophets will appear performing signs and wonders to mislead, if it were possible, even the chosen." (13:22) Some even thought that Jesus would return to give them the power to overcome the Roman oppressors, despite the outcome of the Jewish war with Rome in 66–70 A.D. The destruction of Jerusalem and the Temple was for them a sign of the coming end of the world, and the return of Jesus in power. In support of their view, they used again and again the tradition of Jesus' miracles and healings.

Mark's method of discernment is to present a realistic picture of Jesus as a model to be imitated. The miracle tradition is not ignored. Instead, the inner ingredient of faith is emphasized again and again. It is not some mysterious power of the healer but a deep surrendering trust in God on the part of the recipient. This is summed up in Jesus' words, "Everything is possible to a person who trusts." (9:23) Healings are not a personal prerogative or power; all that is needed is the same faith as Jesus. In consequence, the disciple who has the same humble faith can do all that Jesus did. Lack of faith makes a miracle impossible (9:1–29) As a consequence of this faith, the twelve go out and perform the same exorcisms and healings as their master (6:7–13)

As a criterion for discernment Mark shows how Jesus and the Christian must resist the temptation to use power and violence to bring about the kingdom of God. Even on the cross, Jesus resists this temptation when the chief priests and scribes say, "Let the 'Messiah,' the 'king of Israel,' come down from that cross here and now so that we can see it and believe in him!" (15:32) It is in view of Jesus' example and command that the early Jewish-Christian community refused to take up military weapons to fight against Rome, and even abandoned Jerusalem. (13:14) This was no easy choice to make; it meant that they would be branded as unpatriotic, and even as traitors to their country in their struggle against a foreign oppressor.

In view of this model of a Messiah of peace, Mark presents the picture of a humble, ordinary, suffering Messiah who is willing to give his life in selfless service to others. Mark has three sections on discipleship following a three-fold prediction of the suffering and death of the Son of Man. Each section shows how the Christian is to follow the same way by taking up his or her cross as well. (8:31; 9:30–31; 10:32–33) At the end of the third section Jesus teaches, "The Son of Man has

324

not come to be served but to serve—to give his life in ransom for the many." (10:45) As a kind of climax to the gospel, the centurion after the death of Jesus on the cross "on seeing the *manner of his death*," declared, 'Truly this man was the son of God.' " (15:39) It was the way he died as a faithful, humble servant of God that really showed who he was, not some great act of power. For Mark, Jesus' own humble obedience as far as death is the model of discernment for the Christian.

Matthew likewise is concerned that many Christians will be led astray **The** by teachers who present a path that appears to be a good one. Three **Gospel** times in his gospel he refers to "false prophets." (7:15; 24:11,24) Since **of** a prophet is someone who claims to speak in the name of God, it was **Matthew** quite important to distinguish those who are led by the Spirit of God from those who are led by their one spirit or desires. Matthew appears to be especially worried about what have been called "lawless charismatics"—Christians who pride themselves on special powers or spiritual gifts. In the Sermon on the Mount, Jesus says, "When that day comes, many will plead with me, 'Lord, have we not prophesied in your name? Have we not exorcised demons by its power? Did we not do many miracles in your name as well?' Then I will declare to them solemnly, 'I never knew you. Out of my sight, you evildoers!' " (7:22–23) What made their work so impressive was that they actually identified themselves with Christ and performed wondrous deeds in his name.

Matthew, like Mark, appeals to the example of Jesus' acts of mercy and service to others. To Mark's emphasis on faith in the miracle accounts, Matthew adds that of compassion and identification with others. At the end of a series of miracles, he quotes the prophet Isaiah's text on the suffering, humble servant of the Lord with the words, "It was our infirmities he bore, our sufferings he endured." (8:5; Is. 53:4) In contrast to those who claimed an inner identification with Christ through their special gifts, Matthew emphasizes again and again that what you *do* tells what you are. The verb *do* is repeated again and again in the gospel, especially the Sermon on the Mount. A true prophet can be discerned by his or her actions. Even though a false prophet looks good in sheep's clothing he or she may be underneath a wolf in disguise. (7:15) "You will know them by their deeds." (7:16) It is not enough to just hear Jesus' words; they must be put into practice: "Anyone who hears my words and puts them into practice is like the wise man who built his house on rock." (7:24) To merely hear them is a complete disaster.

For Matthew, the criterion for discernment is the *words of Jesus actually put into practice*. The final instructions of Jesus and the last words of the gospel are the command, "Teach them to carry out everything I have commanded you." (28:20) These words and commands are not generalities; they are spelled out in detail in the Sermon on the Mount as a summary of Jesus' teaching. (chaps. 5–7) The inner basis of these commands is imitation of God's own unconditional love for everyone, whether good or bad: "This will prove that you are sons of your heavenly Father, for his sun rises on the bad and the good, he rains on the just and the unjust." (5:45) Special attention is drawn to brotherly love as the only means to avoid murder (5:21), inner purity of thought and respect for women as persons to avoid adultery and divorce (5:27,31), a deep fidelity to one another that prevents swearing (5:33), a non-violent loving response to hatred, oppression and violence, and finally love even for strangers and enemies to break down a narrow concept of family solidarity. (5:43)

The commands of Jesus are so important for Matthew as a criterion for discernment that the final judgment scene in his gospel concerns the manner in which the Sermon on the Mount has been put into practice. Those who are Christians have become identified with Christ by obeying his commands, and imitating his care and concern for the hungry, the thirsty, the naked, the stranger, the sick and those in prison: "For I was hungry and you gave me food, I was thirsty and you gave me drink. I was a stranger and you welcomed me, naked and you clothed me. I was ill and you comforted me, in prison and you came to visit me." (25:35–36)

It is not some extraordinary gift or power that identifies a Christian but sensitivity to others in the very ordinary events of daily life: "As often as you did it for one of my least brothers, you did it for me." (25:40)

The Gospel of Luke and the Acts of the Apostles In both parts of his two-volume work, Luke is concerned about Christians who might be misguided by some community members into directions that could prove dangerous. In Acts 20:30, Luke has Paul speak in this manner: "From your own number, men will present themselves distorting the truth and leading astray any who follow them." Luke does not specify in detail what these misdirections would be, but there is some evidence that at least part of them would be incorrect ideas about the Spirit and its nature as well as function. This misconception would make the Spirit into a magical personal power that could be given to certain elite persons by a secret transfer in baptism/the laying on of hands. The attention given to the story of Simon Magus illustrates this. Simon was amazed when he saw the power of the Spirit working through Peter and John. He offered them money if they could give him the same power also. (Acts 8:19)

In both Acts and the gospel, Luke indicates definite criteria that distinguish the presence and activity of the Spirit. 1) It is a gift of God, and comes only after fervent prayer. Jesus prays for the coming of the Spirit before his baptism. (Luke 3:21) The first Christians pray together with Mary the mother of Jesus at the coming of the Spirit on the first Pentecost. (Acts 1:14; 2:1ff) 2) The Spirit is intimately connected to the person of Jesus. It acted through him during his earthly life. At his death and resurrection he received the promised fullness of the Spirit from the Father and poured it on the first believers. (Acts 2:33) The Acts of the Apostles shows how the Spirit duplicated and extended all that Jesus had done through Peter, Paul and the early Christian community. The duplication and imitation of the life-style of Jesus is a sign of the presence of the Spirit. In fact, the whole gospel of Luke is written to furnish a model for the Christian who wishes to know how the Spirit worked in Jesus. 3) Luke gives special attention to the presence of the Spirit in all that points toward a oneness that is based on God's most repeated name, "the One" (Hear, O Israel, the Lord your God is one—Dt. 6:4) God's oneness was especially shown in his creative activity as the cause of oneness, beginning from the oneness of male and female (Gn. 2:24) and continuing to the oneness of the human race. (Is. 2:1–4) In the Acts of the Apostles, it is the Spirit that makes possible this oneness of the human race by a new language of the Spirit that unites people from all over the world so they can understand one another at the first Pentecost. (2:5–13) The one Spirit prompts an economic oneness as the early Christians share their food with the hungry. (4:32–35) It is a oneness that breaks down existing social, national, and even sexual barriers. In Luke, women are described as disciples of Jesus and accompanying him on his journeys. (8:1–3) It is noted in the story of Martha and Mary that Mary is seated at the Lord's feet listening to his word, the attitude of a disciple. (11:39; cf. 8:35) Whenever the gospel comes to a new territory or to previously separated people, special note is made of the activity of the Spirit: the Spirit in Philip brings the gospel to the Samaritans (Acts 8). When Peter first addresses the Gentile Cornelius and his friends, the Holy Spirit comes down upon the whole group to create a "Gentile Pentecost." (10:41–48) When Paul converts a group of twelve former followers of John the Baptist in Roman Asia, the Holy Spirit falls on the group and they begin to speak in tongues. (19:6–7) It is the "Spirit of Jesus" that prompts Paul to begin the European apostolate. (16:7–9)

The Gospel of John

In comparison to Luke, John offers few concrete details that would offer a guide to discernment of spirits in regard to orthopraxis. The teachings of Jesus in regard to marriage, divorce, children, riches, etc. that are present in the synoptic gospels are missing. The Sermon on the Mount in Matthew and Luke is nowhere to be found. And yet the missing details may be part of the author's purpose. He may be wishing to point to a deeper level of discernment that could prevent an imitation of Jesus at an external and perhaps slavish level.

John does have a definite criterion in mind for he writes, "This is how all will know you for my disciples: your love for one another." (7:34) When the author uses the term "love," he has something very special in mind. Jesus calls it "a new commandment" (13:34), and "my commandment." (15:12) The injunction follows the story of Jesus washing the feet of his disciples, which is a very personal, selfless service of others. Jesus commands them to imitate him with the words, "What I just did was to give you an example: as I have done, so you must do." (13:15) This example also follows the betrayal of Judas, despite Jesus' special attention to him. Consequently, it is a love that goes out even to a betrayer or enemy. It is a love that accompanies Jesus' announcement of his coming death. (13:13–33) Thus it can be described as a love that goes as far as giving up one's life for another. This will be phrased later in the form,

This is my commandment: love one another as I have loved you. There is no greater love than this: to lay down one's life for one's friends. (15:12–13)

John takes care to show the deeply personal and divine quality of such a love. It flows from an intimate communion between the Risen Jesus and the disciple, which in turn has its source in the same type of communion between Jesus and the Father. Jesus says, "As the Father has loved me, so I have loved you." (15:9) This identification and communion is so close that it is described in terms of identification and even interpenetration:

I pray that they may be one in us, that the world may believe that you sent me. (17:21)

and

I living in them, you living in me—that their unity may be complete. So shall the world know that you sent me. . . . (17:23)

We might say that John's love has its base not in any surface emotion (although certainly accompanied by emotion) but in a deep feeling of oneness and identification resulting from the divine indwelling in both Jesus and the believer.

The First Letter of John This letter seems to have been written as a reaction and response to various Christians who carried some teachings in the gospel of John to a far extreme. While the gospel of John emphasizes the inner gift of the Spirit, there were some who claimed that a special inner illumination gave them a special knowledge and experience of God that made them exempt from sin and human weakness. (1:8–10; 2:4) For them this was the sole criterion of the direction of the Spirit. In contrast, the author points out that this can be self-deception. Admission of sin and human weakness, as well as trust in God's forgiveness, is a much surer sign of closeness to God. (1:9) The inner experience is not nearly as important as obedience to the commands of God, and imitation of Jesus' example. (2:4–6)

In more detail, the author points out that an inner experience of light can only be trusted if it is accompanied by a loving relationship with other human beings: "The man who continues in the light is the one who loves his brother." This in itself is an experience of God and his love, for "God is love." (4:8) Here again it is not just an inner feeling but a very practical response to other human beings in need: "I ask you, how can God's love survive in a man who has enough of this world's goods yet closes his heart to his brother when he sees him in need?" (3:17)

In this letter *orthodoxis* (right belief) is connected with *orthopraxis* (right conduct):

328

Beloved, do not trust every spirit, but put the spirits to a test to see if they belong to God, because many false prophets have appeared in the world. This is how you can recognize God's Spirit: every spirit that acknowledges Jesus Christ come in the flesh belongs to God, while every spirit that fails to acknowledge him does not belong to God. (4:1–3)

In this text, belief in Jesus and his real, concrete human nature means that a person will follow his example and see the reality and need of his saving work, rather than trusting only in inner experiences, however moving they may be.

In First Thessalonians we already see that discernment of spirits is a problem:

Do not stifle the Spirit. Do not despise prophecies. Test everything; retain what is good. Avoid any semblance of evil. (5:19–22)

However, all we can learn from this brief text is that Christian prophets are to be encouraged despite the fact that sometimes they may be misleading. The community is to carefully sift what they say and retain only what is good.

In the letter to the Galatians, the problem is much more clear. There were some Christians who thought that a sign of the presence of the Spirit was a complete freedom in their actions. Paul has to warn them that certain actions are a sign of slavery rather than freedom. How can they distinguish between them? Paul provides a valuable guide in his distinction between the "flesh" and the Spirit. These two are at direct poles of opposition. He writes, "My point is that you should live in accord with the spirit and you will not yield to the cravings of the flesh." (5:16) Then a detailed guide of these latter is furnished:

It is obvious what proceeds from the flesh: lewd conduct, impurity, licentiousness, idolatry, sorcery, hostilities, bickering, jealousy, outbursts of rage, selfish rivalries, dissensions, factions, envy, drunkenness, orgies and the like. (5:19–20)

Looking carefully at this list, we see that these fruits of the flesh are manifested in separating emotions such as anger, jealousy, lustful feelings, etc. They are "cravings," because they look outside for happiness. They are impersonal, or if they are toward people, the people are being used or looked upon as things. They are more than just inclinations of the body such as for food, sex, pleasure, etc. These are good in themselves. In contrast, they are *cravings* or demands placed on other people or things. These have their origin in the mind with its expectations, models and demands, rather than in the natural good inclinations of the body. Giving in to these demands makes for a self-centered life in which people or things outside must somehow come to us and be used exclusively for ourselves.

Paul sees these as directly in contrast to the way of the Spirit. He writes, "I warn you, as I have warned you before: those who do such things will not inherit the kingdom of God." (5:21) Then he provides a list of the fruits of the Spirit:

The fruits of the spirit are love, joy, peace, patient endurance, kindness, generosity, faith, mildness, and chastity. Against such there is no law! Those who belong to Christ Jesus have crucified their flesh with its passions and desires. Since we live by the Spirit, let us follow the Spirit's lead. (5:22–25)

Looking now at the list of the Spirit's fruits, we note that these are manifested in what we might call unifying emotions, such as love, joy, kindness, etc. These emotions draw us closer to other people. In contrast to the first list, this one is very personal in its orientation, with a deep respect and sensitivity for other people. It is characterized by an outward movement that seeks more to love and serve others, than to be inward and self-serving.

Paul the Apostle points out that a real choice must be made between the two ways. It is a choice not only to move outward in the selfless service of others through the Spirit, but a definite attempt to control and overcome the opposing way of the flesh. That is why he writes, "Those who belong to Christ Jesus have crucified their flesh with its passions and desires." (5:24) To further strengthen this, Paul concludes by stating, "Let us never be boastful, or challenging, or jealous toward one another." (5:26)

In the letters to the Corinthians, it is especially in regard to spiritual gifts that discernment of spirits becomes a very important matter. Previous to their conversion, the Corinthian Christians had gone to pagan shrines where they were often raised to an exalted state of consciousness in which they hardly knew what they were saying or doing. Their religious experience of the "spirit" was like a spiritual "trip" in which they felt detached from the earth and at times not even conscious of what they were saying or doing. So first of all, Paul is careful to point out that the experience of the Spirit does not in any way reduce personal responsibility or alertness. He writes,

That is why I tell you that nobody who speaks in the Spirit of God ever says "Cursed be Jesus." And no one can say: "Jesus is Lord," except in the Holy Spirit. (1 Cor. 12:3)

In fact, Paul points out that a characteristic of the possession of the Spirit is full control of one's self, rather than a loss of control. He states, "The spirits of the prophets are under the prophets' control, since God is a God, not of confusion but of peace." (1 Cor. 14:32–33)

A second important area for discernment was in regard to comparison of one's own spiritual gifts to those of others. In the Corinthian community there was a variety of manifestations of the Spirit, many of which we would say today were along the nature of special psychic powers. Among these was the gift of tongues which seemed to be an ecstatic, exhilarating outburst of prayer to God which to bystanders seemed like a babble or a foreign language. In addition there were special gifts of healing, prophecy and wisdom. There was the tendency among Corinthian Christians to earnestly strive after the more showy and personally gratifying gifts such as tongues and healing, and at the same time to downplay those that seemed more ordinary and prosaic in daily life.

Paul provides an important basic criterion to apply to all gifts of the Holy Spirit. For him, the essential quality of the Spirit is that it moves toward oneness with others. For Paul (as we have seen in Luke) the great name of God, repeated thousands of times by each Jew, is "the One." Consequently, a true indication of the presence of the Spirit is that it breaks down every separating barrier whether built on race, sex, or social status: "It was in one Spirit that all of us whether Jew or Greek, slave or free, were baptized into one body. All of us have been given a drink of the one Spirit." (12:13) In Galatians, Paul also added to this "male and female." (3:28) Because of this essential feature of oneness, every genuine gift of the Spirit is meant to build up the whole community. It is not just for one's self, or for mere personal gratification. This is why Paul will write, "To each person the manifestation of the Spirit is given for the *common good*." (12:7) For this reason, Paul asks the community to prefer those gifts that build up others more than those that are oriented more toward building up one's self. This is the reason why he asks them to strive to be prophets, whose gift is more outwardly oriented toward helping others:

The prophet, on the other hand, speaks to men for their upbuilding, their encouragement, their consolation. He who speaks in a tongue builds up himself, but he who prophesies builds up the church. (14:4)

The oneness, however, that Paul speaks about does not consist by any means in uniformity. On the contrary, this oneness is characterized by a remarkable diversity, in which each person realizes that he or she has a unique way to serve and help others. It is this quality or direction that is more important than the specific way that the gift may operate.

To bring out the true meaning of oneness through diversity, Paul uses the image of a human body. Despite the unbelievable amount of specialization in the human body, each member works not for itself but for the benefit of the whole:

Now the body is not one member, it is many. If the foot should say, "Because I am not a hand I do not belong to the body," would it then no longer belong to the body? If the ear should say, "Because I am not an eye I do not belong to the body," would it then no longer belong to the body? If the body were all eye, what would happen to our hearing? If it were all ear, what would happen to our smelling? (12:14–17)

Paul points out that if there were uniformity—if each member did the same thing—then the human body would be an impossibility: "If all the members were alike, where would the body be?" (12:19) The purpose of such variety and specialization is that the members of the body learn to care for one another and know that they need one another:

that there may be no dissension in the body but that all the members may be concerned for one another. If one member suffers, all the members suffer with it; if one member is honored, all the members share its joy. (12:25–26)

We can see, then, that Paul's image of the "body of Christ" points to a discernment based on oneness through appreciation of diversity rather than uniformity. It is easy to be deceived by a certain outward show of unity that does not flow from real interior oneness. It often takes a real process of discernment to distinguish one from the other. For Paul, the ability "to distinguish one spirit from another" (12:10) is in itself a special gift. The truly spiritual person is characterized by a deep wisdom that comes from God. (2:10–16) It was such a wisdom that distinguished the life-style of Jesus. A true person of wisdom can state, "We have the mind of Christ." (2:16)

Leadership Training and Discernment of Spirits: Some Applications 1. Discernment is an exercise of the will, an active choice. Jesus was tempted; i.e., he had to make serious and difficult choices. The process of leadership training implies a continual strengthening of the will in order to be able to make difficult value decisions.

2. The New Testament emphasizes the place of the community as the locus where discernment takes place. (see Thessalonians and Corinthians) A community is a place where one learns to be critical in the original meaning of the word, which is to make a good judgment or decision. The leader receives honest feedback from community members and is willing to acknowledge mistakes and learn from others.

3. Whatever gifts a leader may have are only for the benefit of serving the community—as Paul would express it "for the common good" (1 Cor. 12:7) The temptation to use power and force to win over others is an ever present temptation to the leader, just as the Gospel of Mark shows that it was for Jesus. But the only way to true Christian leadership is that of Jesus—the humble way of the cross and selfless service of others.

4. It is Luke especially who reminds us that the indwelling of the Holy Spirit, the best qualification for a Christian leader, is essentially a gift from God that comes through fervent prayer—like that of Jesus before his baptism (3:21) and that of the early church before the day of Pentecost. (Acts 1:12–14)

5. Matthew's emphasis on the words and example of Jesus shows us that a Christian leader is only so in name unless he or she imitates the life-style of Jesus and initiates others into that life-style through a liv-

ing example, one that stresses peace, non-violence and unconditional love.

6. It is John especially who brings out the pre-eminence of love for others in the Christian leader. It is a love like that of Jesus which goes out even to death in service of others, and embraces even the enemy and betrayer Judas within its scope.

7. Paul is a constant reminder that true leaders should encourage and stimulate diversity within the community. They will see this as a contribution to true oneness in contrast to a uniformity that would only be an external show of unity. Paul's special gift as an apostle was the ability to start new foundations, create new leaders and then to start this over and over again in new places. The best leader, like Paul, is the person who makes himself or herself "useless" by trusting in the gifts of the Holy Spirit within each person and within the community.

BIBLIOGRAPHY

de Guibert, *Theology of the Spiritual Life*, ch. 3, "Discernment of Spirits" (Sheed and Ward, 1954)

Wright, John H., "Discernment of Spirits in the New Testament," in *Communio* 1 (1974) #2

Rahner, Hugo, *Ignatius the Theologian*, ch. 4, "Discernment of Spirits" (London: Chapman, 1968)

Buckley, Michael, "Rules for Discernment of Spirits," in *The Way*, #20, Autumn, 1973

Discernment

Robert L. Schmitt, S.J.
University of Santa Clara

This appendix will briefly explore the interesting and mutually clarifying relationship between Brian Hall's book on the "Genesis Effect" and the Christian tradition on discernment. The key to understanding this relationship is found in their common concern: both approaches focus on gaining and processing pertinent information so that one can make life-giving decisions. Since the reader has already read about the "Genesis Effect," our method of exploration will be to offer a quick, modern sketch of discernment in language that resonates with Brian Hall's work.

This sketch is meant to raise questions and stimulate further reflection and discussion rather than give a satisfying, complete picture. The Christian tradition on discernment is too complex and rich to even dream of such an attempt in so few pages. To simplify the scene, this sketch will focus on discernment as taught by Ignatius of Loyola, a sixteenth century Basque who founded the Jesuit Order (Society of Jesus) and who is recognized as an extraordinary teacher in the area of discernment.

I will begin by presenting a definition of discernment and some suppositions behind the view of discernment offered here. Then I will describe in broad outline two types of discernment: discernment in ordinary day to day living and discernment in the process of major decision-making.

A Starting The interest of growing numbers of Christians in discernment has
Point: mushroomed as their world has become less clear and exterior au-
Definition thority less able to speak definitively to their individual situations. A
and variety of definitions for discernment have been proposed. Edward
Suppositions Malatesta's definition will do well for our starting point. He speaks of
discernment as:

> . . . the process by which we examine, in the light of faith and in the connaturality of love, the nature of the spiritual states we experience in ourselves and in others. The purpose of such examination is to decide, as far as possible, which of the movements we experience lead to the Lord and to a more perfect service of him and our brothers, and which deflect us from this goal.[1]

Hand in hand with contemplation, discernment is not a discrete act but an entire spiritual endeavor, a way of life. It seeks an abiding condition of knowing God, of a life-style based on an experiential, personal knowledge that comes from love. It yearns to live in harmony with the Source of all Reality.

The Christian teaching on discernment flows out of certain common human experiences. These experiences speak to the ambiguity in our lives, to the conflict and diversity within our interior movements (feelings, thoughts, impulses, etc.). Some of these movements lead more toward life and some more toward death. One naturally asks the question: how do I discover which movements are truly life-giving?

Any Christian teaching on discernment also depends upon one's basic suppositions or faith stance. This basic stance helps a person express and thus understand better his or her experiences. It helps give norms for suggesting which movements are truly trust-worthy. We need then to make more explicit the suppositions operative in this presentation.

My starting point is belief in an active, loving God. This God is Creator and Lord of history. He has a goal and a will: seeking to bring creation to fullness of life. God does this not as a force over against us but as the Ground of all that is, as the Horizon within which all takes place. Thus this God does not fulfill his will by playing the puppeteer, manipulating us against our will. This God knows creation as it truly is and is invited to be. Thus he calls us by name and draws us towards fulfillment. Such a God wants us to be ourselves more than we do!

A Jewish story describes well this aspect of God. Rabbi Jacob was dying. His disciples asked him what he thought God would say to him when they met. The Rabbi thought and then responded. He will say: "Rabbi Jacob, why did you try so to be like Moses and David; why didn't you just be more Rabbi Jacob?"

334

God calls us to fullness of life by calling us to be our true selves. God works in mysterious ways, ways that do not go against our own humanity nor against our need to act responsibly, to act as adults. God works through the natural order, leading us both as individuals and as a world to greater life. Our fates are interwoven. We are called then to live in harmony with life as it is evolving within us and in the world around us. Christians, by seeking to find and do God's will, are striving to be more fully alive and human, not less, to be truly integrated, not confined to some small realm like that of the super-ego.

The choice for life sounds so easy. But we all know that it is not. There is within us and around us resistance to life. There is evil and the movement toward death or stagnation. There is the definite possibility of self-deception. Thus one can experience great confusion as he or she seeks to decide what specific deed or choice will truly move oneself and one's world toward completion.

It is in this context that writers speak of the need to learn the art of discernment and to pray for it as a gift. There is so much information within us and outside us as we seek to live our lives and make decisions. In discernment we seek to gather the pertinent information and to process it in a way that enables us to live in a life-fostering way and to make life-nurturing decisions.

Writers will speak then of two types of discernment. One is "discernment of spirits." This treats of normal day to day living and the ways we should listen to and respond to the movements within the day. The other type is called "discernment of God's will." This treats of Christian decision making (major decisions). Let us take a few minutes to sketch certain aspects of each type of discernment.

In daily life a variety of feelings, thoughts, impulses, etc. move about inside us (we will call these interior movements). Recognizing from experience that not all his thoughts and feelings led to life, Ignatius sought to "discern" the differences in these movements. We call this "discernment of spirits." In modern terms, it is a process of taking data (one's interior movements, especially thoughts and feelings) and gathering significant information from them that could lead to more congruent and healthy living of the spiritual life. It involves learning which movements are life-giving and which are not, what they mean, and how to respond to them in life-fostering ways. **Discernment of Spirits**

From an analysis of a vast range of experiences (his own, his directees, and Christian writers through the centuries), Ignatius developed certain guidelines or "rules" to facilitate the discernment process. Ignatius wrote these guidelines as an aid to freedom, to assist one to live more in harmony with one's deepest self and with God. They do this by helping one retrieve useful information from his or her interior experiences.

In this process Ignatius saw the need for a developmental approach. The significance of certain movements could be different depending on where one was in the spiritual journey. Thus Ignatius really has several sets of guidelines depending on the stage of the journey. If there were more time it would be interesting to compare the developmental stages proposed by Ignatius with those proposed by Brian Hall.

In fostering the facility to discern well Ignatius stressed the role of the imagination and of images. Ignatius taught that essential to growth in discernment was the prayerful entering into the images and messages of Scripture. This way one took on more the values of Christ and, behind them, the internal images or "mind" of Christ. By doing this and by seeking to live out Christ's values in one's daily life (the importance of behavior!), one's affectivity and thoughts became more congruent with Christ's. As a result one's sensitivity to movements fostered by God (Life) became more natural and spontaneous. The ability then to distinguish life-giving movements from death-dealing blossomed both in daily life and in making important decisions.

To facilitate daily discernment Ignatius taught a form of prayer called the "examen."[2] This prayer helps one develop a discerning attitude for the entire day. Besides helping one be more aware of God's activity in his or her day, the prayer assists a person to see more clearly what values are operative in one's behavior and what they signify. These elements are critical to Ignatian Spirituality and to the material presented in this book.

In summary, Ignatius stressed that God is a very active Lover present in our daily lives. He saw that to live in harmony with such a God we need to learn his language. Part of that involves learning how to interpret our interior movements, for God is intimately at work within us. In modern terms, we need a way of retrieving the information present in our day that reveals to us how God is present and what he is doing. Ignatius' Rules for Discernment of Spirits are well-tested guidelines for doing that.

Discernment of God's Will   There are certain times in our lives when we must make major decisions. The committed Christian wants those decisions to be in conformity with God's will. "Discernment of God's will" is the process or method of gaining information from all the pertinent data so that one can make a God-directed decision, a decision that comes out of truth and freedom, not ignorance and bondage.

In describing this process two extremes should be avoided. The first makes the process magical. It assumes that God will simply tell us what he wants without any searching on our part. Such a view makes us irresponsible children and denies that God expects us to be adults in our decision-making process. The other extreme assumes that God has no part in the process, that God does not communicate with us. Such a view simply denies the God of the Bible.

The Ignatian method emphasizes our need to use in a spirit of prayer and openness all our human resources. One needs to begin in a spirit of freedom and openness to God's activity. One must gather and evaluate all the pertinent information. Then in prayerful silence one needs to place before God all the information acquired and to listen to the interior movements that occur (gaining information from them with the help of the rules on "discernment of spirits"). Let us describe aspects of this process in a little more detail.

The discernment process demands a high degree of freedom. Being closed to certain possibilities can block a person even being able to retrieve or process pertinent information that may favor those alternatives. The areas of unfreedom may be conscious or hidden deeply in the unconscious. Because of such complexity in us, Ignatius spoke of how difficult it was to make a good discernment process. Granted, we are never totally free. It is always a matter of degree. But for authentic discernment we need to check out our freedom and confront ourselves so that we can see more clearly and thus decide more authentically.

Our freedom is intimately bound together with our internal images. Insight into them offers insight into our inner workings and into what motivates us. We can make contact with these images through discovering the values operative in our lives and their order of priority. If this search for self-knowledge is combined with reaching the unconscious through such vehicles as dreams and journaling, the discerner is truly working for a knowledge that fosters freedom. Ignatius stresses that for sincere discernment one needs such a freedom, a freedom based on a clear order of priorities in one's life. Ignatius expresses that first priority this way:

I must consider only the end for which I am created, that is, for the praise of God our Lord and for the salvation of my soul. Hence, whatever I choose must help me to this end for which I am created.[3]

Any healthy decision-making process is built on collecting the pertinent data and drawing the significant information from it. Even the person who relies heavily on intuition needs such information. Otherwise what is the person intuiting or "looking into"? Intuition is not magic, drawing something out of nothing.

Much writing on discernment focuses on making a decision between two clear alternatives, e.g., move to Toronto or don't move to Toronto. But how does one come up with that set of alternatives in the first place? Usually a great deal needs to be done before that question is chosen. The selecting of the alternatives to be "discerned" is critical! So much can be missed by settling on the wrong question.

Information gathering for discernment demands drinking from all the major sources. That includes the outside world as well as the inner world. In the outer world one needs to carefully discover the pertinent facts and hear opinions, look at the present situation and at possibilities for the future. In the inner world one should draw from both the conscious and the unconscious parts. One should draw from one's affectivity, thoughts, body, imagination, history. One needs to draw from one's "natural" powers and from one's "graced" times of prayer. One needs to look at the data through the prism of Scripture and one's experience of God's movement in his or her life. In all of this one needs to be asking for God's assistance, asking to be open to surprises, to seeing clearly, to being sensitive to the movements of the Spirit.

This entire process can appear overwhelming! Different approaches are offered by writers to help one gather and organize the information available. Information is useless if it drowns a person or leads to simply deciding on one or two issues that seem manageable.

Authors like Irving Janis and Daniel Wheeler offer excellent guidelines for coming to alternatives for decision-making.[4] They suggest processes that enable one to create all kinds of alternatives that help expand one's horizons and clarify the issues. Like Ignatius they suggest writing down all the pros and cons on an alternative. In discernment one then sits in quiet before God waiting to see if movements come from deep within to help clarify the issue.

In coming to the final decision Ignatius says that sometimes (and it can happen anytime in the process) God does move so strongly in the person that he or she knows the choice. Normally this is not the case. Then one places the whole matter, all the pertinent information having been gathered, before oneself and God in prayer. One listens to the movements within oneself, sorting through that data with the help of the rules for discernment of spirits. Sometimes clarity will emerge. One will sense the choice as truly fitting with one's deepest self and relationship with God. Sometimes the movements will not give clarity. Then Ignatius encourages the person to rely more on reason, on stepping back and seeing what one would advise another person or how one would look at oneself at the end of life. One hopes that with time, patience, and sensitivity the graced interior responses of a person in prayer to the information gathered will lead to clarity. One expects God to work through the process.

In summary, Ignatius stressed that God is actively involved in our lives but in a way that works through our natural gifts and processes. Thus discernment of God's will involves a graced human process, a process of using all our resources to gather information, to process it and to make a decision. But part of that information, the all-important part, comes from the way God speaks to us from deep within. Thus discernment of God's will and Ignatius' teaching on "discernment of spirits" come together in those special decision moments of our lives.

Conclusion These few pages have not attempted to explain in detail modern Ignatian teaching on discernment. Such an explanation would be a book in itself. The goal here has been to sketch in broad strokes certain features of Ignatian discernment in a way that might indicate to the reader something of the special relationship between the material offered in this book and Ignatian discernment. To explore that relationship in greater detail, I propose, will stimulate insight into the riches in each approach, into the ways they seek the same goal, and into ways they can help each other assist us in our life-journeys.

NOTES

1. Edward Malatesta (ed.), *Discernment of Spirits*. Collegeville, Minnesota: Liturgical Press, 1970. p. 9.

2. Cf. George A. Aschenbrenner, "Consciousness Examen," *Review for Religious* 31 (1972), pp. 14–21. This is a modern way of explaining what Ignatius suggests for the examen prayer.

3. Ignatius of Loyola, *The Spiritual Exercises of St. Ignatius,* Louis J. Puhl (tr.). Westminster, Maryland: Newman Press. p. 71 (no. 169). For a modern translation of this work, see David L. Fleming. *A Contempory Reading of The Spiritual Exercises.* St. Louis: The Institute of Jesuit Sources, 1976. It is helpful to use a commentary when reading the rules of Ignatius such as: Jules Toner, S.J., *A Commentary on St. Ignatius' Rules for the Discernment of Spirits.* St. Louis: The Institute of Jesuit Sources, 1982; Thomas H. Green, S.J., *Weeds Among the Wheat. Discernment: Where Prayer and Action Meet.* Notre Dame: Ave Maria Press, 1984.

4. Daniel D. Wheeler and Irving L. Janis, *A Practical Guide for Making Decisions.* New York: Free Press, 1980.

BIBLIOGRAPHY

Allen, M.J. and Yen, W.M. *Introduction to Measurement Theory*. Monterey, Ca.: Brooks/ Cole, 1979.

American Psychological Association (APA), *Standards for Educational and Psychological Tests*. Washington, D.C.: Author, 1974.

Anastasi, A. *Psychological Testing* (4th edition). New York: Macmillan, 1976.

Aschenbrenner, George A. "Consciousness Examen." *Review for Religious*, 1972, 31, 14–21.

Ashley, Benedict M. and O'Rourke, Kevin D. *Health Care Ethics: A Theological Analysis*. St. Louis: The Catholic Health Association of the United States, 1982.

Assigioli, R. *Psychosynthesis*. New York: The Viking Press, 1971.

Auel, Jean M. *The Clan of the Cave Bear*. Toronto: Bantam Books, 1980.

Bandler, Richard and Grinder, John. *Frogs into Princes: Neuro Linguistic Programming*. Moab, Utah: Real People Press, 1979.

Bandler, Richard and Grinder, John. *The Structure of Magic: A Book About Language and Therapy*. Palo Alto, Ca: Science & Behavior Books, Inc., 1975.

Bardwick, Judith M. *Psychology of Women*. New York: Harper & Row, 1971.

Bateson, Gregory. *Steps to an Ecology of Mind*. New York: Ballantine Books, 1972.

Bentov, Itzhak. *Stalking the Wild Pendulum: On the Mechanics of Consciousness*. New York: E.P. Dutton, 1977.

Blake, Robert F. and Mouton, Jane S. *Consultation: A Comprehensive Approach to Organizational Development*. Reading, Mass.: Addison-Wesley Publishing Company, 1983.

Blekinsopp, Joseph. *The Men Who Spoke Out*. London: Dalton, 1969.

Boison, Anton T. *The Exploration of the Inner World: A Study of Mental Disorder and Religious Experience*. Philadelphia: University of Pennsylvania Press, 1936.

Bolen, Jean Shinoda, M.D. *Goddesses in Everywoman: A New Psychology of Women*. San Francisco: Harper and Row, Publishers, 1984.

Bradford, Leland P. *Group Development*. La Jolla, Ca.: University Associates, 1978.

Bronowski, J. *The Ascent of Man*. Boston, Toronto: Little, Brown and Company, 1973.

Brownlie, Ian, ed. *Basic Documents on Human Rights*. Oxford: Clarendon Press, 1971, 1981.

Brueggemann, Walter A. *In Man We Trust: The Neglected Side of Biblical Faith*. Atlanta: John Knox, 1972.

Buckley, Michael. "Rules for Discernment of Spirits." *The Way*, 1973, 20.

Bugental, James F.T. *The Search for Authenticity*. New York: Holt, Rinehart & Winston, Inc., 1965.

Bugental, James F.T. *The Search for Existential Identity*. San Francisco: Jossey-Bass Publishers, 1976.

Bullock, Alan. *Hitler: A Study in Tyranny*. New York: Harper & Row, Publishers, 1971.

Burke, James. *Connections*. Boston: Little, Brown and Company, 1978.

Burke, W. Warner and Goodstein, Leonard D., ed. *Trends and Issues in OD: Current Theory and Practice*. San Diego, Ca: University Associates, Inc., 1980.

Cada, Lawrence, *et al. Shaping the Coming Age of Religious Life*. New York: The Seabury Press, 1979.

Campbell, D.T., and Fiske, D.W. "Convergent and Discriminant Validation by the Multitrait-Multimethod Matrix." *Psychological Bulletin*, 1959, 56, 81–105.

Campbell, Joseph, ed. *The Portable Jung*. New York: Penguin Books, 1971.

Caplan, G. and Killilea, M. editors. *Support Systems and Mutual Help*. New York: Grune and Stratton, 1972.

Caplan, Ruth B. et al. *Helping the Helpers to Help: Mental Health Consultation to Aid Clergymen in Pastoral Work*. New York: The Seabury Press, 1972.

Capra, Fritjof. *The Turning Point*. New York: Bantam Books, 1982.

Carretto, Carlo. *Letters from the Desert*. Maryknoll, New York: Orbis Books, 1972.

Cassirer, Ernst. *The Philosophy of Symbolic Forms*. New Haven and London: Yale University Press, 1957.

Chodorow, Nancy. "Family Structure and Feminine Personality." In M.Z. Rosaldo and L. Lamphere, eds. *Woman, Culture and Society*. Stanford: Stanford University Press, 1974.

Chodorow, Nancy. *The Reproduction of Mothering*. Berkeley: University of California Press, 1978.

Claremont de Castillejo, Irene. *Knowing Woman*. New York: Harper & Row, 1973.

Clark, Kenneth. *Civilisation*. New York and Evanston: Harper & Row, Publishers, 1969.

Clements, R.E. *Prophecy and Covenant*. Naperville, Ill.: Allenson, 1965.

Clinebell, Howard. *Contemporary Growth Therapies*. Nashville: Abingdon, 1981.

Corey, Gerald, Corey, Marianne S., and Callanan, Patrick. *Issues and Ethics in the Helping Professions*. Monterey, California: Brooks/Cole Publishing Company, 1984.

Cox, Sue. *Female Psychology: The Emerging Self*. Chicago: Science Research Associates, 1976.

Crenshaw, James L., ed. *Studies in Ancient Israelite Wisdom*. New York: Ktav, 1976.

Cronbach, L.J. "Coefficient Alpha and the Internal Structure of Tests." *Psychometrika*, 1951, 16, 297–334.

Cronbach, L.J. "Validity on Parole: How Can We Go Straight?" *New Directions for Testing and Measurement*, 1980, 5, 99–108.

Cronbach, L.J. *Essentials of Psychological Testing* (3rd Edition). New York: Harper & Row, 1970.

Cronbach, L.J., and Meehl, P.E. "Construct Validity in Psychological Tests." *Psychological Bulletin*, 1955, 52, 281–302.

Davies, Paul. *God and the New Physics*. New York: Simon & Schuster, Inc., 1983.

de Chardin, Pierre Teilhard. *Le Milieu Divin: An Essay on the Interior Life*. New York: Harper & Brothers, 1960.

de Guibert. *Theology of the Spiritual Life*. New York: Sheed and Ward, 1954.

de Laszlo, Violet S. ed. *Psyche and Symbol: A Selection from the Writings of C.G. Jung*. Garden City, New York: Doubleday, 1958.

de Saint-Exupery, Antoine. *The Wisdom of the Sands*. New York: Harcourt, Brace and Company, 1950.

Deal, Terrence E. and Kennedy, Allan A. *Corporate Cultures: The Rites and Rituals of Corporate Life*. Reading, Mass.: Addison-Wesley Publishing Company, 1982.

Dinnerstein, Dorothy. *The Mermaid and the Minotaur: Sexual Arrangements and Human Malaise*. New York: Harper & Row, 1977.

Dix, Dom Gregory. *The Shape of the Liturgy*. London: Dacre Press, 1945.

Douglas, Ann. *The Feminization of American Culture*. New York: Avon Books, 1977.

Dunnette, M.D., and Borman, W.C. "Personnel Selection and Classification Systems." *Annual Review of Psychology*, 1979, *30*, 477–525.

Dyer, William G. *Contemporary Issues in Management and Organization Development*. Reading, Mass.: Addison Wesley Publishing Company, 1983.

Edward, Joyce, Ruskin, Turrini. *Separation-Individuation: Theory and Application*. New York: Gardner Press, 1981.

Elgin, Duane. *Voluntary Simplicity: An Ecological Lifestyle that Promotes Personal and Social Renewal*. Toronto and New York: Bantam Books, 1982.

Erikson, Erik H., ed. *Adulthood*. New York: W.W. Norton & Company, Inc., 1978.

Erikson, Erik H. *Childhood and Society*. New York: W.W. Norton & Company, Inc., 1950, 1963.

Erikson, Erik H. *Gandhi's Truth.*. New York: W.W. Norton & Company, Inc., 1969.

Erikson, Erik H. *Identity: Youth and Crisis*. New York: W. W. Norton & Company, Inc., 1968.

Erikson, Erik H. *Identity and the Life Cycle*. New York: W. W. Norton & Company, Inc., 1980.

Fabry, Joseph B. *The Pursuit of Meaning: Logotherapy Applied to Life*. Boston: Beacon Press, 1968.

The First International Conference on Moral and Religious Development. *Toward Moral and Religious Maturity*. Morristown, New Jersey: Silver Burdett Company, 1980.

Fleming, David L. *A Contemporary Reading of the Spiritual Exercises*. St. Louis: The Institute of Jesuit Sources, 1976.

Fowler, James W. *Stages of Faith*. San Francisco: Harper & Row, Publishers, 1981.

Frankl, Viktor. *The Doctors and the Soul*. New York: Vintage Books, 1955, 1965.

Frankl, Viktor E. *Man's Search for Meaning*. New York: Simon & Schuster, 1959.

Frankl, Viktor E. *Psychotherapy and Existentialism*. New York: Simon & Schuster, 1967.

Freire, Paulo. *Pedagogy in Process*. New York: Seabury Press, 1978.

Freire, Paulo. *Pedagogy of the Oppressed*. New York: Herder and Herder, 1972.

French, Wendell L. and Bell, Cecil H., Jr. *Organization Development*. Englewood Cliffs: Prentice-Hall, Inc., 1978.

Friars Minor of the Franciscan Province of Saint Barbara, translators. *Early Franciscan Classics*. Paterson, New Jersey: Saint Anthony Guild Press, 1962.

Friday, Nancy. *My Mother/My Self*. New York: Dell Books, 1978.

Friedman, H.S. "On Shutting One's Eyes to Face Validity." *Pychological Bulletin*, 1983, *94*, 185–187.

Fromm, Erich. *The Anatomy of Human Destructiveness*. New York: Holt, Rinehart and Winston, 1973.

Fromm, Erich. *Escape from Freedom*. New York: Avon Books, 1941.

Fromm, Erich. *The Heart of Man*. New York: Perennial Library, 1964.

Gerbault, Alain. *Firecrest: Round the World*. New York: David McKay Company, Inc., 1981.

Gerstein, Martin, Pappen-Daniel. *Understanding Adulthood*. Fullerton, Ca.: California Personnel and Guidance Association, 1981.

Gilligan, Carol. *In a Different Voice*. Cambridge, Massachusetts: Harvard University Press, 1982.

Gould, Roger L. *Transformations: Growth and Change in Adult Life*. New York: Simon & Schuster, 1978.

Green, Thomas H., S.J. *Weeds Among the Wheat Discernment: Where Prayer and Action Meet.* Notre Dame: Ave Maria Press, 1984.

Ghiselli, E.E. *Theory of Psychological Measurement.* New York: McGraw-Hill, 1964.

Hall, Brian P. *Developing Leadership by Stages: A Value-Based Approach to Executive Management.* London and New Delhi: Manohar Publications, 1979.

Hall, Brian P. *The Development of Consciousness: A Confluent Theory of Values.* New York: Paulist Press, 1976.

Hall, Brian P. and Tonna, Benjamin. *God's Plans for Us: A Practical Strategy for Discernment of Spirits.* New York: Paulist Press, 1980.

Hall, Brian P. and Thompson, Helen. *Leadership through Values: An Approach to Personal and Organizational Development.* New York: Paulist Press, 1980.

Hall, Brian P. and Osburn, Joseph. *Noq's Vision.* New York: Paulist Press, 1976.

Hall, Brian P. *The Personal Discernment Inventory.* New York: Paulist Press, 1980.

Hall, Brian P. *Shepherds and Lovers.* Ramsey, N.J.: Paulist Press, 1982.

Hall, Brian P. *Value Clarification as Learning Process: A Guidebook.* New York: Paulist Press, 1973.

Hall, Brian P. and Smith, Maury. *Value Clarification as Learning Process: Handbook for Clergy and Christian Educators.* New York: Paulist Press, 1973.

Hall, Brian P. *Value Clarification as Learning Process: A Sourcebook.* New York: Paulist Press, 1973.

Hall, Brian P. *The Wizard of Maldoone.* New York: Paulist Press, 1976.

Haught, John F. *The Cosmic Adventure.* New York/Ramsey: Paulist Press, 1984.

Heschel, A. *The Prophets.* New York: Harper & Row, 1963.

Hillman, James. *The Dream and the Underworld.* New York: Harper & Row, Publishers, 1979.

Howe, Ruel L. *Man's Need and God's Action.* Greenwich, Conn: The Seabury Press, 1953.

Hutchins, Robert Maynard, ed. *Great Books of the Western World.* Chicago: Encyclopaedia Britannica, 1952.

Ignatius of Loyola. *The Spiritual Exercises of St. Ignatius.* Louis J. Puhl (tr.). Westminster, Maryland: Newman Press, (no. 169).

Illich, Ivan. *Celebration of Awareness.* New York: Doubleday & Company, 1969.

Illich, Ivan. *Deschooling Society.* New York: Harper & Row, Publishers, 1971.

Illich, Ivan. *Gender.* New York: Pantheon Books, 1982.

Illich, Ivan. *Tools for Conviviality.* New York: Harper & Row, Publishers, 1973.

Illich, Ivan. *Toward a History of Needs.* New York: Pantheon Books, 1978.

Jackson, Paul, S.J., ed. *Sharafuddin Maneri: The Hundred Letters.* New York: Paulist Press, 1980.

Jaynes, Julian. *The Origin of Consciousness in the Breakdown of the Bicameral Mind.* Boston: Houghton Mifflin Company, 1976.

Johnston, William. *Silent Music: The Science of Meditation.* New York: Harper & Row, Publishers, 1974.

Jung, C. G. *Collected Works.* Bollingen Series, New York: Pantheon Books, 1953–54.

Jung, Carl G. *Memories, Dreams, Reflections.* New York: Pantheon Books, 1963.

Jung, Carl G. *Psychological Types; or, The Psychology of Individuation.* Trans. H. Godwin Baynes. New York: Harcourt, Brace and Company, Inc., 1923.

Jung, C. G. *Tipi Psicologici.* Universale Scientifica (translated by Cesare L. Musatti and Luigi Aurigemma). Editor Boringhieri, Torino, 1977.

344

Kaiser, Hellmuth, ed. by Fierman, Louis B. *Effective Psychotherapy.* New York: The Free Press, 1965.

Kaplan, R.M. and Saccuzzo, D.P. *Psychological Testing: Principles, Applications, and Issues.* Monterey, Ca.: Brooks/Cole, 1982.

Keirsey, D. and Bates, M. *Please Understand Me: An Essay on Temperament Styles.* Del Mar: Prometheus Nemesis Books, 1978.

Kelsey, Morton T. *God, Dreams, and Revelation: A Christian Interpretation of Dreams.* First edition published in 1968 under the title: *Dreams: The Dark Speech of the Spirit.* Minneapolis: Augsburg Publishing House, 1973, 1974.

Kerlinger, F.N. *Behavioral Research: A Conceptual Approach,* New York: Holt, Rinehart, & Winston, 1978.

Kirschenbaum, Howard. *Advanced Value Clarification.* La Jolla, Ca.: University Associates, 1977.

Kirschenbaum, Howard. *On Becoming Carl Rogers.* New York: Delacorte Press, 1979.

Koestenbaum, Peter. *Existential Sexuality: Choosing to Love.* Englewood Cliffs: Prentice-Hall, 1974.

Koestenbaum, Peter. *The New Image of the Person.* Westport, Conn: Greenwood Press, 1978.

Kohlberg, Lawrence. *The Philosophy of Moral Development.* San Francisco: Harper and Row, 1981.

Kraeling, Emil. *The Prophets.* Chicago: Rand McNally, 1969.

Langer, Susanne K. *Philosophy in a New Key.* Cambridge: Harvard University Press, 1957.

Leech, Kenneth. *Soul Friend.* San Francisco: Harper & Row, 1977.

Leslie, Robert E. *Jesus and Logotherapy.* New York, Nashville: Abingdon Press, 1965.

Lever, Janet. "Sex Differences in the Complexity of Children's Play and Games." *American Sociological Review,* 1978, 43, pp. 471–483.

Lever, Janet. "Sex Differences in the Games Children Play." *Social Problems,* 1976, 23, pp. 418–487.

Levinson, Daniel. *The Seasons of a Man's Life.* New York: Alfred A. Knopf, 1978.

Likona, Thomas, ed. *Moral Development and Behavior: Theory, Research, and Social Issues.* New York: Holt, Rinehart and Winston, 1976.

Lindblom, Johannes. *Prophecy in Ancient Israel.* Philadelphia: Fortress, 1965.

Lowen, Alexander. *Narcissism: Denial of the True Self.* New York: Macmillan Publishing Company, 1983.

Loye, David. *The Sphinx and the Rainbow: Brain, Mind and Future Vision.* Boulder, Colorado: Shambhala Publications, Inc., 1983.

Maccoby, Eleanor, ed. *The Development of Sex Differences.* Stanford: Stanford University Press, 1966.

Mahler, Margaret. *Essays in Honor of Margaret S. Mahler: Separation-Individuation.* New York: International University Press, 1971.

Mahler, Margaret. *On Human Symbiosis: The Vicissitudes of Individuation.* New York: Lane Medical Library, 1968.

Mahler, Margaret. *The Psychological Birth of the Human Infant.* New York: Basic Books, 1975.

Malatesta, Edward, ed. *Discernment of Spirits.* Collegeville, Minnesota: Liturgical Press, 1970.

Maly, Eugene. *Prophets of Salvation.* New York: Herder, 1969.

Margolis, Maxine. *Mothers and Such: Views of American Women and Why They Changed.* Berkeley: University of California Press, 1984.

Maslow, Abraham, ed. by Richard J. Lowry. *Dominance, Self-esteem, Self-actualization: Germinal Papers of A.H. Maslow*. Monterey, Ca.: Brooks/Cole Publishing Company, 1973.

Maslow, Abraham. *The Farther Reaches of Human Nature*. New York: Viking Press, 1971.

Maslow, Abraham. *Motivation and Personality*. New York: Harper & Row, 1954, 1970.

Maslow, Abraham, ed. *New Knowledge in Human Values*. New York: Penguin Books, 1959.

Maslow, Abraham. *Religions, Values, and Peak-Experiences*. New York: Penguin Books, 1964, 1976.

Maslow, Abraham. *Toward a Psychology of Being*. New York: D. Van Nostrand Co., 1968.

May, Herbert G., and Metzger, Bruce M., editors. *The New Oxford Annotated Bible With The Apocrypha*. New York: Oxford University Press, 1962.

May, Rollo. *The Meaning of Anxiety*. New York: Washington Square Press, Pocket Books, 1950, 1977.

McGregor, Douglas. *The Human Side of Enterprise*. New York: McGraw-Hill, 1960.

Messick, S. "Test Validity and the Ethics of Assessment." *American Psychologist*, 1980, 35, 1012–1027.

Myers, I. B. *Gifts Differing*. Palo Alto: Consulting Psychologists Press, Inc., 1980.

Miller, Jean Baker. *Toward a New Psychology of Women*. Boston: Beacon Press, 1976.

Milne, A. A. *The House at Pooh Corner*. New York: E.P. Dutton & Co., Inc., 1928.

Mische, Gerald and Mische, Patricia. *Toward a Human World Order*. New York: Paulist Press, 1977.

Mowvley, Harry. *Reading the Old Testament Prophets Today*. Atlanta: John Knox, 1979.

Murphy, J.M. and Gilligan, C. "Moral Development in Late Adolescence and Adulthood: A Critique and Reconstruction of Kohlberg's Theory. "*Human Development*, 1980, 23, pp. 77–104.

Murphy, Roland. *Seven Books of Wisdom*. Milwaukee: Bruce, 1960.

Naisbitt, John. *Megatrends*. New York: Warner Books, 1982.

Needleham, Jacob, translator. *Being-in-the-World: Selected Papers of Ludwig Binswanger*. New York: Harper Torchbooks.

Neumann, Erich. *The Origins and History of Consciousness*. R.F.C. Hull, trans. Princeton: Princeton University Press, 1954.

Nicholls, J., Pearl, R.A., and Licht, B.G. "On the Validity of Inferences About Personality Constructs." *Psychological Bulletin*, 1983, 94, 188–190.

Oden, Thomas C. *The Structures of Awareness*. Nashville: Abingdon Press, 1969.

O'Leary, Virginia E. *Toward Understanding Women*. Monterey, Ca., Brooks/Cole, 1977.

Ouchi, William G. *Theory Z: How American Business Can Meet the Japanese Challenge*. Reading, Massachusetts: Addison-Wesley Publishing Company, 1981.

Ouchi, William G. *The M-Form Society: How American Teamwork Can Capture the Competitive Edge*. Reading, Massachusetts: Addison-Wesley Publishing Company, 1984.

Ornstein, R. *The Psychology of Consciousness*. San Francisco: Freeman, 1975.

Peck, M.S. *People of the Lie: The Hope for Healing Human Evil*. New York: Simon & Schuster, 1983.

Peters, Thomas J. and Waterman, Robert H. Jr. *In Search of Excellence*. New York: Warner Books, 1982.

Pfeiffer, J. William, and Goodstein, Leonard D., ed. *The 1984 Annual: Developing Human Resources*. San Diego, Ca.: University Associates, 1984.

Poulain, Augustin F. *The Graces of Interior Prayer*. Trans. Leonora L. Yorke Smith. Westminster, Vt.: Celtic Cross Books, 1978.

346

Previte-Orton, C.W. *The Shorter Cambridge Medieval History, Volumes I & II*. Great Britain: Cambridge University Press, 1953.

Progoff, Ira. *The Symbolic and the Real: A New Psychological Approach to the Fuller Experience of Personal Existence*. New York: McGraw-Hill, 1963, 1973.

Progoff, Ira. *The Practice of Process Meditation: The Intensive Journal Way to Spiritual Experience*. New York: Dialogue House Library, 1980.

Rad, Gerhard. *The Message of the Prophets*. New York: Harpers, 1977, 1965.

Rad, Gerhard von. *Wisdom in Israel*. James Martin, trans. Nashville: Abingdon, 1972.

Rahner, Hugo. *Ignatius the Theologian*. London: Chapman, 1968.

Raths, Louis E., Harmin, Merrill, and Simon, Sidney B. *Values and Teaching: Working with Values in the Classroom*. Columbus, Ohio: Charles E. Merrill Publishing Company, 1966.

Rawls, John. *A Theory of Justice*. Cambridge: Harvard University Press, 1971.

Reeves, Clement. *The Psychology of Rollo May*. San Francisco: Jossey-Bass Publishers, 1977.

Reid, David P. *What Are They Saying About the Prophets?* New York: Paulist Press, 1980.

Restak, R. "The Hemispheres of the Brain Have Minds of Their Own." *New York Times*, January 25, 1976.

Richards, Sister Innocentia, Ph.D. *Discernment of Spirits*. Collegeville, Minnesota: The Liturgical Press, 1970.

Roberts, David E. *Psychotherapy and a Christian View of Man*. New York: Charles Scribner's Sons, 1950.

Rokeach, Milton. *Beliefs, Attitudes and Values: A Theory of Organization and Change*. San Francisco: Jossey-Bass, 1968.

Rokeach, Milton. *The Nature of Human Values* New York: Free Press, 1973.

Rokeach, Milton, Bonier, Richard, et al. *The Open and Closed Mind: Investigations into the Nature of Belief Systems and Personality Systems*. New York: Basic Books, 1960.

Rokeach, Milton. *The Three Christs of Ypsilanti: A Psychological Study*. New York: Knopf, 1964.

Rokeach, Milton, ed. *Understanding Human Values: Individual and Societal*. New York: Free Press, 1979.

Ross, Maggie. *The Fire of Your Life*. New York: Paulist Press, 1983.

Rubin, Lillian. *Intimate Strangers: Men and Women Together*. New York: Harper & Row, 1983.

Rubin, Lillian. *Worlds of Pain*. New York: Basic Books, 1976.

Ruch, Richard S. and Goodman, Ronald. *Image at the Top*. New York: The Free Press, 1983.

Ryckman, Richard M. *Theories of Personality*. New York: D. Van Nostrand Company, 1978.

Sartre, Jean-Paul. *Being and Nothingness: An Essay on Phenomonological Ontology*. New York: Washington Square Press, 1953, 1956.

Scarf, Maggie. *Unfinished Business*. New York: Doubleday and Co., Inc., 1980.

Schumacher, E.F. *A Guide for the Perplexed*. New York: Harper & Row, 1977.

Schumacher, E.F. *Small is Beautiful*. New York: Harper & Row, 1973.

Scott, R.B.Y. *The Relevance of the Prophets*. New York: Macmillan, 1968.

Scott, R.B.Y. *The Way of Wisdom in the Old Testament*. New York: Macmillan, 1971.

Sebald, Hans. *Momism: The Silent Disease of America*. Chicago: Nelson Hall Co., 1976.

Sheehy, Gail. *Passages*. New York: Dutton, 1976.

Simon, Sidney B., Howe, Leland W., and Kirschenbaum, Howard. *Values Clarification: A Handbook of Practical Strategies for Teachers and Students*. New York: Hart Publishing Company, 1972.

Sobel, Robert. *I.B.M. Colossus in Transition*. New York: Bantam Books, 1983.

Society of Saint Francis. *Manual of the Third Order of Saint Francis*. England: The Society of Saint Francis.

Soleri, Paolo. *Arcology: The City in the Image of Man*. Cambridge, Mass: MIT Press, 1969.

Sowa, J.F. *Conceptual Structures: Information Processing in Mind and Machine*. Palo Alto, Ca.: Addison-Wesley Publishing Company, 1984.

Spence, J.T., and Helmreich, R.L. "Beyond Face Validity: A Solution." *Psychological Bulletin* 1983, *94*, 181–184.

Spencer, Anita. *Mothers Are People Too: A Contemporary Analysis of Motherhood*. New York: Paulist Press, 1984.

Spencer, Anita. *Seasons: Women's Search for Self through Life's Stages*. New York: Paulist Press, 1984.

Springer, S. *Left Brain, Right Brain*. San Francisco: Freeman, 1981.

Stack, Carol B. *All Our Kin*. New York: Harper & Row, 1974.

Stevens, Edward. *Business Ethics*. New York: Paulist Press, 1979.

Tenopyr, M.L. "Content-construct Confusion." *Personnel Psychology* 1977, *30*, 47–54.

Tillich, Paul. *The Courage To Be*. New Haven and London: Yale University Press, 1952.

Toffler, Alvin. *Future Shock*. New York: Random House, 1970.

Toner, Jules, S.J. *A Commentary on St. Ignatius' Rules for the Discernment of Spirits*. St. Louis: The Institute of Jesuit Sources, 1982.

Tonna, Benjamin. *Gospel for the Cities: A Socio-Theology of Urban Ministry*. Translated by William E. Jerman, Ata. Maryknoll, New York: Orbis Books, 1982.

Tournier, Paul. *The Meaning of Persons*. New York: Harper & Row, 1957.

Underhill, Evelyn. *Mysticism*. New York: Meridian Books, 1955.

"Uniform Guidelines on Employee Selection Procedures." *Federal Register*, 1978, *43*, 38296–38309.

Vaillant, George. *Adaptation to Life*. Boston: Little, Brown and Co., 1977.

Van der Hoop, J.H. *Conscious Orientation*. New York: Harcourt Brace, 1939.

Vaughn, F. *Awakening Intuition*. New York: Anchor Books, Doubleday, 1979.

Wadsworth, Barry J. *Piaget's Theory of Cognitive Development*. New York: David McKay Company, Inc., 1971.

Weber, Max. *The Protestant Ethic and the Spirit of Capitalism*. Talcott Parsons, trans. London: George Allen & Unwin, 1976.

Wheeler, Daniel D., and Janis, Irving L. *A Practical Guide for Making Decisions*. New York: Free Press, 1980.

Wilber, Ken. *A Sociable God*. New York: New Press, 1983.

Wilson, Robert R. *Prophecy and Society in Ancient Israel*. Phila: Fortress, 1980.

Wright, John H. "Discernment of Spirits in the New Testament." *Communio*, 1974, *1*, #2.

Wolf, Fred Alan. *Star Wave: Mind, Consciousness, and Quantum Physics*. New York: Macmillan Publishing Company, 1984.

Wyssm, Dieter. *Depth Psychology: A Critical History*. New York: W.W. Norton and Company, Inc., 1966.

Yalom, Irvin D. *Existential Psychotherapy*. New York: Basic Books, Inc., 1980.

Yalom, Irvin D. *Inpatient Group Psychotherapy*. New York: Basic Books, 1983.

Yalom, Irvin D. *The Theory and Practice of Group Psychotherapy*. New York: Basic Books, 1975.

INDEX